DNS on Windows 2000

SECOND EDITION

DNS on Windows 2000

Matt Larson & Cricket Liu

O'REILLY®

Beijing · Cambridge · Farnham · Köln · Paris · Sebastopol · Taipei · Tokyo

DNS on Windows 2000, Second Edition
by Matt Larson and Cricket Liu

Copyright © 2001, 1998 O'Reilly & Associates, Inc. The first edition of this book was titled *DNS on Windows NT*. All rights reserved. Printed in the United States of America.

Portions of this book previously appeared in *DNS and BIND, Fourth Edition*, Copyright © 2001 O'Reilly & Associates, Inc.

Published by O'Reilly & Associates, Inc., 101 Morris Street, Sebastopol, CA 95472.

Editors:	Mike Loukides and Debra Cameron
Production Editor:	Rachel Wheeler
Cover Designer:	Edie Freedman
Interior Designer:	Melanie Wang

Printing History:

October 1998:	First Edition.
September 2001:	Second Edition.

ISBN: 0-596-00230-0

[C]

Table of Contents

Preface

You may not know much about the Domain Name System—yet—but whenever you use the Internet, you use DNS. Every time you send electronic mail or surf the Web, you rely on the Domain Name System.

You see, while you, as a human being, prefer to remember the *names* of computers, computers like to address each other by number. On an internet, that number is 32 bits long, or between zero and four billion or so.* That's easy for a computer to remember because computers have lots of memory ideal for storing numbers, but it isn't nearly as easy for us humans. Pick 10 phone numbers out of the phone book at random, and then try to recall them. Not easy? Now flip to the front of the book and attach random area codes to the phone numbers. That's about how difficult it would be to remember 10 arbitrary internet addresses.

This is part of the reason we need the Domain Name System. DNS handles mapping between hostnames, which we humans find convenient, and internet addresses, which computers deal with. In fact, DNS is the standard mechanism on the Internet for advertising and accessing all kinds of information about hosts, not just addresses. And DNS is used by virtually all internetworking software, including electronic mail, remote terminal programs such as *telnet*, file transfer programs such as *ftp*, and web browsers such as Netscape Navigator and Microsoft Internet Explorer.

Another important feature of DNS is that it makes host information available *all over* the Internet. Keeping information about hosts in a formatted file on a single computer helps only users on that computer. DNS provides a means of retrieving information remotely from anywhere on the network.

More than that, DNS lets you distribute the management of host information among many sites and organizations. You don't need to submit your data to some central site or periodically retrieve copies of the "master" database. You simply make sure

---

* And, with IP Version 6, it's soon to be a whopping 128 bits long, or between zero and a 39-digit decimal number.

your section, called a *zone*, is up to date on your name servers. Your name servers make your zone's data available to all the other name servers on the network.

Because the database is distributed, the system also needs to be able to locate the data you're looking for by searching a number of possible locations. The Domain Name System gives name servers the intelligence to navigate through the database and find data in any zone.

Of course, DNS does have a few problems. For example, the system allows more than one name server to store data about a zone for redundancy's sake, but inconsistencies can crop up between copies of the zone data.

The worst problem with DNS is that despite its widespread use on the Internet, there's really very little documentation about managing and maintaining it. Most administrators on the Internet make do with the documentation their vendors see fit to provide and with whatever they can glean from following the Internet mailing lists and Usenet newsgroups on the subject.

This lack of documentation means that the understanding of an enormously important internet service—one of the linchpins of today's Internet—is either handed down from administrator to administrator like a closely guarded family recipe or relearned repeatedly by isolated programmers and engineers. New zone administrators suffer through the same mistakes made by countless others.

Our aim with this book is to help remedy this situation. We realize that not all of you have the time or the desire to become DNS experts. Most of you, after all, have plenty to do besides managing your zones and name servers: system administration, network engineering, or software development. It takes an awfully big institution to devote a whole person to DNS. We'll try to give you enough information to allow you to do what you need to do, whether that's running a small zone or managing a multinational monstrosity, tending a single name server or shepherding a hundred of them. Read as much as you need to know now, and come back later if you need to know more.

DNS is a big topic—big enough to require two authors, anyway—but we've tried to present it as sensibly and understandably as possible. The first two chapters give you a good theoretical overview and enough practical information to get by, and later chapters fill in the nitty-gritty details. We provide a roadmap up front to suggest a path through the book appropriate for your job or interest.

When we talk about actual DNS software, we'll concentrate on the Microsoft DNS Server, which is a popular implementation of the DNS specs included in Windows 2000 Server (and Windows NT Server 4.0 before it). We've tried to distill our experience in managing and maintaining zones into this book (One of our zones, incidentally, was once one of the largest on the Internet, but that was a long time ago.)

We hope that this book will help you get acquainted with DNS on Windows 2000 if you're just starting out, refine your understanding if you're already familiar with it, and provide valuable insight and experience even if you know it like the back of your hand.

Versions

This book deals with name servers that run on Windows 2000 Server, particularly the Microsoft DNS Server. We will also occasionally mention other name servers that run on Windows 2000, especially ports of BIND, a popular implementation of the DNS specifications. However, if you need a book on BIND, we suggest this book's sister edition, *DNS and BIND* by Paul Albitz and Cricket Liu (O'Reilly). This book is essentially a Windows 2000 edition of *DNS and BIND*.

We use *nslookup*, a name server utility program, a great deal in our examples. The version of *nslookup* we use is the one shipped with Windows 2000 Server. Other versions of *nslookup* provide similar functionality to that in the Windows *nslookup*. We have tried to use commands common to most *nslookup*s in our examples; when this was not possible, we tried to note it.

What's New in This Edition

The first edition of this book was called *DNS on Windows NT* and dealt with Microsoft's DNS implementation for that operating system. This new edition has been comprehensively updated to document the many changes to DNS, large and small, found in Windows 2000. The most significant new feature in Windows 2000 is Active Directory, and this edition describes how Active Directory depends on DNS, including the extra DNS resource records required for a domain controller to function properly. Other new DNS features explained are dynamic update, incremental zone transfer, and storing DNS zone information in Active Directory itself rather than in a text file on disk. The new material appears throughout the book, but many features are described in a new chapter for this edition, Chapter 11. The resolver, or client side of DNS, has also changed in Windows 2000, and Chapter 6 has been updated to document the behavior of the Windows 2000 and Windows 98 resolvers.

Organization

This book is organized, more or less, to follow the evolution of a zone and its administrator. Chapters 1 and 2 discuss Domain Name System theory. Chapters 3 through 6 help you to decide whether to set up your own zones, then describe how to go about it, should you choose to. The middle chapters, 7 through 11, describe how to maintain your zones, configure hosts to use your name servers, plan for the growth of your zones, create subdomains, secure your name servers, and integrate DNS with Active Directory. The last chapters, 12 through 14, deal with common problems and troubleshooting tools.

Here's a more detailed, chapter-by-chapter breakdown:

- Chapter 1, *Background*, provides a little historical perspective and discusses the problems that motivated the development of DNS, then presents an overview of DNS theory.

- Chapter 2, *How Does DNS Work?*, goes over DNS theory in more detail, including the DNS namespace, domains, and name servers. We also introduce important concepts such as name resolution and caching.

- Chapter 3, *Where Do I Start?*, covers how to choose and acquire your DNS software if you don't already have it and what to do with it once you've got it; that is, how to figure out what your domain name should be and how to contact the organization that can delegate your domain to you.

- Chapter 4, *Setting Up the Microsoft DNS Server*, details how to set up your first two name servers, including creating your name server database, starting up your name servers, and checking their operation.

- Chapter 5, *DNS and Electronic Mail*, deals with DNS's MX record, which allows administrators to specify alternate hosts to handle a given destination's mail. The chapter covers mail-routing strategies for a variety of networks and hosts, including networks with security firewalls and hosts without direct Internet connectivity.

- Chapter 6, *Configuring Hosts*, explains how to configure a Windows resolver.

- Chapter 7, *Maintaining the Microsoft DNS Server*, describes the periodic maintenance administrators must perform to keep their domains running smoothly, such as checking name server health and authority.

- Chapter 8, *Growing Your Domain*, covers how to plan for the growth and evolution of your domain, including how to get big and how to plan for moves and outages.

- Chapter 9, *Parenting*, explores the joys of becoming a parent domain. We explain when to become a parent (i.e., create subdomains), what to call your children, how to create them (!), and how to watch over them.

- Chapter 10, *Advanced Features and Security*, goes over less common name server configuration options that can help you tune your name server's operation, secure your name server, and ease administration.

- Chapter 11, *New DNS Features in Windows 2000*, describes the new bells and whistles in Microsoft's DNS implementation for Windows 2000 that weren't present in Windows NT.

- Chapter 12, *nslookup*, shows the ins and outs of the most popular tool for doing DNS debugging, including techniques for digging obscure information out of remote name servers.

- Chapter 13, *Troubleshooting DNS*, covers many common DNS problems and their solutions and then describes a number of less common, harder-to-diagnose scenarios.

- Chapter 14, *Miscellaneous*, ties up all the loose ends. We cover DNS wildcarding; special configurations for networks that connect to the Internet through firewalls; hosts and networks with intermittent Internet connectivity via dial-up; network name encoding; and new, experimental record types.

- Appendix A, *DNS Message Format and Resource Records*, contains a byte-by-byte breakdown of the formats used in DNS queries and responses as well as a comprehensive list of the currently defined resource record types.

- Appendix B, *Installing the DNS Server from CD-ROM*, describes how to load the Microsoft DNS Server from the Windows 2000 Server CD-ROM.

- Appendix C, *Converting from BIND to the Microsoft DNS Server*, covers migrating from an existing BIND 4 name server to the Microsoft DNS Server.

- Appendix D, *Top-Level Domains*, lists the current top-level domains in the Internet domain namespace.

Audience

This book is intended primarily for Windows 2000 system administrators who manage zones and one or more name servers, but it also includes material for network engineers, postmasters, and others. Not all the book's chapters will be equally interesting to a diverse audience, though, and you don't want to wade through 14 chapters to find the information pertinent to your job. We hope this road map will help you plot your way through the book.

System administrators setting up their first zones should read Chapters 1 and 2 for DNS theory, Chapter 3 for information on getting started and selecting a good domain name, then Chapters 4 and 5 to learn how to set up a zone for the first time. Chapter 6 explains how to configure hosts to use the new name servers. Soon after, they should read Chapter 7, which explains how to "flesh out" their implementation by setting up additional name servers and adding additional zone data. Chapters 12 and 13 describe useful troubleshooting tools and techniques.

Experienced administrators may benefit from reading Chapter 6 to learn how to configure DNS resolvers on different hosts and Chapter 7 for information on maintaining their zones. Chapter 8 contains instructions on how to plan for a zone's growth and evolution, which should be especially valuable to administrators of large zones. Chapter 9 explains parenting—creating subdomains—which is essential reading for those considering the big move. Chapter 10 covers security features of the Microsoft DNS Server, many of which may be useful for experienced administrators. The new-to-Windows 2000 features covered in Chapter 11 will be helpful to experienced administrators making the jump from Windows NT. Chapters 12 and 13 describe tools and techniques for troubleshooting, which even advanced administrators may find worth reading.

System administrators on networks without full Internet connectivity should read Chapter 5 to learn how to configure mail on such networks and Chapter 14 to learn how to set up an independent DNS infrastructure.

Network administrators not directly responsible for any zones should still read Chapters 1 and 2 for DNS theory, then Chapter 12 to learn how to use *nslookup*, plus Chapter 13 for troubleshooting tactics.

Postmasters should read Chapters 1 and 2 for DNS theory, then Chapter 5 to find out how DNS and electronic mail coexist. Chapter 12, which describes *nslookup*, will also help postmasters dig mail routing information out of the domain namespace.

Interested users can read Chapters 1 and 2 for DNS theory, and then whatever else they like!

Note that we assume you're familiar with basic Windows 2000 system administration and TCP/IP networking. We don't assume you have any other specialized knowledge, though. When we introduce a new term or concept, we'll do our best to define or explain it. Whenever possible, we'll use analogies from Windows (and from the real world) to help you understand.

Obtaining the Example Programs

The example programs in this book are available from this URL:

> *http://www.oreilly.com/catalog/dnswin2/*

Extract the files from the archive using WinZip by typing:

    C:\temp> winzip dns.zip

If WinZip is not available on your system, get a copy from *http://www.winzip.com*.

Conventions Used in This Book

We use the following font and format conventions:

Italic
> Used for new terms where first defined, Registry values, domain names, filenames, and command lines when they appear in the body of a paragraph exactly as a user would type them (for example: run *dir* to list the files in a directory). *Italic* is also used for Windows commands when they are mentioned in passing and not as part of a command line (for example: to find more information on *nslookup*, a user could consult the Windows help system).

Bold
> Used for menu names and for text appearing in windows and dialog boxes, such as names of fields, buttons, and menu options. For example: enter a domain name in the **Server name** field and then click the **OK** button.

Constant width

Used for excerpts from scripts or configuration files. For example, a snippet of Perl:

```
if ( -x /winnt/system32/dns.exe )
{
    system( /winnt/system32/dns.exe );
}
```

Sample interactive sessions showing command-line input and corresponding output are also shown in a constant width font, with user-supplied input in **constant width bold**:

```
C:\> more <\winnt\system32\drivers\etc\hosts
# Copyright (c) 1993-1999 Microsoft Corp.
#
# This is a sample HOSTS file used by Microsoft TCP/IP for Windows.
#
```

 Indicates a tip, suggestion, or general note.

 Indicates a warning or caution.

How to Contact Us

Please address comments and questions concerning this book to the publisher:

O'Reilly & Associates, Inc.
101 Morris Street
Sebastopol, CA 95472
(800) 998-9938 (in the United States or Canada)
(707) 829-0515 (international/local)
(707) 829-0104 (fax)

There is a web page for this book, which lists errata, examples, and any additional information. You can access this page at:

http://www.oreilly.com/catalog/dnswin2/

To comment or ask technical questions about this book, send email to:

bookquestions@oreilly.com

For more information about books, conferences, software, Resource Centers, and the O'Reilly Network, see the O'Reilly web site at:

http://www.oreilly.com

Quotations

The Lewis Carroll quotations that begin each chapter are from the Millennium Fulcrum Edition 2.9 of the Project Gutenberg electronic text of *Alice's Adventures in Wonderland* and *Through the Looking-Glass*. Quotations in Chapters 1, 2, 5, 6, 8, 11, and 14 come from *Alice's Adventures in Wonderland*, and those in Chapters 3, 4, 7, 9, 10, 12, and 13 come from *Through the Looking-Glass*.

Acknowledgments

The authors would like to thank their technical reviewer for this edition, Levon Esibov, as well as Jon Forrest and David Blank-Edelman, technical reviewers for *DNS on Windows NT*, for their invaluable contributions to this book. Paul Robichaux provided assistance from his wealth of Exchange knowledge for Chapter 5, and John Peterson offered helpful suggestions based on his production Windows 2000 environment.

Matt would like to thank his wife, Sonja, for her support and unflagging patience, and Cricket for asking him to help with this book. He'd also like to thank his manager at VeriSign Global Registry Services, Aristotle Balogh, for his support.

Cricket would like to thank his wife, Paige, for her support during the writing of this book. Thanks also to Walter B and Dakota and Annie, for providing occasional but much-needed relief from writing.

We would also like to thank the folks at O'Reilly & Associates for their hard work and patience. Credit is especially due to our editors, Mike Loukides and Deb Cameron.

Background

The White Rabbit put on his spectacles. "Where shall
I begin, please your Majesty?" he asked.
"Begin at the beginning," the King said, very gravely,
"and go on till you come to the end: then stop."

It's important to know a little ARPANET history to understand the Domain Name System (DNS). DNS was developed to address particular problems on the ARPANET, and the Internet—a descendant of the ARPANET—remains its main user.

If you've been using the Internet for years, you can probably skip this chapter. If you haven't, we hope it'll give you enough background to understand what motivated the development of DNS.

A (Very) Brief History of the Internet

In the late 1960s, the U.S. Department of Defense's Advanced Research Projects Agency, ARPA (later DARPA), began funding an experimental wide area computer network that connected important research organizations in the U.S., called the *ARPANET*. The original goal of the ARPANET was to allow government contractors to share expensive or scarce computing resources. From the beginning, however, users of the ARPANET also used the network for collaboration. This collaboration ranged from sharing files and software and exchanging electronic mail—now commonplace—to joint development and research using shared remote computers.

The *TCP/IP* (Transmission Control Protocol/Internet Protocol) protocol suite was developed in the early 1980s and quickly became the standard host-networking protocol on the ARPANET. The inclusion of the protocol suite in the University of California at Berkeley's popular *BSD Unix* operating system was instrumental in democratizing internetworking. BSD Unix was virtually free to universities. This meant that internetworking—and ARPANET connectivity—were suddenly available cheaply to many more organizations than were previously attached to the

ARPANET. Many of the computers being connected to the ARPANET were being connected to local area networks (LANs), too, and very shortly the other computers on the LANs were communicating via the ARPANET as well.

The network grew from a handful of hosts to tens of thousands of hosts. The original ARPANET became the backbone of a confederation of local and regional networks based on TCP/IP, called the *Internet*.

In 1988, however, DARPA decided the experiment was over. The Department of Defense began dismantling the ARPANET. Another network, funded by the National Science Foundation and called the *NSFNET*, replaced the ARPANET as the backbone of the Internet.

Even more recently, in the spring of 1995, the Internet made a transition from using the publicly-funded NSFNET as a backbone to using multiple commercial backbones, run by long-distance carriers such as MCI and Sprint, and long-time commercial internetworking players such as PSINet and UUNET.

Today, the Internet connects millions of hosts around the world. In fact, a significant proportion of the non-PC computers in the world are connected to the Internet. Some of the new commercial backbones can carry a volume of several gigabits per second, tens of thousands of times the bandwidth of the original ARPANET. Tens of millions of people use the network for communication and collaboration daily.

On the Internet and Internets

A word on "the Internet," and on "internets" in general, is in order. In print, the difference between the two seems slight: one is always capitalized, one isn't. The distinction between their meanings, however, *is* significant. The Internet, with a capital "I," refers to the network that began its life as the ARPANET and continues today as, roughly, the confederation of all TCP/IP networks directly or indirectly connected to commercial U.S. backbones. Seen up close, it's actually quite a few different networks—commercial TCP/IP backbones, corporate and U.S. government TCP/IP networks, and TCP/IP networks in other countries—interconnected by high-speed digital circuits.

A lowercase internet, on the other hand, is simply any network made up of multiple smaller networks using the same internetworking protocols. An internet (little "i") isn't necessarily connected to the Internet (big "I"), nor does it necessarily use TCP/IP as its internetworking protocol. There are isolated corporate internets, and there are Xerox XNS–based internets and DECnet-based internets.

The new term "intranet" is really just a marketing term for a TCP/IP-based "little i" internet, used to emphasize the use of technologies developed and introduced on the Internet within a company's internal corporate network. An "extranet," on the other hand, is a TCP/IP-based internet that connects partner companies, or a company to its distributors, suppliers, and customers.

The History of the Domain Name System

Through the 1970s, the ARPANET was a small, friendly community of a few hundred hosts. A single file, *HOSTS.TXT*, contained a name-to-address mapping for every host connected to the ARPANET. The familiar Unix host table, */etc/hosts*, was compiled from *HOSTS.TXT* (mostly by deleting fields Unix didn't use).

HOSTS.TXT was maintained by SRI's *Network Information Center* (dubbed "the NIC") and distributed from a single host, *SRI-NIC*.* ARPANET administrators typically emailed their changes to the NIC and periodically *ftp*ed to *SRI-NIC* and grabbed the current *HOSTS.TXT* file. Their changes were compiled into a new *HOSTS.TXT* file once or twice a week. As the ARPANET grew, however, this scheme became unworkable. The size of *HOSTS.TXT* grew in proportion to the growth in the number of ARPANET hosts. Moreover, the traffic generated by the update process increased even faster: every additional host meant not only another line in *HOSTS.TXT*, but potentially another host updating from *SRI-NIC*.

When the ARPANET moved to the TCP/IP protocols, the population of the network exploded. Now there was a host of problems with *HOSTS.TXT*:

Traffic and load
> The toll on *SRI-NIC*, in terms of the network traffic and processor load involved in distributing the file, was becoming unbearable.

Name collisions
> No two hosts in *HOSTS.TXT* could have the same name. However, while the NIC could assign addresses in a way that guaranteed uniqueness, it had no authority over hostnames. There was nothing to prevent someone from adding a host with a conflicting name and breaking the whole scheme. Adding a host with the same name as a major mail hub, for example, could disrupt mail service to much of the ARPANET.

Consistency
> Maintaining consistency of the file across an expanding network became harder and harder. By the time a new *HOSTS.TXT* file could reach the farthest shores of the enlarged ARPANET, a host across the network may have changed addresses or a new host may have sprung up.

The essential problem was that the *HOSTS.TXT* mechanism didn't scale well. Ironically, the success of the ARPANET as an experiment led to the failure and obsolescence of *HOSTS.TXT*.

The ARPANET's governing bodies chartered an investigation into a successor for *HOSTS.TXT*. Their goal was to create a system that solved the problems inherent in a unified host table system. The new system should allow local administration of

---

* SRI is the former Stanford Research Institute in Menlo Park, California. SRI conducts research into many different areas, including computer networking.

data, yet make that data globally available. The decentralization of administration would eliminate the single-host bottleneck and relieve the traffic problem. And local management would make the task of keeping data up-to-date much easier. It should use a hierarchical namespace to name hosts. This would ensure the uniqueness of names.

Paul Mockapetris, then of USC's Information Sciences Institute, was responsible for designing the architecture of the new system. In 1984, he released RFCs 882 and 883, which describe the Domain Name System. These RFCs were superseded by RFCs 1034 and 1035, the current specifications of the Domain Name System.[*] RFCs 1034 and 1035 have since been augmented by many other RFCs, which describe potential DNS security problems, implementation problems, administrative gotchas, mechanisms for dynamically updating name servers and for securing zone data, and more.

The Domain Name System, in a Nutshell

The Domain Name System is a distributed database. This structure allows local control of the segments of the overall database, yet data in each segment is available across the entire network through a client/server scheme. Robustness and adequate performance are achieved through replication and caching.

Programs called *name servers* constitute the server half of DNS's client/server mechanism. Name servers contain information about some segments of the database and make that information available to clients, called *resolvers*. Resolvers are often just library routines that create queries and send them across a network to a name server.

The structure of the DNS database, shown in Figure 1-1, is similar to the structure of the Windows filesystem. The whole database (or filesystem) is pictured as an inverted tree, with the root node at the top. Each node in the tree has a text label, which identifies the node relative to its parent. This is roughly analogous to a "relative pathname" in a filesystem, like *bin*. One label—the null label, or ""—is reserved for the root node. In text, the root node is written as a single dot (.). In the Windows filesystem, the root is written as a backslash (\).

Each node is also the root of a new subtree of the overall tree. Each of these subtrees represents a partition of the overall database—a "directory" in the Windows filesystem, or a *domain* in the Domain Name System. Each domain or directory can be further divided into additional partitions, called *subdomains* in DNS, like a filesystem's "subdirectories." Subdomains, like subdirectories, are drawn as children of their parent domains.

---

[*] RFCs are Request for Comments documents, part of the relatively informal procedure for introducing new technology on the Internet. RFCs are usually freely distributed and contain fairly technical descriptions of the technology, often intended for implementers.

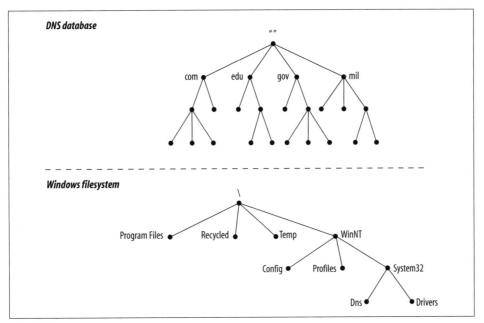

Figure 1-1. The DNS database versus a Windows filesystem

Every domain has a unique name, like every directory. A domain's *domain name* identifies its position in the database, much as a directory's "absolute pathname" specifies its place in the filesystem. In DNS, the domain name is the sequence of labels from the node at the root of the domain to the root of the whole tree, with dots (.) separating the labels. In the Windows filesystem, a directory's absolute pathname is the list of relative names read from root to leaf (the opposite direction from DNS, as shown in Figure 1-2), using a slash to separate the names.

In DNS, each domain can be broken into a number of subdomains, and responsibility for those subdomains can be doled out to different organizations. For example, the InterNIC runs the *edu* (educational) domain, but delegates responsibility for the *berkeley.edu* subdomain to U.C. Berkeley (Figure 1-3). This is similar to remotely mounting a filesystem: certain directories in a filesystem may actually be filesystems on other hosts, mounted from remote hosts. The administrator on host *winken*, for example (again, Figure 1-3), is responsible for the filesystem that appears on the local host as the directory */usr/nfs/winken*.

Delegating authority for *berkeley.edu* to U.C. Berkeley creates a new *zone*, an autonomously administered piece of the namespace. The zone *berkeley.edu* is now independent from *edu*, and contains all domain names that end in *berkeley.edu*. The zone *edu*, on the other hand, contains only domain names that end in *edu* but aren't in delegated zones like *berkeley.edu*. *berkeley.edu* may be further divided into subdomains, like *cs.berkeley.edu*, and some of these subdomains may themselves be separate zones, if the *berkeley.edu* administrators delegate responsibility for them to other

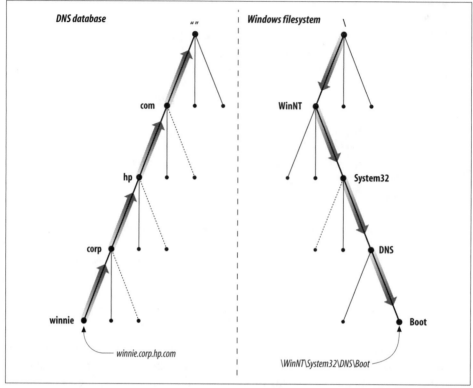

Figure 1-2. Reading names in DNS and in a Windows filesystem

organizations. If *cs.berkeley.edu* is a separate zone, the *berkeley.edu* zone doesn't contain domain names that end in *cs.berkeley.edu* (Figure 1-4).

Domain names are used as indexes into the DNS database. You might think of data in DNS as "attached" to a domain name. In a filesystem, directories contain files and subdirectories. Likewise, domains can contain both hosts and subdomains. A domain contains those hosts and subdomains whose domain names are within the domain.

Each host on a network has a domain name, which points to information about the host (see Figure 1-5). This information may include IP addresses, information about mail routing, etc. Hosts may also have one or more *domain name aliases*, which are simply pointers from one domain name (the alias) to another (the official or *canonical* domain name). In Figure 1-5, *mailhub.nv...* is an alias for the canonical name *rincon.ba.ca....*

Why all the complicated structure? To solve the problems that *HOSTS.TXT* had. For example, making domain names hierarchical eliminates the pitfall of name collisions. Each domain has a unique domain name, so the organization that runs the domain is free to name hosts and subdomains within its domain. Whatever name they choose for a host or subdomain won't conflict with other organizations' domain

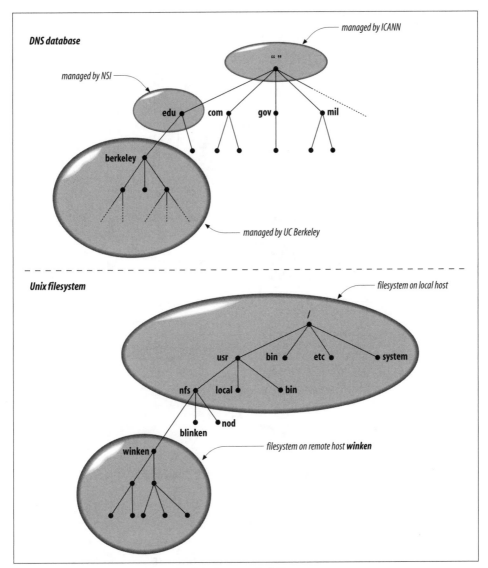

Figure 1-3. Remote management of subdomains and of filesystems

names, since it will end in their unique domain name. For example, the organization that runs *hic.com* can name a host *puella* (as shown in Figure 1-6), since it knows that the host's domain name will end in *hic.com*, a unique domain name.

The History of the Microsoft DNS Server

The first implementation of the Domain Name System was called *JEEVES*, written by Paul Mockapetris himself. A later implementation was *BIND*, an acronym for

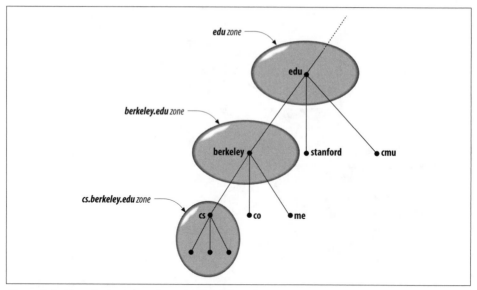

Figure 1-4. The edu, berkeley.edu, and cs.berkeley.edu zones

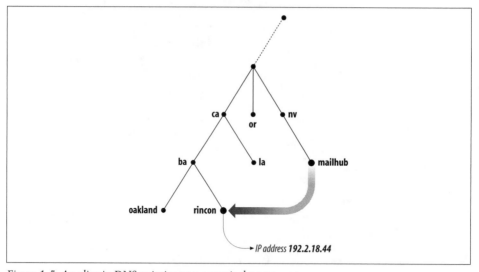

Figure 1-5. An alias in DNS pointing to a canonical name

Berkeley Internet Name Domain, written for Berkeley's 4.3BSD Unix operating system by Kevin Dunlap. BIND is now maintained by the Internet Software Consortium.[*]

Although the Microsoft DNS Server can read BIND's configuration and data files, it is not BIND. Microsoft wrote its server from scratch, according to the DNS

---

[*] For more information on the Internet Software Consortium and its work on BIND, see *http://www.isc.org/ bind.html*.

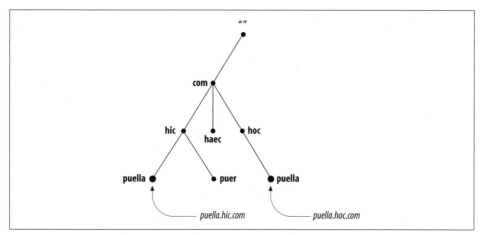

Figure 1-6. Solving the name collision problem

specifications. The first version of the Microsoft DNS Server was a beta version that ran on NT 3.51. Microsoft made it available for some time from one of its FTP servers. The first product version of the DNS server was shipped with Microsoft Windows NT Server 4.0 (but not with NT Workstation 4.0). The server was updated in several NT Service Packs, including the latest (as of this writing), Service Pack 6a. The DNS server shipped with Windows 2000 Server comes from the same code base as the NT DNS server—it's really just a later version.

There are other name servers that run on Windows. For example, the Internet Software Consortium provides a free port of BIND 8.2.4, which runs on Windows NT and Windows 2000. Check Point offers a commercial version of the BIND 8.2.3 server. It also runs on both Windows NT and Windows 2000.

Must I Use DNS?

Despite the usefulness of the Domain Name System, there are some situations in which it doesn't pay to use it. There are other name-resolution mechanisms besides DNS, some of which may be standard with your operating system. Sometimes the overhead involved in managing zones and their name servers outweighs the benefits. On the other hand, there are circumstances in which you have no other choice but to set up and manage name servers. Following are some guidelines to help you make that decision.

If You're Connected to the Internet...

...DNS is a must. Think of DNS as the *lingua franca* of the Internet: nearly all of the Internet's network services use DNS. That includes the World Wide Web, electronic mail, remote terminal access, and file transfer.

On the other hand, this doesn't necessarily mean that you have to set up and run zones *by* yourself *for* yourself. If you've got only a handful of hosts, you may be able to join an existing zone (see Chapter 3) or find someone else to host your zones for you. If you pay an Internet service provider for your Internet connectivity, ask if they'll host your zone for you, too. Even if you aren't already a customer, there are companies who will help out, for a price.

If you have a little more than a handful of hosts, or a lot more, you'll probably want your own zone. And if you want direct control over your zone and your name servers, you'll want to manage it yourself. Read on!

If You Have Your Own TCP/IP-Based Internet...

...you probably want DNS. By an internet, we don't mean just a single Ethernet of workstations using TCP/IP (see the next section if you thought that was what we meant); we mean a fairly complex "network of networks." Maybe you have a forest of AppleTalk nets and a handful of Apollo token rings.

If your internet is basically homogeneous and your hosts don't need DNS (say you have a big DECnet or OSI internet), you may be able to do without it. But if you've got a variety of hosts, especially if some of those run some variety of Unix, you'll want DNS. It'll simplify the distribution of host information and rid you of any kludgy host-table distribution schemes you may have cooked up.

If You Have Your Own Local Area Network or Site Network...

...and that network isn't connected to a larger network, you can probably get away without using DNS. You might consider using Microsoft's Windows Internet Name Service (WINS), host tables, or Sun's Network Information Service (NIS) product.

But if you need distributed administration or have trouble maintaining the consistency of data on your network, DNS may be for you. And if your network is likely to soon be connected to another network, such as your corporate internet or the Internet, it'd be wise to start up your zones now.

How Does DNS Work?

> *"… and what is the use of a book," thought Alice,*
> *"without pictures or conversations?"*

The Domain Name System is basically a database of host information. Admittedly, you get a lot with that: funny dotted names, networked name servers, a shadowy "namespace." But keep in mind that, in the end, the service DNS provides is information about internet hosts.

We've already covered some important aspects of DNS, including its client-server architecture and the structure of the DNS database. However, we haven't gone into much detail, and we haven't explained the nuts and bolts of DNS's operation.

In this chapter, we'll explain and illustrate the mechanisms that make DNS work. We'll also introduce the terms you'll need to know to read the rest of the book (and to converse intelligently with your fellow zone administrators).

First, though, let's take a more detailed look at the concepts introduced in the previous chapter. We'll try to add enough detail to spice it up a little.

The Domain Namespace

DNS's distributed database is indexed by domain names. Each domain name is essentially just a path in a large inverted tree, called the *domain namespace*. The tree's hierarchical structure, shown in Figure 2-1, is similar to the structure of the Windows 2000 filesystem. The tree has a single root at the top.* In the Windows filesystem, this is called the root directory and is represented by a backslash (\). DNS simply calls it "the root." Like a filesystem, DNS's tree can branch any number of ways at each intersection point, or *node*. The depth of the tree is limited to 127 levels (a limit you're not likely to reach).

---

* Clearly this is a computer scientist's tree, not a botanist's.

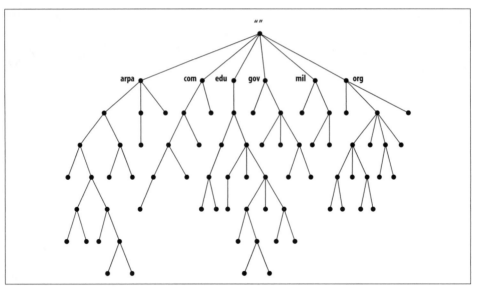

Figure 2-1. The structure of the DNS namespace

Domain Names

Each node in the tree has a text label (without dots) that can be up to 63 characters long. A null (zero-length) label is reserved for the root. The full *domain name* of any node in the tree is the sequence of labels on the path from that node to the root. Domain names are always read from the node toward the root ("up" the tree), with dots separating the names in the path.

If the root node's label actually appears in a node's domain name, the name looks as though it ends in a dot, as in "www.oreilly.com.". (It actually ends with a dot—the separator—and the root's null label.) When the root node's label appears by itself, it is written as a single dot, ".", for convenience. Consequently, some software interprets a trailing dot in a domain name to indicate that the domain name is *absolute*. An absolute domain name is written relative to the root and unambiguously specifies a node's location in the hierarchy. An absolute domain name is also referred to as a *fully qualified domain name*, often abbreviated FQDN. Names without trailing dots are sometimes interpreted as relative to some domain name other than the root, just as directory names without a leading slash are often interpreted as relative to the current directory.

DNS requires that sibling nodes—nodes that are children of the same parent— have different labels. This restriction guarantees that a domain name uniquely identifies a single node in the tree. The restriction really isn't a limitation, because the labels need to be unique only among the children, not among all the nodes in the tree. The same restriction applies to the Windows 2000 filesystem: you can't give two sibling directories or two files in the same directory the same name. As illustrated in Figure 2-2, just as you can't have two *hobbes.pa.ca.us* nodes in the namespace, you can't have two *\Temp* directories. You can, however, have both a *hobbes.pa.ca.us* node and a *hobbes.lg.ca.us* node, as you can have both a *\Temp* directory and a *\WinNT\Temp* directory.

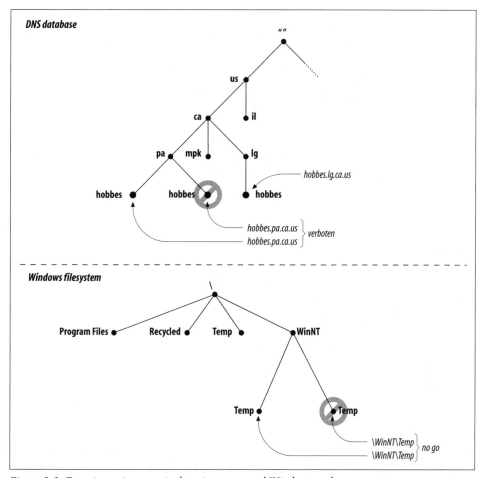

Figure 2-2. Ensuring uniqueness in domain names and Windows pathnames

Domains

A *domain* is simply a subtree of the domain namespace. The domain name of a domain is the same as the domain name of the node at the very top of the domain. So, for example, the top of the *purdue.edu* domain is a node named *purdue.edu*, as shown in Figure 2-3.

Likewise, in a filesystem, at the top of the *\Program Files* directory you'd expect to find a node called *\Program Files*, as shown in Figure 2-4.

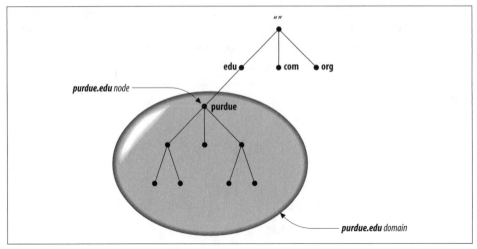

Figure 2-3. The purdue.edu domain

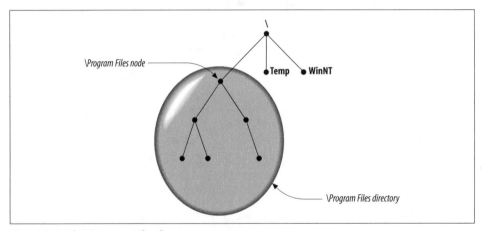

Figure 2-4. The \Program Files directory

Any domain name in the subtree is considered a part of the domain. Because a domain name can be in many subtrees, a domain name can also be in many domains. For example, the domain name *pa.ca.us* is part of the *ca.us* domain and also part of the *us* domain, as shown in Figure 2-5.

So in the abstract, a domain is just a subtree of the domain namespace. But if a domain is simply made up of domain names and other domains, where are all the hosts? Domains are groups of hosts, right?

The hosts are there, represented by domain names. Remember, domain names are just indexes into the DNS database. The "hosts" are the domain names that point to information about individual hosts, and a domain contains all the hosts whose domain names are within the domain. The hosts are related *logically*, often by geography or

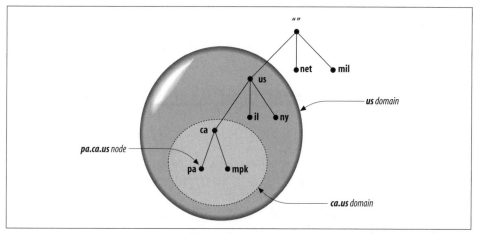

Figure 2-5. A node in multiple domains

organizational affiliation, and not necessarily by network or address or hardware type. You might have 10 different hosts, each of them on a different network and perhaps even in a different country, all in the same domain.

One note of caution: don't confuse domains in DNS with domains in NIS. Though an NIS domain also refers to a group of hosts and both types of domains have similarly structured names, the concepts are quite different. NIS uses hierarchical names, but the hierarchy ends there: hosts in the same NIS domain share certain data about hosts and users, but they can't navigate the NIS namespace to find data in other NIS domains. NT domains, which provide account-management and security services, also don't have any relationship to DNS domains. Active Directory domains, however, are DNS domains. We discuss the relationship between DNS and Active Directory domains in Chapter 11.

Domain names at the leaves of the tree generally represent individual hosts, and they may point to network addresses, hardware information, and mail-routing information. Domain names in the interior of the tree can name a host *and* point to information about the domain; they aren't restricted to one or the other. Interior domain names can represent both the domain they correspond to and a particular host on the network. For example, *hp.com* is both the name of the Hewlett-Packard Company's domain and the domain name of the hosts that run HP's main web server.

The type of information retrieved when you use a domain name depends on the context in which you use it. Sending mail to someone at *hp.com* would return mail-routing information, while *telnet*ing to the domain name would look up the host information (in Figure 2-6, for example, *hp.com*'s IP address).*

---

* The terms "domain" and "subdomain" are often used interchangeably, or nearly so, in DNS documentation. Here, we use "subdomain" only as a relative term: a domain is a subdomain of another domain if the root of the subdomain is within the domain.

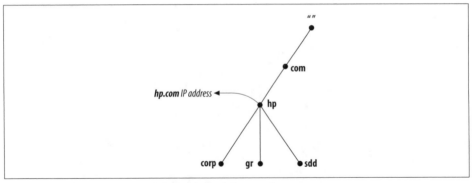

Figure 2-6. An interior node with both host and domain data

A simple way of determining if a domain is a subdomain of another domain is to compare their domain names. A subdomain's domain name ends with the domain name of its parent domain. For example, the domain *la.tyrell.com* must be a subdomain of *tyrell.com*, because *la.tyrell.com* ends with *tyrell.com*. It's also a subdomain of *com*, as is *tyrell.com*.

Besides being referred to in relative terms, as subdomains of other domains, domains are often referred to by *level*. On mailing lists and in Usenet newsgroups, you may see the terms *top-level domain* or *second-level domain* bandied about. These terms simply refer to a domain's position in the domain namespace:

- A top-level domain is a child of the root.
- A first-level domain is a child of the root (a top-level domain).
- A second-level domain is a child of a first-level domain, and so on.

Resource Records

The data associated with domain names is contained in *resource records*, or RRs. Records are divided into classes, each of which pertains to a type of network or software. Currently, there are classes for internets (any TCP/IP-based internet), networks based on the Chaosnet protocols, and networks that use Hesiod software. (Chaosnet is an old network of largely historic significance.) The internet class is by far the most popular. (We're not really sure if anyone still uses the Chaosnet class, and use of the Hesiod class is mostly confined to MIT.) In this book, we concentrate on the internet class.

Within a class, records come in several types, which correspond to the different varieties of data that may be stored in the domain namespace. Different classes may define different record types, though some types are common to more than one class. For example, almost every class defines an *address* type. Each record type in a given class defines a particular record syntax to which all resource records of that class and type must adhere. (For details on all internet resource record types and their syntaxes, see Appendix A.)

If this information seems sketchy, don't worry—we'll cover the records in the internet class in more detail later. The common records are described in Chapter 4, and a comprehensive list is included as part of Appendix A.

The Internet Domain Namespace

So far, we've talked about the theoretical structure of the domain namespace and what sort of data is stored in it, and we've even hinted at the types of names you might find in it with our (sometimes fictional) examples. But this won't help you decode the domain names you see on a daily basis on the Internet.

The Domain Name System doesn't impose many rules on the labels in domain names, and it doesn't attach any *particular* meaning to the labels at a particular level. When you manage a part of the domain namespace, you can decide on your own semantics for your domain names. Heck, you could name your subdomains A through Z and no one would stop you (though they might strongly recommend against it).

The existing Internet domain namespace, however, has some self-imposed structure to it. Especially in the upper-level domains, the domain names follow certain traditions (not rules, really, as they can be and have been broken). These traditions help to keep domain names from appearing totally chaotic. Understanding these traditions is an enormous asset if you're trying to decipher a domain name.

Top-Level Domains

The original top-level domains divided the Internet domain namespace organizationally into seven domains:

com

> Commercial organizations, such as Hewlett-Packard (*hp.com*), Sun Microsystems (*sun.com*), and IBM (*ibm.com*).

edu

> Educational organizations, such as U.C. Berkeley (*berkeley.edu*) and Purdue University (*purdue.edu*).

gov

> Government organizations, such as NASA (*nasa.gov*) and the National Science Foundation (*nsf.gov*).

mil

> Military organizations, such as the U.S. Army (*army.mil*) and Navy (*navy.mil*).

net

> Formerly organizations providing network infrastructure, such as NSFNET (*nsf.net*) and UUNET (*uu.net*). Since 1996, however, *net* has been open to any commercial organization, like *com* is.

org

Formerly noncommercial organizations, such as the Electronic Frontier Foundation (*eff.org*). Like *net,* though, restrictions on *org* were removed in 1996.

int

International organizations, such as NATO (*nato.int*).

Another top-level domain called *arpa* was originally used during the ARPANET's
transition from host tables to DNS. All ARPANET hosts originally had hostnames
under *arpa*, so they were easy to find. Later, they moved into various subdomains of
the organizational top-level domains. However, the *arpa* domain remains in use in a
way you'll read about later.

You may notice a certain nationalistic prejudice in the examples: we've used primarily U.S.-based organizations. That's easier to understand—and forgive—when you
remember that the Internet began as the ARPANET, a U.S.-funded research project.
No one anticipated the success of the ARPANET, or that it would eventually become
as international as the Internet is today.

Today, these original domains are called *generic top-level domains*, or gTLDs. By the
time you read this, we may have a few more of these, such as *biz, pro, info*, and
name, to accommodate the rapid expansion of the Internet and the need for more
domain name "space." The organization now responsible for management of the
Domain Name System, the Internet Corporation for Assigned Names and Numbers,
or ICANN, has decided to add seven new gTLDs. For information on their work, see
http://www.icann.org. We'll talk more about ICANN later in this chapter.

To accommodate the increasing internationalization of the Internet, the implementers of the Internet namespace compromised. Instead of insisting that all top-level
domains describe organizational affiliation, they decided to allow geographical designations, too. New top-level domains were reserved (but not necessarily created) to
correspond to individual countries. Their domain names followed an existing international standard called ISO 3166.* ISO 3166 establishes official, two-letter abbreviations for every country in the world. We've included the current list of top-level
domains as Appendix D.

Further Down

Within these top-level domains, the traditions and the extent to which they are followed vary. Some of the ISO 3166 top-level domains closely follow the U.S.'s original
organizational scheme. For example, Australia's top-level domain, *au*, has subdomains such as *edu.au* and *com.au*. Some other ISO 3166 top-level domains follow the

---

* Except for Great Britain. According to ISO 3166 and Internet tradition, Great Britain's top-level domain
  name should be *gb*. Instead, most organizations in Great Britain and Northern Ireland (i.e., the United Kingdom) use the top-level domain name *uk*. They drive on the wrong side of the road, too.

uk domain's lead and have organizationally oriented subdomains such as *co.uk* for corporations and *ac.uk* for the academic community. In most cases, however, even these geographically oriented top-level domains are divided up organizationally.

That's not true of the *us* top-level domain, though. The *us* domain has 50 subdomains that correspond to—guess what?—the 50 U.S. states.* Each is named according to the standard two-letter abbreviation for the state—the same abbreviation standardized by the U.S. Postal Service. Within each state's domain, the organization is still largely geographical: most subdomains correspond to individual cities. Beneath the cities, the subdomains usually correspond to individual hosts.

Reading Domain Names

Now that you know what most top-level domains represent and how their namespaces are structured, you'll probably find it much easier to make sense of most domain names. Let's dissect a few for practice:

lithium.cchem.berkeley.edu
> You've got a head start on this one, as we've already told you that *berkeley.edu* is U.C. Berkeley's domain. (Even if you didn't already know that, though, you could have inferred that the name probably belongs to a U.S. university because it's in the top-level *edu* domain.) *cchem* is the College of Chemistry's subdomain of *berkeley.edu*. Finally, *lithium* is the name of a particular host in the domain— and probably one of about a hundred or so, if they've got one for every element.

winnie.corp.hp.com
> This example is a bit harder, but not much. The *hp.com* domain in all likelihood belongs to the Hewlett-Packard Company (in fact, we gave you this earlier, too). Their *corp* subdomain is undoubtedly their corporate headquarters. And *winnie* is probably just some silly name someone thought up for a host.

fernwood.mpk.ca.us
> Here you'll need to use your understanding of the *us* domain. *ca.us* is obviously California's domain, but *mpk* is anybody's guess. In this case, it would be hard to know that it's Menlo Park's domain unless you knew your San Francisco Bay Area geography. (And no, it's not the same Menlo Park that Edison lived in— that one's in New Jersey.)

daphne.ch.apollo.hp.com
> We've included this example just so you don't start thinking that all domain names have only four labels. *apollo.hp.com* is the former Apollo Computer subdomain of the *hp.com* domain. (When HP acquired Apollo, it also acquired Apollo's Internet domain, *apollo.com*, which became *apollo.hp.com*.) *ch.apollo.hp.com* is Apollo's Chelmsford, Massachusetts site. *daphne* is a host at Chelmsford.

---

* Actually, there are a few more domains under *us*: one for Washington, D.C., one for Guam, and so on.

Delegation

Remember that one of the main goals of the design of the Domain Name System was to decentralize administration? This is achieved through *delegation*. Delegating domains works a lot like delegating tasks at work. A manager may break up a large project into smaller tasks and delegate responsibility for each of these tasks to different employees.

Likewise, an organization administering a domain can divide it into subdomains. Each of those subdomains can be delegated to other organizations. This means that an organization becomes responsible for maintaining all the data in that subdomain. It can freely change the data nd even divide its subdomain into more subdomains and delegate those. The parent domain retains only pointers to sources of the subdomain's data, so that it can refer queriers there. The domain *stanford.edu*, for example, is delegated to the folks at Stanford who run the university's networks (Figure 2-7).

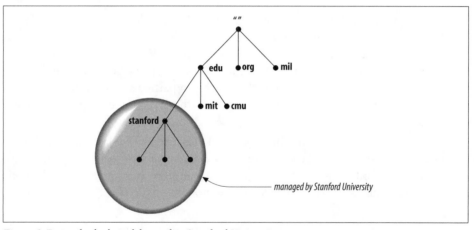

Figure 2-7. stanford.edu is delegated to Stanford University

Not all organizations delegate away their whole domain, just as not all managers delegate all their work. A domain may have several delegated subdomains and also contain hosts that don't belong in the subdomains. For example, the Acme Corporation (it supplies a certain coyote with most of his gadgets), which has a division in Rockaway and its headquarters in Kalamazoo, might have a *rockaway.acme.com* subdomain and a *kalamazoo.acme.com* subdomain. However, the few hosts in the Acme sales offices scattered throughout the U.S. would fit better under *acme.com* than under either subdomain.

We'll explain how to create and delegate subdomains later. For now, it's important only that you understand that the term delegation refers to assigning responsibility for a subdomain to another organization.

Name Servers and Zones

The programs that store information about the domain namespace are called *name servers*. Name servers generally have complete information about some part of the domain namespace, called a *zone*, which they load from a file or from another name server. The name server is then said to have *authority* for that zone. Name servers can be authoritative for multiple zones, too.

The difference between a zone and a domain is important, but subtle. All top-level domains and many domains at the second level and lower, such as *berkeley.edu* and *hp.com*, are broken into smaller, more manageable units by delegation. These units are called zones. The *edu* domain, shown in Figure 2-8, is divided into many zones, including the *berkeley.edu* zone, the *purdue.edu* zone, and the *nwu.edu* zone. At the top of the domain, there's also an *edu* zone. It's natural that the folks who run *edu* would break up the *edu* domain: otherwise, they'd have to manage the *berkeley.edu* subdomain themselves. It makes much more sense to delegate *berkeley.edu* to Berkeley. What's left for the folks who run *edu*? The *edu* zone, which contains mostly delegation information for the subdomains of *edu*.

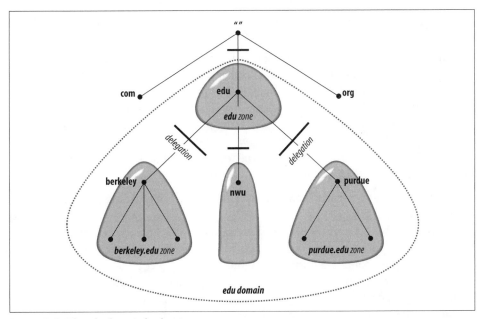

Figure 2-8. The edu domain broken into zones

The *berkeley.edu* subdomain is, in turn, broken up into multiple zones by delegation, as shown in Figure 2-9. There are delegated subdomains called *cc*, *cs*, *ce*, *me*, and more. Each of these subdomains is delegated to a set of name servers, some of which are also authoritative for *berkeley.edu*. However, the zones are still separate and may have totally different groups of authoritative name servers.

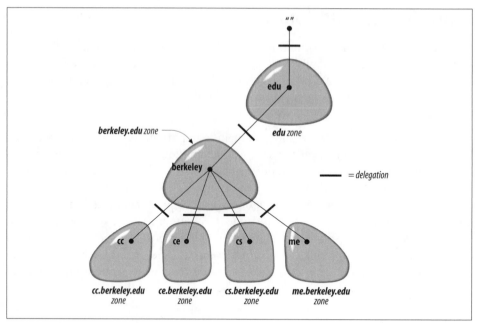

Figure 2-9. The berkeley.edu domain broken into zones

A zone contains all the domain names the domain with the same domain name contains, except for domain names in delegated subdomains. For example, the top-level domain *ca* (for Canada) has subdomains called *ab.ca*, *on.ca*, and *qc.ca*, for the provinces Alberta, Ontario, and Quebec. Authority for the *ab.ca*, *on.ca*, and *qc.ca* domains may be delegated to name servers in each of the provinces. The *domain ca* contains all the data in *ca* plus all the data in *ab.ca*, *on.ca*, and *qc.ca*. However, the *zone ca* contains only the data in *ca* (see Figure 2-10), which is probably mostly pointers to the delegated subdomains. *ab.ca*, *on.ca*, and *qc.ca* are separate zones from the *ca* zone.

The zone also contains the domain names and data in any subdomains that aren't delegated away. For example, the *bc.ca* and *sk.ca* (British Columbia and Saskatchewan) subdomains of the *ca* domain may exist but not be delegated. (Perhaps the provincial authorities in B.C. and Saskatchewan aren't yet ready to manage their subdomains, but the authorities running the top-level *ca* domain want to preserve the consistency of the namespace and implement subdomains for all of the Canadian provinces right away.) In this case, the zone *ca* has a ragged bottom edge, containing *bc.ca* and *sk.ca*, but not the other *ca* subdomains, as shown in Figure 2-11.

Now it's clear why name servers load zones instead of domains: a domain may contain more information than the name server needs, since it can contain data delegated to other name servers.* Since a zone is bounded by delegation, it will never include delegated data.

---

* If a root name server loaded the root domain instead of the root zone, it would load the entire namespace!

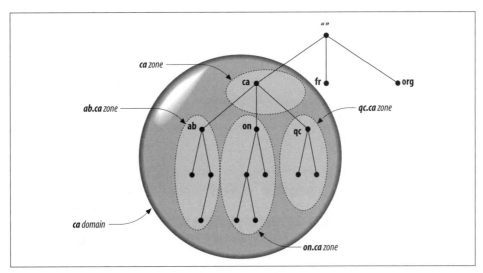

Figure 2-10. The domain ca...

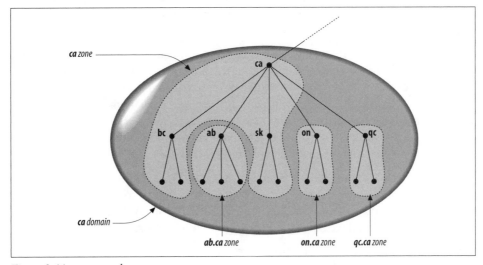

Figure 2-11. ...versus the zone ca

If you're just starting out your domain probably won't have any subdomains. In this case, since there's no delegation going on, your domain and your zone will contain the same data.

Delegating Subdomains

Even though you may not need to delegate parts of your domain just yet, it's helpful to understand a little more about how the process of delegating a subdomain works. Delegation, in the abstract, involves assigning responsibility for some part of your domain to another organization. What really happens, however, is the assignment of authority for your subdomain to different name servers. (Note that we said "name servers," not just "name server.")

Your zone's data, instead of containing information in the subdomain you've delegated, includes pointers to the name servers that are authoritative for that subdomain. Now if one of your name servers is asked for data in the subdomain, it can reply with a list of the right name servers to contact.

Types of Name Servers

The DNS specs define two types of name servers: primary masters and secondary masters. A *primary master* name server for a zone reads the data for the zone from a file on its host. A *secondary master* name server for a zone gets the zone data from the name server that is authoritative for the zone, called its master server. Quite often, the master server is the zone's primary master, but that's not required: a secondary master can load zone data from another secondary. When a secondary starts up, it contacts its master name server and, if necessary, pulls the zone data over. This is referred to as a *zone transfer*. Nowadays, the preferred term for a secondary master name server is a *slave*, though many people (and some software, including Microsoft's DNS console) still use the old term.

Both the primary master and slave name servers for a zone are authoritative for that zone. Despite the somewhat disparaging name, slaves aren't second-class name servers. DNS provides these two types of name servers to make administration easier. Once you've created the data for your zone and set up a primary master name server, you don't need to copy that data from host to host to create new name servers for the zone. You simply set up slave name servers that load their data from the primary master for the zone. The slaves you set up will transfer new zone data when necessary.

Slave name servers are important because it's a good idea to set up more than one name server for any given zone. You'll want more than one for redundancy, to spread the load around, and to make sure that all the hosts in the zone have a name server close by. Using slave name servers makes this administratively workable.

Calling a *particular* name server a primary master name server or a slave name server is a little imprecise, though. We mentioned earlier that a name server can be authoritative for more than one zone. Similarly, a name server can be a primary master for one zone and a slave for another. Most name servers, however, are either primary for most of the zones they load or slave for most of the zones they load. So if we call a particular name server a primary or a slave, we mean that it's the primary master or a slave for *most* of the zones for which it's authoritative.

Data Files

The files from which primary master name servers load their zone data are called, simply enough, *zone data files*. We often refer to them as *data files*. Slave name servers can also load their zone data from data files. Slaves are usually configured to back up the zone data they transfer from a master name server to data files. If the slave is later killed and restarted, it will read the backup data files first, then check to see whether its zone data is current. This both obviates the need to transfer the zone data if it hasn't changed and provides a source of the data if the master is down.

Resolvers

Resolvers are the clients that access name servers. Programs running on a host that need information from the domain namespace use the resolver. The resolver handles:

- Querying a name server
- Interpreting responses (which may be resource records or an error)
- Returning the information to the programs that requested it

In Windows 2000, the resolver is just a set of library routines that is linked into programs such as *telnet* and *ftp*. It's not even a separate process. It has the smarts to put together a query, to send it and wait for an answer, and to resend the query if it isn't answered, but that's about all. Most of the burden of finding an answer to the query is placed on the name server. The DNS specs call this kind of resolver a *stub resolver*.

Other implementations of DNS have had smarter resolvers that can do more sophisticated things, such as build up a cache of information already retrieved from name servers. In fact, Windows 2000 includes a caching resolver.

Resolution

Name servers are adept at retrieving data from the domain namespace. They have to be, given the limited intelligence of most resolvers. Not only can they give you data about zones for which they're authoritative, they can also search through the domain namespace to find data for which they're not authoritative. This process is called *name resolution* or simply *resolution*.

Because the namespace is structured as an inverted tree, a name server needs only one piece of information to find its way to any point in the tree: the domain names and addresses of the root name servers (is that more than one piece?). A name server can issue a query to a root name server for any domain name in the domain namespace, and the root name server will start the name server on its way.

Root Name Servers

The root name servers know where there are authoritative name servers for each of the top-level zones. (In fact, some of the root name servers are authoritative for the generic top-level zones.) Given a query about any domain name, the root name servers can at least provide the names and addresses of the name servers that are authoritative for the top-level zone the domain name ends in. In turn, the top-level name servers can provide the list of name servers that are authoritative for the domain name's second-level zone. Each name server queried either gives the querier information about how to get "closer" to the answer it's seeking or provides the answer itself.

The root name servers are clearly important to resolution. Because they're so important, DNS provides mechanisms—such as caching, which we'll discuss a little later—to help offload the root name servers. But in the absence of other information, resolution has to start at the root name servers. This makes the root name servers crucial to the operation of DNS; if all the Internet root name servers were unreachable for an extended period, all resolution on the Internet would fail. To protect against this, the Internet has 13 root name servers (as of this writing) spread across different parts of the network. One is on PSINet, a commercial Internet backbone; one is on the NASA Science Internet; two are in Europe; and one is in Japan.

Being the focal point for so many queries keeps the roots busy; even with 13, the traffic to each root name server is very high. A recent informal poll of root name server administrators showed some roots receiving thousands of queries per second.

Despite the load placed on root name servers, resolution on the Internet works quite well. Figure 2-12 shows the resolution process for the address of a real host in a real domain, including how the process corresponds to traversing the domain namespace tree.

The local name server queries a root name server for the address of *girigiri.gbrmpa. gov.au* and is referred to the *au* name servers. The local name server asks an *au* name server the same question, and is referred to the *gov.au* name servers. The *gov.au* name server refers the local name server to the *gbrmpa.gov.au* name servers. Finally, the local name server asks a *gbrmpa.gov.au* name server for the address and gets the answer.

Recursion

You may have noticed a big difference in the amount of work done by the name servers in the previous example. Four of the name servers simply returned the best answer they already had—mostly referrals to other name servers—to the queries they received. They didn't have to send their own queries to find the data requested. But one name server—the one queried by the resolver—had to follow successive referrals until it received an answer.

Why couldn't the local name server simply have referred the resolver to another name server? Because a stub resolver wouldn't have had the intelligence to follow a referral. And how did the name server know not to answer with a referral? Because the resolver issued a *recursive* query.

Queries come in two flavors, *recursive* and *iterative*, also called *nonrecursive*. Recursive queries place most of the burden of resolution on a single name server. *Recursion,*

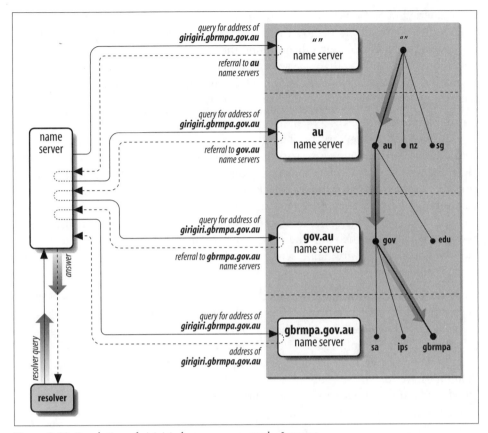

Figure 2-12. Resolution of girigiri.gbrmpa.gov.au on the Internet

or *recursive resolution*, is just a name for the resolution process used by a name server when it receives recursive queries. As with recursive algorithms in programming, the name server repeats the same basic process (querying a remote name server and following any referrals) until it receives an answer.

Iteration, or *iterative resolution*, on the other hand, refers to the resolution process used by a name server when it receives iterative queries.

In recursion, a resolver sends a recursive query to a name server for information about a particular domain name. The queried name server is then obliged to respond with the requested data or with an error stating either that data of the requested type doesn't exist or that the domain name specified doesn't exist.[*] The name server can't just refer the querier to a different name server, because the query was recursive.

---

[*] The Microsoft DNS Server can be configured to ignore recursive queries; see Chapter 10 for how and why you'd want to do this.

If the queried name server isn't authoritative for the data requested, it will have to query other name servers to find the answer. It can send recursive queries to those name servers, thereby obliging them to find the answer and return it (and passing the buck), or it can send iterative queries and possibly be referred to other name servers "closer" to the domain name it's seeking. Current implementations are polite and do the latter, following the referrals until an answer is found.[*]

A name server that receives a recursive query that it can't answer itself will query the "closest known" name servers. The closest known name servers are the servers authoritative for the zone closest to the domain name being looked up. For example, if the name server receives a recursive query for the address of the domain name *girigiri.gbrmpa.gov.au*, it will first check whether it knows which name servers are authoritative for *girigiri.gbrmpa.gov.au*. If it does, it will send the query to one of them. If not, it will check whether it knows the name servers for *gbrmpa.gov.au*, and after that *gov.au*, and then *au*. The default, where the check is guaranteed to stop, is the root zone, since every name server knows the domain names and addresses of the root name servers.

Using the closest known name servers ensures that the resolution process is as short as possible. A *berkeley.edu* name server receiving a recursive query for the address of *waxwing.ce.berkeley.edu* shouldn't have to consult the root name servers; it can simply follow delegation information directly to the *ce.berkeley.edu* name servers. Likewise, a name server that has just looked up a domain name in *ce.berkeley.edu* shouldn't have to start resolution at the root to look up another *ce.berkeley.edu* (or *berkeley.edu*) domain name; we'll show how this works in the upcoming section on caching.

The name server that receives the recursive query always sends the same query that the resolver sent it; for example, for the address of *waxwing.ce.berkeley.edu*. It never sends explicit queries for the name servers for *ce.berkeley.edu* or *berkeley.edu*, though this information is also stored in the namespace. Sending explicit queries could cause problems: there may be no *ce.berkeley.edu* name servers (that is, *ce.berkeley.edu* may be part of the *berkeley.edu* zone). Also, it's always possible that an *edu* or *berkeley.edu* name server would know *waxwing.ce.berkeley.edu*'s address. An explicit query for the *berkeley.edu* or *ce.berkeley.edu* name servers would miss this information.

Iteration

Iterative resolution doesn't require nearly as much work on the part of the queried name server. In iterative resolution, a name server simply gives the best answer *it already knows* back to the querier. No additional querying is required. The queried

---

[*] The exception is a name server configured to forward all unresolved queries to a designated name server, called a *forwarder*. See Chapter 10 for more information on using forwarders.

name server consults its local data (including its cache, which we'll talk about shortly), looking for the data requested. If it doesn't find the answer there, it finds the names and addresses of the name servers closest to the domain name in the query in its local data and returns that as a referral to help the querier continue the resolution process. Note that the referral includes *all* of the name servers listed in the local data; it's up to the querier to choose which one to query next.

Choosing Between Authoritative Name Servers

Some of the card-carrying Mensa members in our reading audience may be wondering how the name server that receives the recursive query chooses between the name servers authoritative for the zone. For example, we said that there are 13 root name servers on the Internet today. Does the name server simply query the one that appears first in the referral? Does it choose randomly?

The Microsoft DNS Server uses *roundtrip time* (RTT) to choose between name servers authoritative for the same zone. Roundtrip time is a measurement of how long a remote name server takes to respond to queries. Each time a Microsoft DNS Server sends a query to a remote name server, it starts an internal stopwatch. When it receives a response, it stops the stopwatch and makes a note of how long that remote name server took to respond. When the name server must choose which of a group of authoritative name servers to query, it simply chooses the one with the lowest roundtrip time.

Before a Microsoft DNS Server has queried a name server, it gives it a random roundtrip time value lower than any real-world value. This ensures that the server queries all of the name servers authoritative for a given zone in a random order before playing favorites.

On the whole, this simple but elegant algorithm allows Microsoft DNS Servers to "lock on" to the closest name servers quickly and without the overhead of an out-of-band mechanism to measure performance.

The Whole Enchilada

What this amounts to is a resolution process that, taken as a whole, looks like Figure 2-13.

A resolver queries a local name server, which then sends iterative queries to a number of other name servers in pursuit of an answer for the resolver. Each name server it queries refers it to another name server that is authoritative for a zone further down in the namespace and closer to the domain name sought. Finally, the local name server queries the authoritative name server, which returns an answer. All the while, the local name server uses each response it receives—whether a referral or the answer—to update the RTT of the responding name server, which will help it decide which name servers to query to resolve domain names in the future.

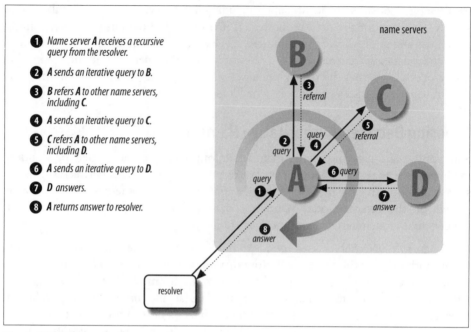

1. Name server **A** receives a recursive query from the resolver.

2. **A** sends an iterative query to **B**.

3. **B** refers **A** to other name servers, including **C**.

4. **A** sends an iterative query to **C**.

5. **C** refers **A** to other name servers, including **D**.

6. **A** sends an iterative query to **D**.

7. **D** answers.

8. **A** returns answer to resolver.

Figure 2-13. The resolution process

Mapping Addresses to Names

One major piece of functionality missing from the resolution process as explained so far is how addresses get mapped back to domain names. Address-to-name mapping is used to produce output that is easier for humans to read and interpret (e.g., in log files). It's also used in some authorization checks. Unix hosts map addresses to domain names to compare against entries in *.rhosts* and *hosts.equiv* files, for example. When using host tables, address-to-name mapping is trivial. It requires a straightforward sequential search through the host table for an address. The search returns the official hostname listed. In DNS, however, address-to-name mapping isn't so simple. Data, including addresses, in the domain namespace is indexed by name. Given a domain name, finding an address is relatively easy. But finding the domain name that maps to a given address would seem to require an exhaustive search of the data attached to every domain name in the tree.

Actually, there's a better solution that's both clever and effective. Because it's easy to find data once you're given the domain name that indexes that data, why not create a part of the domain namespace that uses addresses as labels? In the Internet domain namespace, this portion of the namespace is the *in-addr.arpa* domain.

Nodes in the *in-addr.arpa* domain are labeled after the numbers in the dotted-octet representation of IP addresses. (Dotted-octet representation refers to the common method of expressing 32-bit IP addresses as four numbers in the range 0 to 255, separated by dots.) The *in-addr.arpa* domain, for example, could have up to 256 subdomains, one corresponding to each possible value in the first octet of an IP address. Each of these subdomains could have up to 256 subdomains of its own, corresponding to the possible values of the second octet. Finally, at the fourth level down, there are resource records attached to the final octet giving the full domain name of the host at that IP address. That makes for an awfully big domain: *in-addr. arpa*, shown in Figure 2-14, is roomy enough for every IP address on the Internet.

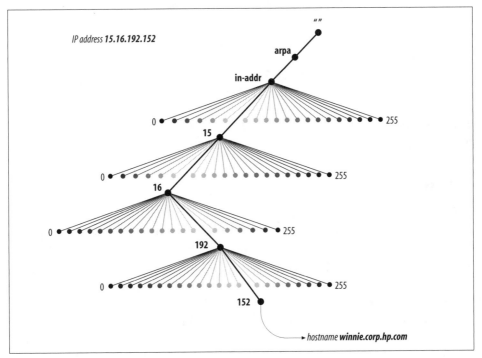

Figure 2-14. The in-addr.arpa domain

Note that when read in a domain name, the IP address appears backward because the name is read from leaf to root. For example, if *winnie.corp.hp.com*'s IP address is 15.16.192.152, the corresponding node in the *in-addr.arpa* domain is *152.192.16.15. in-addr.arpa*, which maps back to the domain name *winnie.corp.hp.com*.

IP addresses could have been represented the opposite way in the namespace, with the first octet of the IP address at the bottom of the *in-addr.arpa* domain. That way, the IP address would have read correctly (forward) in the domain name. IP addresses are hierarchical, however, just like domain names. Network numbers are doled out much as domain names are, and administrators can then subnet their address space and further delegate numbering. The difference is that IP addresses get more specific from left to right, while domain names get less specific from left to right. Figure 2-15 shows what we mean.

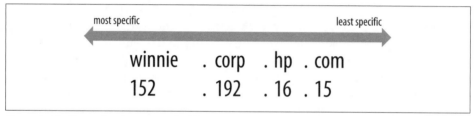

Figure 2-15. Hierarchical names and addresses

Making the first octets in the IP address appear highest in the tree gives administrators the ability to delegate authority for *in-addr.arpa* zones along network lines. For example, the *15.in-addr.arpa* zone, which contains the reverse-mapping information for all hosts whose IP addresses start with 15, can be delegated to the administrators of network 15.0.0.0. This would be impossible if the octets appeared in the opposite order. If the IP addresses were represented the other way around, *15.in-addr.arpa* would consist of every host whose IP address *ended* with 15—not a practical zone to try to delegate.

Caching

The whole resolution process may seem awfully convoluted and cumbersome to someone accustomed to simple searches through the host table. Actually, though, it's usually quite fast. One of the features that speeds it up considerably is *caching*.

A name server processing a recursive query may have to send out quite a few queries to find an answer. However, it discovers a lot of information about the domain namespace as it does so. Each time it's referred to another list of name servers, it learns that those name servers are authoritative for some zone, and it learns the addresses of those servers. At the end of the resolution process, when it finally finds the data the original querier sought, it can store that data for future reference, too. The Microsoft DNS Server even implements *negative caching*: if an authoritative name server responds to a query with an answer that says the domain name or data type in the query doesn't exist, the local name server will also temporarily cache that information.

Name servers cache all this data to help speed up successive queries. The next time a resolver queries the name server for data about a domain name the name server knows something about, the process is shortened quite a bit. The name server may have cached the answer, positive or negative, in which case it simply returns the answer to the resolver. Even if it doesn't have the answer cached, it may have learned the identities of the name servers that are authoritative for the zone the domain name is in and be able to query them directly.

For example, say our name server has already looked up the address of *eecs.berkeley.edu*. In the process, it cached the names and addresses of the *eecs.berkeley.edu* and *berkeley.edu* name servers (plus *eecs.berkeley.edu*'s IP address). Now if a resolver were to query our name server for the address of *baobab.cs.berkeley.edu*, our name server could skip querying the root name servers. Recognizing that *berkeley.edu* is the closest ancestor of *baobab.cs.berkeley.edu* about which it knows, our name server would start by querying a *berkeley.edu* name server, as shown in Figure 2-16. On the other hand, if our name server had discovered that there was no address for *eecs.berkeley.edu*, the next time it received a query for the address, it could simply have responded appropriately from its cache.

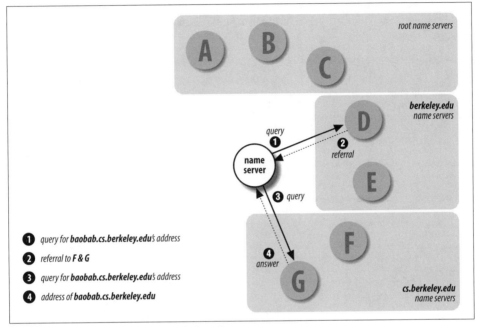

Figure 2-16. Resolving baobab.cs.berkeley.edu

In addition to speeding up resolution, caching obviates a name server's need to query the root name servers to answer any queries it can't answer locally. This means it's not as dependent on the roots, and the roots won't suffer as much from all its queries.

Time to Live

Name servers can't cache data forever, of course. If they did, changes to that data on the authoritative name servers would never reach the rest of the network; remote name servers would just continue to use cached data. Consequently, the administrator of the zone that contains the data decides on a *time to live* (TTL) for the data. The time to live is the amount of time that any name server is allowed to cache the data. After the time to live expires, the name server must discard the cached data and get new data from the authoritative name servers. This also applies to negatively cached data: a name server must time out a negative answer after a period in case new data has been added on the authoritative name servers.

Deciding on a time to live for your data is essentially deciding on a trade-off between performance and consistency. A small TTL will help ensure that data in your zones is consistent across the network, because remote name servers will time it out more quickly and be forced to query your authoritative name servers more often for new data. On the other hand, this will increase the load on your name servers and lengthen the average resolution time for information in your zones.

A large TTL will shorten the average time it takes to resolve information in your zones because the data can be cached longer. The drawback is that your information will be inconsistent for a longer time if you make changes to the data on your name servers.

But enough of this theory—I'll bet you're antsy to get on with things. Some home-work is necessary before you can set up your zones and your name servers, though, and we'll assign it in the next chapter.

CHAPTER 3

Where Do I Start?

"What do you call yourself?" the Fawn said at last.
Such a soft sweet voice it had!

"I wish I knew!" thought poor Alice. She answered,
rather sadly, "Nothing, just now."

"Think again," it said: "that won't do."

Alice thought, but nothing came of it. "Please, would
you tell me what you call yourself?" she said timidly.
"I think that might help a little."

"I'll tell you, if you come a little further on,"
the Fawn said. "I can't remember here."

Now that you understand the theory behind the Domain Name System, we can attend to more practical matters. Before you set up your zones, you may need to get name server software. While a name server is included as a standard part of Windows 2000 Server, you may want to look at alternatives. Once you've got the software to run your name server, you need to decide on a domain name for your main zone—which may not be quite as easy as it sounds, because it entails finding an appropriate place in the Internet namespace. That decided, you need to contact the administrators of the parent of the zone whose domain name you've chosen.

One thing at a time, though. Let's talk about how to decide on name server software and where to get it.

Which Name Server?

If you plan to set up your own domain and run name servers for it, you'll need name server software first. Even if you're planning on having someone else run your domain, it's helpful to have the software around. For example, you can use your local name server to test your data files before giving them to your remote domain administrator.

Microsoft ships a name server on the Windows 2000 Server CD-ROM, but you have to install it separately. This server, which we call the Microsoft DNS Server, is the server we cover in this book. It's notable because it sports a nice graphical frontend for configuring the server. This isn't the only name server available for Windows 2000, however. There are several others. Most are ports of BIND, which has traditionally been a Unix-based name server. If you're more comfortable configuring BIND than learning to configure a new name server (even with a GUI), you might consider these options:

Meta IP/DNS
> Meta IP/DNS is a commercial port (that is, you gotta pay for it) of the BIND 8.2.3 server to Windows 2000. As such, it supports DNS NOTIFY, dynamic updates, and all the security features BIND 8.2.3 offers. Meta IP/DNS is also integrated with WINS and can forward- and reverse-map NetBIOS names with the help of a WINS server. It runs on Windows 2000 as well as on Windows NT Workstation and Server.

> Meta IP/DNS is actually part of a larger IP-management product called Meta IP, but it's available separately, too. For more information, see *http://www.checkpoint.com/products/metaip/index.html*.

The Internet Software Consortium's BIND 8.2.4 distribution
> The BIND 8.2.4 name server now compiles for Windows NT and Windows 2000 without any modification to the source code. Since few people have the necessary software to compile it, the Internet Software Consortium distributes a compiled version on its web site. See *http://www.isc.org/products/BIND/bind8.html*.

If you decide to use one of these ports of BIND to Windows 2000, we suggest you pick up a copy of *DNS and BIND*. That book concentrates on the BIND implementation; this book emphasizes the Microsoft DNS Server.

Getting the DNS Server

If you've read to this section, we'll assume you've decided to use the Microsoft DNS Server. Before proceeding, you'll need to install the DNS server and its configuration frontend from the Windows 2000 Server CD-ROM. For detailed instructions on this process, see Appendix B.

Handy Mailing Lists and Usenet Newsgroups

Now that you've installed your name server, it's important to keep abreast of DNS and name server developments. Two Usenet newsgroups are helpful for this: *microsoft.public.win2000.dns* and *comp.protocols.dns.bind*. *microsoft.public.win2000.dns* concentrates on the Microsoft DNS Server and is a good place to find out about new bugs. *comp.protocols.dns.bind* is more BIND-centric (as the name indicates) but is an excellent source of information about the art and practice of running domains and name servers. It arguably has a better signal-to-noise ratio than the Microsoft newsgroup and is also available as a mailing list, *bind-users@isc.org*.* A searchable archive of the list can be found at *http://www.isc.org/ml-archives/bind-users/*.

Microsoft's online support site, at *http://support.microsoft.com/support/*, is a valuable source of information about known bugs in the DNS server and updates to the code. Also, be sure to check Andras Salamon's "DNS Resource Directory" at *http://www.dns.net/dnsrd/* for pointers to online DNS resources and documentation.

Another mailing list you might be interested in is the *namedroppers* list. Folks on the *namedroppers* mailing list are involved in the IETF working group that develops extensions to the DNS specifications, DNSEXT. For example, the discussion of a new, proposed DNS record type would probably take place on *namedroppers* instead of the BIND users mailing list. For more information on DNSEXT's charter, see *http://www.ietf.org/html.charters/dnsext-charter.html*.

The address for the *namedroppers* mailing list is *namedroppers@ops.ietf.org*, and it is gatewayed into the Internet newsgroup *comp.protocols.dns.std*. To join the *namedroppers* mailing list, send mail to *namedroppers-request@ops.ietf.org* with the text "subscribe namedroppers" as the body of the message.

Finding IP Addresses

You'll notice that we gave you a number of domain names of hosts that have *ftp*able software, and the mailing lists we mentioned include domain names. This should underscore the importance of DNS: see what valuable software and advice you can get with the help of DNS? Unfortunately, it's also something of a chicken-and-egg problem: you can't send email to an address with a domain name in it unless you've got DNS set up, so how can you ask someone on the list how to set up DNS?

Well, we could give you the IP addresses for all the hosts we mentioned, but since IP addresses change often (in publishing timescales, anyway), we'll show you how you can *temporarily* use someone else's name server to find the information instead. As long as your host has Internet connectivity and the *nslookup* program, you can retrieve information from the Internet namespace.

To look up the IP address for *ftp.microsoft.com*, for example, you could use:

```
C:\> nslookup ftp.microsoft.com. 207.69.188.185
```

---

* To ask a question on an Internet mailing list, all you need to do is send a message to the mailing list's address. If you'd like to join the list, however, you have to send a message to the list's maintainer first, requesting that he or she add your email address to the list. Don't send this message to the list itself; that's considered rude. The Internet convention is that you can reach the maintainer of a mailing list by sending mail to *list-request@domain*, where *list@domain* is the address of the mailing list. So, for example, you can reach the BIND users mailing list's administrator by sending mail to *bind-users-request@isc.org*.

This instructs *nslookup* to query the name server running on the host at the IP address 207.69.188.185 to find the IP address for *ftp.microsoft.com* and should produce output like:

```
Server:  ns1.mindspring.com
Address:  207.69.188.185


Name:    ftp.microsoft.com
Address: 198.105.232.1
```

Now you can *ftp* to *ftp.microsoft.com*'s IP address, 198.105.232.1.

How did we know that the host at IP address 207.69.188.185 runs a name server? Our ISP, Mindspring, told us—it's one of their name servers. If your ISP provides name servers for its customers' use (and most do), use one of them. If your ISP doesn't provide name servers (shame on them!), you can *temporarily* use one of the name servers listed in this book. As long as you only use it to look up a few IP addresses or other data, the administrators probably won't mind. It's considered very rude, however, to point your resolver or query tool at someone else's name server permanently.

Of course, if you already have access to a host with Internet connectivity *and* have DNS configured, you can use it to *ftp* what you need.

Once you've got a working version of the Microsoft DNS Server, you're ready to start thinking about your domain name.

Choosing a Domain Name

Choosing a domain name is more involved than it may sound, because it entails both choosing a name *and* finding out who runs the parent zone. In other words, you need to find out where you fit in the Internet domain namespace, then find out who runs that particular corner of the namespace.

The first step in picking a domain name is finding where in the existing domain namespace you belong. It's easiest to start at the top and work your way down: decide which top-level domain you belong in, then which of that top-level domain's subdomains you fit into.

Note that in order to find out what the Internet domain namespace looks like (beyond what we've already told you), you'll need access to the Internet. You don't need access to a host that already has name service configured, but it would help a little. If you don't have access to a host with DNS configured, you'll have to "borrow" name service from other name servers (as in our previous *ftp.microsoft.com* example) to get you going.

On Registrars and Registries

Before we go any further, we need to define a few terms: registry, registrar, and registration. These terms aren't defined anywhere in the DNS specs. Instead, they apply to the way the Internet namespace is managed today.

A *registry* is an organization responsible for maintaining a top-level domain's (well, zone's, really) data files, which contain the delegation to each subdomain of that top-level domain. Under the current structure of the Internet, a given top-level domain can have no more than one registry. A *registrar* acts as an interface between customers and the registry, providing registration and value-added services. It submits to the registry the zone data and other data (including contact information) for each of its customers in a single top-level domain.

Registration is the process by which a customer tells a registrar which name servers to delegate a subdomain to and provides the registrar with contact and billing information. The registrar makes these changes through the registry.

VeriSign, Inc. currently acts as both the exclusive registry and as a registrar for the *com*, *net*, *org*, and *edu* top-level domains. And now, back to our story.

Where in the World Do I Fit?

If your organization is attached to the Internet outside of the United States, you first need to decide whether you'd rather request a subdomain of one of the generic top-level domains, such as *com*, *net*, and *org*, or a subdomain of your country's top-level domain. The generic top-level domains aren't exclusively for U.S. organizations. If your company is a multi- or transnational company that doesn't fit in any one country's top-level domain, or if you'd simply prefer a generic top-level to your country's top-level domain, you're welcome to register in one. If you choose this route, skip to the section "The generic top-level domains" later in this chapter.

If you opt for a subdomain under your country's top level, you should check whether your country's top-level domain is registered and, if it is, what kind of structure it has. Consult our list of the current top-level domains (Appendix D) if you're not sure what the name of your country's top-level domain would be.

Some countries' top-level domains, such as New Zealand's *nz*, Australia's *au*, and the United Kingdom's *uk*, are divided organizationally into second-level domains. The names of their second-level domains, such as *co* or *com* for commercial entities, reflect organizational affiliation. Others, like France's *fr* domain and Denmark's *dk* domain, are divided into a multitude of subdomains managed by individual universities and companies, such as the University of St. Etienne's domain, *univ-st-etienne.fr*, and the Danish Unix Users Group's *dkuug.dk*. Many top-level domains have their own web sites that describe their structure. If you're not sure of the URL for your country's top-level domain's web site, start at *http://www.allwhois.com*, a directory of links to such web sites.

If your country's top-level domain doesn't have a web site explaining how it's organized, you may have to use a tool like *nslookup* to grope around and figure out its structure. (If you're uncomfortable with our rushing headlong into *nslookup* without giving it a proper introduction, you might want to skim Chapter 12.) For example, here's how you could list the *au* domain's subdomains using *nslookup*:

```
C:\> nslookup - 207.69.188.185      --Use the name server at 207.69.188.185
Default Server:  ns1.mindspring.com
Address:  207.69.188.185

> set type=ns      --Find the name servers (ns)
> au.              --for the au domain
Server:  ns1.mindspring.com
Address: 207.69.188.185

au      nameserver = MUNNARI.OZ.AU
au      nameserver = MULGA.CS.MU.OZ.AU
au      nameserver = NS.UU.NET
au      nameserver = NS.EU.NET
au      nameserver = NS1.BERKELEY.EDU
au      nameserver = NS2.BERKELEY.EDU
au      nameserver = VANGOGH.CS.BERKELEY.EDU
MUNNARI.OZ.AU      internet address = 128.250.1.21
MULGA.CS.MU.OZ.AU      internet address = 128.250.1.22
MULGA.CS.MU.OZ.AU      internet address = 128.250.37.150
NS.UU.NET      internet address = 137.39.1.3
NS.EU.NET      internet address = 192.16.202.11
NS1.BERKELEY.EDU  internet address = 128.32.136.9
NS1.BERKELEY.EDU  internet address = 128.32.206.9
NS2.BERKELEY.EDU      internet address = 128.32.136.12
NS2.BERKELEY.EDU      internet address = 128.32.206.12

> server ns.uu.net.      --Now query one of these name servers—preferably a close one!
Default Server:  ns.uu.net
Addresses:  137.39.1.3

> ls -t au.      --List the au zone.
                 --The zone's NS records mark delegation to subdomains
                 --and will give you the names of the subdomains.
                 --Note that not all name servers will allow you to list zones,
                 --for security reasons.
 [ns.uu.net]
$ORIGIN au.
@                     3D IN NS        mulga.cs.mu.OZ
                      3D IN NS        vangogh.CS.Berkeley.EDU.
                      3D IN NS        ns1.Berkeley.EDU.
                      3D IN NS        ns2.Berkeley.EDU.
                      3D IN NS        ns.UU.NET.
                      3D IN NS        ns.eu.NET.
                      3D IN NS        munnari.OZ
```

```
    ORG                     1D IN NS        mulga.cs.mu.OZ
                            1D IN NS        rip.psg.COM.
                            1D IN NS        munnari.OZ
                            1D IN NS        yalumba.connect.COM
    info                    1D IN NS        ns.telstra.net.
                            1D IN NS        ns1.telstra.net.
                            1D IN NS        munnari.oz
                            1D IN NS        svc01.apnic.net.
    otc                     4H IN NS        ns2.telstra.com
                            4H IN NS        munnari.oz
                            4H IN NS        ns.telstra.com
    OZ                      1D IN NS        mx.nsi.NASA.GOV.
                            1D IN NS        munnari.OZ
                            1D IN NS        mulga.cs.mu.OZ
                            1D IN NS        dmssyd.syd.dms.CSIRO
                            1D IN NS        ns.UU.NET.
    csiro                   1D IN NS        steps.its.csiro
                            1D IN NS        munnari.OZ
                            1D IN NS        manta.vic.cmis.csiro
                            1D IN NS        dmssyd.nsw.cmis.csiro
                            1D IN NS        zoiks.per.its.csiro
    COM                     1D IN NS        mx.nsi.NASA.GOV.
                            1D IN NS        yalumba.connect.COM
                            1D IN NS        munnari.OZ
                            1D IN NS        mulga.cs.mu.OZ
                            1D IN NS        ns.ripe.NET.
    > ^D
```

The basic technique we used is straightforward: look up the list of name servers for the top-level domain—because they're the only ones with complete information about the corresponding zone—then query one of those name servers and list the name servers for the delegated subdomains.

If you can't tell from the names of the subdomains which one you belong in, you can look up the contact information for the corresponding zone and send email to the technical contact asking, politely, for advice. Similarly, if you think you should be part of an existing subdomain but aren't sure, you can always ask the folks who administer that subdomain to double-check.

To find out who to ask about a particular subdomain, you'll have to look up the corresponding zone's start of authority (SOA) record. In each zone's SOA record, there's a field that contains the electronic mail address of the zone's technical contact.* (The other fields in the SOA record provide general information about the zone—we'll discuss them in more detail later.)

---

* The subdomain and the zone have the same domain name, but the SOA record really belongs to the zone, not the subdomain. The person at the zone's technical contact email address may not manage the whole subdomain (there may be additional delegated subdomains beneath), but he should certainly know the purpose of the subdomain.

You can look up the zone's SOA record with *nslookup*, too. For example, if you're curious about the purpose of the *csiro* subdomain, you can find out who runs it by looking up *csiro.au*'s SOA record:

```
C:\> nslookup - 207.69.188.185
Default Server:  ns1.mindspring.com
Address:  207.69.188.185

> set type=soa       --Look for start of authority data
> csiro.au.          --for csiro.au
Server:  ns1.mindspring.com
Address: 207.69.188.185

csiro.au
        origin = steps.its.csiro.au
        mail addr = hostmaster.csiro.au
        serial = 2000041301
        refresh = 10800 (3H)
        retry   = 3600 (1H)
        expire  = 3600000 (5w6d16h)
        minimum ttl = 86400 (1D)
```

The *mail addr* field is the Internet address of *csiro.au*'s contact. To convert the address into Internet email address format, you'll need to change the first "." in the address to an "@". So *hostmaster.csiro.au* becomes *hostmaster@csiro.au*.[*]

whois

The *whois* service can also help you figure out the purpose of a given domain. Unfortunately, there are many *whois* servers—most good administrators of top-level domains run one—and they don't talk to each other, like name servers do. Consequently, the first step to using *whois* is finding the right *whois* server.

One of the easiest places to start your search for the right *whois* server is at *http://www.allwhois.com* (Figure 3-1). We mentioned earlier that this site has a list of the web sites for each country code's top-level domain; it also has a list of top-level domains with *whois* URLs—pages with HTML-based interfaces to query *whois* servers.

Scrolling down to **Australia (au)**, you can click on **Jump to Whois** and go directly to a page where you can enter *csiro.au*, as shown in Figure 3-2.

Clicking on **Submit** retrieves the information in Figure 3-3 for you.

Perhaps even more interesting for the inertially challenged is the work done by WebMagic to provide a unified whois lookup service on the Web. Their web site, at

---

[*] This form of Internet mail address is a vestige of two former DNS records, MB and MG. MB (mailbox) and MG (mail group) were to be DNS records specifying Internet mailboxes and mail groups (mailing lists) as subdomains of the appropriate domain. MB and MG never took off, but the address format they would have dictated is used in the SOA record, maybe for sentimental reasons.

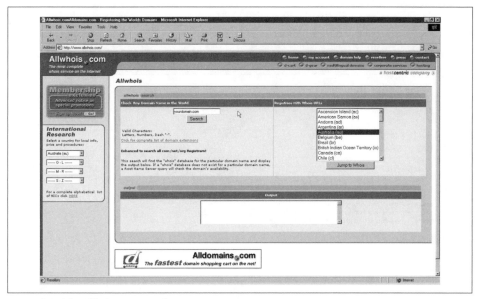

Figure 3-1. The Allwhois.com web site

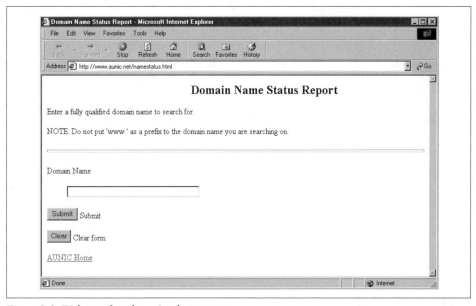

Figure 3-2. Web interface for au's whois server

http://www.webmagic.com/whois/index.html, lets you choose the top-level domain (and sometimes the second-level domain) in which the subdomain you're looking for resides, then transparently contacts the right *whois* server.

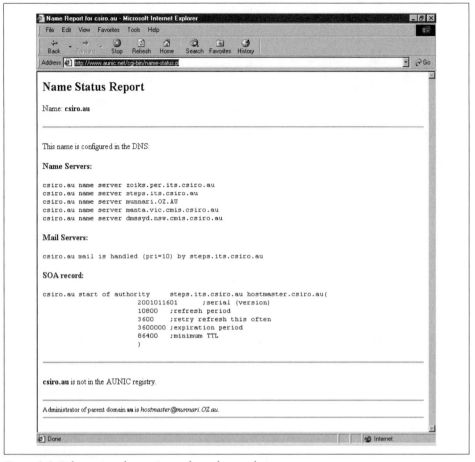

Figure 3-3. Information about csiro.au from the au whois server

Obviously, these are both useful web sites if you're looking for the contact for a domain outside of the U.S.

Once you've found the right web site or the right contact, you've probably found the registrar. Outside the U.S., most domains have a single registrar. A few, though, such as Denmark's *dk* and Great Britain's *co.uk* and *org.uk*, have multiple registrars. However, the process described above will still lead you to them.

Back in the U.S.A.

In true cosmopolitan spirit, we covered international domains first. But what if you're from the good ol' U.S. of A.?

If you're in the U.S., where you belong depends mainly upon what your organization does, how you'd like your domain names to look, and how much you're willing to pay. If your organization falls into one of the following categories, you're encouraged to join *us*:

- K-12 (kindergarten through twelfth grade) schools
- Community colleges and technical vocational schools
- State and local government agencies

Even if you don't fall into one of these categories, if you'd like a domain name that indicates your location, like *acme.boulder.co.us*, you can register in the *us* top-level domain. The *us* domain delegates subdomains under third-level domains largely named after "localities" (usually cities or counties); the second-level domains correspond to the appropriate U.S. Postal Service two-letter state abbreviation (recall our discussion in the section called "The Internet Domain Namespace" in Chapter 2). So, for example, if all you need is a subdomain to hold the two internetworked hosts in your basement in Colorado Springs, Colorado, you can register *toms-basement.colorado-springs.co.us*.

Finally, there's the issue of cost. It's usually cheaper to register a subdomain of the *us* top-level domain than to register under *com*, *net*, or *org*, and sometimes it's even free.

If you'd like more detailed information on the structure of the *us* domain and the rules that govern it, check out the U.S. NIC's web site, at *http://www.nic.us*.

Of course, folks in the U.S. can also ask for a subdomain of one of the generic top-level domains. As long as you don't ask for one that's already taken, you should get the one you request. We'll cover registration under the generic top-level domains later in this chapter.

The us domain

Let's go through an example to give you an idea of how to comb the *us* domain namespace for the perfect domain name. Say you're helping out your son's kindergarten in Boulder, Colorado, and you want to register a domain name for the school.

Using an account you still have on a host at Colorado University (from your undergrad days), you can check to see whether a domain for Boulder exists. (If you didn't have an account there, but you did have Internet connectivity, you could still use *nslookup* to query a well-known name server.)

```
C:\> nslookup
Default Server:  boulder.colorado.edu
Address: 128.138.238.18, 128.138.240.1

> set type=ns      --Look up the name servers
> co.us.           --for co.us
Default Server:  boulder.colorado.edu
Address:  128.138.238.18, 128.138.240.1
```

```
co.us    nameserver = VENERA.ISI.EDU
co.us    nameserver = NS.ISI.EDU
co.us    nameserver = RSO.INTERNIC.NET
co.us    nameserver = NS.UU.NET
co.us    nameserver = ADMII.ARL.MIL
co.us    nameserver = EXCALIBUR.USC.EDU
```

This gives you the names of the *co.us* name servers. Without exiting *nslookup*, change to one of the *co.us* name servers, say *venera.isi.edu*, and check to see if there are any subdomains:

```
> server venera.isi.edu.    --Change server to venera.isi.edu
Default Server:  venera.isi.edu
Address:  128.9.0.32

> ls -t co.us.    --List the co.us zone to look for NS records
[venera.isi.edu]
$ORIGIN co.us.
@                          1W IN NS        NS.ISI.EDU.
                           1W IN NS        RSO.INTERNIC.NET.
                           1W IN NS        NS.UU.NET.
                           1W IN NS        ADMII.ARL.MIL.
                           1W IN NS        EXCALIBUR.USC.EDU.
                           1W IN NS        VENERA.ISI.EDU.
officemate1.monument       1W IN NS        ns1.direct.ca.
                           1W IN NS        ns2.direct.ca.
la-junta                   1D IN NS        ns2.cw.net.
                           1D IN NS        usdns.beltane.com.
                           1D IN NS        usdns2.beltane.com.
morrison                   1W IN NS        NS1.WESTNET.NET.
                           1W IN NS        NS.UTAH.EDU.
littleton                  1W IN NS        NS1.WESTNET.NET.
                           1W IN NS        NS.UTAH.EDU.
mus                        1W IN NS        NS1.WESTNET.NET.
                           1W IN NS        NS.UTAH.EDU.
ci.palmer-lake             1W IN NS        DNS1.REGISTEREDSITE.COM.
                           1W IN NS        DNS2.REGISTEREDSITE.COM.
co.adams                   1W IN NS        ns1.rockymtn.net.
                           1W IN NS        ns2.rockymtn.net.
[...]
```

Aha! So there *is* life in Colorado! There are subdomains called *la-junta*, *morrison*, *littleton*, *mus*, and many others. There's even a subdomain for Boulder (called, not surprisingly, *boulder*):

```
boulder                    1W IN NS        NS1.WESTNET.NET.
                           1W IN NS        NS.UTAH.EDU.
```

How do you find out how to contact the administrator of *boulder.co.us*? You can try *whois*, but since *boulder.co.us* isn't a top-level country domain or a subdomain of a generic top-level domain, you won't find much. Fortunately, the U.S. NIC provides a list of email addresses of contacts for each third-level subdomain of *us* at *http://www.isi.edu/in-notes/us-domain-delegated.txt*. If you can't find the information you need there, you can use *nslookup* to find the SOA record for the *boulder.co.us* zone, just as you did to find out whom to ask about *csiro.au*. Though the person or persons who read mail sent to the address in the SOA record may not handle registration themselves (technical and administrative functions for the zone may be divided), it's a good bet they know the folks who do and can direct you to them.

Here's how you'd use *nslookup* to dig up the SOA record for *boulder.co.us*:

```
C:\> nslookup
Default Server:  boulder.colorado.edu
Address:  128.138.238.18, 128.138.240.1

> set type=soa       --Look up SOA record
> boulder.co.us.     --for boulder.co.us
Default Server:  boulder.colorado.edu
Address:  128.138.238.18, 128.138.240.1

boulder.co.us
        origin = ns1.westnet.net
        mail addr = cgarner.westnet.net
        serial = 200004101
        refresh = 21600 (6H)
        retry  = 1200 (20M)
        expire  = 3600000 (5w6d16h)
        minimum ttl = 432000 (5D)
```

As in the *csiro.au* example, you need to swap the first "." in the *mail addr* field with an "@" before you use it. Thus, *cgarner.westnet.net* becomes *cgarner@westnet.net*.

To request delegation of a subdomain of *boulder.co.us*, you can download a copy of the registration form template from *http://www.nic.us/cgi-bin/template.pl* and mail it to the contact. If, however, you find that the subdomain for your locality hasn't yet been created, read through the *us* domain's delegation policy at *http://www.nic.us/register/locality.html*. Then fill out the registration form at *http://www.nic.us/cgi-bin/template.pl*.

The generic top-level domains

As we said, there are many reasons why you might want to ask for a subdomain of one of the generic top-level domains, like *com*, *net*, and *org*: you work for a multi- or transnational company, you like the fact that they're better-known, or you just prefer the sound of your domain name with "com" on the end. Let's go through a short example of choosing a domain name under a generic top-level domain.

Imagine you're the network administrator for a think tank in Hopkins, Minnesota. You've just gotten a connection to the Internet through a commercial ISP. Your company has never had so much as a UUCP link, so you're not currently registered in the Internet namespace.

Since you're in the United States, you have the choice of joining either *us* or one of the generic top-level domains. Your think tank is world-renowned, though, so *us* wouldn't be a good choice. A subdomain of *com* would be best.

The think tank is known as The Gizmonic Institute, so you decide *gizmonics.com* might be an appropriate domain name. Now you've got to check whether the name *gizmonics.com* has been taken by anyone, so you use an account you have at the University of Minnesota:

```
C:\> nslookup
Default Server:  ns.unet.umn.edu
Address:  128.101.101.101

> set type=any       --Look for any records
> gizmonics.com.     --for gizmonics.com
Server:  ns.unet.umn.edu
Address:  128.101.101.101

gizmonics.com    nameserver = NS2.SFO.WENET.NET
gizmonics.com    nameserver = NS1.SFO.WENET.NET
```

Whoops! Look like *gizmonics.com* is already taken (who would have thought?).[*] Well, *gizmonic-institute.com* is a little longer, but still intuitive:

```
C:\> nslookup
Default Server:  ns.unet.umn.edu
Address:  128.101.101.101

> set type=any              --Look for any records
> gizmonic-institute.com.   --for gizmonic-institute.com
Server:  ns.unet.umn.edu
Address:  128.101.101.101

*** ns.unet.umn.edu can't find gizmonic-institute.com.: Non-existent host/domain
```

gizmonic-institute.com is free, so you can go on to the next step: picking a registrar.

Choosing a registrar

Choose a registrar? Welcome to the brave new world of competition! Before the spring of 1999, a single company, Network Solutions, Inc., was both the registry and sole registrar for *com*, *net*, and *org*, as well as *edu*. To register a subdomain of any of the generic top-level domains, you had to go to Network Solutions.

In June 1999, ICANN, the organization that manages the domain namespace (we mentioned them in the last chapter) introduced competition to the registrar function of *com*, *net*, and *org*. There are now dozens of *com*, *net*, and *org* registrars from which you can choose (see *http://www.internic.net/regist.html*).

We won't presume to tell you how to pick a registrar, but take a look at the price and any other services the registrar might provide that interest you. See if you can get a nice package deal on registration and aluminum siding, for example.

---

[*] Actually, *gizmonics.com* is taken by Joel Hodgson, the guy who dreamed up The Gizmonic Institute and "Mystery Science Theater 3000" in the first place.

Checking That Your Network Is Registered

Before proceeding, you should check whether or not your IP network or networks are registered. Some registrars won't delegate a subdomain to name servers on unregistered networks, and network registries (we'll talk about them shortly) won't delegate an *in-addr.arpa* zone that corresponds to an unregistered network.

An IP network defines a range of IP addresses. For example, the network 15/8 is made up of all IP addresses in the range 15.0.0.0 to 15.255.255.255. The network 199.10.25/24 starts at 199.10.25.0 and ends at 199.10.25.255.

The InterNIC was once the official source of all IP networks; they assigned all IP networks to Internet-connected networks and made sure no two address ranges overlapped. Nowadays, the InterNIC's old role has been largely assumed by Internet service providers (ISPs), who allocate space from their own networks for customers to use. If you know your network came from your ISP, the larger network from which your network was carved is probably registered (to your ISP). You may still want to double-check that your ISP took care of registering their network, but you don't have to (and probably can't) do anything yourself, except nag your ISP if they didn't register their network. Once you've verified their registration, you can skip the rest of this section and move on.

If your network was assigned by the InterNIC, way back when, or you *are* an ISP, you should check to see whether your network is registered. Where do you go to check whether your network is registered? Why, to the same organizations that register networks, of course. These organizations, called (what else?) *network registries*, each handle network registration in some part of the world. In the Western Hemisphere, ARIN, the American Registry of Internet Numbers (*http://www.arin.net*), hands out IP address space and registers networks. In Asia and the Pacific, APNIC, the Asia Pacific Network Information Center (*http://www.apnic.net*), serves the same function. In Europe, it's the RIPE Network Coordination Centre (*http://www.ripe.net*). Each registry may also delegate registration authority for a region; for example, ARIN delegates registration authority for Mexico and Brazil to network registries in each country. Be sure to check for a network registry local to your country.

If you're not sure your network is registered, the best way to find out is to use the *whois* services provided by the various network registries to look for your network. Here are the URLs for each registry's *whois* page:

ARIN
 http://www.arin.net/whois/index.html
APNIC
 http://whois.apnic.net
RIPE
 http://www.ripe.net/cgi-bin/whois/

A Sidebar on CIDR

Once upon a time, when we wrote the first edition of this book, the Internet's 32-bit address space was divided up into three main classes of networks: Class A, Class B, and Class C. Class A networks were networks in which the first octet (the first eight bits) of the IP address identified the network, and the remaining bits were used by the organization assigned the network to differentiate hosts on the network. Most organizations with Class A networks also subdivided their networks into subnetworks, or subnets, adding another level of hierarchy to the addressing scheme. Class B networks devoted two octets to the network identifier and two to the host; Class C networks gave three octets to the network identifier and one to the host.

Unfortunately, this small/medium/large system of networks didn't work well for everyone. Many organizations were large enough to require more than a Class C network, which could accommodate at most 254 hosts, but too small to warrant a full Class B network, which could serve 65534 hosts. Many of these organizations were allocated Class B networks anyway. Consequently, Class B networks quickly became scarce.

To help solve this problem and create networks that were just the right size for all sorts of organizations, Classless Inter-Domain Routing, or CIDR (pronounced "cider"), was developed. As the name implies, CIDR does away with the old Class A, Class B, and Class C network designations. Instead of allocating either one, two, or three octets to the network identifier, the allocator could assign any number of contiguous bits of the IP address to the network identifier. So, for example, if an organization needed an address space roughly four times as large as a Class B network, the powers-that-be could assign it a network identifier of 14 bits, leaving 18 bits (four Class Bs' worth) of space to use.

Naturally, the advent of CIDR made the "classful" terminology outdated—although it's still used a good deal in casual conversation. Now, to designate a particular CIDR network, we specify the particular high-order bit value assigned to an organization, expressed in dotted octet notation, and how many bits identify the network. The two terms are separated by a slash. So 15/8 is the old, Class A–sized network that begins with the eight-bit pattern 00001111. The old, Class B–sized network 128.32.0.0 is now 128.32/16. And the network 192.168.0.128/25 consists of the 128 IP addresses from 192.168.0.128 to 192.168.0.255.

If you find out your network isn't registered, you'll need to get it registered before setting up your *in-addr.arpa* zones. Each registry has a different process for registering networks, but most involve money changing hands (from your hands to theirs, unfortunately).

You may find out that your network is already assigned to your ISP. If this is the case, you don't need to register independently with the network registry.

Once all your Internet-connected hosts are on registered networks, you can register your zones.

Registering Your Zones

Different registrars have different registration policies and procedures, but most, at this point, handle registration online, through their web sites. Since you found or chose your registrar earlier in the chapter, we'll assume you know which web site to use.

The registrar will need to know the domain names and addresses of your name servers and enough information about you to send you a bill or charge your credit card. If you're not connected to the Internet, give them the addresses of the Internet hosts that will act as your name servers. Some registrars also require that you already have operational name servers for your zone. (Those that don't may ask for an estimate of when the name servers will be fully operational.) If that's the case with your registrar, skip ahead to Chapter 4 and set up your name servers. Then contact your registrar with the requisite information.

Most registrars will also ask for some information about your organization, including an administrative contact and a technical contact for your zone (who can be the same person). If your contacts aren't already registered in the registrar's *whois* database, you'll also need to provide information to register them in *whois*. This includes their names, surface mail addresses, phone numbers, and electronic mail addresses. If they are already registered in *whois*, just specify their *whois* "handles" (unique alphanumeric IDs) in the registration.

There's one more aspect of registering a new zone that we should mention: cost. Most registrars are commercial enterprises and charge money for registering domain names. Network Solutions, the original registrar for *com*, *net*, and *org*, charges $35 per year to register subdomains under the generic top-level domains. (If you already have a subdomain under *com*, *net*, or *org* and haven't received a bill from Network Solutions recently, it'd be a good idea to check your contact information with *whois* to make sure they've got a current address and phone number for you.)

If you're directly connected to the Internet, you should also have the *in-addr.arpa* zones corresponding to your IP networks delegated to you. For example, if your company was allocated the network 192.201.44/24, you should manage the *44.201.192. in-addr.arpa* zone. This will let you control the IP address-to-name mappings for hosts on your network. Chapter 4 also explains how to set up your *in-addr.arpa* zones.

In the last section, "Checking That Your Network Is Registered," we asked you to find the answers to several questions: is your network a slice of an ISP's network? Is your network, or the ISP network that your network is part of, registered? If so, in which network registry? You'll need these answers to have your *in-addr.arpa* zones delegated to you.

If your network is part of a larger network registered to an ISP, you should contact the ISP to have the appropriate subdomains of their *in-addr.arpa* zone delegated to you. Each ISP uses a different process for setting up *in-addr.arpa* delegation. Your

ISP's web page is a good place to research that process. If you can't find the information there, try looking up the SOA record for the *in-addr.arpa* zone that corresponds to your ISP's network. For example, if your network is part of UUNET's 153.35/16 network, you could look up the SOA record of *35.153.in-addr.arpa* to find the email address of the technical contact for the zone.

If your network is registered directly with one of the regional network registries, contact them to get your *in-addr.arpa* zone registered. Each network registry makes information on its delegation process available on its web site.

Now that you've registered your zones, you'd better take some time to get your house in order. You've got some name servers to set up, and in the next chapter, we'll show you how.

## CHAPTER 4

Setting Up the Microsoft DNS Server

*"It seems very pretty," she said when she had
finished it, "but it's rather hard to understand!"
(You see she didn't like to confess, even to herself,
that she couldn't make it out at all.) "Somehow
it seems to fill my head with ideas—only I
don't exactly know what they are!"*

If you have been diligently reading each chapter of this book, you're probably anxious to get a name server running. This chapter is for you. Let's set up a couple of name servers. Some of you may have read the table of contents and skipped directly to this chapter. (Shame on you!) If you are one of those people who cuts corners, be aware that we may use concepts from earlier chapters and expect you to understand them.

Several factors influence how you should set up your name servers. The biggest factor is what sort of access you have to the Internet: complete access (for example, you can *ftp* to *ftp.uu.net*), limited access (limited by a security firewall), or no access at all. This chapter assumes you have complete access. We'll discuss the other cases in Chapter 14.

In this chapter, we'll set up two name servers for a fictitious domain as an example for you to follow in setting up your own domain. We'll cover the topics in this chapter in enough detail for you to get your first two name servers running. Subsequent chapters will fill in the holes and go into greater depth. If you already have your name servers running, skim through this chapter to familiarize yourself with the terms we use or just to verify that you didn't miss something when you set up your servers.

Our Zone

Our fictitious zone serves a college. Movie University studies all aspects of the film industry and researches novel ways to distribute films. One of our most promising projects is research into using IP as a distribution medium. After visiting our registrar's web site, we have decided on the domain name *movie.edu*. A recent grant has enabled us to connect to the Internet.

Movie U. currently has two Ethernets, and we have plans for another network or two. The Ethernets have network addresses 192.249.249/24 and 192.253.253/24. A portion of our host table contains the following entries:

```
127.0.0.1      localhost

# These are our killer machines

192.249.249.2  robocop.movie.edu robocop
192.249.249.3  terminator.movie.edu terminator bigt
192.249.249.4  diehard.movie.edu diehard dh

# These machines are in horror(ible) shape and will be replaced
# soon.

192.253.253.2  misery.movie.edu misery
192.253.253.3  shining.movie.edu shining
192.253.253.4  carrie.movie.edu carrie

# A wormhole is a fictitious phenomenon that instantly transports
# space travelers over long distances and is not known to be
# stable. The only difference between wormholes and routers is
# that routers don't transport packets as instantly--especially
# ours.

192.249.249.1  wormhole.movie.edu wormhole wh wh249
192.253.253.1  wormhole.movie.edu wormhole wh wh253
```

The network is pictured in Figure 4-1.

The DNS Console

To manage a Microsoft DNS Server and maintain your DNS data, you'll use a tool called the *DNS console*, a snap-in for the Microsoft Management Console (MMC). (MMC is a general-purpose program that hosts administrative tools. It's new for Windows 2000 and replaces the "one-off" administrative tools found in Windows NT 4.0, such as DNS Manager, WINS Manager, DHCP Manager, and the like.) The DNS console has a graphical user interface (surprise) and is capable of managing multiple name servers. The DNS console is located on the **Administrative Tools** menu, provided you've already installed the DNS service. The DNS console communicates with the Microsoft DNS Server using a proprietary management protocol built on Microsoft's RPC (remote procedure call). That means the DNS console manages only the Microsoft DNS Server and not other name servers, such as BIND.

The main DNS console window looks like Figure 4-2 (or will look like it, after we've set everything up in the course of this chapter).

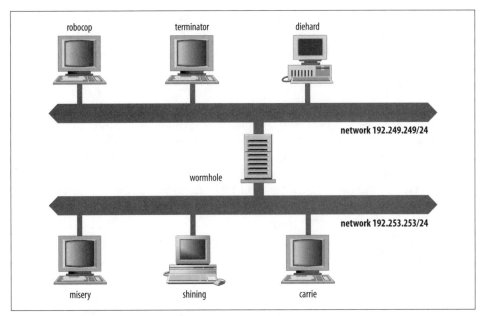

Figure 4-1. The Movie University network

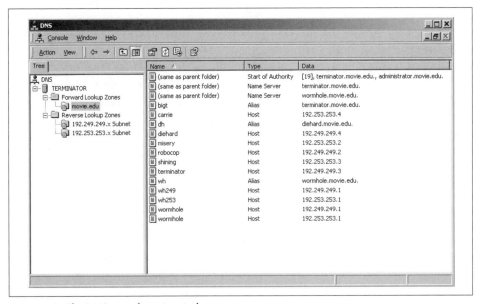

Figure 4-2. The DNS console main window

The left pane is called the *console tree*. It shows name servers, zones, and domains, while the right pane shows either informational messages or resource records.

This particular DNS console knows about only one name server, *terminator*. That name server is authoritative for three zones: *movie.edu*, *249.249.192.in-addr.arpa*, and

253.253.192.in-addr.arpa. The DNS console segregates *forward lookup zones* (which hold primarily address records) and *reverse lookup zones* (which hold primarily pointer records). If any of these zones had subdomains, they would show up as subfolders under the appropriate zone. For example, *comedies.movie.edu* would be represented as a folder called *comedies* under *movie.edu*.

There are two rows of menus. The top row, which lists the **Console**, **Window**, and **Help** menus, are menus for the MMC application itself and, to be honest, they're not that interesting. The **Console** menu has only one choice: **Exit**. The **Window** menu has the expected options to manage MMC subwindows, but you'll find that all the DNS administrative action happens in a single window for the DNS console snap-in. Choosing **New Window** produces another DNS console window; we haven't found a need to have more than one DNS console window open, but you might find multiple windows useful. Finally, the **Help** menu also has the usual suspects: **Help Topics** brings up the MMC help system, which offers quick jumps to help with the MMC application and the DNS console snap-in.

The second row holds the **Action** and **View** menus, which all other MMC plug-ins also have. The really important commands are in the **Action** menu: adding new name servers, creating zones and domains, and creating resource records. You can also delete objects and view objects' properties. We'll explain the various commands throughout this chapter.

But let's take a moment to go over the choices on the **View** menu. Since this is a standard MMC menu, not all the options are useful with the DNS console. An example is the first choice, **Choose Columns…**, which allows you to customize the columns in the right pane. That's nice, except that they don't need customization: you'll always want to see all three columns showing a resource record's name, type, and data. The next set of choices is **Large Icons**, **Small Icons**, **List**, and **Detail**, and the selection determines the display format in the right pane. We recommend choosing **Detail** when you first start the DNS console and leaving the view that way forever: otherwise you don't see the aforementioned three columns and their useful information about each resource record.

Next is **Advanced**, which toggles between a more basic, or beginner's, view and an advanced view more suitable for you DNS experts out there. There are a couple differences. The first is the display value in the type column of the right pane: in basic mode you'll see a description of the type of resource record; advanced mode shows the actual type you'd see in a DNS zone data file. For example, in the basic view you see **Start of Authority** records versus the advanced view's **SOA** records. The second difference is whether or not the DNS console displays some additional information in the console tree on the left. Advanced mode shows the three zones for which every Microsoft DNS Server is authoritative—*0.in-addr.arpa*, *127.in-addr.arpa*, and *255.in-addr.arpa*—as well as an icon allowing access to the name server's cache of records from previous lookups. We'll talk more about these zones and the cache later in this chapter.

The **Filter...** selection brings up a dialog box like the one shown in Figure 4-3. Filtering is handy when you've got a really large zone with hundreds or even thousands of resource records. Rather than displaying them all in the righthand pane, you can limit the display with this option.

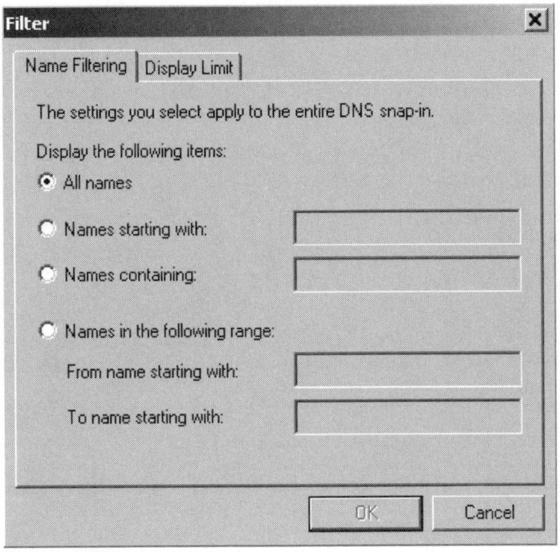

Figure 4-3. Filter dialog box

Customize is another choice standard to the **View** menu on all MMC snap-ins. It controls which MMC menus and toolbars appear. We recommend leaving these options at their default settings, as shown in Figure 4-4, since those settings are optimal.

But enough about the DNS console's generic knobs and switches. Let's move on to some DNS administrative tasks.

Setting Up DNS Data

Let's configure the first of Movie U.'s name servers. We'll use the DNS console for most of this process, so start it up if you haven't already done so. You don't have to run the DNS console on the machine running the name server, but for now it's easier if you do. You'll also need to have Administrator privileges to use the DNS console; otherwise, you'll only be able to start the application, not manage any name servers with it.

Adding a New Server to the DNS Console

The first step is configuring the DNS console to manage the *primary master name server* for your zone. The primary master for a zone—also called just the *primary*—

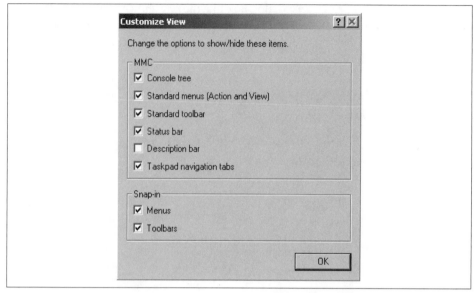

Figure 4-4. Customize dialog box

stores information about the zone on its disk. You make all changes to your zone on the primary master.

Select **Action → Connect To Computer…** and specify where the name server you want manage—the primary master—is running, either on the local machine or somewhere else. If the name server isn't local, enter its name or IP address. The DNS console adds an icon in the left pane for that name server, as in Figure 4-5.

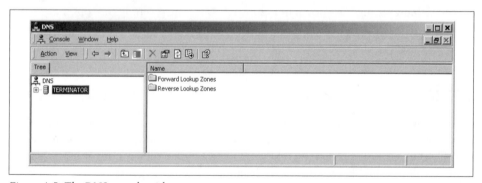

Figure 4-5. The DNS console with a new server

It's important to understand what we just did here. We told the DNS console about a name server for it to manage and it added that name server to its configuration. The DNS console did *not* start the name server on the target machine. If the name server isn't already installed and running, the DNS console can't manage it and will complain with the message, "The server is unavailable. Would you like to add it anyway?"

Selecting **Connect To Computer** adds that name server to the list of servers the DNS console knows about. As you might expect, selecting the server and choosing **Action →** **Delete** (or just pressing the **Delete** key) removes the server from the DNS console's configuration but doesn't change anything on the name server itself. The server will still be running—you can use **Connect To Computer...** to add it, and you'll be right back where you started.

Creating a New Zone

Now it's time to create the *movie.edu* zone. Select the name server on the left where you want to create the zone. (There's only one server now, *terminator*, but the DNS console could know about multiple servers.) Choose **Action → New Zone**. You'll see the New Zone Wizard, as in Figure 4-6.

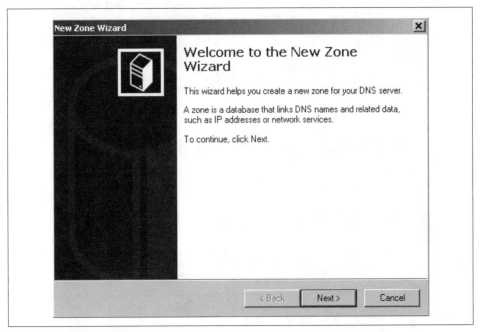

Figure 4-6. New Zone Wizard, first window

To continue, click **Next**. In the next window (Figure 4-7), you have three choices for the type of zone: **Active Directory integrated**, **Standard primary** and **Standard secondary**. For now, choose **Standard primary** and click **Next**. We'll talk more about Active Directory integration of zones in Chapter 11.

Now you need to choose the whether this is a forward- or reverse-mapping zone, as shown in Figure 4-8. *movie.edu* is, of course, a forward-mapping zone, so make that selection and click **Next**.

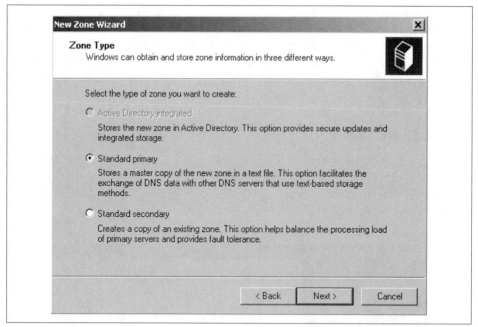

Figure 4-7. New Zone Wizard, second window

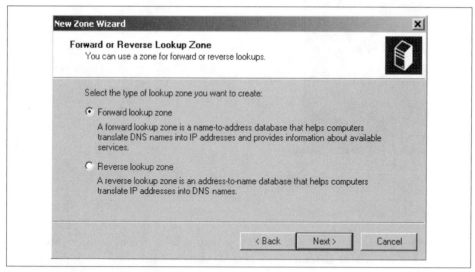

Figure 4-8. New Zone Wizard, third window

Getting tired of all these windows yet? In the next one, shown in Figure 4-9, type the domain name of the zone, which is *movie.edu*. Click **Next**.

Now you need to specify the file that will hold all the zone information, as shown in Figure 4-10.

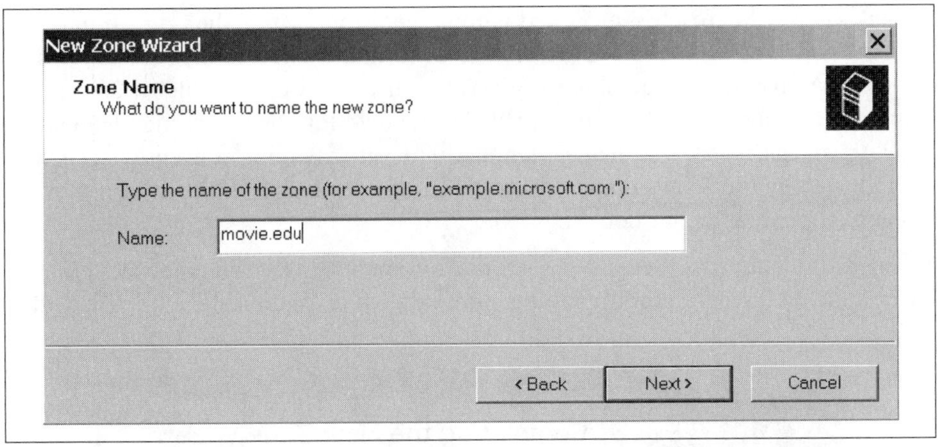

Figure 4-9. New Zone Wizard, fourth window

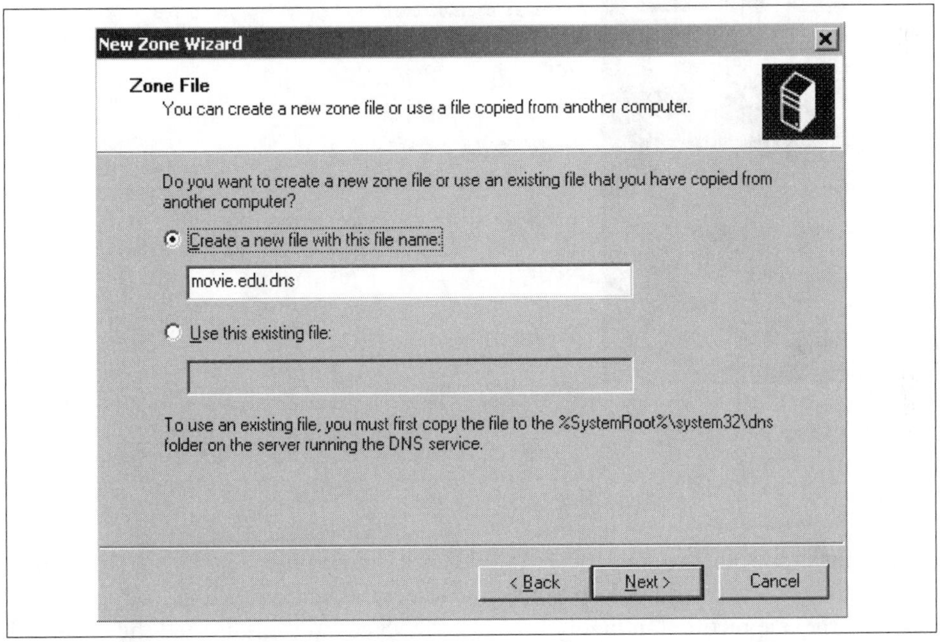

Figure 4-10. New Zone Wizard, fifth window

The zone file, also called a *zone data file*, is the zone's permanent storage location. It's the file on the name server's disk where all the information about the zone is stored: it contains all the zone's resource records. Other name servers require you to edit the zone data file to make changes to the zone, but the DNS console allows you to avoid any hand-editing. As a result, you probably won't see the zone data files very much. We'll talk about their format later in this chapter.

Even if you won't be looking at it often, you need to specify a zone data filename when you create a zone. The server expects these files to be in *%SystemRoot%*

System32\DNS. Microsoft's suggested naming convention uses the domain name of the zone followed by the *.dns* extension. (Notice that the DNS console has filled in the filename based on the zone name.) You can name the zone file whatever you want, but as long as the DNS console fills in the field for you, we recommend sticking with its suggestion. You may be familiar with other naming conventions, such as *db.* followed by the zone's domain name (e.g., *db.movie.edu*). In fact, that's the recommendation in our sister book, *DNS and BIND*.

When you've entered a filename (or left the automatically chosen name alone), click **Next**, and you'll see the confirmation window shown in Figure 4-11.

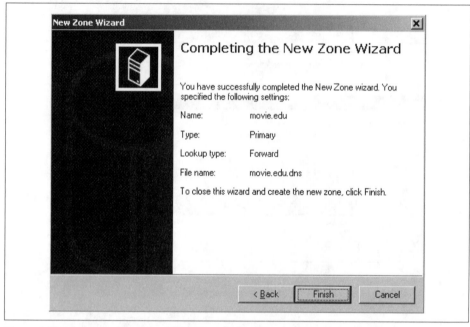

Figure 4-11. New Zone Wizard confirmation window

Click **Finish** to create the zone. If we double-click on *terminator* in the left pane, then double-click on **Forward Lookup Zones** and select the *movie.edu* zone, we see a window like the one pictured in Figure 4-12. The DNS console has created the zone and a few resource records. Let's talk about them one by one.

The SOA record

The first record displayed is the start of authority, or SOA,[*] resource record for the *movie.edu* zone. It's a little tricky to see that the name of this record is really *movie.edu*,

---

[*] Here's where a difference between normal (i.e., nonadvanced) and advanced mode comes in. Figure 4-12 shows the record type as **Start of Authority** because the DNS console is in basic mode. In advanced mode, the record type would show up as simply **SOA**.

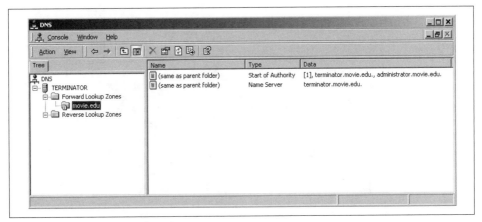

Figure 4-12. The DNS console with a new zone

since the DNS console displays (**same as parent folder**) in the **Name** column. You need to look at the domain name selected in the left pane to know the domain name of this resource record.

The SOA record indicates that this name server is the best source of information for the data within this zone. Our name server is authoritative for the *movie.edu* zone because of the SOA record. An SOA record is required in each zone, and there can be one, and only one, SOA record in a zone.

Double-click the SOA record to view its details. You'll see a window like the one in Figure 4-13.

Let's skip that first field, **Serial number**, for now—don't worry, we'll cover it later in the chapter—and go on to the next field. The second field is the name of the primary master name server for this zone. (You may hear it called the MNAME field, which is its official name.) The third field contains the email address of the person in charge of the zone (if you replace the first dot with an at sign, @). The DNS console defaults to a username of *administrator*, but in other zones you'll often see *root*, *postmaster*, or *hostmaster* as the email address. Name servers won't use these names—they are meant for human consumption. If you notice a problem in someone's zone, you can send an email message to the listed email address.

Most of the remaining fields are for use by slave name servers and are discussed when we introduce slave name servers later in this chapter. For now, assume these are reasonable values.

The NS record

The next record is an NS (name server) resource record. There should be one NS record for each name server authoritative for the zone. Like the SOA record, NS records are attached to the zone's domain name. In our example, the NS records are

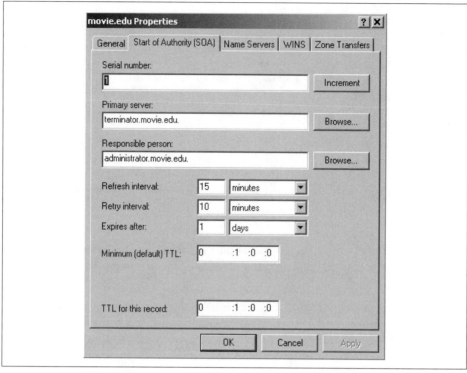

Figure 4-13. The movie.edu SOA record

attached to *movie.edu*. Right now there's only one name server (the primary master), but as we configure slave name servers, we'll add NS records. The DNS console created an NS record for *terminator* because it's a name server—the primary master name server—for *movie.edu*.

The missing A record

Unfortunately, we're missing a required record: the address (A) record for *terminator. movie.edu*, the host running the name server. Address records fulfill the main purpose of DNS: they provide name-to-address mapping. Each A record maps a domain name, like *terminator.movie.edu*, to an IP address, like 192.249.249.3.

Every NS record needs a corresponding A record in some zone. Think about it: an NS record says, "To find out information about this zone, go to this name server." To use the NS record, you need the IP address of the name server it specifies. In this case, the name of the name server, *terminator.movie.edu*, is contained in the *movie. edu* zone we just created, so we need an A record for *terminator.movie.edu* in our zone that will specify its IP address. We're bringing this up now because those of you familiar with Windows NT 4.0 might remember that DNS Manager (the former incarnation of the DNS console) would have automatically created an A record for *terminator.movie.edu* when the *movie.edu* zone was created. We will have to manually add this A record, but not just yet: it's best to create the reverse-mapping (*in-addr.arpa*) zones first.

Creating a New Reverse-Mapping Zone

Zones like *movie.edu* handle mapping names to addresses using A records. But mapping addresses back to names—reverse mapping—is just as important. As you may recall from Chapter 2, a special portion of the namespace, the *in-addr.arpa* domain, is designated for reverse mapping. There's one domain name in *in-addr.arpa* for every possible IP address, and PTR (pointer) records attached to a domain name provide the actual reverse mapping. Just think of a PTR record as the opposite of an A record.

So after we create *movie.edu*, we're not done. Movie U. has two /24 networks, 192. 249.249/24 and 192.253.253/24. We need to create the corresponding *in-addr.arpa* zones for reverse mapping with the DNS console: *249.249.192.in-addr.arpa* and *253. 253.192.in-addr.arpa*.

The process for creating an *in-addr.arpa* zone is the same as that for creating any other zone. Select *terminator* in the left pane and choose **Action → New Zone...**. Follow the prompts in the New Zone Wizard as we did earlier, except this time choose **Reverse lookup zone** in the third window. Figure 4-14 shows the fourth window of the New Zone Wizard when creating a reverse-mapping zone.

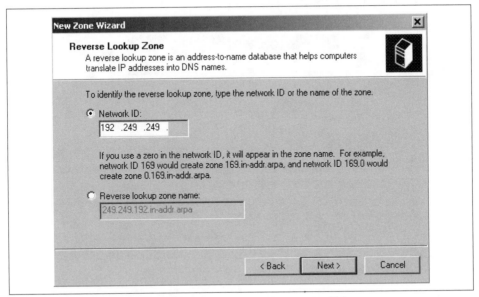

Figure 4-14. Specifying the network number or name of a reverse-mapping zone

We specified the network number (see the selected field), and the DNS console automatically calculated the zone name (see the grayed-out field). Click **Next** and the wizard concludes as shown earlier.

Select the newly created zone in the left pane to see its contents in the right pane. Note that, just as it did with the *movie.edu* zone, the DNS console automatically creates the SOA record and an NS record.

For Movie U., we'll repeat this process to create the *253.253.192.in-addr.arpa* zone. You will create *in-addr.arpa* zones according to the networks you have. Usually there's one *in-addr.arpa* zone per /24 (or smaller) network. Larger networks are often broken into several *in-addr.arpa* zones to make management easier. The zones usually correspond to subnets. This topic is covered in more detail in Chapter 9.

Adding Resource Records

Now that we've created Movie U.'s zones, we can add information about all its machines. Each machine requires two resource records: an A record in the *movie.edu* zone to provide name-to-address mapping and a PTR record in the appropriate *in-addr. arpa* zone to provide address-to-name mapping. Adding the A record is intuitive, but it's easy to forget about the PTR record. The DNS console makes the job easier with the **New Host** command, which creates an A record and a PTR record in one pass.

Select a forward-mapping zone (like *movie.edu*) and choose **Action → New Host…**. Enter the name of the host and its IP address. To create the PTR record as well, you also need to check the **Create associated pointer (PTR) record** box. The window looks like the one in Figure 4-15.

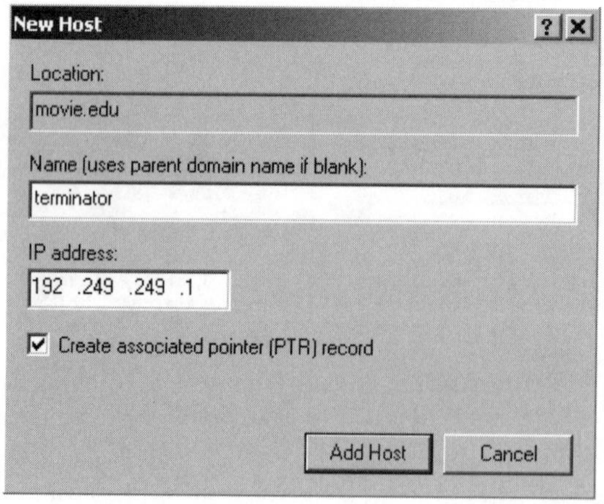

Figure 4-15. The New Host window

You'll notice that we typed a relative domain name (*terminator*) and not a fully qualified domain name (*terminator.movie.edu.*) The DNS console requires a relative domain name in this field. (It won't even let you type a period!) It appends the domain name of the zone selected in the DNS console's left pane (and shown in the **Location** field in the window) to create a fully qualified domain name.

Aliases

Looking back at Movie U.'s host table in the beginning of the chapter, you'll see that some hosts have aliases. (The aliases are any additional names after the first one listed.) For example, *terminator* is also known as *bigt*. A special resource record called the CNAME record is used to make an alias. The name of this record is confusing because CNAME is short for canonical name, which means the "real" name of the host. But a CNAME record doesn't make a canonical name; it makes an alias. All other types of records make a canonical name. We recommend thinking of it this way: CNAME records *point* to canonical names while other record types *make* canonical names.

To create an alias, select the zone to which you want to add the record on the left, and choose **Action → New Alias....** You'll see a window that looks like the one in Figure 4-16.

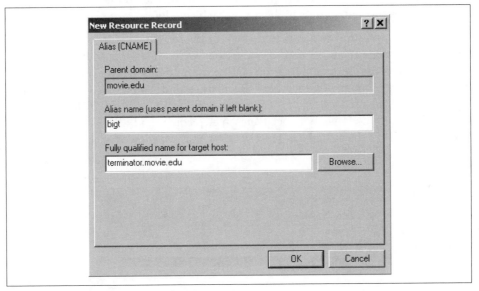

Figure 4-16. Creating a CNAME record

The input in Figure 4-16 will generate an alias from *bigt.movie.edu* to *terminator. movie.edu*. The **Parent domain** field is just a reminder of the current domain. As was the case with the **New Host** command, you must enter a single-label (that is, no periods) name in the **Alias name** field: the **Alias name** field is always relative to the current domain. There is no such restriction for the canonical name field (labeled **Fully qualified name for target host**)—you can point this alias anywhere. We could alias *bigt.movie.edu* to *www.whitehouse.gov* if we wanted to. An important note, however: if you leave off the domain in the canonical name field, the zone's domain name is *not* appended automatically (as was the case with DNS Manager in Windows NT 4.0). You should always enter a fully qualified domain name in the last field.

It's important to know that the name server handles CNAME records in a different manner than aliases are handled in the host table. When a name server looks up a name and finds a CNAME record, it replaces the alias name with the canonical name and looks up the new name. For example, when the name server looks up *bigt.movie. edu*, it finds a CNAME record pointing to *terminator.movie.edu*. Then it looks up *terminator.movie.edu*, and its address is returned.

One thing you must remember about aliases like *bigt* is that they should never appear in the data portion (that is, on the right side) of a resource record. Stated differently, always use the canonical name (*terminator*) in the data portion of the resource record. Notice that the NS records use the canonical name.

Sometimes you can use an A record to get the effect of an alias. Suppose you have a router, like *wormhole*, and you want to check one of the interfaces. One common troubleshooting technique is to *ping* the interface to verify that it is responding. If you *ping* the name *wormhole*, the name server returns the addresses of both interfaces. *ping* uses the first address in the list. But which address is first?

The solution is to create two A records for *wormhole*. We could use the **New Host** command to create them as we did above, but we'll show you another way. The **Other New Records** command lets you choose from 19 different resource records to create. Choose **Action → Other New Records...** and you'll see a window like Figure 4-17. Select a record type to see its description. We've selected **Host** (which is the nonadvanced-mode way of specifying an A record), and after we select **Create Record...** we'll see the same **New Host** window that we showed earlier, which we'll use to add an A record for *wh249.movie.edu*.

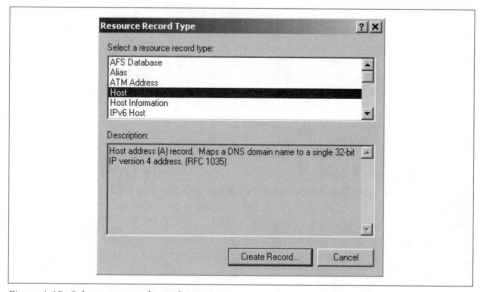

Figure 4-17. Other new records window

With the host table, we chose the address we wanted by using either *wh249* or *wh253*—each name referred to *one* of the host's addresses. To provide equivalent capability with DNS, we didn't make *wh249* and *wh253* into aliases (CNAME records). That would result in both addresses for *wormhole* being returned when we looked up the alias. Instead, we used address records. Now, to check the operation of the 192.253.253.1 interface on *wormhole*, we *ping wh253* since it refers to only one address. The same applies to *wh249*.

To state this as a general rule: if a host is multihomed (i.e., has more than one network interface), create an address (A) record for each alias unique to one address. Create a CNAME record for each alias common to all the addresses.

One more note about PTR records

We now have two A records, *wormhole.movie.edu* and *wh249.movie.edu*, pointing to the same address, 192.249.249.1. We also have a PTR record pointing from *1.249. 249.192.in-addr.arpa* to *wormhole.movie.edu*. (This record was added automatically to the *249.249.192.in-addr.arpa* zone by the **New Host** command. Remember that addresses are looked up as names: the IP address is reversed, and *in-addr.arpa* is appended.) Thus, 192.249.249.1 maps to *wormhole.movie.edu* and not to *wh249. movie.edu*. Should you create another PTR record that maps 192.249.249.1 to *wh249.movie.edu*? You *can* create two PTR records—it's perfectly legal—but most systems are not prepared to see more than one name for an address. We recommend that you don't bother with multiple PTR records since so few systems can use them.

Where Is All This Information Stored?

You may be wondering what's happened to all the resource records we've been entering. Where are they being stored? The answer is: in the memory of the DNS server process. We mentioned earlier that the DNS console communicates with the DNS server using an RPC mechanism. As you add records to a zone with the DNS console, they are added "on the fly" to the name server's memory. Of course, the name server's memory is transient—when the name server process stops, its memory is lost. Obviously it needs a permanent storage location, too.

This is where the zone data files we specified when we created the zones come in. The zone data files are the zones' permanent storage location, holding all the zones' resource records. If you use the DNS console to make a change to a zone, the copy of the zone in the name server's memory is changed, and a flag is set to update that zone's data file. The name server updates the zone data file when it exits, unless you tell it to update the file sooner. The command **Action → Update Server Data Files** causes the name server to update the zone data files of all the zones for which it's a primary (if the version of a zone in the server's memory is more recent than the version on disk). To avoid losing data, we recommend using **Action → Update Server**

Data Files after any changes—use it like you use the **Save** command in other applications. Of course, the difference here is that the server will save your data if it exits gracefully. You don't have to use **Action** → **Update Server Data Files** after a batch of changes, but it doesn't hurt anything and you'll be able to sleep better.

As you've probably guessed, when the name server starts up, it reads the zone data files into memory. When you select **Action** → **Refresh** or press **F5**, the DNS console queries the name server and updates the console's display.

If you've been keeping track, you'll realize that DNS information exists in three places: zone data files, the name server's memory, and the DNS console's window. The diagram in Figure 4-18 helps explain how the information flows.

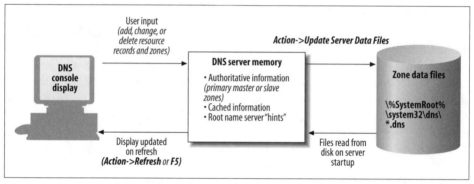

Figure 4-18. Where everything is stored

The Zone Data Files

Let's take a look at the zone data files for Movie U. After inputting the remaining host table entries, we end up with the display shown previously in Figure 4-2. (Of course, this view shows only the contents of *movie.edu*. The *249.249.192.in-addr.arpa* and *253.253.192.in-addr.arpa* zones are populated with PTR records.)

Next we select **Action** → **Update Server Data Files**, and the server generates three files in *%SystemRoot%\System32\DNS*: *movie.edu.dns*, *249.249.192.in-addr.arpa.dns*, and *253.253.192.in-addr.arpa.dns*. They look like the following.

Contents of *movie.edu.dns*:

```
;
;   Data file movie.edu.dns for movie.edu zone.
;       Zone version:  41
;

@               IN      SOA terminator.movie.edu.  administrator.movie.edu. (
                        1               ; serial number
                        3600            ; refresh
                        600             ; retry
```

```
                        86400        ; expire
                        3600         ) ; minimum TTL

;
;   Zone NS records
;

@                IN     NS terminator

;
;   Zone records
;

bigt                    IN      CNAME    terminator
carrie                  IN      A 192.253.253.4
dh                      IN      CNAME      diehard
diehard                 IN      A 192.249.249.4
misery                  IN      A 192.253.253.2
robocop                 IN      A 192.249.249.2
shining                 IN      A 192.253.253.3
terminator              IN      A 192.249.249.3
wh                      IN      CNAME      wormhole
wh249                   IN      A 192.249.249.1
wh253                   IN      A 192.253.253.1
wormhole                IN      A 192.249.249.1
                        IN      A 192.253.253.1
```

Contents of *249.249.192.in-addr.arpa.dns*:

```
;
;   Data file 249.249.192.in-addr.arpa.dns for 249.249.192.in-addr.arpa zone.
;      Zone version: 51
;

@                IN     SOA terminator.movie.edu.   administrator.movie.edu.   (
                        5            ; serial number
                        3600         ; refresh
                        600          ; retry
                        86400        ; expire
                        3600         ) ; minimum TTL


;
;   Zone NS records
;

@                IN     NS terminator.movie.edu.


;
;   Zone records
;

1                       IN      PTR wormhole.movie.edu.
2                       IN      PTR robocop.movie.edu.
3                       IN      PTR terminator.movie.edu.
4                       IN      PTR diehard.movie.edu.
```

Contents of 253.253.192.in-addr.arpa.dns:

```
;
; Data file 253.253.192.in-addr.arpa.dns for 253.253.192.in-addr.arpa zone.
;       Zone version:  41
;

@               IN      SOA terminator.movie.edu.   administrator.movie.edu.   (
                        4               ; serial number
                        3600            ; refresh
                        600             ; retry
                        86400           ; expire
                        3600            ) ; minimum TTL


;
; Zone NS records
;

@               IN      NS terminator.movie.edu.


;
; Zone records
;

1                       IN      PTR wormhole.movie.edu.
2                       IN      PTR misery.movie.edu.
3                       IN      PTR shining.movie.edu.
4                       IN      PTR carrie.movie.edu.
```

Zone Data File Format

The format of zone data files is specified in the DNS standards. That means all name servers, whether Microsoft DNS Server or the BIND name server, can read each other's zone data files.

You've probably already guessed that the semicolon is the comment character. It can appear anywhere on a line, and anything to the right is considered a comment and is ignored by the name server. Blank lines are okay, too.

Each resource record must start in the first column of the file—no preceding whitespace. (Don't be confused by the examples in this book, which are indented because of the way the book is formatted.) Resource records are case-insensitive—you can use uppercase or lowercase. The name server doesn't preserve the case, though. It matches the case of the reply to the case of the query. For example, if a record is written as *terminator* in the zone data file but you query for *Terminator*, the server responds with *Terminator*.

Resource records are broken up into fields, with any amount of whitespace (tabs or spaces) separating the fields.

The first field, called the owner, is the domain name of the record. Put another way, it's the node in the namespace to which the resource record is attached. You've seen the domain name on the *left* side of the *right* pane of the DNS console. (Got that?)

The next field in our examples is the class, IN, which stands for Internet. There are other classes, but none of them are currently in widespread use. Our examples use only the IN class.

The field after that is the record type. We've already discussed the SOA, NS, A, PTR, and CNAME record types, and you've probably browsed through the list of other record types in the DNS console's **Other New Records** window. The type simply specifies what type of data is associated with the domain name on the right: A means IP address, NS means the name of an authoritative name server, and so on.

That's a good lead-in to the final field, the RDATA or resource record data. This field holds the kind of data specified by the record type. It can be divided into multiple subfields, depending on the type. For example, A records may specify only one parameter, an IP address, but the SOA record specifies seven parameters (remember all those fields in Figure 4-13?).

Speaking of the SOA record, you'll notice in the examples that it's the only record spanning multiple lines. If you ever have to edit zone data files by hand, you can use parentheses to allow a resource record to span multiple lines. This trick works for all record types, not just SOA.

Domain names appear a lot in resource records. The left side of every resource record is a domain name, and the right side (RDATA field) of many record types also contains domain names (for example, NS and SOA records). Using a fully qualified domain name in each case is perfectly legal, but it would be a lot of work: imagine having to type *movie.edu* at the end of every hostname if you were entering these files by hand. Fortunately, abbreviations are allowed. You need to understand the abbreviations because the Microsoft DNS Server uses them in records it generates.

Appending domains

Every zone has a domain name: it's just the name of the zone. (This probably strikes you as pretty obvious.) This domain name is the key to the most useful shortcut. This domain name is the *origin* of all the data in the data file. The origin is appended to all domain names in the file not ending in a dot. The origin is different for each file because each file is associated with a different zone, each of which has a different domain name.

Since the origin is appended to names, instead of entering *robocop*'s address in *movie.edu.dns* as this:

```
robocop.movie.edu.    IN A    192.249.249.2
```

the server generated it like this:

```
robocop    IN A     192.249.249.2
```

In *192.249.249.in-addr.arpa.dns*, this is the long way to write this record:

```
2.249.249.192.in-addr.arpa.  IN PTR robocop.movie.edu.
```

But since *249.249.192.in-addr.arpa* is the origin, the server generated:

```
2 IN PTR robocop.movie.edu.
```

Notice that all the fully qualified domain names in the file end in a dot. That tells the server that this domain name is complete and should be left alone. Suppose you forgot the trailing dot. An entry like this:

```
robocop.movie.edu    IN A     192.249.249.2
```

turns into an entry for *robocop.movie.edu.movie.edu*, which you didn't intend at all.

@ notation

If the domain name is the *same* as the origin, the name can be specified with an at sign (@). This is most often seen in the SOA record in data files generated by hand, but the Microsoft DNS Server also uses the @ notation in the NS records. In the *movie.edu.dns* file in the previous example, the @ stands for *movie.edu*. Of course, in the *249.249.192.in-addr.arpa.dns* file, the @ stands for *249.249.192.in-addr.arpa*, and in the *253. 253.192.in-addr.arpa.dns* file... well, you get the idea.

Repeat last name

If there is a space or a tab in column one, the name from the last resource record is used. This shortcut gets used when there are multiple resource records for a name. Here is an example where there are two address records for one name:

```
wormhole   IN A     192.249.249.1
           IN A     192.253.253.1
```

In the second address record, the name *wormhole* is implied. You can use this shortcut even if the resource records are of different types—for example, if *wormhole* also had a TXT (arbitrary text) record.

The Loopback Address

Those of you familiar with the BIND name server may be wondering if we forgot about the loopback address. If we were setting up a BIND name server, it would need one additional zone data file to cover the *loopback* network: the special address that hosts use to direct traffic to themselves. This network is (almost) always 127.0. 0.0, and the host number is (almost) always 127.0.0.1. Therefore, the name of this file would be *0.0.127.in-addr.arpa.dns*, and it would look like the other *in-addr.dns* files.

The following would be the contents of the *0.0.127.in-addr.arpa.dns* file:

```
@                   IN      SOA terminator.movie.edu.   administrator.movie.edu.   (
                            1           ; serial number
                            3600        ; refresh
                            600         ; retry
                            86400       ; expire
                            3600      ) ; minimum TTL

;
;  Zone NS records
;

@                   IN      NS terminator.movie.edu.

;
;  Zone records
;

1                   IN      PTR localhost.
```

Why do name servers need this file? Think about it for a second. No one was given responsibility for network 127.0.0.0, yet systems use it for a loopback address. Since no one has direct responsibility, everyone who uses it is responsible for it individually. If you omit this file on a BIND name server, it will still operate. However, a lookup of 127.0.0.1 might fail: the name server will send the query to a root name server that might not be configured to map 127.0.0.1 to a name.

With the Microsoft DNS Server, you don't have to worry about creating this file and making your name server authoritative for the *in-addr.arpa* zone corresponding to network 127.0.0.0. The server is authoritative for this zone by default. It's called an *automatically created zone* and is visible in the DNS console only in advanced mode. Select **View** → **Advanced** and you can see the three automatically created zones shown in Figure 4-19.

We've drilled down into the *127.in-addr.arpa* zone to show that there's a PTR record for *1.0.0.127.in-addr.arpa* pointing to the domain name *localhost*. In other words, a Microsoft DNS Server will reverse-map the IP address 127.0.0.1 to the domain name *localhost* "out of the box" without any work on your part.

The *0.in-addr.arpa* and *255.in-addr.arpa* zones are empty, save for NS and A records. Some hosts attempt to reverse-map the IP addresses 0.0.0.0 and 255.255.255.255, and these zones cause the local server to return an immediate NXDOMAIN (name not found) error for those queries rather than asking a root name server.

The Root Hints Data

Besides your local information, the name server also needs to know where the name servers for the root zone are. (Remember that the resolution process starts at the root zone, so knowing which name servers are authoritative for the root zone is critical.)

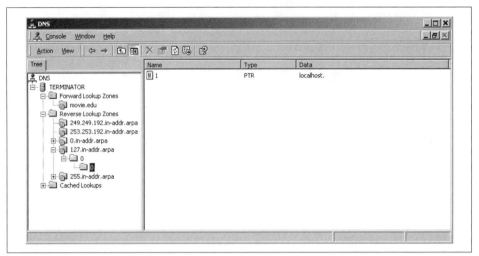

Figure 4-19. The DNS console showing automatically created zones

This information is stored in a file called the *root name server hints file*, which is named *%SystemRoot%\System32\DNS\cache.dns* on your name server. The Microsoft DNS Server ships with a version of this file that looks like this (or at least it did when this book was published):

```
;       This file holds the information on root name servers needed
;       to initialize cache of Internet domain name servers
;       (e.g., reference this file in the "cache  . <file>"
;       configuration file of BIND domain name servers).
;
;       This file is made available by InterNIC registration services
;       under anonymous FTP as
;           file                /domain/named.root
;           on server           FTP.RS.INTERNIC.NET
;       -OR- under Gopher at    RS.INTERNIC.NET
;           under menu          InterNIC Registration Services (NSI)
;               submenu         InterNIC Registration Archives
;           file                named.root
;
;       last update:    Aug 22, 1997
;       related version of root zone:   1997082200
;
;
; formerly NS.INTERNIC.NET
;
.                       3600000  IN  NS   A.ROOT-SERVERS.NET.
A.ROOT-SERVERS.NET.     3600000      A    198.41.0.4
;
; formerly NS1.ISI.EDU
;
.                       3600000      NS   B.ROOT-SERVERS.NET.
B.ROOT-SERVERS.NET.     3600000      A    128.9.0.107
;
```

```
; formerly C.PSI.NET
;
.                      3600000      NS      C.ROOT-SERVERS.NET.
C.ROOT-SERVERS.NET.    3600000      A       192.33.4.12
;
; formerly TERP.UMD.EDU
;
.                      3600000      NS      D.ROOT-SERVERS.NET.
D.ROOT-SERVERS.NET.    3600000      A       128.8.10.90
;
; formerly NS.NASA.GOV
;
.                      3600000      NS      E.ROOT-SERVERS.NET.
E.ROOT-SERVERS.NET.    3600000      A       192.203.230.10
;
; formerly NS.ISC.ORG
;
.                      3600000      NS      F.ROOT-SERVERS.NET.
F.ROOT-SERVERS.NET.    3600000      A       192.5.5.241
;
; formerly NS.NIC.DDN.MIL
;
.                      3600000      NS      G.ROOT-SERVERS.NET.
G.ROOT-SERVERS.NET.    3600000      A       192.112.36.4
;
; formerly AOS.ARL.ARMY.MIL
;
.                      3600000      NS      H.ROOT-SERVERS.NET.
H.ROOT-SERVERS.NET.    3600000      A       128.63.2.53
;
; formerly NIC.NORDU.NET
;
.                      3600000      NS      I.ROOT-SERVERS.NET.
I.ROOT-SERVERS.NET.    3600000      A       192.36.148.17
;
; temporarily housed at NSI (InterNIC)
;
.                      3600000      NS      J.ROOT-SERVERS.NET.
J.ROOT-SERVERS.NET.    3600000      A       198.41.0.10
;
; housed in LINX, operated by RIPE NCC
;
.                      3600000      NS      K.ROOT-SERVERS.NET.
K.ROOT-SERVERS.NET.    3600000      A       193.0.14.129
;
; temporarily housed at ISI (IANA)
;
.                      3600000      NS      L.ROOT-SERVERS.NET.
L.ROOT-SERVERS.NET.    3600000      A       198.32.64.12
;
; housed in Japan, operated by WIDE
;
.                      3600000      NS      M.ROOT-SERVERS.NET.
M.ROOT-SERVERS.NET.    3600000      A       202.12.27.33
; End of File
```

This information can also be retrieved from the Internet host *ftp.rs.internic.net* (198. 41.0.7). Use anonymous FTP to retrieve the file *named.root* from the *domain* subdirectory. The domain name "." refers to the root zone. Since the root zone's name servers change over time, don't assume this list is current. Pull a new version of *named.root*.

You can also view this information from within the DNS console: select a name server in the left pane and choose **Action → Properties**. Then select the **Root Hints** tab to see a window like the one shown in Figure 4-20.

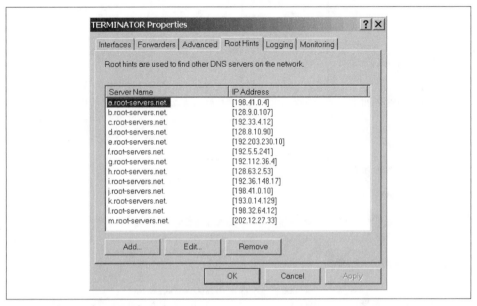

Figure 4-20. Root hints window

It's worth noting that the root NS records are not put into the cache and used directly. Rather, upon startup the server queries one of the root servers in the cache file for the list of root servers. The list returned is the one used by the name server to start the resolution process and is the list you see when you double-click the Cache icon.

You may be wondering what the *3600000*s are for. In older versions of this file, this number was *99999999*. It dates back to the behavior of early versions of BIND, the reference implementation of the name server. The BIND name server used to put the contents of the cache file directly into its cache, and it had to know how long to keep these records active. The *99999999*s meant a *very long time*. The root name server data was to be kept active for as long as the server ran. Since both BIND and the Microsoft DNS Server now store the cache file data in a special place and don't discard it if it times out, the TTL is unnecessary. But it's not harmful to have the *3600000*s, and it makes for interesting DNS folklore when you pass responsibility to the next name server administrator.

Running a Primary Master Name Server

Your primary name server is already up and running; you've been talking to it via the DNS console. You've created a zone and populated it with information. Then you directed the server to write out zone data files with the **Action → Update Server Data Files** command. To be sure that everything is okay, you should stop and restart the server and then check the Event Log for any messages or errors.

Starting and Stopping the DNS Server

There are several ways to start and stop the DNS server. First, you can control it just like any other Windows 2000 service: with the Services MMC snap-in. Select **Start → Programs → Administrative Tools → Services**. You'll see a window like Figure 4-21.

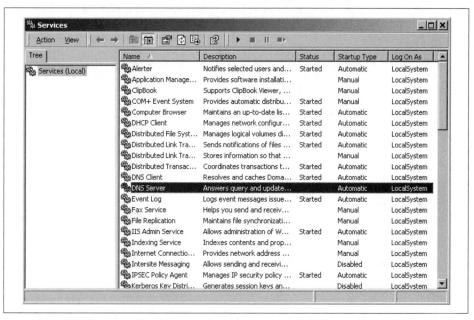

Figure 4-21. Windows 2000 Services control window

Your system should look like this: the server should be running (that is, it should be started). Select the server as we've done by clicking anywhere on the **DNS Server** line. Select **Action → Stop**. After the server stops, select **Action → Start**. In a few seconds, the server should be running again.

While you've got this window open, check to make sure that the DNS server is being started automatically on bootup. You want to see **Automatic** in the **Startup Type** column (and not **Manual** or **Disabled**). To change the startup behavior, double-click on the service and choose the appropriate behavior in the **Startup Type** field of the resulting window.

You can also start and stop the DNS server from within the DNS console. With the server selected in the left pane, select **Action** → **All Tasks**. You'll see a menu with choices that include **Start**, **Stop**, and **Restart**. (The latter does just what you'd expect: stops, then starts, the server.)

Finally, you can start and stop the DNS server from the good old DOS command line: *net start dns* will start the server, and *net stop dns* stops it. Of course, this command must be run on the system on which the DNS server is running, which is not necessarily the same system on which the DNS console is running.

Check the Event Log for Messages and Errors

Now you need to check the Event Log. Start the Event Viewer by selecting **Start** → **Programs** → **Administrative Tools** → **Event Viewer**. Under Windows 2000, the DNS server has its own category in the Event Log. Select **DNS Server** in the left pane and you should see a window like the one in Figure 4-22.

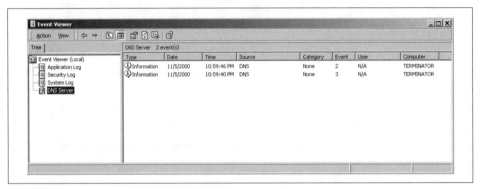

Figure 4-22. Event Viewer

DNS Server Event ID 3 is "The DNS server has shutdown." and Event ID 2 is "The DNS server has started." (More events are listed in Chapter 7.) These two events are just what you want to see: a normal server shutdown and startup. We're reading from bottom to top since Event Viewer's default view shows newest events first. We also cleared the Event Log before we stopped and started the server—that's why only these two events are showing.

If there were any other messages or errors, we'd take steps to correct them now. To be honest, we didn't expect any problems because we entered all the data via the DNS console. Since it performs some syntax and sanity checking, it's hard to enter bad data to make the name server upset enough to complain in the Event Log. Still, it doesn't hurt to check. If you ever start editing zone data files by hand (which we don't recommend), you definitely need to check the Event Log.

Testing Your Setup with nslookup

If you have correctly set up your local domain and your connection to the Internet is up, you should be able to look up a local and a remote domain name. We'll step you through the lookups with *nslookup*. This book contains an entire chapter on this topic (Chapter 12), but we will cover *nslookup* in enough detail here to do basic name-server testing.

Look up a local name

You can use *nslookup* to look up any type of resource record, and it can be directed to query any name server. By default, it looks up A (address) records using the name server on the local system. To look up a host's address with *nslookup*, run *nslookup* with the host's name as the only argument. A lookup of a local name should return almost instantly.

We ran *nslookup* to look up *carrie*:

```
C:\> nslookup carrie
Server:  terminator.movie.edu
Address:  192.249.249.3

Name:    carrie.movie.edu
Address:  192.253.253.4
```

If looking up a local name works, your local name server has been configured properly for your domain. If the lookup fails, you'll see something like this:

```
*** terminator.movie.edu can't find carrie: Non-existent domain
```

This means that either *carrie* is not in your data—check the DNS console or the zone data file—or some name server error occurred (but you should have caught the error when you checked the Event Log).

Look up a local address

When *nslookup* is given an address to look up, it knows to make a PTR query instead of an address query. We ran *nslookup* to look up *carrie*'s address:

```
C:\> nslookup 192.253.253.4
Server:  terminator.movie.edu
Address:  192.249.249.3

Name:    carrie.movie.edu
Address:  192.253.253.4
```

If looking up an address works, your local name server has been configured properly for your *in-addr.arpa* domain. If the lookup fails, you'll see the same error message as when you looked up a name.

Look up a remote name

The next step is to use the local name server to look up a remote name, such as *ftp.uu. net* or another system you know on the Internet. Don't forget to add a period at the end of your input so the system doesn't automatically append the origin, *movie.edu*.

This command may not return as quickly as the last one. If *nslookup* fails to get a response from your name server, it will wait a little over a minute before giving up:

```
C:\> nslookup ftp.uu.net.
Server:  terminator.movie.edu
Address:  192.249.249.3

Name:    ftp.uu.net
Address:  192.48.96.9
```

If this lookup works, your name server knows where the root name servers are and how to contact them to find information about domains other than your own. If it fails, there is a problem with the cache file or the network. The cache file might be empty or missing address records for the root name servers. Or perhaps the network is broken somewhere and you can't reach the name servers for the remote domain. Try a different remote domain name.

If these first three lookups succeeded, congratulations! You have a primary master name server up and running. At this point, you are ready to start configuring your slave name server.

One more test

While you are testing, though, run one more test. Try having a remote name server look up a name in your zone. This will work only if your parent name servers have already delegated your zone to the name server you just set up. If your parent required you to have your two name servers running before delegating your zone, skip ahead to the next section.

To make *nslookup* use a remote name server to look up a local name, give the local host's name as the first argument and the remote server's name as the second argument. Again, if this doesn't work, it may take a little longer than a minute before *nslookup* gives you an error message. For instance, to have *gatekeeper.dec.com* look up *carrie*, we'd enter:

```
C:\> nslookup carrie gatekeeper.dec.com.
Server:  gatekeeper.dec.com.
Address:  204.123.2.2

Name:    carrie.movie.edu
Address:  192.253.253.4
```

If the first two lookups worked but using a remote name server to look up a local name failed, you may not be registered with your parent name server. That is not a problem at first because systems within your zone can look up the names of other systems within and outside your zone. You'll be able to send email and *ftp* to local and remote systems. Some systems won't allow FTP connections if they can't map your address back to a name. But not being registered will shortly become a problem. Hosts outside of your zone cannot look up names within your zone. You will be able to send email to friends in remote domains, but you won't get their responses. To fix this problem, contact someone responsible for your parent zone and have them check the delegation of your zone.

Running a Slave Name Server

You need to set up another name server for robustness. You can (and probably will) set up more than two name servers. Two servers are the minimum. If you have only one name server and it goes down, no one can look up names in your zone. A second name server splits the load with the first server or handles the whole load if the first server is down. You *could* set up another primary master name server, but we don't recommend it. Set up a slave name server instead.

How does a server know if it is a primary master or a slave for a zone? The DNS server configuration information in the Registry tells the server it is a primary master or a slave on a per zone basis. The NS records don't tell us which server is the primary master for a zone and which servers are slaves for a zone—they only say who the servers are. (Globally, DNS doesn't care; as far as the actual name resolution goes, slave servers are as good as primary master servers.)

What is different between a primary master name server and a slave name server? The crucial difference is where the server gets its data. A primary master name server reads its data from files. A slave name server loads its data over the network from another name server. This process is called a *zone transfer*.

A slave name server is not limited to loading zones from a primary master name server; a slave server can load from another slave server. The big advantage of slave name servers is that you maintain only one set of zone data files, the ones on the primary master name server. You don't have to worry about synchronizing the files among name servers; the slaves do that for you.

A slave name server doesn't need to retrieve *all* of its data files over the network; the *cache.dns* file is the same as on a primary master, so keep a local copy on the slave.

 One point about slaves may become confusing: slaves used to be called secondary master name servers. We'll use the term slave in this book, but you'll see that the DNS console still uses the term secondary. As we said, the two are synonymous.

Add a New Server to the DNS Console

The first step in configuring a slave server is to add the server to the DNS console's world view. Just as we did when configuring the primary master, select **Action** →

Connect To Computer..., then enter the IP address of the slave. In this case our slave will be *wormhole* with IP address 192.249.249.1. Of course, the DNS server has to be installed and running on the slave-to-be for the DNS console to be able to manage it.

Create a New Zone

This new server will be a slave for every zone on the primary, so we'll have to go through the new zone process for each zone. Let's start with *movie.edu*. Select **Action → New Zone...**. This time, select **Standard secondary** (remember, this is synonymous with *slave*) in the second window of the wizard. In the third window, select **Forward lookup zone**. The fourth window is shown in Figure 4-23.

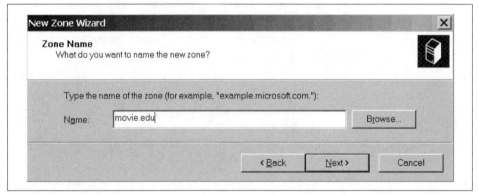

Figure 4-23. Creating a new secondary zone: specifying the zone's domain name

In the **Name** field, enter the domain name of the zone (in this case, *movie.edu*). In the **Server** field, enter the IP address of the primary master name server. You can type this information or take advantage of a shortcut offered by the DNS console. When you click the **Browse** button, the DNS console shows you a view of the zones on all the name servers it's managing. So rather than typing out *movie.edu,* we could have drilled down to find that zone in the **Browse** window, as shown in Figure 4-24.

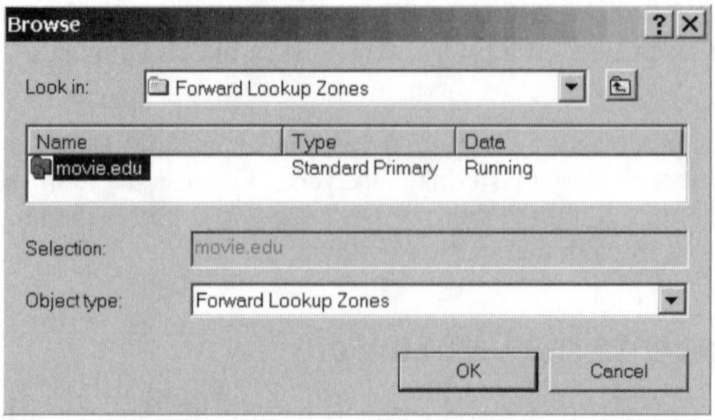

Figure 4-24. Finding a zone with the Browse window

Whether you enter the zone and server manually or use the **Browse** shortcut, click **Next** to get the next window, shown in Figure 4-25.

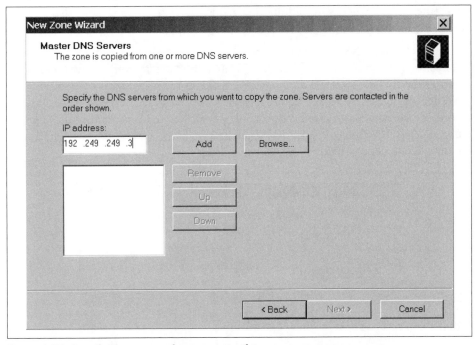

Figure 4-25. Creating a new secondary zone: specifying master servers

At this point, the process of creating a primary master zone and a slave zone really diverge. This is the screen where you specify where this name server will get the zone data. In this example, we're making *wormhole* a slave for the *movie.edu* zone. We need to tell *wormhole* to load the zone from *terminator*, the primary master. In fact, on this screen you can specify multiple IP addresses. In advanced (and complicated) configurations, sometimes there are multiple primaries or multiple sources from which a slave can get the zone information. The DNS console supports those configurations. You could also just specify the IP address of another slave after that of the primary: in case the primary is down, this slave can load from another slave. Of course, Movie U. doesn't have another slave (yet).

For now, we just specify *terminator*'s IP address, 192.249.249.3. (Once again you can click the **Browse** button and find *terminator* among the DNS console's list of known name servers to avoid having to type its IP address.) Then click **Next**. The final window in the process is the same as when creating a primary zone: it just tells you that you're done now and asks you to click **Finish**. We'll omit showing it to you.

When you're done, the new slave immediately initiates a zone transfer to the primary to download the zone. Within a few seconds you should be able to double-click the slave's icon for the zone and see the records in the zone.

Add an NS Record for the New Slave Name Server

Your new slave won't be much good if the rest of the world doesn't know about it. As a general rule, when you add another name server for a zone, you also need to add an NS record for it. (We'll discuss the exceptions to this in Chapter 8.)

You need to add an NS record on the zone's primary. (Remember that all changes to a zone are made on the primary and propagate automatically to the slaves. Don't get confused by the fact that the DNS console lets you see all your name servers—you make the changes only to the zone's primary.) In our case, we need to add an NS record for *wormhole* to the *movie.edu* zone. So we highlight *movie.edu* under *terminator* and select **Action → Properties**. Click on the **Name Servers** tab and you'll see a window like the one in Figure 4-26.

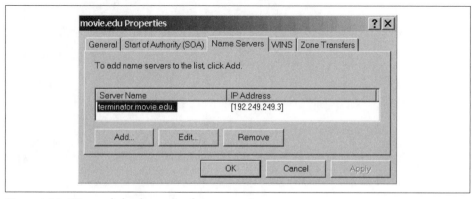

Figure 4-26. NS records for the movie.edu zone

This window shows that right now there's only one NS record for the *movie.edu* zone, which specifies *terminator.movie.edu* as an authoritative name server. To add another, click **Add...** and you'll see the window shown in Figure 4-27.

Enter the name and IP address of the slave name server and click **OK**.

Don't Forget the in-addr.arpa Zones!

Now repeat this slave zone creation process with the *249.249.192.in-addr.arpa* and *253.253.192.in-addr.arpa* zones.

SOA Values

Remember this SOA record for the *movie.edu* zone?

```
@   IN  SOA terminator.movie.edu.    administrator.movie.edu.    (
                        1           ; serial number
                        3600        ; refresh
                        600         ; retry
                        86400       ; expire
                        3600      ) ; minimum TTL
```

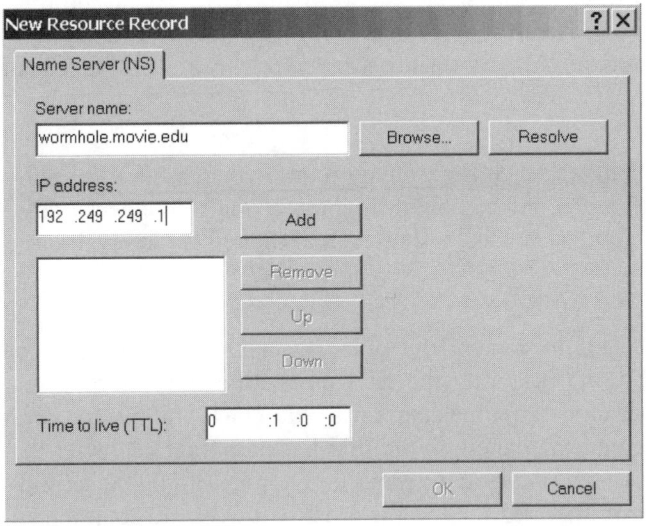

Figure 4-27. Adding an NS record

We never explained what the values in between the parentheses were for.

The serial number applies to all the data within the zone. We chose to start our serial number at 1, a logical place to start. The DNS console automatically increments the serial number in a zone's SOA record whenever you make a change to the zone. If you've maintained zone data files by hand, you might have encoded the date in the serial number—for example, 2000102301. This format is YYYYMMDDNN, where YYYY is the year, MM is the month, DD is the day, and NN is a count of how many times the zone data were modified that day. Unfortunately, you can't use that convention with the DNS console. It just increments the serial number by one each time a change is made and doesn't understand the date encoding.

When a slave name server contacts a primary master server for zone data, it first asks for the serial number of the data. If the slave's serial number is lower than the primary's, the slave's zone data is out of date. In this case, the slave pulls a new copy of the zone. As you might guess, if you ever modify the zone data files on the primary master by hand, you must increment the serial number, too. Updating zone data files is covered in Chapter 7.

The next four fields specify various time intervals in seconds:

refresh
> The refresh interval tells the slave how often to check that its data is up to date. To give you an idea of the system load this feature causes, a slave will make one SOA query per zone per refresh interval. The default value generated by the DNS console when the zone was created, one hour, is reasonably aggressive. Most users will tolerate a delay of half a working day for things like name server data to propagate when they are waiting for their new workstation to be operational.

If you provide one-day service for your site, consider raising this value to eight hours. If your data doesn't change very often, or if all your slaves are spread over long distances (as the root name servers are), consider a longer value, such as 24 hours.

retry

If a slave fails to reach the primary name server(s) after the refresh period (the hosts or hosts could be down), it starts trying to connect every *retry* seconds. The retry interval is usually shorter than the refresh interval, but it doesn't have to be.

expire

If a slave fails to contact the primary server(s) for *expire* seconds, the slave expires its data. Expiring the data means the slave stops giving out answers about the data because the data is too old to be useful. Essentially, this field says: at some point, the data is so old that having no data is better than having stale data. We think Microsoft's default expire time of 86,400 seconds (24 hours) is awfully short. Expire times on the order of a week are common, and the interval can be longer (up to a month) if you frequently have problems reaching your updating source. The expiration time should always be much larger than the retry and refresh intervals; if the expire time is smaller than the refresh interval, your slaves will expire their data before trying to load new data.

minimum TTL

TTL stands for time to live. This value applies to all the resource records in the zone data file. The name server supplies this TTL in query responses, allowing other servers to cache the data for the TTL interval. If your data doesn't change much, you might consider using a minimum TTL of several days. One week is about the longest value that makes sense. Again, the default value of 3,600 seconds (one hour) is very short, which we don't recommend because of the amount of DNS traffic it causes.

What values you choose for your SOA record will depend upon the needs of your site. In general, longer times cause less loading on your systems and lengthen the propagation of changes; shorter times increase the load on your systems and speed up the propagation of changes. We find the following values work well for most sites; they're also a good starting point if you're not sure what values to use:

```
  10800 ;  Refresh       3 hours
   3600 ;  Retry         1 hours
2592000 ;  Expire       30 days
  86400 ;  Minimum TTL   1 day
```

One final note about TTL values: the DNS console displays them in a somewhat cryptic fashion. Take a look back at the NS record we added in Figure 4-27. Notice the TTL specified as 0: 1: 0: 0. "What the heck is that?" you ask. Well, the first field is days, then hours, minutes, and seconds. So rather than display a value in seconds and make you do the math, the DNS console lets you specify a TTL in a (slightly) more convenient way.

Adding More Zones

Now that you have your name servers running, you might want to handle more zones. What needs to be done? Nothing special, really. Just use the DNS console to select the appropriate server in the left pane, then choose **Action → New Zone...**. Follow the instructions earlier in this chapter according to whether you are creating a primary or a slave (secondary) zone.

At this point, it's useful to repeat something we said in an earlier chapter. Calling a *given* name server a primary master name server or slave name server is a little silly. Name servers can be authoritative for more than one zone. A name server can be a primary master for one zone and a slave for another. Most name servers, however, are either primary master for most of the zones they load or slave for most of the zones they load. So if we call a particular name server a primary master or a slave, we mean that it's the primary master or a slave for *most* of the zones it loads.

DNS Properties

Let's finish this chapter with an explanation of the **Action → Properties** selection. The **Properties** selection on the **Action** menu is context-sensitive. When selected, the DNS console displays the properties of the resource record, zone, or server that is highlighted.

Resource Record Properties

Select a resource record on the right by single-clicking it. Then choose **Action → Properties**. The window should look familiar: it's the same one you used to add the record. You can get the same effect by simply double-clicking the record, too.

Zone Properties

The zone properties window is viewed by selecting a zone on the left and choosing **Action → Properties**. Unlike resource record properties, some zone information can be changed only from this window. It has five tabs:

General
> This window shows the name of the zone's data file as well as indicating if it's a primary or slave (secondary) zone. The type of the zone can be changed from primary to slave or vice versa. Dynamic updates and aging/scavenging are advanced topics that we'll cover in Chapter 11. The window for the *movie.edu* zone is shown in Figure 4-28.

Start of Authority (SOA)
> This window shows the zone's SOA record. The display is the same as the window shown way back in Figure 4-13 and is no different than if you double-click the SOA record in the right panel.

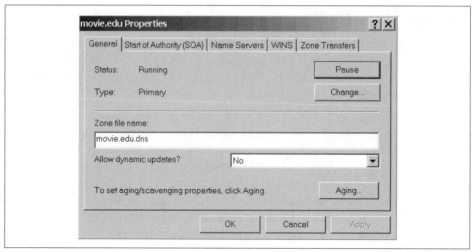

Figure 4-28. Zone properties window, General tab

Name Servers
> We've already seen this window—see Figure 4-26.

WINS
> The **WINS** tab is covered in Chapter 10.

Zone Transfers
> The **Zone Transfers** tab and **Notify** settings are also covered in Chapter 10.

Server Properties

You can view the server properties by selecting a server on the left and choosing **DNS Properties**. It has three tabs:

Interfaces
> This window allows you to specify the interfaces on which the server will listen for queries. If you have multiple interfaces (as for virtual web hosting), you might not need them all to be listed here. The default behavior is for the server to listen on all interfaces. The window is shown in Figure 4-29.

Forwarders, Advanced, Logging, and Monitoring
> These tabs are all covered in Chapter 10.

Root Hints
> We discussed this window earlier—see Figure 4-20.

What Next?

In this chapter, we showed you how to set up a primary master and a slave name server. There is more work to do to complete setting up your local domain: you need

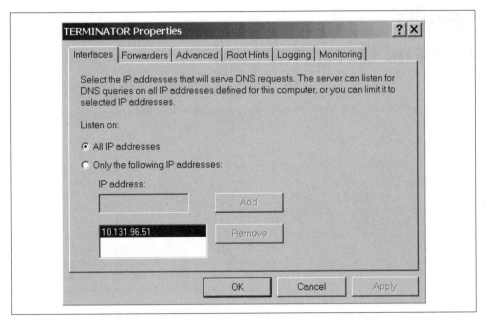

Figure 4-29. Server properties, Interfaces tab

to modify your DNS data for email, configure the other hosts in your domain to use name servers, and possibly start up more name servers. These topics are covered in the next few chapters.

CHAPTER 5
DNS and Electronic Mail

And here Alice began to get rather sleepy, and went on saying to herself, in a dreamy sort of way, "Do cats eat bats? Do cats eat bats?" and sometimes "Do bats eat cats?" for, you see, as she couldn't answer either question, it didn't much matter which way she put it.

I'll bet you're drowsy too, after that looong chapter. Thankfully, this next chapter discusses a topic that will probably be very interesting to you system administrators and postmasters: how DNS impacts electronic mail. And even if it isn't interesting to you, at least it's shorter than the last chapter.

One of the advantages of the Domain Name System over host tables is its support of advanced mail routing. When mailers had only the *HOSTS.TXT* file (and its derivatives, */etc/hosts* in the Unix world and *%SYSTEM ROOT%\system32\drivers\etc\ HOSTS* under Windows) to work with, the best they could do was to attempt delivery to a host's IP address. If that failed, they could either defer delivery of the message and try again later or bounce the message back to the sender.

DNS offers a mechanism for specifying backup hosts for mail delivery. The mechanism also allows hosts to assume mail-handling responsibilities for other hosts. This lets diskless hosts that don't run mailers, for example, have mail addressed to them processed by their servers.

DNS, unlike host tables, allows arbitrary names to represent electronic mail destinations. You can—and most organizations on the Internet do—use the domain name of your main forward-mapping zone as an email destination. Or you can add domain names to your zone that are purely email destinations and don't represent any particular host. A single logical email destination may also represent several mail servers. With host tables, mail destinations were hosts, period.

Together, these features give administrators much more flexibility in configuring electronic mail on their networks.

MX Records

DNS uses a single type of resource record to implement enhanced mail routing, the MX record. Originally, the MX record's function was split between two records, the MD (mail destination) and MF (mail forwarder) records. MD specified the final destination to which a message addressed to a given domain name should be delivered. MF specified a host that would forward mail on to the eventual destination, should that destination be unreachable.

Early experience with DNS on the Internet showed that separating the functions didn't work very well. A mailer needed both the MD and MF records attached to a domain name (if both existed) to decide where to send mail—one or the other alone wouldn't do. But an explicit lookup of one type or another (either MD or MF) would cause a name server to cache just that record type. So mailers either had to do two queries, one for MD and one for MF data, or they could no longer accept cached answers. This meant that the overhead of running mail was higher than that of running other services, which was eventually deemed unacceptable.

The two records were integrated into a single record type, MX, to solve this problem. Now a mailer just needed all the MX records for a particular domain name destination to make a mail routing decision. Using cached MX records was fine, as long as the TTLs matched.

MX records specify a *mail exchanger* for a domain name: a host that will *either* process *or* forward mail for the domain name (through a firewall, for example). "Processing" the mail means either delivering it to the individual to whom it's addressed or gatewaying it to another mail transport, such as X.400. "Forwarding" means sending it to its final destination or to another mail exchanger "closer" to the destination via SMTP, the Internet's Simple Mail Transfer Protocol. Sometimes forwarding the mail involves queuing it for some amount of time, too.

In order to prevent mail routing loops, the MX record has an extra parameter, besides the domain name of the mail exchanger: a *preference value*. The preference value is an unsigned 16-bit number (between 0 and 65535) that indicates the mail exchanger's priority. For example, the MX record:

```
peets.mpk.ca.us.    IN    MX    10 relay.hp.com.
```

specifies that *relay.hp.com* is a mail exchanger for *peets.mpk.ca.us* at preference value 10.

Taken together, the preference values of a destination's mail exchangers determine the order in which a mailer should use them. The preference value itself isn't important, only its relationship to the values of other mail exchangers: is it higher or lower than the values of this destination's other mail exchangers? Unless there are other records involved, this:

```
plange.puntacana.dr.  IN  MX  1 listo.puntacana.dr.
plange.puntacana.dr.  IN  MX  2 hep.puntacana.dr.
```

does exactly the same thing as:

```
plange.puntacana.dr.  IN  MX  50   listo.puntacana.dr.
plange.puntacana.dr.  IN  MX  100  hep.puntacana.dr.
```

Mailers should attempt delivery to the mail exchangers with the *lowest* preference values first. This may seem a little counterintuitive—the *most* preferred mail exchanger has the *lowest* preference value. But since the preference value is an unsigned quantity, this lets you specify a "best" mail exchanger at preference value 0.

If delivery to the most preferred mail exchanger(s) fails, mailers should attempt delivery to less preferred mail exchangers (those with *higher* preference values), in order of increasing preference value. That is, mailers should try more-preferred mail exchangers before they try less-preferred mail exchangers. More than one mail exchanger may share the same preference value, too. This gives the mailer its choice of which to send to first. The mailer must try all the mail exchangers at a given preference value before proceeding to the next higher value, though.

For example, the MX records for *oreilly.com* might be:

```
oreilly.com.   IN   MX   0 ora.oreilly.com.
oreilly.com.   IN   MX   10 ruby.oreilly.com.
oreilly.com.   IN   MX   10 opal.oreilly.com.
```

Interpreted together, these MX records instruct mailers to attempt delivery to *oreilly.com* by sending to:

1. *ora.oreilly.com* first
2. Either *ruby.oreilly.com* or *opal.oreilly.com* next, and finally
3. The remaining preference 10 mail exchanger (the one not used in step 2)

Of course, once the mailer successfully delivers the mail to one of *oreilly.com*'s mail exchangers, it can stop. A mailer successfully delivering *oreilly.com* mail to *ora.oreilly.com* doesn't need to try *ruby.oreilly.com* or *opal.oreilly.com*.

Note that *oreilly.com* isn't a particular host; it's the domain name of O'Reilly & Associates' main forward-mapping zone. O'Reilly & Associates uses the domain name as the email destination for everyone who works there. It's much easier for correspondents to remember the single email destination *oreilly.com* than to remember which host—*ruby.oreilly.com? amber.oreilly.com?*—each employee has an email account on.

This requires, of course, that the mailer on *ora.oreilly.com* keep track of the host on which each user at O'Reilly & Associates has an email account. That's usually done by maintaining a master *aliases* file on *ora.oreilly.com* that forwards email from *ora.oreilly.com* to its eventual destination.

What if a destination doesn't have any MX records, but it has one or more A records? Will a mailer simply not deliver mail to that destination? It depends on the mail server. Both Exchange and the SMTP servers provided with Windows 2000 require the presence of a valid MX record for any domain to which you want to deliver mail. However, *sendmail*, a popular mail transport agent from the Unix world, is different. Recent versions of *sendmail* can be compiled with the functionality to deliver mail to a destination with no MX records but at least one A record. Most vendors have compiled their *sendmail*s with this more forgiving feature: if no MX records exist but one or more A records do, they'll at least attempt delivery to the address. *sendmail* Version 8, compiled "out of the box," will try the address of a mail destination without MX records. Check your vendor's documentation if you're not sure whether your mail server will send mail to destinations with only address records. Even though nearly all mailers will deliver mail to a destination with just an address record and no MX records, it's still a good idea to have at least one MX record for each legitimate mail destination. Most mailers, including *sendmail*, will always look up the MX records for a destination first when there is mail to deliver. If the destination doesn't have any MX records, a name server—usually one of your authoritative name servers—still must answer that query, and then *sendmail* will go on to look up A records. That takes extra time, slows mail delivery, and adds a little load to your zone's authoritative name servers. If you simply add an MX record for each destination pointing to a domain name that maps to the same address that an address lookup would return, the mailer will have to send only one query, and the mailer's local name server will cache the MX record for future use.

Adding MX Records with the DNS Console

Now that you're familiar with MX records as they appear in zone data files, let's cover how to add them with the DNS console. First, right-click on the domain name of the zone to which you'd like to add the MX record. You'll access the drop-down menu shown in Figure 5-1.

Choose **New Mail Exchanger...** from the pop-up menu. A small window, shown in Figure 5-2, will be displayed.

In Figure 5-2, we're adding an MX record for *terminator.movie.edu* at preference 10, pointing to *terminator.movie.edu* itself. The record that's added to the zone data file looks like this:

```
terminator   IN MX 10 terminator
```

What's a Mail Exchanger, Again?

The idea of a mail exchanger is probably new to many of you, so let's go over it in a little more detail. A simple analogy should help here: imagine that a mail exchanger is an airport, and instead of setting up MX records to instruct mailers where to send messages, you're advising your in-laws on which airport to fly into when they come to visit you.

Say you live in Los Gatos, California. The closest airport for your in-laws to fly into is San Jose, the second closest is San Francisco, and the third Oakland. (We'll ignore

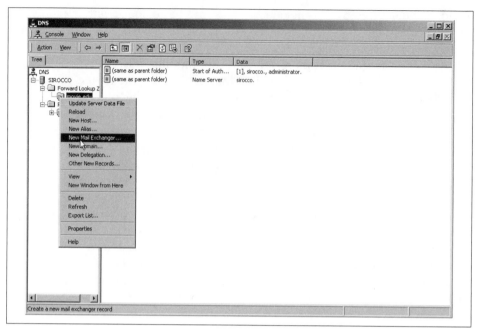

Figure 5-1. Adding an MX record to a zone

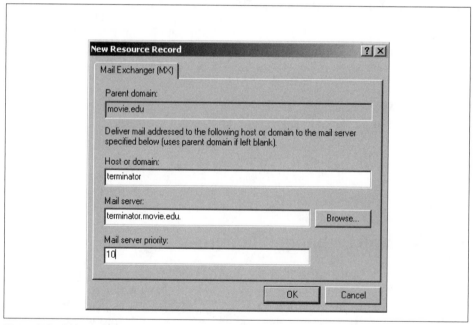

Figure 5-2. Adding an MX record for terminator.movie.edu

other factors such as price of the ticket, Bay Area traffic, etc.) Don't see the parallel? Then picture it like this:

```
los-gatos.ca.us.    IN    MX    1 san-jose.ca.us.
los-gatos.ca.us.    IN    MX    2 san-francisco.ca.us.
los-gatos.ca.us.    IN    MX    3 oakland.ca.us.
```

The MX list is just an ordered list of destinations that tells mailers (your in-laws) where to send messages (fly) if they want to reach a given email destination (your house). The preference value tells them how desirable it is to use that destination—you can think of it as a logical "distance" from the eventual destination (in any units you choose), or simply as a "top ten"–style ranking of the proximity of those mail exchangers to the final destination.

With this list, you're saying, "Try to fly into San Jose, and if you can't get there, try San Francisco and Oakland, in that order." It *also* says that if you reach San Francisco, you should take a commuter flight to San Jose. If you wind up in Oakland, you should try to get a commuter to San Jose or at least to San Francisco.

What makes a good mail exchanger, then? The same qualities that make a good airport:

Size

You wouldn't want to fly into tiny Reid-Hillview Airport to get to Los Gatos, because the airport's not equipped to handle large planes or many people. (You'd probably be better off landing a big jet on Interstate 280 than at Reid-Hillview.) Likewise, you don't want to use an emaciated, underpowered host as a mail exchanger; it won't be able to handle the load.

Uptime

You know better than to fly through Denver International Airport in the winter, right? Then you should know better than to use a host that's rarely up or available as a mail exchanger.

Connectivity

If your relatives are flying in from far away, you've got to make sure they can get a direct flight to at least one of the airports in the list you give them. You can't tell them their only choices are San Jose and Oakland if they're flying in from Helsinki. Similarly, you've got to make sure that at least one of your hosts' mail exchangers is reachable to anyone who might conceivably send you mail.

Management and administration

How well an airport is managed has a bearing on your safety while flying into or just through the airport and on how easy it is to use. Think of these factors when choosing a mail exchanger. The privacy of your mail, the speed of its delivery during normal operations, and how well your mail is treated when your hosts go down all hinge upon the quality of the administrators who manage your mail exchangers.

Keep this example in mind, because we'll use it again later.

The MX Algorithm

That's the basic idea behind MX records and mail exchangers, but there are a few more wrinkles you should know about. To avoid routing loops, mailers need to use a slightly more complicated algorithm than what we've described when they determine where to send mail.*

Imagine what would happen if mailers didn't check for routing loops. Let's say you send mail from your workstation to *nuts@oreilly.com*, raving (or raging) about the quality of this book. Unfortunately, *ora.oreilly.com* is down at the moment. No problem! Recall *oreilly.com*'s MX records:

```
oreilly.com.    IN    MX    0 ora.oreilly.com.
oreilly.com.    IN    MX    10 ruby.oreilly.com.
oreilly.com.    IN    MX    10 opal.oreilly.com.
```

Your mailer falls back and sends your message to *ruby.oreilly.com*, which is up. *ruby. oreilly.com*'s mailer then tries to forward the mail on to *ora.reilly.com* but can't because *ora.oreilly.com* is down. Now what? Unless *ruby.oreilly.com* checks the sanity of what she is doing, she'll try to forward the message to *opal.oreilly.com* or maybe even to herself. That's certainly not going to help get the mail delivered. If *ruby.oreilly.com* sends the message to herself, we have a mail routing loop. If *ruby. oreilly.com* sends the message to *opal.oreilly.com*, *opal.oreilly.com* will either send it back to *ruby.oreilly.com* or send it to herself, and we again have a mail routing loop.

To prevent this from happening, mailers discard certain MX records before they decide where to send a message. A mailer sorts the list of MX records by preference value and looks in the list for the canonical domain name of the host on which it's running. If the local host appears as a mail exchanger, the mailer discards that MX record and all MX records in which the preference value is equal or higher (that is, equally or less-preferred mail exchangers). That prevents the mailer from sending messages to itself or to mailers "farther" from the eventual destination.

Let's think about this in the context of our airport analogy. This time, imagine you're an airline passenger (a message) trying to get to Greeley, Colorado. You can't get a direct flight to Greeley, but you can fly to either Fort Collins or Denver (the two next-highest mail exchangers). Since Fort Collins is closer to Greeley, you opt to fly to Fort Collins.

Now, once you've arrived in Fort Collins, there's no sense in flying to Denver, away from your destination (a lower-preference mail exchanger). (And flying from Fort Collins to Fort Collins would be silly, too.) So the only acceptable flight to get you to your destination is now a Fort Collins–Greeley flight. You eliminate flights to less-preferred destinations to prevent frequent-flyer looping and wasteful travel time.

---

* This algorithm is based on RFC 974, which describes how Internet mail routing works.

One caveat: most mailers will look *only* for their local host's *canonical* domain name in the list of MX records. They don't check for aliases (domain names on the left side of CNAME records). Unless you always use canonical names in your MX records, there's no guarantee that a mailer will be able to find itself in the MX list, and you'll run the risk of having your mail loop.

If you do list a mail exchanger by an alias and it unwittingly tries to deliver mail to itself, most mailers will detect the loop and bounce the mail with an error. Here's the error message from recent versions of *sendmail*:

```
554 MX list for movie.edu points back to relay.isp.com
554 <root@movie.edu>... Local configuration error
```

The moral: in an MX record, always use the mail exchanger's canonical name.

One more caveat: the hosts you list as mail exchangers *must* have address records. A mailer needs to find an address for each mail exchanger you name or else it can't attempt delivery there.

To go back to our *oreilly.com* example, when *ruby.oreilly.com* received the message from your workstation, her mailer would have checked the list of MX records:

```
oreilly.com.    IN    MX    0 ora.oreilly.com.
oreilly.com.    IN    MX    10 ruby.oreilly.com.
oreilly.com.    IN    MX    10 opal.oreilly.com.
```

Finding the local host's domain name in the list at preference value 10, *ruby.oreilly.com*'s mailer would discard all the records at preference value 10 or higher (the records in bold):

```
oreilly.com.    IN    MX    0 ora.oreilly.com.
oreilly.com.    IN    MX    10 ruby.oreilly.com.
oreilly.com.    IN    MX    10 opal.oreilly.com.
```

leaving only:

```
oreilly.com.    IN    MX    0 ora.oreilly.com.
```

Since *ora.oreilly.com* is down, *ruby.oreilly.com* would defer delivery until later and queue the message.

What happens if a mailer finds *itself* at the highest preference (lowest preference value) and has to discard the whole MX list? Some mailers attempt delivery directly to the destination host's IP address as a last-ditch effort. In most mailers, however, it's an error. It may indicate that DNS thinks the mailer should be processing (not just forwarding) mail for the destination, but the mailer hasn't been configured to know that. Or it may indicate that the administrator has ordered the MX records incorrectly by using the wrong preference values.

Say, for example, the folks who run *acme.com* add an MX record to direct mail addressed to *acme.com* to a mailer at their Internet service provider:

```
acme.com.    IN    MX    10 mail.isp.net.
```

Most mailers need to be configured to identify their aliases and the names of other hosts for which they process mail. Unless the mailer on *mail.isp.net* is configured to recognize email addressed to *acme.com* as local mail, it will assume it's being asked to relay the mail and attempt to forward the mail to a mail exchanger closer to the final destination.* When it looks up the MX records for *acme.com*, it will find itself as the most-preferred mail exchanger and will bounce the mail back to the sender.

You may have noticed that we tend to use multiples of 10 for our preference values. Ten is convenient because it allows you to insert other MX records temporarily at intermediate values without changing the other weights, but otherwise there's nothing magical about it. We could just as easily have used increments of 1 or 100—the effect would have been the same.

DNS and Exchange

If you're running Microsoft Exchange Server, you need to know how it interoperates with DNS, whether or not you're using the Microsoft DNS Server. There are some subtle differences between various versions of Exchange and Windows NT or Windows 2000:

- If you're using Exchange 4.x or 5.x on Windows NT, you can run Exchange without DNS. However, before you can install the Internet Mail Service (which is what Microsoft calls its SMTP server), you must have A and MX records defined for the host and domain on which you're installing the IMS. You also need to make sure that the Exchange server's DNS settings are set correctly so it can look up mail forwarders for outgoing mail.

- If you're using the SMTP server that comes with the Windows NT Option Pack, Internet Information Server 4.x, or Windows 2000, you need an MX record if you want to receive mail; to send mail you only need access to a name server.

- If you're using Windows 2000 Active Directory, you'll find that your need for DNS is pervasive—Active Directory depends on DNS to find domain controllers, logon servers, and other services. We'll cover the DNS needs of Active Directory in Chapter 11.

- Exchange 2000 uses Active Directory as its directory service, so it is totally dependent on the underlying OS's DNS setup. In particular, Exchange 2000 needs access to SRV records so it can find global catalog servers, instant messaging hosts, and domain controllers. Don't worry—SRV records are also covered in Chapter 11.

---

* Unless, of course, *mail.isp.net*'s mailer is configured not to relay mail for unknown domains. In this case, it would simply reject the mail.

CHAPTER 6

Configuring Hosts

*They were indeed a queer-looking party that
assembled on the bank—the birds with draggled
feathers, the animals with their fur clinging close to
them, and all dripping wet, cross, and uncomfortable.*

Now that you or someone else in your organization has set up name servers for your
zones, you'll want to configure the hosts on your network to use them. That involves
configuring those hosts' resolvers, which you can do by telling the resolvers which
name servers to query and which domain names to search. This chapter covers these
topics and focuses on the Windows 2000 resolver. It also briefly describes configuring the resolver in Windows 95, Windows 98, and Windows NT.

The Resolver

We introduced resolvers way back in Chapter 2, but we didn't say much more about
them. The resolver, you'll remember, is the client half of the Domain Name System.
It's responsible for translating a program's request for host information into a query
to a name server and for translating the response into an answer for the program.

We haven't done any resolver configuration yet because the occasion for it hasn't
arisen. When we set up our name servers in Chapter 4, the resolver's default behavior worked just fine for our purposes. But if we'd needed the resolver to do more than
or behave differently from the default, we would have had to configure the resolver.

There's one thing we should mention up front: what we describe in the next few sections is the behavior of the Windows 2000 resolver. There are lots of other resolvers,
though. Every version of Windows has its own resolver, and the configuration and
behavior of each one is slightly different.* Unix hosts normally use some variant of
the BIND resolver, discussed in O'Reilly's *DNS and BIND*, and many Unix vendors

---

* Installing a Service Pack or a different Winsock version (e.g., upgrading to Windows 95 OSR2) can also
change resolver behavior.

have extended their resolvers' functionality. Still, the basic concepts behind the operation of each resolver are quite common.

Resolver Configuration

So, what exactly does the resolver allow you to configure? Most resolvers let you configure at least three aspects of their behavior: the DNS suffix,* the search list, and the name server(s) that the resolver queries.

DNS Suffix

The DNS suffix is the DNS domain in which a system resides. Under certain circumstances, the resolver uses the DNS suffix to generate the search list (which we discuss next). Don't confuse the DNS suffix, which is obviously a DNS domain name, with the name of the Active Directory domain of which the system is a member. The two values are usually the same because the DNS suffix defaults to a host's Active Directory domain, but they don't have to be. As we'll see in a moment, you can configure a host's DNS suffix to be different from the Active Directory domain of which it's a member. We're going to talk much more about domain names—both DNS and Active Directory—in Chapter 11. For now, though, it's not necessary to know anything more about Active Directory domains to understand resolver configuration.

All configuration options for the Windows NT 4.0 resolver were found in a single window. The Windows 2000 resolver configuration settings, however, are located on three separate windows. The first of these windows is where you change a host's DNS suffix. To get there, open the **Control Panel** and double-click on **System**, then click the **Network Identification** tab to display the window shown in Figure 6-1.

Here you see the host's fully qualified domain name, which Windows 2000 refers to as the **Full computer name**. It's the concatenation of the host's single-label computer name and its primary DNS suffix. The value listed as **Domain** is not the DNS suffix; it's the host's Active Directory domain. To change the primary DNS suffix, click **Properties**, and you'll see a window like the one shown in Figure 6-2.

You can change the computer name—the first label of the host's name—only from this window. The **Member of** box again refers to Active Directory domain membership, which, strictly speaking, doesn't affect resolver behavior. To change the DNS suffix, click on **More…** to display the window shown in Figure 6-3.

Here—finally!—is where you can change the DNS suffix. This window also shows the only linkage between Active Directory and DNS resolver behavior. A host's DNS suffix stays the same as its Active Directory domain as long as the **Change primary DNS**

---

* We're using the Windows 2000 term here for clarity. You may know the DNS suffix as the default domain if you've configured the BIND resolver before.

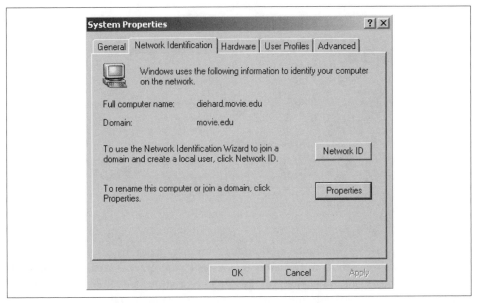

Figure 6-1. Network Identification tab

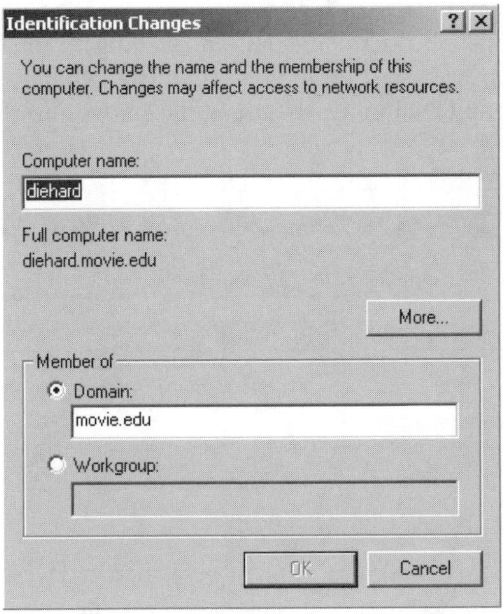

Figure 6-2. Identification Changes window

suffix when domain membership changes box is checked, which is the default set-ting. By unchecking this box and changing the **Primary DNS suffix of this computer** setting, you can decouple the DNS default domain and Active Directory domain. You

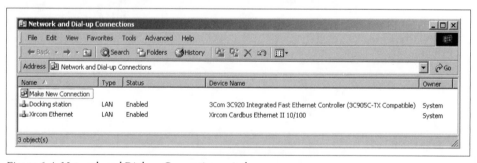

Figure 6-3. DNS Suffix window

do this only if you want your hosts to reside in (that is, be named in) a different domain than your Active Directory domain. Few organizations who set up Active Directory want to do this, and Microsoft does not recommend setting the primary DNS suffix to any value other than the DNS name of an Active Directory domain to which the computer is joined. But enough about Active Directory until Chapter 11.

The Windows 2000 resolver also supports a different DNS suffix for each network interface on the system. In fact, each network interface (or *adapter* in Windows 2000 parlance) has its own resolver configuration. Getting to the connection-specific resolver configuration windows is a little involved, though: click on **Start**, then **Settings**, then **Network and Dial-up Connections**. This brings up the window shown in Figure 6-4.

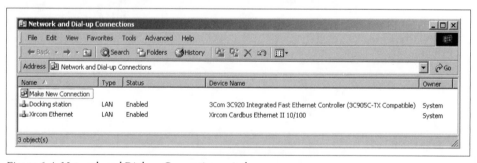

Figure 6-4. Network and Dial-up Connections window

This particular Windows 2000 host has two network interfaces. (We've gone to the trouble of naming them because the default names assigned by Windows were *Local Area Connection* and *Local Area Connection 2*—how boring!) Right-click on a local area network adapter and choose **Properties**. This brings up a window like the one shown in Figure 6-5.

Double-click on **Internet Protocol (TCP/IP)**. This displays the second of the three windows used for resolver configuration, which is shown in Figure 6-6.

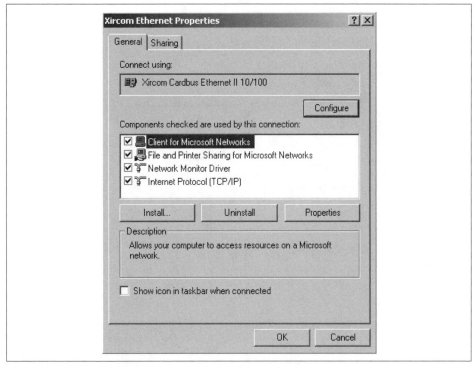

Figure 6-5. Local area connection properties window

Further resolver configuration options are available by clicking the **Advanced...** button and selecting the **DNS** tab, which produces the third and final window with resolver settings; it's shown in Figure 6-7.

The connection-specific DNS suffix is set in the **DNS suffix for this connection** field. Connection-specific DNS suffixes do affect resolver behavior (as we'll talk about in the next section, which discusses the search list), but their primary purpose is to assist with DNS registration. As we'll discuss in Chapter 11, Windows 2000 hosts automatically register their names in DNS. You'd specify a connection-specific suffix if your host connects to multiple networks and needs a different fully qualified domain name on each network. For example, perhaps one interface is connected to a network in which the host is named *diehard.movie.edu*, and another interface is connected to a network in which the host has a different fully qualified domain name, such as *diehard.fx.movie.edu*.

Search List

The primary DNS suffix and any connection-specific suffixes determine the default *search list*. The search list was designed to make users' lives a little easier by saving them some typing. The idea is to search one or more domains for incomplete names—that is, names that might not be fully qualified domain names.

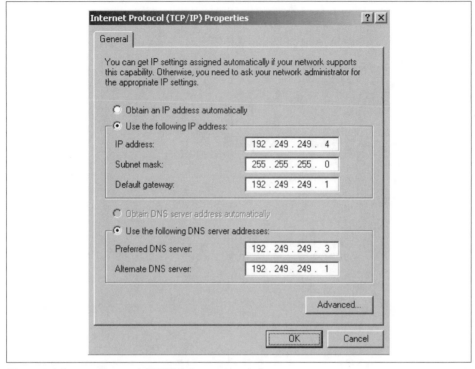

Figure 6-6. Internet Protocol (TCP/IP) Properties window

Most Windows networking commands that take a domain name as an argument, such as *ftp* and *ping*, apply the search list to those arguments.

With the Windows 2000 resolver, a user can indicate that a domain name is fully qualified by adding a trailing dot to it.* For example, the trailing dot in the command:

```
C:\> ftp ftp.oreilly.com.
```

means "don't bother searching any other domains; this domain name is fully qualified." This is analogous to the leading backslash in full pathnames in the Windows filesystem. Pathnames without a leading backslash are interpreted as relative to the current working directory while pathnames with a leading backslash are absolute, anchored at the root.

The default search list includes the primary DNS suffix and any connection-specific suffixes. If the **Append parent suffixes of the primary DNS suffix** box is checked (see Figure 6-7), each of the primary DNS suffix's parent domains with two or more labels is also included in the default search list. So on a Windows 2000 host configured with

---

* Note that we said the resolver can handle a trailing dot. Some programs, particularly mail user agents, don't deal correctly with a trailing dot in email addresses. They cough even before they hand the domain name in the address to the resolver.

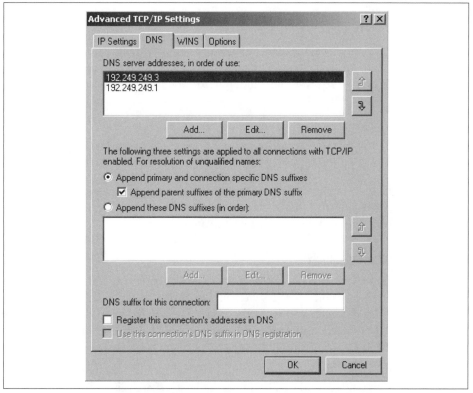

Figure 6-7. Advanced TCP/IP Settings window, DNS tab

a primary DNS suffix of *cv.hp.com* and the **Append parent suffixes of the primary DNS suffix** box checked, the default search list would contain first *cv.hp.com*, the primary DNS suffix, then *hp.com* (the primary DNS suffix's parent), but not *com*, as it has only one label.*

The search list is usually applied after the name is tried as-is. As long as the argument you type has at least one dot in it, it's looked up exactly as you typed it before any element of the search list is appended. If that lookup fails, the search list is applied.

Why is it better to try the argument first if it contains one or more dots? From experience, people who wrote resolvers found that, more often than not, if a user bothered to type in a name with even a single dot in it, she was probably typing in a fully qualified domain name without the trailing dot. Better to see right away whether the name was a fully qualified domain name than to create nonsense domain names unnecessarily by appending the elements of the search list to it.

---

* One reason resolvers don't append just the top-level domain is that there are few hosts at the second level of the Internet's namespace, so just tacking on *com* or *edu* to *foo* is unlikely to result in the domain name of a real host. Also, looking up the address of *foo.com* or *foo.edu* might well require sending a query to a root name server, which taxes the roots and can be time-consuming.

Thus, a user typing:

```
C:\> telnet pronto.cv.hp.com
```

causes a lookup of *pronto.cv.hp.com* first since the name contains three dots, which is certainly more than one. If the resolver doesn't find an address for *pronto.cv.hp.com*, it then tries *pronto.cv.hp.com.cv.hp.com*, and, if necessary, *pronto.cv.hp.com.hp.com*.

A user typing:

```
C:\> telnet asap
```

on the same host causes the resolver to look up first *asap.cv.hp.com* and then *asap.hp.com*, if necessary, but not just *asap*.

Note that application of the search list stops as soon as a prospective domain name finds the needed data. In the *asap* example, the search list would never get around to appending *hp.com* if *asap.cv.hp.com* resolved to an address.

Setting the search list manually

What if you don't like the default search list you get when you set your local domain? Windows lets you set the search list explicitly, domain name by domain name, in the order in which you want the domains searched. You do this with the **Append these DNS suffixes (in order)** field on the main resolver configuration window (Figure 6-8).

You can add as many domain names as you like to this field,[*] in the order in which you want them appended, and this becomes the host's search list. Setting the search list with **Append these DNS suffixes (in order)** overrides the default search list.

The user interface is simple to use: click **Add...** to add a domain name to the list; select a domain name and click **Remove** to remove it from the list; or click **Edit...** to change the domain name. You can also use the **Up** and **Down** arrow buttons to reorder the list. The basic search algorithm still applies: the resolver looks up domain name arguments as-is if they contain at least one dot.

The settings shown in Figure 6-8, for example, instruct the resolver to search the *corp.hp.com* domain first, then *paloalto.hp.com*, then both domains' parent, *hp.com*.

This setup might be useful on a host whose users frequently access hosts in both *corp.hp.com* and *paloalto.hp.com*. On the other hand, the configuration shown in Figure 6-9 has the resolver search only *corp.hp.com* (and not that domain's parent, *hp.com*) when the search list is applied.

This might be useful if the host's users access hosts only in the local domain or if connectivity to the parent name servers isn't good, because the configuration minimizes unnecessary queries to the parent name servers.

---

[*] Or so it appears: we stopped after adding 10.

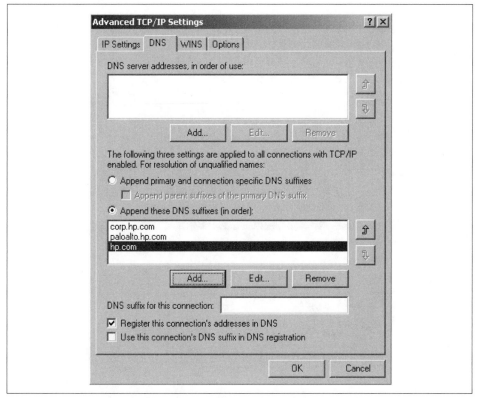

Figure 6-8. A search order example

Name Servers to Query

This section discusses how to tell your resolver which name servers to query. By default, the resolver looks for a name server running on the local host, which is why we could use *nslookup* on *terminator* and *wormhole* right after we configured their name servers. You can, however, instruct the resolver to look to another host for name service. This configuration is sometimes called a *DNS client*.

The **DNS server addresses, in order of use** field (see Figure 6-7) tells the resolver the IP addresses of the name server(s) to query. What's potentially confusing is that the information in this field is linked to the **Use the following DNS server addresses** field in the main TCP/IP properties window (see Figure 6-6). You can specify as many name servers as you want in the **DNS server addresses, in order of use** field.* As with the list of DNS suffixes in Figure 6-8, the **Add...**, **Edit...**, and **Remove** buttons have the expected effect. You can also use the **Up** and **Down** arrows to reorder the list of addresses. The first two addresses show up as the **Preferred DNS server** and

---

* As with the DNS suffix list, we stopped after entering 10 values.

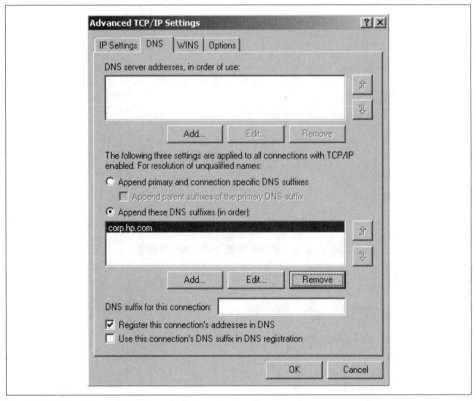

Figure 6-9. Another search order example

Alternate DNS server[*] on the main TCP/IP properties window. Likewise, changes made to the **Preferred DNS server** and **Alternate DNS server** fields are reflected in this list.

The settings in Figure 6-7 instruct the resolver to send queries to the name servers running at IP addresses 192.249.249.3 and 192.249.249.1. Typically, you configure the resolvers on your hosts to query your own name servers, but you can configure your resolver to query almost anyone's name server. Of course, configuring your host to use someone else's name server without first asking permission is presumptuous, if not downright rude, and using one of your own usually gives you better performance, so we'll consider this only an emergency option.

If you want the resolver to query the name server running on the local host, you have two choices: you can specify the address of one of the host's adapters, or you can specify the loopback IP address of 127.0.0.1.

---

[*] Kudos to Microsoft for clarifying their labels. In previous versions of Windows, name servers were sometimes labeled *Primary DNS* and *Secondary DNS*. This sometimes misled users into listing the primary master and slave (secondary master) name servers for some zone or another in those fields. Besides, "DNS" is an abbreviation for "Domain Name System," not "domain name server."

Query behavior

The way the Windows 2000 resolver determines which of the name servers you specify to query is significantly different than in other versions of Windows. Older versions of Windows send a query to the first name server specified. If that name server doesn't respond—say it's down or there's a network problem—the resolver tries subsequent name servers in the order configured, waiting a few seconds between each query. If it queries all configured name servers without getting a response, it cycles through the list again—six more times on some Windows resolvers! In the case of Windows NT SP3, if three name servers are configured and none of them are responding, the resolver tries for 75 seconds before finally giving up.

Microsoft's customers must have complained about this long resolver timeout, because things changed drastically with the release of Service Pack 4 for Windows NT. The resolver retransmission algorithm became much more aggressive. The Windows 2000 resolver exhibits the same behavior.

Here's how the Windows 2000 resolver behaves after it applies the search list to determine the name to look up:

1. The resolver first checks its local cache, which is systemwide (and therefore shared by all applications calling the resolver). If the desired record is not in the cache, the resolver has to send at least one query to a name server.

2. The resolver queries the first name server of the preferred network adapter and waits just one second.

3. If no answer is received, the resolver resends the query simultaneously to the first name server configured for each network adapter and waits two seconds. If the host has only one network adapter, this step is skipped.

4. If no answer is received, the resolver resends the query simultaneously to all name servers configured for all adapters and waits two seconds.

5. If no answer is received, the resolver resends the query simultaneously to all name servers configured for all adapters and waits four seconds.

6. If no answer is received, the resolver resends the query simultaneously to all name servers configured for all adapters and waits eight seconds.

7. If after all this time no name server has returned an answer, the resolver gives up.

What does the resolver do after it gives up? It times out and returns an error to the calling application. Typically this results in an error like:

```
C:\> ping tootsie
Bad IP address tootsie.
```

Adding up all the waiting time, you can see that the maximum timeout is much less than in older resolvers: 17 seconds (1+2+2+4+8), as opposed to 75 seconds for Windows NT SP3—quite a difference!

As soon as the resolver receives a positive answer during this process, it stops and returns that answer to the calling application. A positive answer is a list of resource records answering the query. If the resolver receives a negative answer (indicating that a domain name doesn't exist or that the particular type of record queried doesn't exist for a domain name), it doesn't immediately halt and return that answer. Instead, it just removes from consideration all name servers configured on the network adapter from which it received a negative answer for the duration of that query round. Only if it receives a negative answer from a name server configured for each adapter does it return a negative answer. If the resolver receives even a single positive answer from a name server, it returns that. The net effect of this mechanism is that if the resolver is configured to query name servers on multiple adapters that have different "views" of the namespace, the resolver sees the aggregate view.

The resolver also tracks the response time of individual name servers and shuffles the fastest-responding one to the top of the list. In other words, it adaptively changes the order of the name servers you specify (although these changes are not permanent, nor are they reflected in the resolver configuration windows). As you can see from the retransmission algorithm, the first name server gets only two or three seconds to reply before the resolver begins blasting queries to all configured name servers. By tracking how fast individual name servers respond and favoring the best performer, the resolver tries to minimize simultaneous querying.

The Windows 2000 Professional resolver adds another twist: if no name servers from a particular adapter respond during a query round, all name servers from that adapter are ignored—that is, not queried—for 30 seconds. This penalty-box treatment cuts down on unnecessary retransmission: if a network connection appears to be dead, there's no sense trying its name servers for every query.

Advanced Resolver Features

The Windows 2000 resolver has some advanced features that are worth describing here.

Caching

The Windows 2000 resolver stores every record it receives in a shared cache available to all programs on the system. The Windows NT 4.0 resolver caches, but only on a per-process basis. For example, if you have two different web browsers running (say, Internet Explorer and Netscape Navigator), each has its own copy of the resolver with a separate cache. Windows 98, 95, and 3.1 resolvers don't do any caching.

The Windows 2000 resolver obeys the TTL (time to live) field on resource records it caches, up to a maximum of 24 hours by default. So if a record specifies a TTL longer than that, the resolver rounds down to 24 hours. This maximum TTL is configurable with a Registry setting:

```
MaxCacheEntryTtlLimit
HKEY_LOCAL_MACHINE\SYSTEM\CurrentControlSet\Services\DNSCache\Parameters
```

```
Data type: REG_DWORD
Range: 0x0 - 0xFFFFFFFF seconds
Default value: 0x15180 (86,400 seconds = 24 hours)
```

The Windows 2000 resolver also supports negative caching. It caches negative responses for five minutes by default. This negative caching timeout is also configurable with a Registry setting:

```
NegativeCacheTime
HKEY_LOCAL_MACHINE\SYSTEM\CurrentControlSet\Services\DNSCache\Parameters
Data type: REG_DWORD
Range: 0x0 - 0xFFFFFFFF seconds
Default value: 0x12C (300 seconds = 5 minutes)
```

To disable negative caching altogether, set this value to zero.

To view the resolver's cache, use *ipconfig /displaydns*. To clear the cache, type *ipconfig /flushdns*.

Subnet Prioritization

This feature is analogous to the BIND resolver's address-sorting feature. When the resolver receives multiple address records for the same domain name, it examines the IP address in each record and adjusts the order of the records before returning the list to the calling application: any records with IP addresses on the same subnets as the host on which the resolver is running are moved to the top of the list. Since most applications use addresses in the order returned by the resolver, this behavior causes traffic to remain on local networks.

For example, Movie University has two mirrored web servers on two different subnets:

```
www.movie.edu.   IN   A   192.253.253.101
www.movie.edu.   IN   A   192.249.249.101
```

Let's say the resolver on *terminator.movie.edu* (192.249.249.3) sends a query and receives these records. It sorts the record with address 192.249.249.101 to the top of the list because *terminator* shares a network with that address.

Note that this behavior defeats the round-robin feature implemented by most name servers. *Round robin* refers to the name server behavior of rotating the order of multiple address records in successive responses to distribute the load among the servers (again taking advantage of the behavior of most applications to use the first address in the list returned by the resolver). With subnet prioritization enabled, the order of the records is subject to shuffling by the resolver. You can disable subnet prioritization with a Registry setting:

```
PrioritizeRecordData
HKEY_LOCAL_MACHINE\SYSTEM\CurrentControlSet\Services\DNSCache\Parameters
Data type: REG_DWORD
Range: 0 - 1
Default value: 1 (Subnet prioritization enabled)
```

Loose Response Acceptance

By default, the Windows 2000 resolver accepts and caches any response it receives, even if it arrives from an unexpected source (i.e., a name server the resolver did not query)! We think this behavior is more than a little dangerous because it opens up your resolver to spoofing attacks. It's easy to forge a DNS response and send it to an unsuspecting resolver, which then caches it. Fortunately, this behavior can be disabled with a Registry setting:

```
QueryIpMatching
HKEY_LOCAL_MACHINE\SYSTEM\CurrentControlSet\Services\DNSCache\Parameters
Data type: REG_DWORD
Range: 0 - 1
Default value: 0 (IP addresses of responses are not checked)
```

Other Windows Resolvers

Since you probably have hosts running older versions of Windows on your network, it's helpful to know how these older resolvers behave, too.

Windows 95

Windows 95 includes its own TCP/IP stack with a DNS resolver. In fact, Windows 95 actually includes two TCP/IP stacks: one for TCP/IP over LANs and another for TCP/IP over dial-up connections. To get to the main DNS configuration panel, go to the **Control Panel**, then select **Network**. Select **TCP/IP**, then click the **Properties** button. This brings up a new dialog, which looks similar to the one in Figure 6-10. Choose the tab labeled **DNS Configuration**.

Configuration using this panel is fairly self-explanatory: first select **Enable DNS** to turn on DNS resolution, then fill in the PC's hostname (in this case, the first label of its domain name) in the **Host** field and the local domain name (everything after the first dot) in the **Domain** field. Add the IP addresses of up to three name servers you want to query, in the order in which you want to query them, under **DNS Server Search Order**. Finally, fill in the domain names in the search list under **Domain Suffix Search Order** in the order in which you want them appended. If you leave out the **Domain Suffix Search Order**, the Windows 95 resolver derives one from the local domain name in the same way a Windows 2000 resolver does: appending successive parent domains with at least two labels.

One interesting note about the current version of Windows 95: you can configure a different set of name servers for each dial-up connection you might have to an ISP in the Dial-Up Networking (DUN) configuration. To configure DUN-specific resolver settings, double-click on the **My Computer** icon on your desktop, then double-click on **Dial-Up Networking**, right-click on the name of the connection whose resolver

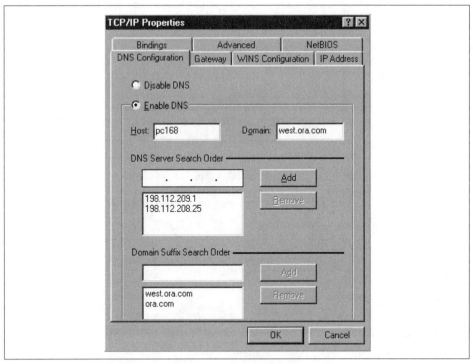

Figure 6-10. Resolver configuration under Windows 95

settings you'd like to configure, and select **Properties**. Select the **Server Types** tab and click on **TCP/IP Settings**. You'll see the window shown in Figure 6-11.

If you leave the **Server assigned name server addresses** radio button checked, the resolver retrieves the name servers it should query from the server you dial into. If you check **Specify name server addresses** and specify the addresses of one or two name servers, Windows 95 tries to use those name servers when the DUN connection is active.

This is really useful if you use multiple ISPs and each has its own name servers. However, configuring name servers in the **TCP/IP Properties** panel overrides the DUN-specific name servers. To use the DUN-specific name server feature, you must leave the **TCP/IP Properties** panel blank except for enabling DNS and specifying the local hostname. This limitation is due to a lack of integration between the dial-up and LAN TCP/IP stacks and is corrected in DUN 1.3. See Knowledge Base article Q191494 for details.[*]

---

[*] To access a Microsoft Knowledge Base article by article ID number, go to *http://search.support.microsoft.com/ kb/* and check the **Specific article ID number** radio button, then type the article ID number in the search field.

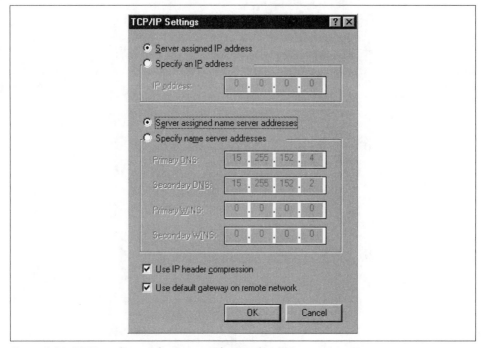

Figure 6-11. DUN resolver configuration under Windows 95

Windows 98

The resolver in Windows 98 is almost identical to Windows 95's resolver. (Graphically, in fact, it *is* identical, so we won't show you any screen shots.) The major differences between the two resolvers are due to the fact that Windows 98 ships with Winsock 2.0.* Winsock 2.0, for example, sorts responses as we described in the previous section on subnet prioritization. For details, see Knowledge Base article Q182644.

Configuring DUN-specific name servers also works with Windows 98. The resolver queries the name servers listed in the **TCP/IP Properties** panel and the DUN-specific name servers simultaneously and takes the first positive answer it receives from either set. If the resolver receives only negative answers, it returns a negative answer.

Windows NT 4.0

In Windows NT, LAN resolver configuration is done from a single panel that looks remarkably similar to Windows 95's, since NT 4.0 incorporated the Windows 95 "shell." In fact, other than the presence of the new **Edit** button and the handy little

---

* The version of Winsock in Windows 95 can be upgraded to 2.0; see Knowledge Base article Q182108.

arrows that allow you to reorder name servers and elements of the search list, there's really no semantic difference between them, as shown in Figure 6-12.

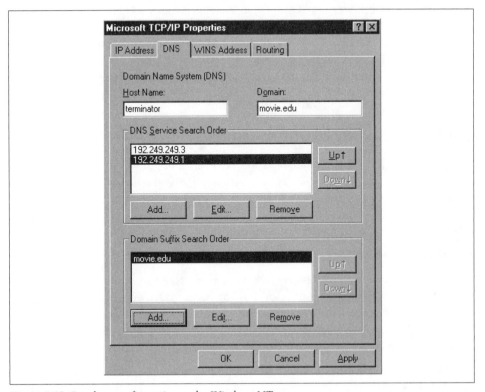

Figure 6-12. Resolver configuration under Windows NT

To get to the **DNS Configuration** panel, go to the **Control Panel**, click on **Network**, and select the **Protocols** tab. Double-click on **TCP/IP Protocol**, then select the **DNS** tab.

Windows NT also allows users to configure resolver settings specific to particular dial-up networking connections. To configure these, click on the **My Computer** icon, select **Dial-Up Networking**, pull down the top selection box, and choose the name of the DUN connection whose resolver you'd like to configure. Then click on the **More** pull-down and select **Edit Entry** then **Modem Properties**. Select the **Server** tab on the resulting window, and click on the **TCP/IP Settings** button. You'll see the same window you'd see in Windows 95 (shown earlier).

If you leave the **Server assigned name server addresses** radio button checked, the resolver retrieves the name servers it should query from the server you dial into. If you check **Specify name server addresses** and specify the addresses of one or two name servers, Windows NT uses those name servers when the DUN connection is active. When you drop the DUN connection, NT reverts to using the LAN resolver's settings.

The Windows NT 4.0 resolver caches name-to-address mappings on a per-process basis, according to the TTL on the returned address records, as mentioned earlier.

Microsoft updated the resolver fairly extensively in Windows NT 4.0, Service Pack 4. The SP4 resolver supports subnet prioritization. See Microsoft Knowledge Base article Q196500 for details. The SP4 resolver also lets you turn off caching in the resolver using a Registry value. For details, see Knowledge Base article Q187709. The SP4 resolver uses the same, more aggressive retransmission algorithm as the Windows 2000 resolver. See Knowledge Base article Q198550 for details.

Sample Resolver Configurations

Let's go over what some Windows 2000 resolver configurations look like on real hosts. Resolver configuration needs vary depending on whether or not a host runs a local name server, so we'll cover both cases: hosts using remote name servers and hosts running name servers locally.

Remote Name Server

We, as the administrators of *movie.edu*, have been asked to configure a professor's new workstation, which doesn't run a name server. Deciding which domain the workstation belongs in is easy: there's only *movie.edu* to choose from. However, the professor *is* working with researchers at Pixar on new shading algorithms, so perhaps it'd be wise to put *pixar.com* in her workstation's list of DNS suffixes to append.

The new workstation is on the 192.249.249.0 network, so the closest name servers are *wormhole.movie.edu* (192.249.249.1) and *terminator.movie.edu* (192.249.249.3). As a rule, you should configure hosts to first use the closest name server available. (The closest possible name server is a name server on the local host; the next closest is a name server on the same subnet or network.) In this case, both name servers are equally close, but we know that *wormhole* is bigger (it's a faster host, with more capacity).

Since this particular professor is known to get awfully vocal when she has problems with her computer, we'll also add *terminator.movie.edu* (192.249.249.3) as a backup name server. That way, if *wormhole* is down for any reason, the professor's workstation can still get name service (assuming *terminator* and the rest of the network are up).

Figure 6-13 shows what her workstation's resolver configuration will look like.

Local Name Server

Next, we have to configure the university mail hub, *postmanrings2x*, to use DNS. *postmanrings2x* is shared by all groups in the *movie.edu* domain. We've recently

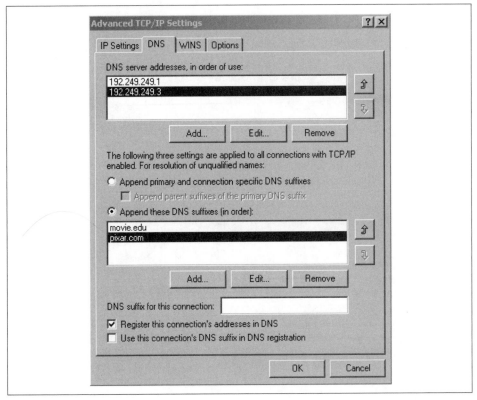

Figure 6-13. Example resolver configuration

configured a name server on the host to help cut down the load on the other name servers, so we should make sure the resolver queries the name server on the local host first.

If we decide we need a backup name server—a prudent decision—we can add a name server to the **DNS server addresses, in order of use** field. Whether or not we configure a backup name server depends largely on the reliability of the local name server. A robust name server implementation will keep running for longer than some operating systems, so there may be no need for a backup. If the local name server has a history of problems, though—say it hangs occasionally and stops responding to queries—it's prudent to add a backup name server.

To add a backup name server, we just list the local name server first in the list of DNS suffixes to append and then list one or two backup name servers. Since we'd rather be safe than sorry, we're going to add two backup name servers. *postmanrings2x* is on the 192.249.249.0 network, too, so *terminator* and *wormhole* are the closest name servers to it (besides its own). The final configuration is shown in Figure 6-14.

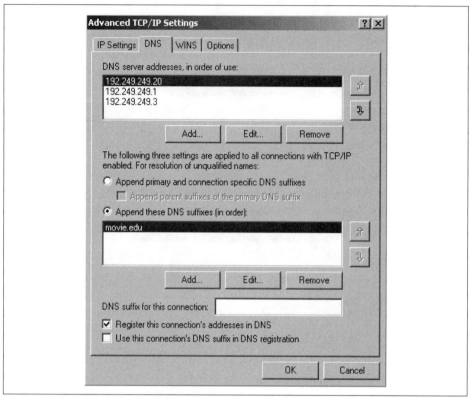

Figure 6-14. Another example resolver configuration

## CHAPTER 7

Maintaining the Microsoft DNS Server

> *"Well, in our country," said Alice, still panting a little,*
> *"you'd generally get to somewhere else—if you ran*
> *very fast for a long time as we've been doing."*
>
> *"A slow sort of country!" said the Queen. "Now, here,*
> *you see, it takes all the running you can do, to keep in*
> *the same place. If you want to get somewhere else,*
> *you must run at least twice as fast as that!"*

This chapter discusses a number of related topics pertaining to name server maintenance. We'll talk about commands you can (and can't) send to a running name server, modifying the zone data files, and keeping the root name server cache file up to date. We'll also list common Event Log messages.

This chapter doesn't cover troubleshooting problems. Maintenance involves keeping your data current and watching over your name servers as they operate. Troubleshooting involves putting out fires—those little DNS emergencies that flare up periodically. Firefighting is covered in Chapter 13.

What About Signals?

Those of you familiar with the BIND name server know that it's possible to signal a running name server to perform certain tasks, such as rereading its configuration file or turning on debugging information. The Microsoft DNS Server has no exact analog to a BIND name server's signals, but you can still make it perform certain tasks while running. We'll go over the tasks possible using signals on a BIND name server and show how to accomplish the same thing (if possible) with the Microsoft DNS Server:

Restart the name server

You can signal a BIND name server to reread its configuration file and zone data files. There's no comparable Microsoft DNS Server command. If the server obtains its configuration information from the Registry (the default mode), this command isn't necessary: as you make configuration changes with the DNS console, they take effect immediately in the running name server. If the server is using a BIND-style boot file, you must stop and restart the server after making a change to the boot file. For more information on the server "boot method," see Appendix C.

Dump a copy of the name server's internal database to a file

A BIND server can dump its entire memory database of authoritative data, cached data, and root name server "hints" to a file. There's no direct Microsoft DNS Server equivalent, but you can come close—all this information is visible in the DNS console. To see authoritative data, just select the appropriate zone. By selecting the **Cached Lookups** folder, you can see the contents of the name server's cache as well as the list of root name servers it's using.*

Dump name server statistics to a file

You can't dump the Microsoft DNS Server's usage statistics to a file, but you can view them from System Monitor (a Microsoft Management Console snap-in). Statistics are covered in detail at the end of this chapter.

Start/stop writing debugging information to a file

The Microsoft DNS Server can log several different kinds of debugging-related information to a file. This behavior is controlled from the **Logging** tab of the server properties window, where you can select the types of debugging information that should be logged.

Log all queries

As with a BIND server, you can also direct the Microsoft DNS Server to log individual queries processed. Use the **Query** option on the **Logging** tab.

The main thing you can do to a running Microsoft DNS Server is stop it and start it again. What happens when you stop and start the server? Remember that the name server answers queries from its in-memory database. This database includes three kinds of information: authoritative data (zones for which the server is a primary master or slave), cached data (answers from other name servers), and root name server "hints" (the list of root name servers from the root name server cache file, *cache.dns*). When you stop the name server, this data is lost.

When you restart the server, it reloads the authoritative data from the zone data files on its disk. Zones for which the server is a primary master are loaded and not read again for the lifetime of the server process. (Of course, you can make a change to a primary zone with the DNS console and direct the server to *write* to the zone data file with **Action → Update Server Data Files**, but the server *reads* the zone data file only at startup.) Zones for which the server is a slave are also loaded from the zone data files. But for each zone, the server queries its master (usually the zone's primary

---

* You can see the *Cached Lookups* folder only if the DNS console is showing the advanced view: select **View → Advanced**.

master) for the SOA record to compare serial numbers. If the master's serial number is larger than the serial number in the zone just loaded from disk, the server performs a zone transfer.

The server also reads *cache.dns* at startup. In Chapter 4, we described how root name server information is used not directly, but as a "hint" to find the current list of root name servers: the server queries a root name server from *cache.dns* for the current list of root name servers, and the results are the first records in the cache. Remember, the cache is empty when the server starts up.

Logging

The version of the Microsoft DNS Server shipped with Windows 2000 is much improved over its Windows NT 4.0 predecessor when it comes to logging and debugging. Previous versions of the server were like a "black box" you couldn't see inside of. But now you can direct the server to write several different kinds of helpful logging and debugging information while it's running.

To enable this feature, right-click on a server in the left pane of the DNS console, choose **Properties**, then select the **Logging** tab. The window looks like the one shown in Figure 7-1.

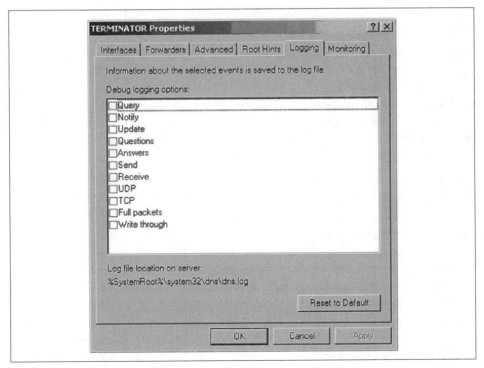

Figure 7-1. Server properties, Logging tab

Updating Zone Data

For nearly all changes to your zones, you'll use the DNS console. In Chapter 4 we described how to add a name server to the DNS console, create zones, and create resource records. Deleting these objects is easy: just select the object by left-clicking it, then press **Delete** (or select **Action → Delete**). Modifying objects is also straightforward. Name server names and zone names cannot be changed but must be deleted and added with the new name. For example, if the name of a name server you're managing changes, you have to delete the name server within the DNS console and replace it with the new name. The same thing goes if you change the name of a zone, say from *movie.edu* to *movie.net*.

Changing resource record data is easy, too. Just double-click the record in the right pane (or select it with a single click and choose **Action → Properties**). You'll see the same window as when you added the record. Note that you can change resource record data (also called *RDATA*) but not the name of the record (the owner). In other words, you can change the right side of the record but not the left side (as viewed in the DNS console's right pane or in the zone data file). So you can change the IP address of *terminator*'s A record, but you can't change *terminator* to *terminator2*. If you need to change the owner, you'll have to delete the record and replace it with the new owner.

Adding and Deleting Resource Records by Hand

Most of the time, you really should use the DNS console to make changes to your zones. The DNS console is much more versatile than its Windows NT 4.0 predecessor, the DNS Manager, but still isn't suited for some tasks—sometimes you might want to edit the zone data files by hand. For example, adding, deleting, or changing a lot of records at once is tough with the DNS console but easy with a little Perl code or a good text editor. If you run a name server for long enough, you'll eventually want to make a change outside the DNS console.

Editing by hand is a little complicated because you have to manually perform some steps that the DNS console does for you automatically. The following list describes what to do:

1. Remember that all changes must be made on a zone's primary master name server. This is the case whether you're using the DNS console or editing by hand. If you make changes to the zone data file on a slave, the next zone transfer from the primary master will overwrite your work.

2. If you've made any changes using the DNS console since you started the name server (that usually means since the last reboot), stop the name server. Here's why: when you change a zone with the DNS console, the change takes effect in the primary master name server's memory right away, but the zone data file on disk is not updated immediately. The name server sets an internal "update

pending" flag to remind itself that that zone's data file needs updating. If you select **Action → Update Server Data Files**, all the zone data files of changed zones are updated and any flags are cleared. But if the server stops (whether it's halted by you or by a system reboot—or for any other reason) and some zones have their update pending flags set, the server updates the corresponding zone data files before terminating. So you can see what happens if you make a change by hand but forget about a recent change made with the DNS console: when you stop and restart the server to put the manual change into effect, the zone data file gets updated, and your manual editing is lost.

3. Find the zone data file of the zone you want to change. Recall from Chapter 4 that the zone data files are stored in *%SystemRoot%\system32\dns* and the default naming convention is the name of the zone followed by the *.dns* extension—for example, *movie.edu.dns*.

4. Bring up the zone data file in your favorite text editor. Notepad is a good choice; Microsoft Word isn't. Whatever you use, make sure you eventually save the file in plain text format. That's why we like Notepad—you can't save a file as anything but plain text.

5. Increment the serial number in the SOA record at the top of the file. (See the next section for more information on SOA serial numbers.) Since the SOA record is at the top of the file, it's a good idea to update it first so you won't forget to do it later.

6. Make whatever changes you need to make. If you're adding a host, you might need MX records in addition to the A record. For example, we added the following resource records to *movie.edu.dns* when we added the new host *cujo* to our network:

```
cujo  IN  A   192.253.253.5
      IN MX   10 cujo
      IN MX   20 terminator
```

7. When you're done, don't forget to save the file!

8. Don't forget to add PTR records! If you're adding a host, you should add a PTR record to the appropriate *in-addr.arpa* zone for each of its IP addresses. This step is easy to forget, because the DNS console adds PTR records for you automatically. And remember—if you change a zone, don't forget to increment the serial number in its SOA record. Our new host *cujo* has only one IP address, 192.253. 253.5, so we added one PTR record to the *253.253.192.in-addr.arpa.dns* file:

```
5 IN PTR cujo.movie.edu.
```

Your changes won't take effect until you restart the primary master name server: stop it, and then start it again. This is another task handled by the DNS console. When you make changes with the DNS console, the changes take effect immediately in the name server's memory and get written to disk later. Editing by hand reverses the process: you make the changes first on disk and have to restart the name server to get the changes into its memory.

Slave name servers will load the new data after some length of time within the time interval defined in the SOA record for refreshing their data. Sometimes your users won't want to wait for the slaves to pick up the new data—they'll want it available right away. (Are you wincing or nodding knowingly as you read this?) Can you force a slave to load the new information right away? If you've enabled zone change notification, the slaves will pick up the new data quickly because the primary master notifies the slave of changes within 15 minutes of the change. (See Chapter 10 for more information on zone change notification.) If you don't have notification set up, you should! But you can get the same effect the hard way by restarting the name server on each of the slaves. When the name server starts up, it does a serial number compare with its master for every zone for which it's a slave. If it discovers an out-of-date zone, it immediately performs a zone transfer.

To delete a host, remove all the resource records pertaining to it from the appropriate zone data files. Make sure you remove the A record, any MX records, and the PTR record. Also be sure to increment the serial number in each zone data file you modify and restart your primary master name server. (But, realistically, deleting hosts is best done with the DNS console.)

SOA Serial Numbers

Every zone has a serial number. Every time the data in a file is changed, the zone's serial number must be incremented. If the serial number is not incremented, slave name servers for the zone will not pick up the updated data. The change is simple. If the original data file had the following SOA record:

```
movie.edu. IN SOA terminator.movie.edu. al.robocop.movie.edu. (
                        100     ; Serial
                        10800   ; Refresh
                        3600    ; Retry
                        604800  ; Expire
                        86400 ) ; Minimum TTL
```

the updated data file would have the following SOA record:

```
movie.edu. IN SOA terminator.movie.edu. al.robocop.movie.edu. (
                        101     ; Serial
                        10800   ; Refresh
                        3600    ; Retry
                        604800  ; Expire
                        86400 ) ; Minimum TTL
```

This simple change is the key to distributing the data to all of your slaves. Failing to increment the serial number is the most common mistake made when updating by hand. The first few times you make a change manually, you'll remember to update the serial number because this process is new and you are paying close attention. After modifying zone data files becomes second nature (we bet you can't wait for *that*), you'll make some "quickie" little change, forget to update the serial number... and none of the slaves will pick up the new data. Eternal vigilance is the price of modifying zone data files by hand.

There are several good ways to manage integer serial numbers. The obvious way is just to use a counter: increment the serial number by one each time the file is modified. That's what the DNS console does. Every time it updates a zone, it increments the zone's serial number. If you make changes with the DNS console, you're locked into this method. If you modify the zone data files only by hand, you have other options, such as deriving the serial number from the date. For example, you could use the eight-digit number formed by *<year><month><day>*. Suppose today is March 5, 2001. In this form, your serial number would be 20010305. This scheme allows only one update per day, though, and that may not be enough. Add another two digits to this number to indicate how many times the file has been updated that day. The first number for March 5, 2001, would then be 2001030500. The next modification that day would change the serial number to 2001030501. This scheme allows 100 updates per day. Whatever scheme you choose (or are forced to go along with), the serial number must fit in a 32-bit integer. And since you probably want to use the DNS console at least some of the time, you may just want to follow its numbering scheme.

Additional Records

After you've been running a name server for a while, you may want to add data to your name server to help you manage your domain. Have you ever been stumped when someone asked you *where* one of your hosts is? Maybe you don't even remember what kind of host it is. Administrators have to manage larger and larger populations of hosts these days, making it easy to lose track of this information. The name server can help you out. And if one of your hosts is acting up and someone notices remotely, the name server can help them get in touch with you.

So far, we've covered records critical to everyday operation: SOA, NS, A, CNAME, MX, and PTR. Name servers need these records to operate, and applications look up data of these types. Two other useful resource record types are TXT (text) and RP (Responsible Person); these can be used to tell you the machine's location and who is responsible for it. But DNS defines still more data types. For a complete list of the resource records, see Appendix A.

General text information

TXT stands for TeXT. These records contain simply a list of strings. The Microsoft DNS Server supports one string of up to 255 characters per TXT record. TXT records can be used for anything you want; a common use is to list a host's location. Creating a TXT record is easy: just highlight the zone or domain in the DNS console's left pane and select **Action → Other New Records...**. In the **Resource Record Type** window, choose **TXT** and select **Create Record...**, then fill in the fields as shown in Figure 7-2.

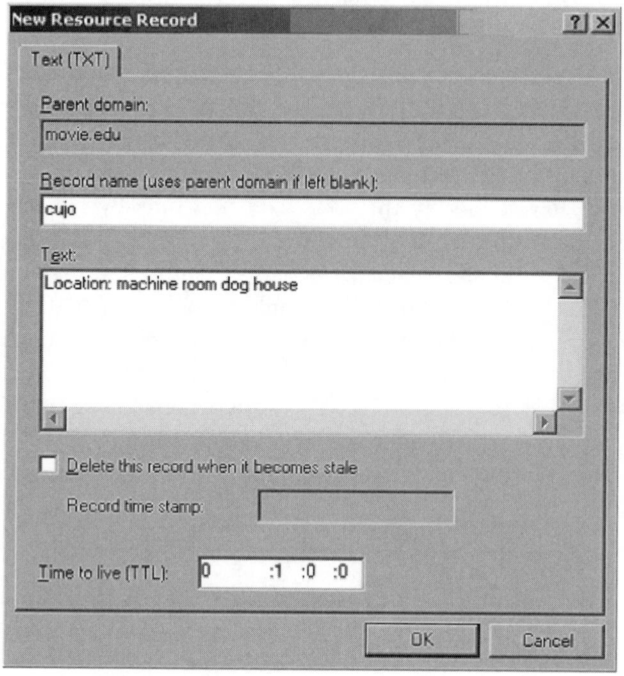

Figure 7-2. Creating a TXT record

The TXT record shown in Figure 7-2 looks like this in a zone data file:

```
cujo  IN  TXT  "Location: machine room dog house"
```

Responsible Person

Domain administrators will undoubtedly develop a love/hate relationship with the Responsible Person (RP) record. The RP record can be attached to any domain name, internal or leaf, and indicates who is responsible for that host or domain. This enables you to locate the miscreant responsible for the host peppering you with DNS queries, for example. But it also leads people to you when one of your hosts acts up.

The record takes two arguments as its record-specific data: an electronic mail address, in domain name format; and a domain name, which points to additional data about the contact. The electronic mail address is in the same format the SOA record uses: it substitutes a dot (.) for the at sign (@). The next argument is a domain name, which must have a TXT record associated with it. The TXT record contains free-format information about the contact, such as a full name and phone number. You can omit either field and specify the root (.) as a placeholder instead. For example, let's say that the Movie U. Network Hotline is responsible for the host *robocop*. It also happens that the Movie U. hotline reads all mail sent to *root@movie.edu*. You'd add the RP record shown in Figure 7-3 with **Action → Other New Records....**

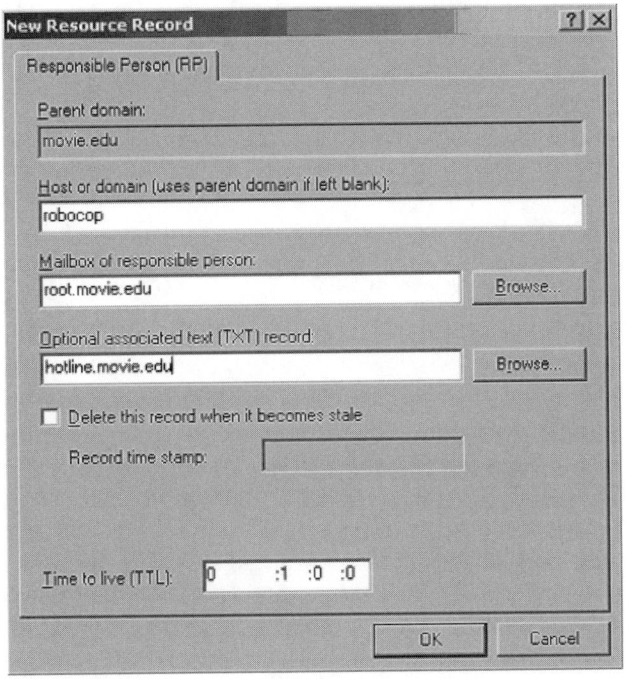

Figure 7-3. Creating an RP record

You'd also add the TXT record shown in Figure 7-4 for *hotline.movie.edu.*

Here's what these records would look like in a zone data file:

```
robocop      IN  RP   root.movie.edu.  hotline.movie.edu.
hotline      IN  TXT  "Movie U. Network Hotline, (415) 555-4111"
```

Note that a TXT record for *root.movie.edu* isn't necessary since it's only the domain name encoding of an electronic mail address, not a real domain name.

Keeping db.cache Current

As we explained in Chapter 4, the *cache.dns* file tells your server where the servers for the root zone are. We also explained that, unlike a BIND name server (which never modifies the cache file), a Microsoft DNS Server updates *cache.dns* with its current notion of the root name servers every time it exits.

The root name servers don't change very often, but they do change. A Microsoft DNS Server that starts with a proper cache file should, in theory, always have the current list of root name servers in its cache file. A good practice and a part of maintaining your name server is to check your *cache.dns* file a couple times a year. In Chapter 4, we told you to get the current cache file by *ftp*ing to *ftp.rs.internic.net.* That's probably the best method to keep the file current. Remember that you must

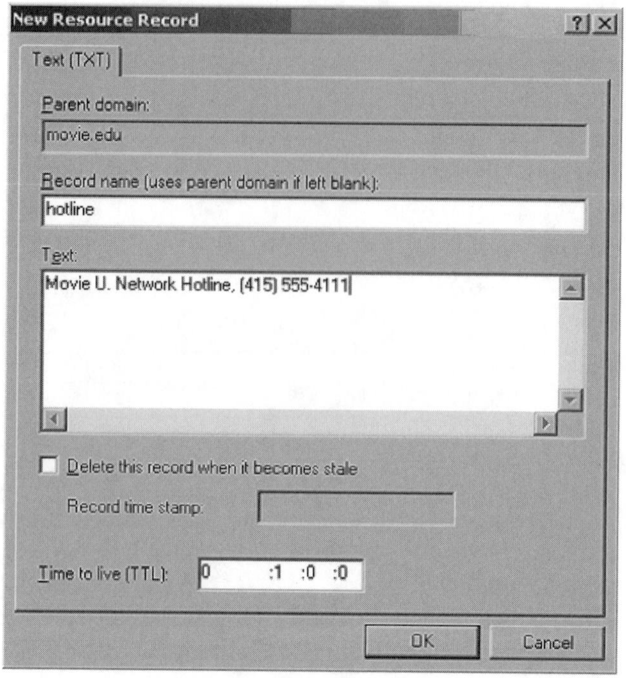

Figure 7-4. Creating an associated TXT record

stop the name server before updating *cache.dns*! If you don't, the cache file you install will be overwritten the next time the server does stop.

You can use *dig*,* a utility that works like *nslookup*, to retrieve the current list of roots just by running:

```
C:\> dig @a.root-servers.net  .  ns > cache.dns
```

Zone Data File Controls

The data files for all name servers, whether Microsoft or BIND, can include two control entries: $ORIGIN and $INCLUDE. $ORIGIN changes the origin, and $INCLUDE inserts a new file into the current file. These control entries are not resource records; they facilitate the maintenance of DNS data. They were designed back in the "good old days" as a shortcut for people who had to edit zone data files by hand. If you make changes to your zones with the DNS console only, you won't encounter these controls: the Microsoft DNS Server doesn't use them in the zone

---

* *dig* is a powerful DNS query tool that comes with BIND. Unfortunately, it isn't shipped with Windows 2000, but you can get a version of *dig* that runs on Windows 2000 from *ftp://ftp.isc.org/isc/bind/contrib/ntbind-8.2.4/ BIND8.2.4Tools.zip*.

data files it generates. However, some day you might need to work with zone data files created by hand, so it's important that you understand these controls.

Changing the Origin in a Data File

The default origin for a DNS data file is just the domain name of the zone. The origin is a domain name that is appended automatically to all names not ending in a dot. This origin can be changed within the zone data file using $ORIGIN, which must be followed by a domain name. (Don't forget the trailing dot if you give the full domain name!) From that point in the file on, the new will be origin appended to all names not ending in a dot.

If we didn't have the DNS console to make changes and had to edit files by hand, we'd run into times when $ORIGIN would save us some work. For example, if your name server were responsible for a number of subdomains, you could use the $ORIGIN entry to reset the origin and simplify the files. For example, from the *movie.edu* zone data file:

```
$ORIGIN classics.movie.edu.
maltese      IN  A  192.253.253.100
casablanca   IN  A  192.253.253.101

$ORIGIN comedy.movie.edu.
mash         IN  A  192.253.253.200
twins        IN  A  192.253.253.201
```

We'll discuss creating subdomains in Chapter 9.

Including Other Data Files

To continue our example of editing zone data files by hand: once you've subdivided your domain like this, you might find it more convenient to keep the subdomain records in separate files. The $INCLUDE statement would let you do this:

```
$ORIGIN classics.movie.edu.
$INCLUDE classics.dns

$ORIGIN comedy.movie.edu.
$INCLUDE comedy.dns
```

To simplify the file even further, the new origin can be specified on the $INCLUDE line:

```
$INCLUDE classics.dns classics.movie.edu.
$INCLUDE comedy.dns   comedy.movie.edu.
```

When you specify the origin on the $INCLUDE line, it applies only to the particular file that you're including. For example, the *comedy.movie.edu* origin applies only to the names in *comedy.dns*. After *comedy.dns* has been included, the origin returns to what it was before $INCLUDE, even if *comedy.dns* contained an $ORIGIN entry.

Remember that, strictly speaking, you don't need to know anything about these directives to create subdomains with the DNS console, and the Microsoft DNS Server doesn't generate zone data files using these shortcuts. But you do need to know about them to complete your knowledge of zone data files.

Keeping Everything Running Smoothly

A significant part of maintenance is being aware when something has gone wrong—before it becomes a real problem. If you catch a problem early, chances are it'll be that much easier to fix. As the adage says, an ounce of prevention is worth a pound of cure.

This isn't quite troubleshooting—we'll devote an entire chapter to troubleshooting (Chapter 13)—but you can think of it as "pre-troubleshooting." Troubleshooting (the pound of cure) is what you have to do if you ignore maintenance, after your problem has developed complications, when you need to identify the problem by its symptoms.

The next two sections deal with preventive maintenance: looking periodically at the Event Log and the name server statistics to see whether any problems are developing. Consider this a name server's medical checkup.

Common Event Log Messages

The Microsoft DNS Server logs events to the System Log. To view the events, use the Event Viewer, which you start with **Start → Programs → Administrative Tools → Event Viewer**. The DNS server logs to a special category called, appropriately enough, DNS Server. Make sure you're looking at the correct log messages by selecting **DNS Server** in the left pane. To save space, when we describe an event we won't show a screen shot of the complete event. Instead, we'll list just the description from the event detail. (Double-click an event to see its details.) We'll also list the Event ID in parentheses after the text of the event.

When the server starts up (either at boot time or because you restarted it) and is ready to answer queries, you'll see this event:

```
The DNS Server has started.  (ID 2)
```

For a healthy server, you should see this event after booting. If you stop the server manually, you'll see this event:

```
The DNS Server has shutdown.  (ID 3)
```

If a server is a slave for a zone, it will notify you every time it performs a zone transfer:

```
A more recent version, version 2000120500 of zone movie.edu was found at DNS server
at 192.249.249.3. Zone transfer is in progress.  (ID 6522)

The DNS server wrote version 2000120500 of zone movie.edu to file movie.edu.dns.
(ID 3150)
```

You'll also see that last message on the primary master when you make a change to a zone through the DNS console and select **Action → Update Server Data Files**. After the server writes the updated file to disk, it logs that event.

If the primary master is not authoritative for the zone—another error condition— you'll see this on the slave:

```
Zone transfer request for secondary zone movie.edu refused by master server at 192.
249.249.3. Check the zone at the master server 192.249.249.3 to verify that zone
transfer is enabled to this server. To do so, use the DNS console, and select master
server 192.249.249.3 as the applicable server, then in secondary zone movie.edu
Properties, view the settings on the Zone Transfers tab. Based on the settings you
choose, make any configuration adjustments there (or possibly in the Name Servers
tab) so that a zone transfer can be made to this server. (ID 6525)
```

Unfortunately, if the name server simply can't reach the primary master (e.g., if it has gone down), the DNS server never logs an error.

On the other hand, a server that's a primary master for a zone will notify you when a slave does a zone transfer:

```
The DNS server successfully completed transfer of zone movie.edu to DNS server at
192.249.249.1. (ID 6001)
```

If you're missing the cache file, *cache.dns*, or a zone data file, the server will log a flurry of messages. A missing or empty cache file produces these events:

```
The DNS server could not open the file dns\cache.dns. Check that the file exists in
the %SystemRoot%\System32\Dns directory and that it contains valid data. The event
data is the error code. (ID 1000)
```

```
The DNS server could not find or open zone file dns\cache.dns. in the %SystemRoot%\
System32\Dns directory.  Verify that the zone file is located in this directory and
that it contains valid data.  (ID 1004)
```

```
The DNS server is not root authoritative and no root hints were specified in the
cache.dns file.
Where the server is not a root server, this file must specify root hints in the form
of at least one name server (NS) resource record, indicating a root DNS server and a
corresponding host (A) resource record for that root DNS server.  Otherwise, the DNS
server will be unable to contact the root DNS server on startup and will be unable to
answer queries for names outside of its own authoritative zones.  To correct this
problem, use the DNS console to update the server root hints.  For more information,
see the online Help.  (ID 707)
```

```
The DNS server does not have a cache or other database entry for root name servers.
Either the root hints file, cache.dns, or Active Directory must have at least one
name server (NS) resource record, indicating a root DNS server and a corresponding
host (A) resource record for that root DNS server.  Otherwise, the DNS server will be
unable to contact the root DNS server on startup and will be unable to answer queries
for names outside of its own authoritative zones.  To correct this problem, use the
DNS console to update the server root hints.  For more information, see the online
Help.  (ID 706)
```

The somewhat cryptic message "The event data is the error code" makes more sense when viewing the message in Event Viewer. This message means there's a specific error code listed in the **Data** field at the bottom of the **Event Properties** window for this event.

A missing zone data file, say *movie.edu.dns*, generates these events:

```
The DNS server could not open the file dns\movie.edu.dns.  Check that the file exists
in the %SystemRoot%\System32\Dns directory and that it contains valid data. The event
data is the error code.  (ID 1000)

The DNS server could not find or open zone file dns\movie.edu.dns.  in the
%SystemRoot%\System32\Dns directory.  Verify that the zone file is located in this
directory and that it contains valid data.  (ID 1004)
```

The server also logs a syntax error in a zone data file. If you always make changes to your zones using the DNS console, you shouldn't see syntax errors. Editing by hand can get you into trouble, though. Here's what happens when the server encounters a syntax error:

```
The DNS server unexpected end of line, in zone file movie.edu.dns at line 5.  To
correct the problem, fix this line in the zone file, which is located in the
%SystemRoot%\System32\Dns directory.  (ID 1505)

The DNS server is ignoring an invalid resource record in zone file movie.edu.dns at
line 5.
See the previously logged event for a description of the error.
Although the DNS server continues to load, ignoring this RR, it is recommended that
you investigate the error associated with this record and either correct it or remove
it from the zone file.  (ID 1508)
```

If you put an invalid IP address (such as an IP address not corresponding to a network interface on the server) in the **DNS Server IP Addresses** field of the **Server Properties Interfaces** window, you'll see this:

```
The DNS server list of restricted interfaces contains IP addresses that are not
configured for use at the server computer.
Use the DNS manager server properties, interfaces dialog, to verify and reset the IP
addresses the DNS server should listen on.  For more information, see "To restrict a
DNS server to listen only on selected addresses" in the online Help.  (ID 409)
```

Note that the server will *not* receive queries sent to the wildcard address 0.0.0.0.

For a list of most of the events logged by a Microsoft DNS Server, see article Q259302 in the Microsoft Knowledge Base: *http://support.microsoft.com/support/kb/articles/Q259/3/02.ASP*.

Understanding Name Server Statistics

You should periodically look over the statistics on some of your name servers. Name server statistics are viewed with the System Monitor. To start it, select **Start** → **Administrative Tools** → **Performance**. Make sure **System Monitor** is selected in the left pane, right-click in the right pane, and select **Add Counters...**. Select **DNS** in the **Performance object** pull-down list. You'll see a list of all the server parameters that you can monitor in real time. A brief explanation of each parameter is available in the Windows 2000 online help system document entitled "Monitoring server performance." To view this document, choose **Start** → **Help**, select the **Index** tab, and type *Performance, DNS servers*.

Selecting all parameters is not useful—it produces too much information. To get an idea of the amount of memory being used by the server, choose **Caching Memory** and **Database Node Memory**. To see how busy the server is—that is, how many queries it is handling—look at **Total Query Received/sec** and **Total Response Sent/sec**. To select several parameters, hold down the **Ctrl** key while single-clicking. When you've selected all the ones you want, choose **Add**, then **Close**. Note that you have to save this list if you want to avoid selecting the list of parameters again. Select **Console** → **Save As...** to produce a *.msc* file that you can use for subsequent monitoring sessions.

Growing Your Domain

> *"What size do you want to be?" it asked.*
> *"Oh, I'm not particular as to size,"*
> *Alice hastily replied; "only one doesn't like*
> *changing so often, you know…."*
> *"Are you content now?" said the Caterpillar.*
> *"Well, I should like to be a little larger, sir,*
> *if you wouldn't mind…."*

How Many Name Servers?

We set up two name servers in Chapter 4. Two servers are as few as you'll ever want to run and, depending on the size of your network, you may need to run many more. It is not uncommon to run from five to seven servers, with one of them off-site. How many name servers are enough? You'll have to decide that based on your network. Here are some guidelines to help out:

- Run at least one name server on each network or subnet you have. This removes routers as a point of failure. Make the most of any multihomed hosts you may have since they are (by definition) attached to more than one network.

- If you have a file server and some diskless nodes, run a name server on the file server to serve this group of machines.

- Run name servers near, but not necessarily on, large multiuser computers. The users and their processes probably generate a lot of queries and, as administrators, you will work harder to keep a multiuser host up. But balance their needs against the risk of running a name server—a security-critical server—on a system to which lots of people have access.

- Run one name server off-site. This makes your data available when your network isn't. You might argue that it's useless to look up an address when you can't reach the host. Then again, the off-site name server may be available if your network is reachable but your other name servers are down. If you have a close relationship with an organization on the Internet—say another university or a business partner—they may be willing to run a slave for you.

Figure 8-1 shows a sample topology and a brief analysis to show you how this might work.

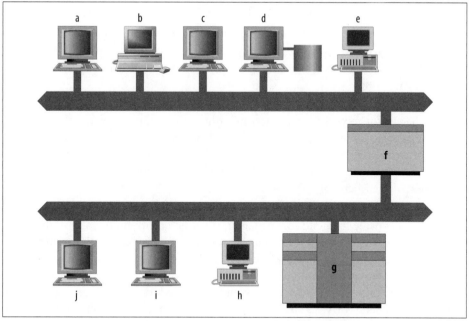

Figure 8-1. Sample network topology

Notice that if you follow our guidelines, there are still a number of places you could choose to run a name server. Host *d*, the file server for hosts *a*, *b*, *c*, and *e*, could run a name server. Host *g*, a big, multiuser host, is another good candidate. But probably the best choice is host *f*, the smaller host with interfaces on both networks. You'll need to run only one name server, instead of two, and it will run on a closely watched host. If you want more than one name server on either network, you can also run one on *d* or *g*.

Where Do I Put My Name Servers?

In addition to giving you a rough idea of how many name servers you'll need, these criteria should help you decide *where* to run name servers (e.g., on file servers and multihomed hosts). But there are other important considerations when choosing the right host.

Other factors to keep in mind are the host's connectivity, the software it runs (for example, the Microsoft DNS Server or BIND), the security of your host, and maintaining the homogeneity of your name servers:

Connectivity

It's important that name servers be well connected. Running a name server on the fastest, most reliable host on your network won't do you any good if the host is mired in some backwater subnet of your network behind a slow, flaky serial line. Try to find a host close to your link to the Internet (if you have one), or find a well-connected Internet host to act as a slave for your zone. On your own network, try to run name servers near the hubs.

It's doubly important that your primary master name server be well connected. The primary needs good connectivity to all the slaves that update from it, for reliable zone transfers. And, like any name server, it will benefit from fast, reliable networking.

Software

Another factor to consider in choosing a host for a name server is the software the host runs. If you bought this book, we'll assume it's because you want to run the Microsoft DNS Server. Keep in mind that you'll be able to manage remote name servers with the DNS console only if they're running the Windows 2000 version of the Microsoft DNS Server.

If managing servers with the DNS console isn't important to you (maybe you like the DNS console frontend for managing zone data, but you're comfortable editing BIND configuration files by hand), you might consider running some BIND name servers on your network. Newer BIND name servers are fast and robust and can interoperate with Microsoft's DNS Server. If you do decide to implement some BIND name servers, it would be a good idea to run the most recent version of BIND, BIND 9. BIND 9 servers can use a more efficient zone transfer protocol with Microsoft DNS Servers. (See Chapter 10 and Chapter 13 for more information on interoperability between the Microsoft DNS Server and BIND.)

Security

Since you would undoubtedly prefer that hackers not commandeer your name server to assist them in attacking your own hosts or other networks across the Internet, it's important to run your name server on a secure host. Don't run a name server on a big, multiuser system if you can't trust its users. Computers that are dedicated to hosting network services but don't permit general logins are good candidates for running name servers. If you have only one or a few really secure hosts, consider running the primary master name server on one of those, since its compromise would be more significant than the compromise of the slaves.

Homogeneity

One last thing to take into account is the homogeneity of your name servers. Hopping between Windows 2000 and different versions of Unix can be frustrating and confusing. Avoid running name servers on lots of different platforms, if you can. You can waste a lot of time porting your scripts (or ours!) from one operating system to another or looking for the location of *nslookup* on three different operating systems.

Though these are really secondary considerations—it's more important to have a name server on a given subnet than to have it running on the perfect host—do keep these criteria in mind when deciding where to run your name servers.

Capacity Planning

If you have heavily populated networks or users who do a lot of name server–intensive work, you may find you need more name servers than we've recommended to handle the load. Likewise, our recommendations may be fine for a little while, but as people add hosts to your networks or install new name server–intensive programs, you may find your name servers bogged down by queries.

Just which tasks are "name server–intensive"? Surfing the Web can be, as can sending electronic mail, especially to large mailing lists. Programs that make lots of remote procedure calls to different hosts can also be name server–intensive. Even running certain graphical user environments can tax your name server. The astute (and precocious) among you may be asking, "But how do I know when my name servers are overloaded? What do I look for?" An excellent question!

Memory utilization is probably the most important aspect of a name server's operation to monitor. *dns.exe*, the name server process, can get very large on a name server that is authoritative for many zones. If *dns.exe*'s size, plus the size of the other processes you run, exceeds the size of your host's real memory, your host may swap furiously ("thrash") and not get anything done. Another criterion you can use to measure the load on your name server is the load the name server process places on the host's CPU. Correctly configured name servers don't use much CPU time, so high CPU usage is often symptomatic of a configuration error. Windows 2000's Performance tool can help you characterize your name server's average CPU utilization. To see the name server's CPU utilization, start the Performance tool (**Start Programs** → **Administrative Tools** → **Performance**) and select **System Monitor** in the left pane. Click on the **Add** icon (shaped like a plus sign) in the right pane. In the resulting window, choose **Process** under **Performance object**, then choose **% Processor Time** in the left list and **DNS** in the right list, as in Figure 8-2. Click on the **Add** button, then the **Close** button. A chart now shows the percentage of processor time the name server is using.

Unfortunately, there are no absolute rules when it comes to acceptable CPU utilization. We offer a rough rule of thumb, though: 5% average CPU utilization is probably acceptable; 10% is a bit high, unless the host is dedicated to providing name service.

Another statistic to look at is the number of queries the name server receives per minute (or second, if you have a busy name server). Again, there are no absolutes here: a multiprocessor server with oodles of RAM running Windows 2000 can handle thousands of queries per second without breaking into a sweat, while a less powerful PC might have problems with more than a few queries per second.

To check the volume of queries your name server is receiving, use the Performance tool again. This time, select **DNS** under **Performance object**. You'll see there are several counters to choose from: you can monitor many different aspects of the DNS server's behavior. To see how busy your server is, pay particular attention to these

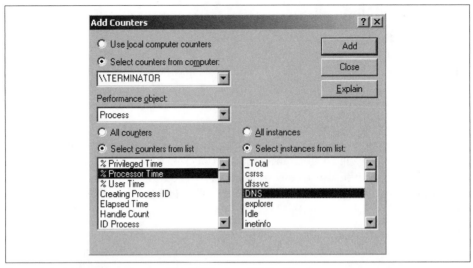

Figure 8-2. Adding counters to monitor DNS server CPU utilization

counters: **Total Query Received**, **Total Query Received/sec**, **Total Response Sent**, and **Total Response Sent/sec**. More information about using the Performance tool to monitor DNS server performance can be found in the section "Understanding Name Server Statistics" in Chapter 7.

You should pay special attention to peak periods. For example, Monday morning is often busy because many people like to respond to mail they've received over the weekend first thing on Mondays.

You might also want to take a sample starting just after lunch, when people are returning to their desks and getting back to work—all at about the same time. Of course, if your organization is spread across several time zones, you'll have to use your judgment to determine a busy time.

Even if your host is fast enough to handle the volume of queries it receives, you should make sure the DNS traffic isn't placing undue load on your network. On most LANs, DNS traffic will be too small a proportion of the network's bandwidth to worry about. Over slow leased lines or dial-up connections, though, DNS traffic could consume enough bandwidth to merit concern.

To get a rough estimate of the volume of DNS traffic on your LAN, multiply the number of queries received plus the number of answers sent in an hour by 800 bits (100 bytes, a rough average size for a DNS message), and divide by 3,600 (seconds per hour) to find the bandwidth utilized. This should give you a feeling for how much of your network's bandwidth is being consumed by DNS traffic.

To give you an idea of what's normal, the last NSFNET traffic report (in April 1995) showed that DNS traffic constituted just over 5% of the total traffic volume (in bytes) on their backbone. The NSFNET's figures were based upon actual traffic sampling, not calculations like ours using the name server's statistics.* If you want to get a more accurate idea of the traffic your name server is receiving, you can always do your own traffic sampling with a LAN protocol analyzer.

If you find that your name servers are overworked, what then? First, it's a good idea to make sure that your name servers aren't being bombarded with queries by a misbehaving program. To do that, you'll need to find out the sources of all the queries.

Fortunately, Microsoft added some slick logging capabilities to the Windows 2000 DNS Server (the Windows NT DNS Server was woefully lacking in this area). Logging is configured through the **Logging** tab of the server properties window (right-click on a server in the DNS console and choose **Properties**, then click on the **Logging** tab). You'll want to enable the **Query** category, which logs a record of every query to the file *%SystemRoot%\system32\dns\dns.log*. A sample logging properties window is shown in Figure 8-3.

Figure 8-3. The Logging tab of the properties window

---

* We're not sure how representative of the current state of the Internet these numbers are, because it's extremely difficult to wheedle equivalent numbers out of the commercial backbone providers that succeeded the NSFNET.

When poring over the example, look for hosts sending repeated queries, especially for the same or similar information. That may indicate a misconfigured or buggy program running on the host or a foreign name server pelting your name server with queries.

If all the queries appear to be legitimate, add a new name server. Don't put the name server just anywhere, though; use the logging information to help you decide where it's best to run one. If DNS traffic is gobbling up your LAN, it won't help to choose a host at random and create a name server there. You need to consider which hosts are sending most of the queries, then figure out how to best provide them name service. Here are some hints to help you decide:

- Look for queries from resolvers on hosts that share the same file server. You could run a name server on that file server.

- Look for queries from resolvers on large, multiuser hosts. You could run a name server there.

- Look for queries from resolvers on another subnet. Those resolvers should be configured to query a name server on their local subnet. If there isn't one on that subnet, create one.

- Look for queries from resolvers on the same bridged segment (if you use bridging). If you run a name server on the bridged segment, the traffic won't need to be bridged to the rest of the network.

- Look for queries from hosts connected to each other via another, lightly loaded network. You could run a name server on the other network.

Adding More Name Servers

When you need to create new name servers for your domain, the simplest recourse is to add slaves. You already know how—we went over it in Chapter 4—and once you've set up one slave, cloning it is a piece of cake. But you can run into trouble if you add slaves indiscriminately.

If you run a large number of slave servers for a zone, the primary master name server can take quite a beating just keeping up with the slaves' polling to check that their zone data is current. There are a number of courses of action to take for this problem, as described in the sections that follow:

- Eliminate the slave name servers altogether by using Active Directory integration.
- Increase the refresh interval so that the slaves don't check so often.
- Direct some of the slave name servers to load from other slave name servers.
- Create caching-only name servers.
- Create partial-slave name servers.

Active Directory Integration

We discuss this new feature for Windows 2000 in Chapter 11. Briefly, this feature eliminates the load on the primary master from slaves' polling by eliminating the slaves! Remember that the main purpose of the primary master/slave relationship is zone data replication: the DNS designers created the zone transfer mechanism as a way to spread zone data among multiple authoritative name servers. Windows 2000 stores all kinds of information about the network in Active Directory and replicates this information, too. With Windows 2000, you have the option of storing the definitive version of your zones' data in Active Directory rather than in zone data files on the primary master. All authoritative name servers load the zone data stored in Active Directory, which also takes care of replicating changes to the data. See Chapter 11 for more details and instructions on setting up this new feature.

Slave Servers

You can have some of your slaves load zone data from other slave name servers instead of from a primary name server. The slave name server can't tell if it's loading from a primary or another slave. It's only important that the name server serving the zone transfer is authoritative for the zone. There's no trick to configuring this. Instead of specifying the IP address of the primary in the slave's configuration, you simply specify the IP address of another slave.

When you go to this second level of distribution, though, be aware that it can take up to twice as long for the data to percolate from the primary name server to all the slaves. Remember that the *refresh interval* is the period after which the slave servers check to make sure that their zone data is still current. Therefore, it can take the first-level slave servers the entire length of the refresh interval to get a new copy of the zone from the primary master server. Similarly, it can take the second-level slave servers the entire refresh interval to get a new copy of the zone from the first-level slave servers. The propagation time from the primary master server to all the slave servers can therefore be twice the refresh interval.

Fortunately, using the DNS NOTIFY feature, which we'll describe in Chapter 10, avoids this delay. This feature is on by default and will trigger zone transfers soon after the zone is updated on the primary master. Unfortunately, it doesn't work with any BIND Version 4 slaves (they'll receive the NOTIFY messages but will not understand them). Active Directory integration, described in Chapter 11, also avoids zone synchronization delays.

If you decide to configure your network with two (or more) tiers of slave servers, be careful to avoid updating loops. If we configured *wormhole* to update from *diehard* and then accidentally configured *diehard* to update from *wormhole*, neither would ever get data from the primary master. They would merely check their out-of-date serial numbers against each other and perpetually decide that they were both up-to-date.

Caching-Only Servers

Creating *caching-only name servers* is another alternative when you need more servers. Caching-only name servers are name servers not authoritative for any zones (except *0.0.127.in-addr.arpa*). The name doesn't imply that primary master and slave name servers don't cache—they do—but rather that the *only* function this server performs is looking up data and caching it. As with primary master and slave name servers, a caching-only name server needs a *cache.dns* file and the automatically created zones, *0.in-addr.arpa*, *127.in-addr.arpa*, and *255.in-addr.arpa*. The configuration of a caching-only server looks like Figure 8-4.

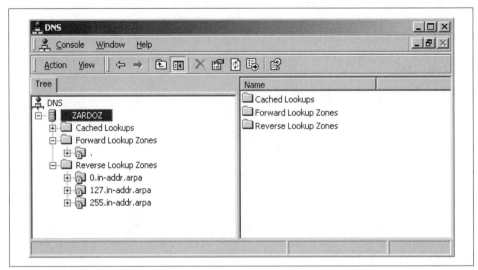

Figure 8-4. The DNS console showing a caching-only name server

A caching-only name server can look up domain names inside and outside your zone, as can primary master and slave name servers. The difference is that when a caching-only name server initially looks up a name within your zone, it ends up asking one of the primary master or slave name servers in your zone for the answer. A primary or slave would answer the same question out of its authoritative data. Which primary or slave does the caching-only server ask? As with name servers outside of your domain, it finds out which name servers serve your zone from one of the name servers for your parent zone. Is there any way to prime a caching-only name server's cache so it knows which hosts run primary and slave name servers for your zone? No, there isn't. You can't use *cache.dns*—the *cache.dns* file is only for root name server hints.

A caching-only name server's real value comes after it builds up its cache. Each time it queries an authoritative name server and receives an answer, it caches the records in the answer. Over time, the cache will grow to include the information most often requested by the resolvers querying the caching-only name server. And you avoid the overhead of zone transfers—a caching-only name server doesn't need to do them.

Partial-Slave Servers

In between a caching-only name server and a slave name server is another variation: a name server that is a slave for only a few of the local zones. We call this a *partial-slave name server* (although probably nobody else does). Suppose *movie.edu* had 20 /24-sized (the old Class C) networks (and a corresponding 20 *in-addr.arpa* zones). Instead of creating a slave server for all 21 zones (all the *in-addr.arpa* subdomains plus *movie.edu*), we could create a partial-slave server for *movie.edu* and only those *in-addr.arpa* zones the host itself is in. If the host had two network interfaces, its name server would be a slave for three zones: *movie.edu* and the two *in-addr.arpa* zones.

Let's say we scare up the hardware for another name server. We'll call the new host *zardoz.movie.edu*, with IP addresses 192.249.249.9 and 192.253.253.9. We'll create a partial-slave name server on *zardoz*, with the configuration shown in Figure 8-5.

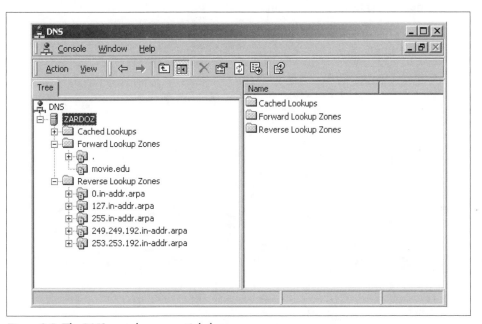

Figure 8-5. The DNS console on a partial-slave server

This server is a slave for *movie.edu* and only 2 of the 20 *in-addr.arpa* zones. A "full" slave would have 21 different zone statements in *named.conf*.

What's so useful about a partial-slave name server? They're not much work to administer because their configuration doesn't change much. On a server authoritative for all the *in-addr.arpa* zones, we'd need to add and delete *in-addr.arpa* zones as our network changed. That can be a surprising amount of work on a large network.

A partial slave can still answer most of the queries it receives, though. Most of these queries will be for data in *movie.edu* and the two *in-addr.arpa* zones. Why? Because most of the hosts querying the name server are on the two networks to which it's connected, 192.249.249/24 and 192.253.253/24. And those hosts probably communicate primarily with other hosts on their own network. This generates queries for data within the *in-addr.arpa* zone that corresponds to the local network.

Registering Name Servers

When you get around to setting up more and more name servers, a question may strike you—do I need to register *all* of my primary and slave name servers with my parent zone? The answer is no. Only those servers you want to make available to name servers outside of your zone need to be registered with your parent. For example, if you run nine name servers for your zone, you may choose to tell the parent zone about only four of them. Within your network, you use all nine servers. Five of those nine servers, however, are queried only by resolvers on hosts that are configured to query them. Their parent name servers don't delegate to them, so they'll never be queried by remote name servers. Only the four servers registered with your parent zone are queried by other name servers, including caching-only and partial-slave name servers on your network. This setup is shown in Figure 8-6.

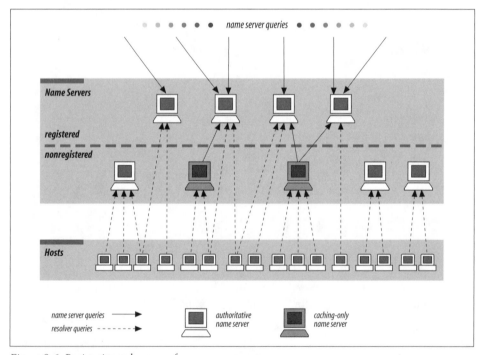

Figure 8-6. Registering only some of your name servers

Besides being able to pick and choose which of your name servers are hammered by outside queries, there's a technical motivation for registering only some of your zone's name servers: there is a limit to how many servers will fit in a UDP response packet. In practice, around 10 name server records should fit. Depending on the data (how many servers are in the same domain), you can get more or fewer.* There's not much point in registering more than 10 servers, anyway—if none of those 10 servers can be reached, it's unlikely the destination host can be reached.

If you've set up a new authoritative name server and you decide it should be registered, make a list of the parents of the zones for which it's authoritative. You'll need to contact the administrators for each of these parent zones. For example, let's say we want to register the name server we just set up on *zardoz*. To get this slave registered in all the right zones, we'll need to contact the administrators of *edu* and *in-addr.arpa*. (For help determining who runs your parent zones, turn back to Chapter 3.)

When you contact the administrators of a parent zone, be sure to follow the process they specify (if any) on their web site. If there's no standard modification process, you'll have to send them the domain name of the zone (or zones) for which the new name server is authoritative. If the new name server is in the new zone, you'll also need to give them the IP address(es) of the new name server. In fact, if there's no official format for submitting the information, it's often best just to send your parent the complete list of registered name servers for the zone, plus any addresses necessary, in zone data file format. That avoids any potential confusion.

Since our networks were originally assigned by the InterNIC, we used the web-based process at *http://www.arin.net/cgi-bin/amt.pl* to change our registration. (If we'd preferred to do things manually, we could have sent them the form at *http://www.arin.net/regserv/templates/modifytemplate.txt*.) If they hadn't had a template for us to use, our message to the administrator of *in-addr.arpa* might have read something like this:

```
Howdy!

I've just set up a new slave name server on zardoz.movie.edu for the
249.249.192.in-addr.arpa and 253.253.192.in-addr.arpa zones. Would you
please add NS records for this name server to the in-addr.arpa zone?
That would make our delegation information look like:

253.253.192.in-addr.arpa. 86400 IN NS terminator.movie.edu.
253.253.192.in-addr.arpa. 86400 IN NS wormhole.movie.edu.
253.253.192.in-addr.arpa. 86400 IN NS zardoz.movie.edu.

249.249.192.in-addr.arpa. 86400 IN NS terminator.movie.edu.
249.249.192.in-addr.arpa. 86400 IN NS wormhole.movie.edu.
```

---

* The domain names of the Internet's root name servers were changed because of this. All the roots were moved into the same domain, *root-servers.net*, to take the most advantage of domain-name compression and to allow information about as many roots as possible to be stored in a single UDP packet.

```
249.249.192.in-addr.arpa. 86400 IN NS zardoz.movie.edu.
```

Thanks!

Albert LeDomaine
al@robocop.movie.edu

Notice that we specified explicit TTLs on the NS and A records. That's because our parent name servers aren't authoritative for those records; *our* name servers are. By including them, we're indicating our choice of a TTL for our zone's delegation. Of course, our parent may have other ideas about what the TTL should be.

In this case, glue data—A records for each of the name servers—isn't necessary, since the domain names of the name servers aren't within the *in-addr.arpa* zones. They're within *movie.edu*, so a name server that was referred to *terminator.movie.edu* or *wormhole.movie.edu* could still find their addresses by following delegation to the *movie.edu* name servers.

Is a partial-slave name server a good name server to register with your parent zone? Actually, it's not ideal because it's authoritative for only *some* of your *in-addr.arpa* zones. Administratively, it may be easier to register only servers backing up *all* the local zones; that way, you don't need to keep track of which name servers are authoritative for which zones. All of your parent zones can delegate to the same set of name servers: your primary master and your "full" slaves.

If you don't have many name servers, though, or if you're good at remembering which name servers are authoritative for which zones, go ahead and register a partial-slave.

Caching-only name servers, on the other hand, must *never* be registered. A caching-only name server rarely has complete information for any given zone; it just has the bits and pieces of the zone that it has looked up recently. If a parent name server were to mistakenly refer a foreign name server to a caching-only name server, the foreign name server would send the caching-only name server a nonrecursive query. The caching-only name server might have the data cached, but then again, it might not. If it didn't have the data, it would refer the querier to the best name servers it knew (those closest to the domain name in the query)—which might include the caching-only name server itself! The poor foreign name server might never get an answer. This kind of misconfiguration—actually, delegating a zone to any name server not authoritative for that zone—is known as *lame delegation*.

Changing TTLs

An experienced domain administrator needs to know how to set the time to live on his zone's data to his best advantage. The TTL on a resource record, remember, is the time for which any server can cache that record. So if the TTL for a particular resource record is 3,600 seconds and a server outside your network caches that record, it will have to remove the entry from its cache after an hour. If it needs the same data after the hour is up, it'll have to query your name servers again.

When we introduced TTLs, we emphasized that your choice of a TTL would dictate how current you would keep copies of your data, at the cost of increased load on your name servers. A low TTL would mean that name servers outside your network would have to get data from your name servers often and that the data would therefore be kept current. On the other hand, your name servers would be peppered by the name servers' queries.

You don't *have* to choose a TTL once and for all, though. You can—and experienced administrators do—change TTLs periodically to suit your needs.

Suppose we know that one of our hosts is about to be moved to another network. This host houses the *movie.edu* film library, a large collection of files our site makes available to hosts on the Internet. During normal operation, outside name servers cache the address of our host according to the minimum (default) TTL in the SOA record. (We set the *movie.edu* TTL to be one day in our sample files.) A name server caching the old address record just before the change could have the wrong address for as long as a day. A loss of connectivity for a full day is unacceptable, though. What can we do to minimize the loss of connectivity? We can lower the TTL so that outside servers cache the address record for a shorter period. By reducing the TTL, we force the outside servers to update their data more frequently, which means that any changes we make when we actually move the system will be propagated to the outside world quickly. How short can we make the TTL? Unfortunately, we can't safely use a TTL of zero, which should mean "don't cache this record at all." Some older BIND Version 4 name servers can't cope with a zero TTL. Small TTLs, like 30 seconds, are okay, though. The easiest change is to lower the TTL in the *movie.edu* SOA record. If you don't place an explicit TTL on resource records, the name server applies this minimum (default) TTL from the SOA record to each resource record. If you lower the minimum (default) TTL field, though, the new, lower TTL applies to all zone data, not just the address of the host being moved. The drawback to this approach is that your name server will be answering a lot more queries since the querying servers will cache *all* the data in your zone for a shorter period. A better alternative is to put a different TTL only on the affected address record.

To add an explicit TTL on an individual resource record, you'll need to be in the DNS console's "advanced" view so that you can actually see individual records' TTLs: choose **View → Advanced**.

Click on the domain name of the zone in the left panel, then double-click the record when it appears in the right panel. The **Properties** window is displayed, and you can type the TTL. Recall that the subfields in the TTL field are (from left to right) days, hours, minutes, and seconds.

Figure 8-7 provides an example of an explicit TTL from *movie.edu*.

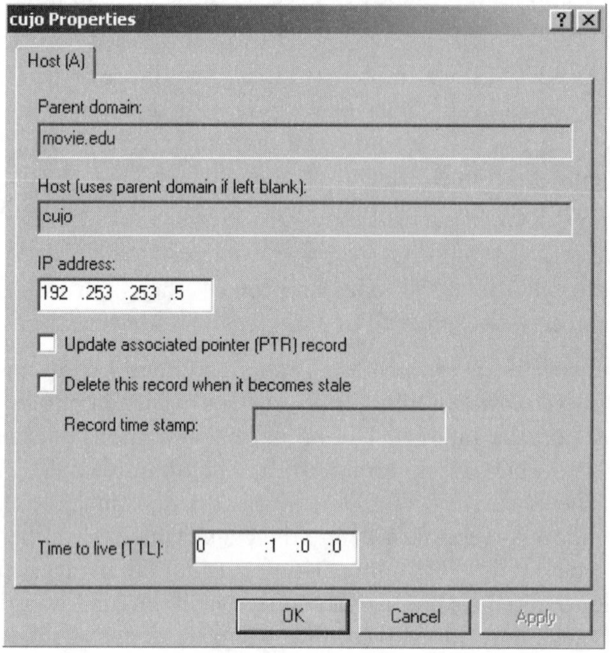

Figure 8-7. An explicit TTL on cujo.movie.edu

The record the DNS console adds to the *movie.edu* zone data file looks like this:

```
cujo 3600 IN A 192.253.253.5
```

Note the explicit TTL of 3,600 seconds (one hour) in the TTL field, overriding the TTL in the zone's SOA record.

You may have seen the last field of the SOA record called simply the "minimum" field (some versions of *nslookup* display it that way, for example). So why does it show up in the DNS console as "Minimum (default)"? (To see what we mean, take a look at the SOA record shown back in Chapter 4, in Figure 4-14.) If the Microsoft DNS Server followed the DNS RFCs, the TTL field in the SOA record would really define the minimum TTL value for all resource records in the zone. Thus, you could only specify explicit TTLs larger than this minimum. Neither Microsoft nor BIND name servers work this way, though. In other words, in real life, "minimum" is not really minimum. Instead, the name server implements the minimum TTL field in the SOA record as a "default" TTL—hence the "Minimum (default)" wording. If there is no TTL on a record, the minimum applies. If there is a TTL on the resource record, the name server allows it even if it is smaller than the minimum. That one record is sent out in responses with the smaller TTL, while all other records are sent out with the "Minimum (default)" TTL from the SOA record.

You should also know that when giving out answers, a slave supplies the same TTL a primary master does—that is, if a primary gives out a TTL of one hour for a particular record, a slave will, too. The slave doesn't decrement the TTL according to how long it has been since it loaded the zone. So, if the TTL of a single resource record is set smaller than the SOA minimum, both the primary and slave name servers give out the resource record with the same, smaller TTL. If the slave name server has reached the expiration time for the zone, it expires the whole zone. It will never expire an individual resource record within a zone.

So the Microsoft DNS Server does allow you to put a small TTL on an individual resource record if you know that the data is going to change shortly. Thus, any server caching that data caches it only for a brief time. Unfortunately, while the name server makes tagging records with a small TTL possible, most administrators don't take the time to do it. When a host changes addresses, you often lose connectivity to it for a while.

More often than not, the host having its address changed is not one of the main hubs on the site, so the outage impacts few people. If one of the mail hubs or a major web server or *ftp* archive—like the film library—is moving, though, a day's loss of connectivity may be unacceptable. In cases like this, the administrator should plan ahead and reduce the TTL on the data to be changed.

Remember that the TTL on the affected data will need to be lowered *before* the change takes place. Reducing the TTL on a workstation's address record and changing the workstation's address simultaneously may do you little or no good; the address record may have been cached seconds before you made the change and may linger until the old TTL times out. You must also be sure to factor in the time it'll take your slaves to load from your primary master. For example, if your minimum TTL is 12 hours and your refresh interval is 3 hours, be sure to lower the TTLs at least 15 hours ahead of time, so that by the time you move the host, all the old, longer TTL records will have timed out. Of course, if all of your slaves are using NOTIFY, the slaves shouldn't take the full refresh interval to sync up.

Changing Other SOA Values

We briefly mentioned increasing the refresh interval as a way of offloading your primary name server. Let's discuss refresh in a little more detail and go over the remaining SOA values, too.

The *refresh* value, you'll remember, controls how often a slave checks whether its zone data is up-to-date. The *retry* value becomes the refresh time after the first failure to reach a master name server. The *expire* value determines how long zone data can be held before it's discarded when a master is unreachable. Finally, the *minimum TTL* sets how long zone information may be cached.

Suppose we've decided we want the slaves to pick up new information every hour instead of every three hours. We change the refresh value to one hour in each of the zones. Since retry is related to refresh, we should probably reduce retry, too—to every 15 minutes or so. Typically, retry is less than refresh, but that's not required.

Although lowering the refresh value will speed up the distribution of zone data, it will also increase the load on the server from which data is being loaded, since the slaves will check more often. The added load isn't much, though; each slave makes a single SOA query during each zone's refresh interval to check its master's copy of the zone. So with two slave name servers, changing the refresh time from three hours to one hour will generate only four more queries (per zone) to the primary master in any three-hour span.

If all of your slaves use NOTIFY, of course, refresh doesn't mean as much. But if you have even one BIND Version 4 slave, your zone data may take up to the full refresh interval to reach it.

Some older versions of BIND slaves stopped answering queries during a zone load. As a result, BIND was modified to spread out the zone loads, reducing the periods of unavailability. So, even if you set a low refresh interval, your slaves may not check exactly as often as you request. BIND Version 4 name servers attempt a certain number of zone loads and then wait 15 minutes before trying another batch. On the other hand, BIND Version 4.9 and later may also refresh *more often* than the refresh interval. These newer BINDs will wait a random number of seconds between one-half of the refresh interval and the full refresh interval to check serial numbers.

Expiration times on the order of a week—longer if you frequently have problems reaching your updating source—are common. The expiration time should always be much larger than the retry and refresh intervals; if the expire time is smaller than the refresh interval, your slaves will expire their data before trying to load new data. If your zone's data doesn't change much, you might consider raising the minimum (default) TTL. The SOA's minimum (default) TTL value is typically one day (86,400 seconds), but you can make it longer. One week is about the longest value that makes sense for a TTL. If it's longer than that, you may find yourself unable to change bad, cached data in a reasonable amount of time.

Planning for Disasters

It's a fact of life on a network that things go wrong. Hardware fails, software has bugs, and people occasionally make mistakes. Sometimes this results in minor inconveniences, like having a few users lose connections. Sometimes the results are catastrophic and involve the loss of important data and valuable jobs.

Because the Domain Name System relies so heavily on the network, it is vulnerable to network outages. Thankfully, the design of DNS takes into account the imperfection of networks: it allows for multiple, redundant name servers, retransmission of queries, retrying zone transfers, and so on.

DNS doesn't protect itself from every conceivable calamity, though. There are types of network failures—some of them quite common—that DNS doesn't or can't protect against. But with a small investment of time and money, you can minimize the threat of these problems.

Outages

Power outages, for example, are relatively common in many parts of the world. In some parts of the U.S., thunderstorms or tornadoes may cause a site to lose power, or to have only intermittent power, for an extended period. Elsewhere, typhoons, volcanoes, or construction work may interrupt your electrical service. And at the time of this writing, those of you in California might lose power in a rolling blackout from lack of electrical capacity.

If all your hosts are down, of course, you don't need name service. Quite often, however, sites have problems when power is *restored*. Following our recommendations, they run their name servers on file servers and big, multiuser machines. And when the power comes up, those machines are naturally the last to boot—because all those disks need to be checked and fixed first! Which means that all the on-site hosts that are quick to boot do so without the benefit of name service.

This can cause all sorts of wonderful problems, depending on what services your hosts access when they boot. For example, your PCs may mount your servers' drives (via *net use*) when they boot. If they do, they almost certainly specify the servers' domain names or NetBIOS names.

Using hostnames in commands is admirable because it allows administrators to change the servers' IP addresses without changing all the startup files on-site. However, if name service isn't available when your PCs boot, the *net use* command will fail, which may cause successive commands to fail, too. This will certainly not help your users' productivity.

Recommendations

Our recommendation is to add the names and IP addresses of critical hosts to your PCs' *HOSTS* files. Any host whose name is referenced during the boot process should appear in this file. You can synchronize the file by copying it from share to share. On Windows 2000, the default location for the file is *%ServerRoot%\System32\Drivers\Etc*, often *C:\WinNT\System32\Drivers\Etc*. The format of the file is just like the format of the Unix */etc/hosts* file: each line consists of an IP address (in dotted-octet notation), which starts in the first column, followed by whitespace and the canonical name of the host. Optionally, one or more aliases may follow the canonical name. For example:

```
192.249.249.1 wormhole.movie.edu wormhole
192.249.249.3 terminator.movie.edu terminator
```

Now, if your PC needs to look up *wormhole* or *wormhole.movie.edu* when it boots, it will be able to resolve the name.

However, there's some danger in using *HOSTS* files: unless you take care to keep the files up-to-date, the information in them may become stale. And since the Windows 2000 resolver uses *HOSTS* before querying a name server, a stale entry can cause resolution failures that are hard to diagnose.

The best solution to this problem is to run a name server on a host with uninterruptible power. If you rarely experience extended power loss, battery backup might be enough. If your outages are longer and name service is critical to you, you should consider an uninterruptible power system (UPS) with a generator of some kind.

If you can't afford luxuries like these, you might just try to track down the fastest-booting host around and run a name server on it. Hosts with small filesystems should boot quickly, since they don't have many disks to check.

Once you've located the right host, you'll need to make sure the host's IP address appears in the resolver configurations of all of your hosts that need full-time name service. You'll probably want to list the backed-up host last since, during normal operation, hosts should use the name server closest to them. Then, after a power failure, your critical applications will still have name service, albeit at a small sacrifice in performance.

Coping with Disaster

When disaster strikes, it really helps to know what to do. Knowing to duck under a sturdy table or desk during an earthquake can save you from being pinned under a toppling monitor. Knowing how to turn off your gas can save your house from conflagration.

Likewise, knowing what to do in a network disaster (or even just a minor mishap) can help you keep your network running.

Long Outages (Days)

If you lose network connectivity for a long time, your name servers may have problems. If they lose connectivity to the root name servers for an extended period, they'll stop resolving queries outside their authoritative zone data. If the slaves can't reach their master, sooner or later they'll expire the zone.

In case your name service really goes haywire because of the connectivity loss, it's a good idea to keep a sitewide or workgroup *HOSTS* file around, as we recommended earlier in this chapter. If your name servers all go down, your hosts will still be able to resolve the names of hosts in the *HOSTS* file.

As for slaves, you can reconfigure a slave that can't reach its master to run temporarily as a primary master. Just right-click on the zone's domain name in the DNS console, select **Properties**, make sure the **General** tab is selected, and click on

Change... to change the zone type from secondary to primary. If more than one slave for the same zone is cut off, you can configure one as a primary master temporarily and reconfigure the other to load from the temporary primary.

Really Long Outages (Weeks)

If an extended outage cuts you off from the Internet—say for a week or more—you may need to restore connectivity to root name servers artificially to get things working again. Every name server needs to talk to a root name server occasionally. It's a bit like therapy: the name server needs to contact the root to regain its perspective on the world.

To provide root name service during a long outage, you can set up your own root name servers, *but only temporarily*. Once you're reconnected to the Internet, you *must* shut off your temporary root servers. The most obnoxious vermin on the Internet are name servers that believe they're root name servers but don't know anything about most top-level domains. A close second is the Internet name server configured to query—and report—a false set of root name servers.

That said, and our alibis in place, here's what you have to do to configure your own root name server. First, you need to create the root zone. The root zone will delegate to the highest-level zones in your isolated network. For example, if *movie.edu* were to be isolated from the Internet, we might create a root zone data file, *root.dns*, for *terminator*:

```
. IN SOA terminator.movie.edu. al.robocop.movie.edu. (
                1       ; Serial
                10800   ; Refresh after 3 hours
                3600    ; Retry after 1 hour
                604800  ; Expire after 1 week
                86400 ) ; Minimum TTL of 1 day

; Refresh, retry, and expire really don't matter since all
; roots are primaries.  Minimum TTL could be longer, since
; the data is likely to be stable.

  IN NS terminator.movie.edu. ; terminator is the temp. root

; Our root only knows about movie.edu and our two
; in-addr.arpa domains

movie.edu. IN NS terminator.movie.edu.
        IN NS wormhole.movie.edu.

249.249.192.in-addr.arpa. IN NS terminator.movie.edu.
                          IN NS wormhole.movie.edu.

253.253.192.in-addr.arpa. IN NS terminator.movie.edu.
                          IN NS wormhole.movie.edu.
```

```
terminator.movie.edu.  IN A 192.249.249.3
wormhole.movie.edu.    IN A 192.249.249.1
                       IN A 192.253.253.1
```

Then we need to add the zone with the DNS console and update all of our name servers (except the new, temporary root) with a *cache.dns* file that includes just the temporary root name server (it's best to move the old cache file aside—we'll need it later, once connectivity is restored).

Here are the contents of the *db.cache* file:

```
.  99999999  IN  NS  terminator.movie.edu.

terminator.movie.edu.  IN  A  192.249.249.3
```

This process will keep *movie.edu* name resolution going during the outage. Then, once Internet connectivity is restored, we can delete the root zone on *terminator* and restore the original cache files on all our other name servers.

## CHAPTER 9

Parenting

The way Dinah washed her children's faces was this: first she held the poor thing down by its ear with one paw, and then with the other paw she rubbed its face all over, the wrong way, beginning at the nose: and just now, as I said, she was hard at work on the white kitten, which was lying quite still and trying to purr— no doubt feeling that it was all meant for its good.

Once your domain reaches a certain size, or you decide you need to distribute the management of parts of your domain to various entities within your organization, you'll want to divide the domain into subdomains. These subdomains will be the children of your current domain on the domain tree; your domain will be the parent. If you delegate responsibility for your subdomains to another organization, each becomes its own zone, separate from its parent zone. We like to call the management of your subdomains—your children—*parenting*.

Good parenting starts with carving up your domain sensibly, choosing appropriate names for your subdomains, and then delegating the subdomains to create new zones. A responsible parent also works hard at maintaining the relationship between the name servers authoritative for her zone and its children; she ensures that delegation from parent to child is current and correct.

Good parenting is vital to the success of your network, especially as name service becomes critical to navigating between sites. Incorrect delegation to a child zone's name servers can render a site effectively unreachable, while the loss of connectivity to the parent zone's name servers can leave a site unable to reach any hosts outside the local zone.

In this chapter we present our views on when to create subdomains, and we go over how to create and delegate them in some detail. We also discuss management of the parent-child relationship and, finally, how to manage the process of carving up a large domain into smaller subdomains with minimal disruption and inconvenience.

When to Become a Parent

Far be it from us to *tell* you when you should become a parent, but we will be so bold as to offer you some guidelines. You may find some compelling reason to implement subdomains that isn't on our list, but here are some of the most common reasons:

- A need to delegate or distribute management of the domain to a number of organizations
- The large size of your domain—dividing it would make it easier to manage and offload the name servers for the domain
- A need to distinguish hosts' organizational affiliations by including them in particular subdomains

Once you've decided to have children, the next question to ask yourself is, naturally, how many children to have.

How Many Children?

Of course, you won't simply say, "I want to create four subdomains." Deciding how many subdomains to implement is really choosing the organizational affiliations of those subdomains. For example, if your company has four branch offices, you might decide to create four subdomains, each of which corresponds to a branch office.

Should you create subdomains for each site, for each division, or even for each department? You have a lot of latitude in your choice because of DNS's scalability. You can create a few large subdomains or many small subdomains. There are trade-offs whichever you choose, though.

Delegating to a few large subdomains isn't much work for the parent, because there's not much delegation to keep track of. However, you wind up with larger subdomains, which require more memory to load and faster name servers, and administration isn't as distributed. If you implement site-level subdomains, for example, you may force autonomous or unrelated groups at a site to share a single namespace and a single point of administration.

Delegating to many smaller subdomains can be a headache for the parent's administrator. Keeping delegation data current involves keeping track of which hosts run name servers and which zones they're authoritative for. The data changes each time a subdomain adds a new name server or the address of a name server for the subdomain changes. If the subdomains are all administered by different people, that means more administrators to train, more relationships for the parent's administrator to maintain, and more overhead for the organization overall. On the other hand, the subdomains are smaller and easier to manage, and the administration is more widely distributed, allowing closer management of zone data.

Given the advantages and disadvantages of either alternative, it may seem difficult to make a choice. Actually, there's probably a natural division in your organization.

Some companies manage computers and networks at the site level; others have decentralized, relatively autonomous workgroups that manage everything themselves. Here are a few basic rules to help you find the right way to carve up your namespace:

- Don't shoehorn your organization into a weird or uncomfortable domain structure. Trying to fit 50 independent, unrelated U.S. divisions into four regional subdomains may save you work (as the administrator of the parent zone), but it won't help your reputation. Decentralized, autonomous operations demand different zones—that's the raison d'être of the Domain Name System.

- The structure of your domain should mirror the structure of your organization, especially your organization's support structure. If departments run networks, assign IP addresses, and manage hosts, they should also manage the subdomains.

- If you're not sure or can't agree about how the namespace should be organized, try to come up with guidelines for when a group within your organization can carve off its own subdomain (for example, how many hosts are needed to create a new subdomain and what level of support the group must provide) and grow the namespace organically, only as needed.

What to Name Your Children

Once you've decided how many subdomains you'd like to create and what they correspond to, you must choose names for them. Rather than unilaterally deciding on your subdomains' names, it's considered polite to involve your future subdomain administrators and their constituencies in the decision. In fact, you can leave the decision entirely to them if you like.

This can lead to problems, though. It's preferable to use a relatively consistent naming scheme across your subdomains. This practice makes it easier for users in one subdomain, or outside your domain entirely, to guess or remember your subdomain names and to figure out in which domain a particular host or user lives.

Leaving the decision to the locals can result in naming chaos. Some will want to use geographical names; others will insist on organizational names. Some will want to abbreviate; others will want to use full names.

Therefore, it's often best to establish a naming convention before choosing subdomain names. Here are some suggestions from our experience:

- In a dynamic company, the names of organizations can change frequently. Naming subdomains organizationally in a climate like this can be disastrous. One month the Relatively Advanced Technology group seems stable enough, the next month they've been merged into the Questionable Computer Systems organization, and the following quarter they're all sold to a German conglomerate. Meanwhile, you're stuck with well-known hosts in a subdomain whose name no longer has any meaning.

- Geographical names are more stable than organizational names but sometimes not as well known. You may know that your famous Software Evangelism Business Unit is in Poughkeepsie or Waukegan, but people outside your company may have no idea where it is (and might have trouble spelling either name).

- Don't sacrifice readability for convenience. Two-letter subdomain names may be easy to type, but impossible to recognize. Why abbreviate "Italy" to "it" and have it confused with your Information Technology organization when for a paltry three more letters you can use the full name and eliminate any ambiguity?

- Too many companies use cryptic, inconvenient domain names. The general rule seems to be the larger the company, the more indecipherable the domain names. Buck the trend: make the names of your subdomains obvious!

- Don't use existing or reserved top-level domain names as subdomain names. It might seem sensible to use two-letter country abbreviations for your international subdomains or to use organizational top-level domain names like *net* for your networking organization, but doing so can cause nasty problems. For example, naming your Communications department's subdomain *com* might impede your ability to communicate with hosts under the top-level *com* domain. Imagine the administrators of your *com* subdomain naming their new Sun workstation *sun* and their new HP 9000 *hp* (they aren't the most imaginative folks): users anywhere within your domain sending mail to friends at *sun.com* or *hp.com* could have their letters end up in your *com* subdomain, since the name of your parent zone may be in some of your hosts' search lists.

How to Become a Parent: Creating Subdomains

Once you've decided on names, creating the child domains is easy. But first, you've got to decide how much autonomy you're going to give your subdomains. Odd that you have to decide that before you actually create them....

Thus far, we've assumed that if you create a subdomain, you'll want to delegate it to another organization, thereby making it a separate zone from the parent. Is this always true, though? Not necessarily.

Think carefully about how the computers and networks within a subdomain are managed when choosing whether or not to delegate it. It doesn't make sense to delegate a subdomain to an entity that doesn't manage its own hosts or networks. For example, in a large corporation, the personnel department probably doesn't run its own computers: the MIS (Management Information Systems) or IT (Information Technology—same animal as MIS) department manages them. So while you may want to create a subdomain for personnel, delegating management for that subdomain to them is probably wasted effort.

Creating a Subdomain in the Parent's Zone

You can create a subdomain without delegating it, however. How? By creating resource records that refer to the subdomain within the parent's zone.

Say one day a group of students approaches us, asking for a DNS entry for a web server for student home pages. The name they'd like is *www.students.movie.edu*. You might think that we'd need to create a new zone, *students.movie.edu*, and delegate to it from the *movie.edu* zone. Well, that's one way to do it, but there's an easier way: just create an A record for *www.students.movie.edu* in the *movie.edu* zone. We find that few people realize this is perfectly legal. You don't need a new zone for each new level in the namespace. A new zone would make sense if the students were going to run *students.movie.edu* by themselves and wanted to administer their own name servers. But they just want one A record, so creating a whole new zone is more work than necessary.

It's easy to add this record with the DNS console. First create a *students.movie.edu* subdomain in the *movie.edu* zone, then add the *www.students.movie.edu* A record. To create the subdomain, right-click on the zone in the left pane and select **New Domain...**. You'll see the window shown in Figure 9-1.

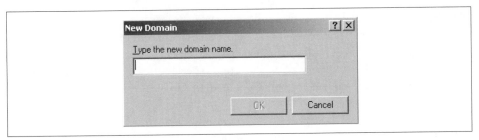

Figure 9-1. Creating a subdomain in a zone

Enter the name of the new subdomain. You don't need to append *movie.edu*—the DNS console knows what you mean. You'll then see a folder icon for the new domain in the DNS console, as shown in Figure 9-2.

To enter the *www.students.movie.edu* A record, just select the *students* folder and follow the procedures described previously to add a new host.

Now users can access *www.students.movie.edu* to get to the students' home pages. We could make this setup especially convenient for students by adding *students. movie.edu* to their PCs' or workstations' search lists; they'd need to type only *www* as the URL to get to the right host.

Notice there's no SOA record for *students.movie.edu*? There's no need for one since the *movie.edu* SOA record indicates the start of authority for the entire *movie.edu* zone. Since there's no delegation to *students.movie.edu*, it's part of the *movie.edu* zone.

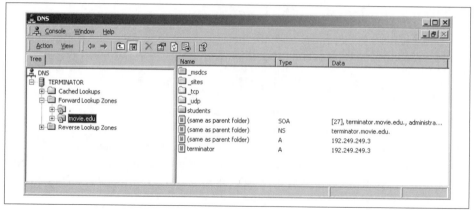

Figure 9-2. The students.movie.edu subdomain in the movie.edu zone

Creating and Delegating a Subdomain

If you decide to delegate your subdomains—to send your children out into the world, as it were—you'll need to do things a little differently. We're in the process of doing it now, so you can follow along with us.

We need to create a new subdomain of *movie.edu* for our special-effects lab. We've chosen the name *fx.movie.edu*—short, recognizable, unambiguous. Because we're delegating *fx.movie.edu* to administrators in the lab, it'll be a separate zone. The hosts *bladerunner* and *outland*, both within the special-effects lab, will serve as the zone's name servers (*bladerunner* will serve as the primary master). We've chosen to run two name servers for the zone for redundancy—a single *fx.movie.edu* name server would be a single point of failure that could effectively isolate the entire special-effects lab. Since there aren't many hosts in the lab, though, two name servers should be enough.

The special-effects lab is on *movie.edu*'s new 192.253.254/24 network. Here are the partial contents of *HOSTS*:

```
192.253.254.1 movie-gw.movie.edu movie-gw
# fx primary
192.253.254.2 bladerunner.fx.movie.edu bladerunner br
# fx secondary
192.253.254.3 outland.fx.movie.edu outland
192.253.254.4 starwars.fx.movie.edu starwars
192.253.254.5 empire.fx.movie.edu empire
192.253.254.6 jedi.fx.movie.edu jedi
```

First, we make sure the Microsoft DNS Server is installed on the new server, *bladerunner*. Then we create the new zone *fx.movie.edu* on *bladerunner* using the process described in the section "Creating a New Zone" in Chapter 4. We also create the corresponding *in-addr.arpa* zone, *254.253.192.in-addr.arpa*. Next, we populate the zone with all the hosts from our snippet of *HOSTS,* making sure the DNS console automatically adds the PTR records that correspond to our A records. We then add MX records for all of our hosts, pointing to *starwars.fx.movie.edu* and *wormhole.movie.edu*, at preferences 10 and 100, respectively.

The zone data file we end up with, called *fx.movie.edu.dns,* looks like this:

```
;
;   Data file fx.movie.edu.dns for fx.movie.edu zone.
;       Zone version:  27
;

@               IN  SOA bladerunner.fx.movie.edu.  administrator.fx.movie.edu. (
                        27          ; serial number
                        900         ; refresh
                        600         ; retry
                        86400       ; expire
                        3600        ) ; minimum TTL


;
;   Zone NS records
;

@               NS      bladerunner.fx.movie.edu.
@               NS      outland.fx.movie.edu.


;
;   Zone records
;

@               MX      10      starwars.
@               MX      100     wormhole.movie.edu.
bladerunner     A       192.253.254.2
                MX      10      starwars.
                MX      100     wormhole.movie.edu.
br              CNAME       bladerunner.fx.movie.edu.
empire          A       192.253.254.5
                MX      10      starwars.
                MX      100     wormhole.movie.edu.
jedi            A       192.253.254.6
                MX      10      starwars.
                MX      100     wormhole.movie.edu.
outland         A       192.253.254.3
                MX      10      starwars.
                MX      100     wormhole.movie.edu.
starwars        A       192.253.254.4
                MX      10      starwars.
                MX      100     wormhole.movie.edu.
```

The *254.253.192.in-addr.arpa.dns* file ends up looking like this:

```
;
;   Data file 254.253.192.in-addr.arpa.dns for 254.253.192.in-addr.arpa zone.
;       Zone version:  11
;
```

```
@               IN  SOA terminator.movie.edu.  administrator.movie.edu. (
                    11              ; serial number
                    900             ; refresh
                    600             ; retry
                    86400           ; expire
                    3600        ) ; minimum TTL

;
;  Zone NS records
;

@               NS      terminator.movie.edu.


;
;  Zone records
;

1               PTR     movie-gw.movie.edu.
2               PTR     bladerunner.fx.movie.edu.
3               PTR     outland.fx.movie.edu.
4               PTR     starwars.fx.movie.edu.
5               PTR     empire.fx.movie.edu.
6               PTR     jedi.fx.movie.edu.
```

Notice that the PTR record for *1.254.253.192.in-addr.arpa* points to *movie-gw. movie.edu*. That's intentional. The router connects to the other *movie.edu* networks, so it really doesn't belong in *fx.movie.edu*. There's no requirement that all the PTR records in *254.253.192.in-addr.arpa* map into a single zone, although they should correspond to the canonical names for those hosts.

Now we need to configure *bladerunner*'s resolver. Following the directions in Chapter 6, we configure *bladerunner* to send queries to its own IP address. Then we set *bladerunner*'s domain to *fx.movie.edu*.

Now we'll use *nslookup* to look up a few hosts in *fx.movie.edu* and in *254.253.192. in-addr.arpa*:

```
C:\> nslookup
Default Server:  bladerunner.fx.movie.edu
Address:  192.253.254.2

> jedi
Server:  bladerunner.fx.movie.edu
Address:  192.253.254.2

Name:    jedi.fx.movie.edu
Address:  192.253.254.6

> set type=mx
> empire
Server:  bladerunner.fx.movie.edu
Address:  192.253.254.2
```

```
empire.fx.movie.edu      MX preference = 10, mail exchanger = starwars
empire.fx.movie.edu      MX preference = 100, mail exchanger = wormhole.movie.edu

> ls fx.movie.edu
[bladerunner.fx.movie.edu]
 fx.movie.edu.            NS      server = bladerunner.fx.movie.edu
 fx.movie.edu.            NS      server = outland.fx.movie.edu
 bladerunner              A       192.253.254.2
 empire                   A       192.253.254.5
 jedi                     A       192.253.254.6
 outland                  A       192.253.254.3
 starwars                 A       192.253.254.4
> set type=ptr
> 192.253.254.3
Server:  bladerunner.fx.movie.edu
Address:  192.253.254.2

3.254.253.192.in-addr.arpa      name = outland.fx.movie.edu
> ls 254.253.192.in-addr.arpa
[bladerunner.fx.movie.edu]
 254.253.192.in-addr.arpa.    NS      server = terminator.movie.edu
 1                            PTR     host = movie-gw.movie.edu
 2                            PTR     host = bladerunner.fx.movie.edu
 3                            PTR     host = outland.fx.movie.edu
 4                            PTR     host = starwars.fx.movie.edu
 5                            PTR     host = empire.fx.movie.edu
 6                            PTR     host = jedi.fx.movie.edu
> exit
```

The output looks reasonable, so it's safe to set up a slave name server for *fx.movie. edu* and then delegate *fx.movie.edu* from *movie.edu*.

An fx.movie.edu slave

Setting up the slave name server for *fx.movie.edu* is simple: use the DNS console to add *outland* as a new server, then add two slave (secondary) zones, according to the instructions in Chapter 4.

Like *bladerunner*, *outland*'s resolver will point to the local name server, and we'll configure the local domain to be *fx.movie.edu*.

On the movie.edu primary master name server

All that's left now is to delegate the *fx.movie.edu* subdomain to the new *fx.movie.edu* name servers on *bladerunner* and *outland*. The whole delegation process is much improved in Windows 2000's DNS console. Right-click on the parent domain, *movie.edu*, in the left pane and choose **New Delegation...**, which starts the New Delegation Wizard. Click **Next** in the welcome screen to display a screen like the one shown in Figure 9-3. The first step is entering the name of the delegated subdomain, which we've done.

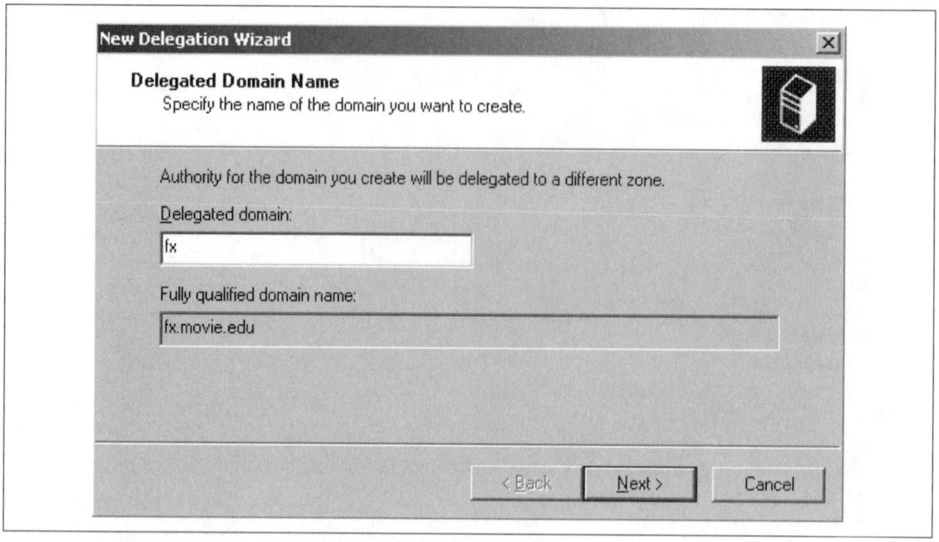

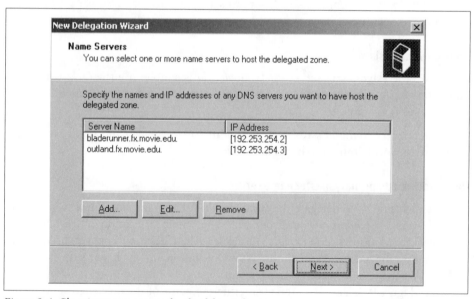

Figure 9-3. Entering the name of the delegated subdomain

Click **Next** and you'll be presented with a window to choose the name servers to host (i.e., be authoritative for) the delegated zone. Our two servers are *bladerunner. fx.movie.edu* and *outland.fx.movie.edu*, so we enter the appropriate information by clicking **Add...** (we have to run through the add process twice, once for each name server), resulting in a window like Figure 9-4.

Figure 9-4. Choosing name servers for the delegated zone

The final window of the wizard is just for confirmation, so we won't bother to show it. Click **Finish** and you've delegated a zone. The DNS console adds a special gray icon for delegated zones; if you select this icon, you'll see the NS records added by the wizard. These records perform the actual delegation. A sample DNS console view showing the *fx.movie.edu* delegation appears in Figure 9-5.

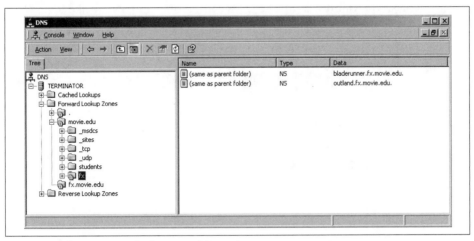

Figure 9-5. The DNS console showing a delegated zone

According to RFC 1034, the domain names in the resource record–specific portion (the "right side") of the *bladerunner.fx.movie.edu* and *outland.fx.movie.edu* NS records must be the canonical domain names for the name servers. A remote name server following delegation expects to find one or more address records attached to that domain name, not an alias (CNAME) record. Actually, the RFC extends this restriction to any type of resource record that includes a domain name as its value—all must specify the canonical domain name.

These two records alone aren't enough, though. Do you see the problem? How can a name server outside of *fx.movie.edu* look up information within *fx.movie.edu*? Well, a *movie.edu* name server would refer it to the name servers authoritative for *fx.movie. edu*, right? That's true, but the NS records in *db.movie.edu* give only the *names* of the *fx.movie.edu* name servers. The foreign name server needs the IP addresses of the *fx. movie.edu* name servers in order to send queries to them. Who can give it those addresses? Only the *fx.movie.edu* name servers. A real chicken-and-egg problem!

The solution is to include the addresses of the *fx.movie.edu* name servers in *movie.edu*. While these aren't strictly part of the *movie.edu* zone, delegation to *fx.movie.edu* won't work without them. Of course, if the name servers for *fx.movie.edu* weren't within *fx.movie.edu*, these addresses—called *glue records*—wouldn't be necessary. A foreign name server would be able to find the address it needed by querying other name servers.

We don't have to worry about adding these records, though—the New Delegation Wizard takes care of it for us.

Also, remember to keep the glue up-to-date. If *bladerunner* gets a new network interface, and hence another IP address, you'll need to update the glue data. The DNS console doesn't let you edit the glue records directly, though. You have use the name server modification window. With the DNS console showing a view like Figure 9-5, double-click on an NS record in the right pane to produce a window like the one shown in Figure 9-6.

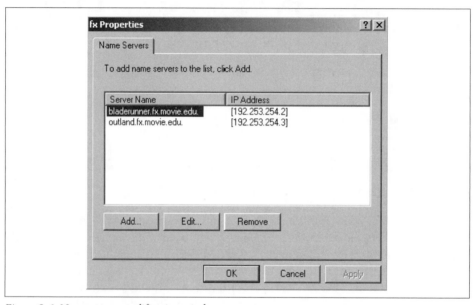

Figure 9-6. Name server modification window

If *fx.movie.edu*'s delegation changes—i.e., a name server gets added or deleted or a name server's IP address changes—use the **Add...**, **Edit...**, or **Remove** buttons to make the appropriate changes.

We might also want to include aliases for any hosts moving into *fx.movie.edu* from *movie.edu*. For example, if we move *plan9.movie.edu*, a server with an important library of public-domain special-effects algorithms, into *fx.movie.edu*, we should create an alias under *movie.edu* pointing the old domain name to the new one. In the zone data file, the record would look like this:

```
plan9   IN  CNAME  plan9.fx.movie.edu.
```

This will allow people outside of *movie.edu* to reach *plan9* even though they're using its old domain name, *plan9.movie.edu*.

Don't get confused about the zone in which this alias belongs. The *plan9* alias record is actually in the *movie.edu* zone, so it belongs in *movie.edu.dns*. An alias pointing *p9.fx.movie.edu* to *plan9.fx.movie.edu*, on the other hand, is in the *fx.movie.edu* zone and belongs in *fx.movie.edu.dns*.

Delegating an in-addr.arpa zone

We almost forgot to delegate the *254.253.192.in-addr.arpa* zone! This is a little trickier than delegating *fx.movie.edu* because we don't manage the parent zone.

First, we need to figure out what *254.253.192.in-addr.arpa*'s parent zone is and who runs it. Figuring this out may take some sleuthing; we covered how to do this in Chapter 3.

As it turns out, the *in-addr.arpa* zone is *254.253.192.in-addr.arpa*'s parent. And, if you think about it, that makes sense. There's no reason for the administrators of *in-addr.arpa* to delegate *253.192.in-addr.arpa* or *192.in-addr.arpa* to a separate authority because, unless 192/8 or 192.253/16 is all one big CIDR block, networks like 192. 253.253/24 and 192.253.254/24 don't have anything in common with each other. They may be managed by totally unrelated organizations.

You might remember (from Chapter 3) that the *in-addr.arpa* zone is managed by ARIN, the American Registry of Internet Numbers. (Of course, if you didn't remember, you could always use *nslookup* to find the contact address in *in-addr.arpa*'s SOA record, like we showed you in Chapter 3.) All that's left is for us to use the web-based "ARIN Modify Tool" at *http://www.arin.net/cgi-bin/amt.pl* to request registration of our reverse-mapping zone.

Adding a movie.edu slave

If the special-effects lab gets big enough, it may make sense to put a *movie.edu* slave somewhere on the 192.253.254/24 network. That way, a larger proportion of DNS queries from *fx.movie.edu* hosts can be answered locally. It seems logical to make one of the existing *fx.movie.edu* name servers into a *movie.edu* slave, too—that way, we can make better use of an existing name server instead of setting up a brand-new name server.

We've decided to make *bladerunner* a slave for *movie.edu*. This won't interfere with *bladerunner*'s primary mission as the primary master name server for *fx.movie.edu*. A single name server, given enough memory, can be authoritative for literally thousands of zones. One name server can load some zones as a primary master and others as a slave.[*]

The configuration change is simple: we use the DNS console to add a slave (secondary) zone to *bladerunner* and tell *bladerunner* to get the *movie.edu* zone data from *terminator*'s IP address, per the instructions in Chapter 4.

---

[*] Clearly, though, a name server can't be both the primary master and a slave for a single zone. The name server gets the data for a given zone either from a local zone data file (and is a primary master for the zone) or from another name server (and is a slave for the zone).

Subdomains of in-addr.arpa Domains

Forward-mapping domains aren't the only domains you can divide into subdomains and delegate. If your *in-addr.arpa* namespace is large enough, you may need to divide it, too. Typically, you divide the domain that corresponds to your network number into subdomains that correspond to your subnets. How that works depends on the type of network you have and on your network's subnet mask.

Subnetting on an Octet Boundary

Since Movie U. has just three /24 (Class C–sized) networks, one per segment, there's no particular need to subnet those networks. However, our sister university, Altered State, has a Class B–sized network, 172.20/16. Their network is subnetted between the third and fourth octet of the IP address; that is, their subnet mask is 255.255.255. 0. They've already created a number of subdomains of their domain: *altered.edu*, including *fx.altered.edu* (okay, we copied them); *makeup.altered.edu*; and *foley. altered.edu*. Since each of these departments also runs its own subnet (their Special Effects department runs subnet 172.20.2/24, Makeup runs 172.20.15/24, and Foley runs 172.20.25/24), they'd like to divvy up their *in-addr.arpa* namespace appropriately, too.

Delegating *in-addr.arpa* subdomains is no different from delegating subdomains of forward-mapping domains. First, they or their departments create three new zones, *2.20.172.in-addr.arpa*, *15.20.172.in-addr.arpa*, and *25.20.172.in-addr.arpa*. The *20. 172.in-addr.arpa* administrators also need to add the NS records with the New Delegation Wizard, as we described in the *fx.movie.edu* example earlier in this chapter.

After running the New Delegation Wizard, the NS records in *20.172.in-addr.arpa.dns* would look something like the following partial listing of the file's contents:

```
;
;  Delegated sub-zone:  15.20.172.in-addr.arpa.
;
15                                 NS     prettywoman.makeup.altered.edu.
prettywoman.makeup.altered.edu.    A      172.20.15.2
15                                 NS     priscilla.makeup.altered.edu.
priscilla.makeup.altered.edu.      A      172.20.15.3
;  End delegation


;
;  Delegated sub-zone:  2.20.172.in-addr.arpa.
;
2                                  NS     gump.fx.altered.edu.
gump.fx.altered.edu.               A      172.20.2.1
2                                  NS     toystory.fx.altered.edu.
toystory.fx.altered.edu.           A      172.20.2.5
;  End delegation
```

```
;
; Delegated sub-zone:  25.20.172.in-addr.arpa.
;
25                              NS      blowup.foley.altered.edu.
blowup.foley.altered.edu.       A       172.20.25.10
25                              NS      muppetshow.foley.altered.edu.
muppetshow.foley.altered.edu.   A       172.20.25.2
; End delegation
```

The Altered State administrators needed to use the fully qualified domain names of the name servers in the NS records because the default origin in this file is *20.172.in-addr.arpa*. Strictly speaking, those glue address records aren't needed since the names of the name servers to which they delegated the zone weren't in the delegated zones. We were a little chagrined to discover that the DNS console forced us to enter IP addresses for these name servers and then put them in *20.172.in-addr.arpa.dns*. The server even includes them in a zone transfer of the *20.172.in-addr.arpa* zone. Since the glue records are not required, all that is unnecessary.

Subnetting on a Nonoctet Boundary

What do you do about networks that aren't subnetted neatly on octet boundaries, like subnetted /24 (Class C–sized) networks? In these cases, you can't delegate along lines that match the subnets. This forces you into one of two situations: you have multiple subnets per *in-addr.arpa* zone or you have multiple *in-addr.arpa* zones per subnet. Neither is particularly pleasing.

Class A and B networks

Let's take the case of the /8 (Class A–sized) network 15/8, subnetted with the subnet mask 255.255.248.0 (a 13-bit subnet field and an 11-bit host field, or 8,192 subnets of 2,048 hosts). In this case, the subnet 15.1.200.0, for example, extends from 15.1. 200.0 to 15.1.207.255. Therefore, the delegation for that single subdomain in *db.15*, the zone data file for *15.in-addr.arpa*, might look like this:

```
200.1.15.in-addr.arpa.      86400   IN      NS      ns-1.cns.hp.com.
200.1.15.in-addr.arpa.      86400   IN      NS      ns-2.cns.hp.com.
201.1.15.in-addr.arpa.      86400   IN      NS      ns-1.cns.hp.com.
201.1.15.in-addr.arpa.      86400   IN      NS      ns-2.cns.hp.com.
202.1.15.in-addr.arpa.      86400   IN      NS      ns-1.cns.hp.com.
202.1.15.in-addr.arpa.      86400   IN      NS      ns-2.cns.hp.com.
203.1.15.in-addr.arpa.      86400   IN      NS      ns-1.cns.hp.com.
203.1.15.in-addr.arpa.      86400   IN      NS      ns-2.cns.hp.com.
204.1.15.in-addr.arpa.      86400   IN      NS      ns-1.cns.hp.com.
204.1.15.in-addr.arpa.      86400   IN      NS      ns-2.cns.hp.com.
205.1.15.in-addr.arpa.      86400   IN      NS      ns-1.cns.hp.com.
205.1.15.in-addr.arpa.      86400   IN      NS      ns-2.cns.hp.com.
206.1.15.in-addr.arpa.      86400   IN      NS      ns-1.cns.hp.com.
206.1.15.in-addr.arpa.      86400   IN      NS      ns-2.cns.hp.com.
```

```
207.1.15.in-addr.arpa.      86400    IN    NS    ns-1.cns.hp.com.
207.1.15.in-addr.arpa.      86400    IN    NS    ns-2.cns.hp.com.
```

That's a lot of delegation for one subnet!

You'd set this up with the DNS console by adding two levels of subdomains under *15.in-addr.arpa* and then running the New Delegation Wizard (eight times!) with the *1.15.in-addr.arpa* zone selected.

/24 (Class C–sized) networks

In the case of a subnetted /24 (Class C-sized) network, say 192.253.254/24, subnetted with the mask 255.255.255.192, you have a single *in-addr.arpa* zone, *254.253. 192.in-addr.arpa*, that corresponds to subnets 192.253.254.0/26, 192.253.254.64/26, 192.253.254.128/26, and 192.253.254.192/26. This can be a problem if you want to let different organizations manage the reverse-mapping information that corresponds to each subnet. You can solve this in one of three ways, none of which is pretty.

Solution 1. The first solution is to administer the *254.253.192.in-addr.arpa* zone as a single entity and not even try to delegate. This requires either cooperation between the administrators of the four subnets involved or the use of a tool like the DNS console to allow each of the four administrators to take care of his own data.

Solution 2. The second solution is to delegate at the *fourth* octet. That's even nastier than the /8 delegation we just showed. You'll need at least a couple of NS records per IP address. To set this up with the DNS console, you'd need to create the *254. 253.192.in-addr.arpa* zone and run the new delegation wizard 254 times, one for each usable value in the fourth octet. Here's how the *254.253.192.in-addr.arpa.dns* file might end up looking (we've removed the unnecessary glue A records for clarity and brevity):

```
;
; Delegated sub-zone:  1.254.253.192.in-addr.arpa.
;
1           IN          NS          ns1.foo.com.
1           IN          NS          ns2.foo.com.
; End delegation


;
; Delegated sub-zone:  2.254.253.192.in-addr.arpa.
;
2           IN          NS          ns1.foo.com.
2           IN          NS          ns2.foo.com.
; End delegation

...

; Delegated sub-zone:  65.254.253.192.in-addr.arpa.
```

```
;
65              IN          NS          gw.bar.com.
65              IN          NS          relay.bar.com.
;  End delegation


;  Delegated sub-zone:  66.254.253.192.in-addr.arpa.
;
66              IN          NS          gw.bar.com.
66              IN          NS          relay.bar.com.
;  End delegation


...


;
;  Delegated sub-zone:  129.254.253.192.in-addr.arpa.
;
129             IN          NS          mail.baz.com.
129             IN          NS          www.baz.com
;  End delegation


;
;  Delegated sub-zone:  193.254.253.192.in-addr.arpa.
;
193             IN          NS          mail.baz.com.
192             IN          NS          www.baz.com
;  End delegation
```

And so on, all the way down to *254.254.253.192.in-addr.arpa*. Of course, on *ns1.foo. com*, you'd also expect the name server to be authoritative for *1.254.253.192.in-addr. arpa*, and in the zone data file for *1.254.253.192.in-addr.arpa*, you'd find just the one PTR record (plus an SOA and two NS records):

```
@    IN    SOA    ns1.foo.com.    root.ns1.foo.com.    (
                          1          ; Serial
                          10800      ; Refresh
                          3600       ; Retry
                          608400     ; Expire
                          86400      ; Default TTL

     IN    NS     ns1.foo.com.
     IN    NS     ns2.foo.com.

     IN    PTR    thereitis.foo.com.
```

Note that the PTR record is attached to the zone's domain name, since the zone's domain name corresponds to just one IP address. (And, as far as we can tell, it's not possible to create a PTR record with the same name as the zone—as in the earlier example zone—with the DNS console. You have to create that zone by hand.) Now, when a *254.253.192.in-addr.arpa* name server receives a query for the PTR record for *1.254.253.192.in-addr.arpa*, it will refer the querier to *ns1.foo.com* and *ns2.foo.com*, which will respond with the one PTR record in the zone.

Solution 3. Finally, there's a clever technique that obviates the need to maintain a separate zone data file for each IP address.[*] The organization responsible for the overall /24 network creates CNAME records for each of the domain names in the zone, pointing to domain names in new subdomains, which are then delegated to the proper servers. These new subdomains can be called just about anything, but names like *0-63*, *64-127*, *128-191*, and *192-255* clearly indicate the range of addresses each subdomain will reverse map. Each subdomain then contains only the PTR records in the range for which the subdomain is named.

Here are the partial contents of the *254.253.192.in-addr.arpa.dns* file:

```
1.254.253.192.in-addr.arpa.   IN  CNAME  1.0-63.254.253.192.in-addr.arpa.
2.254.253.192.in-addr.arpa.   IN  CNAME  2.0-63.254.253.192.in-addr.arpa.

...

0-63.254.253.192.in-addr.arpa.   86400   IN   NS   ns1.foo.com.
0-63.254.253.192.in-addr.arpa.   86400   IN   NS   ns2.foo.com.

65.254.253.192.in-addr.arpa. IN  CNAME  65.64-127.254.253.192.in-addr.arpa.
66.254.253.192.in-addr.arpa. IN  CNAME  66.64-127.254.253.192.in-addr.arpa.

...

64-127.254.253.192.in-addr.arpa.   86400   IN   NS   relay.bar.com.
64-127.254.253.192.in-addr.arpa.   86400   IN   NS   gw.bar.com.

129.254.253.192.in-addr.arpa.  IN  CNAME  129.128-191.254.253.192.in-addr. arpa.
130.254.253.192.in-addr.arpa.  IN  CNAME  130.128-191.254.253.192.in-addr. arpa.

...

128-191.254.253.192.in-addr.arpa.   86400   IN   NS   mail.baz.com.
128-191.254.253.192.in-addr.arpa.   86400   IN   NS   www.baz.com.
```

The zone data file for *0-63.254.253.192.in-addr.arpa*, *0-63.254.253.192.in-addr. arpa.dns*, can contain just PTR records for IP addresses 192.253.254.1 through 192. 253.254.63.

Here are the partial contents of the *0-63.254.253.192.in-addr.arpa.dns* file:

```
@   IN   soa   ns1.foo.com.   root.ns1.foo.com.   (
                        1       ; Serial
                        10800   ; Refresh
                        3600    ; Retry
                        608400  ; Expire
                        86400 ) ; Default TTL


    IN   NS   ns1.foo.com.
```

[*] We first saw this explained by Glen Herrmansfeldt at CalTech in the newsgroup *comp.protocols.tcp-ip. domains*. It's now codified as RFC 2317.

```
           IN    NS     ns2.foo.com.

     1     IN    PTR    thereitis.foo.com.
     2     IN    PTR    setter.foo.com.
     3     IN    PTR    mouse.foo.com.
     ...
```

The way this setup works is a little tricky, so let's go over it. A resolver requests the PTR record for *1.254.253.192.in-addr.arpa*, causing its local name server to go look up that record. The local name server ends up asking a *254.253.192.in-addr.arpa* name server, which will respond with the CNAME record indicating that *1.254.253. 192.in-addr.arpa* is actually an alias for *1.0-63.254.253.192.in-addr.arpa* and that the PTR record is attached to that name. The response will also include NS records telling the local name server that the authoritative name servers for *0-63.254.253.192. in-addr.arpa* are *ns1.foo.com* and *ns2.foo.com*. The local name server then queries either *ns1.foo.com* or *ns2.foo.com* for the PTR record for *1.0-63.254.253.192.in-addr. arpa* and receives the PTR record.

Good Parenting

Now that the delegation to the *fx.movie.edu* name servers is in place, we—responsible parents that we are—should check that delegation using *host*. What? We haven't given you *host* yet? A version of *host* that works on Windows 2000 is available via anonymous *ftp* from *ftp://ftp.nikhef.nl/pub/network/host_970908.exe.Z*. To uncompress *host,* you'll need WinZip or a similar Windows utility. WinZip is available from *http://www.winzip.com*.

Once you uncompress *host_970908.exe*, install it as *host.exe* somewhere on your computer. (We install it in the same directory as *nslookup.exe*.) Next, set up a *resolv.conf* file in your *%WINDIR%* directory. (If you're not sure where *%WINDIR%* is, type *set* from a DOS prompt.)

host makes it easy to check delegation. With *host,* you can look up the NS records for your zone on your parent zone's name servers. If those look good, you can use *host* to query each name server listed for the zone's SOA record. The query is nonrecursive, so the name server queried doesn't query other name servers to find the SOA record. If the name server replies, *host* checks the reply to see whether the *aa* (authoritative answer) bit in the reply packet is set. If it is, the name server checks to make sure that the packet contains an answer. If both these criteria are met, the name server is flagged as authoritative for the zone. Otherwise, the name server is not authoritative, and *host* reports an error.

Why all the fuss over bad delegation? Incorrect delegation can slow name resolution or cause the propagation of old and erroneous root name server information. When a name server is queried for data in a zone for which it is not authoritative, it does its best to provide useful information to the querier. This "useful information" comes in the form of NS records for the closest ancestor zone the name server knows. (We mentioned this briefly in Chapter 8, when we discussed why you shouldn't register a caching-only name server.)

For example, say one of the *fx.movie.edu* name servers mistakenly receives an iterative query for the address of *carrie.horror.movie.edu*. It knows nothing about the *horror.movie.edu* zone (except for what it might have cached), but it likely has NS records for *movie.edu* cached since those are its parent name servers. So it would return those records to the querier.

In that scenario, the NS records may help the querying name server get an answer. However, it's a fact of life on the Internet that not all administrators keep their root hints files up-to-date. If one of your name servers follows a bad delegation and queries a remote name server for records it doesn't have, look what can happen:

```
C:\> nslookup
Default Server:  terminator.movie.edu
Address:  192.249.249.3
> set type=ns
> .
Server:  terminator.movie.edu
Address:  192.249.249.3

Non-authoritative answer:
(root)   nameserver = D.ROOT-SERVERS.NET
(root)   nameserver = E.ROOT-SERVERS.NET
(root)   nameserver = I.ROOT-SERVERS.NET
(root)   nameserver = F.ROOT-SERVERS.NET
(root)   nameserver = G.ROOT-SERVERS.NET
(root)   nameserver = A.ROOT-SERVERS.NET
(root)   nameserver = H.ROOT-SERVERS.NETNIC.NORDU.NET
(root)   nameserver = B.ROOT-SERVERS.NET
(root)   nameserver = C.ROOT-SERVERS.NET
(root)   nameserver = A.ISI.EDU             --These three name
(root)   nameserver = SRI-NIC.ARPA          --servers are no longer
(root)   nameserver = GUNTER-ADAM.ARPA      --roots
```

A remote name server tried to "help out" our local name server by sending it the current list of roots. Unfortunately, the remote name server was corrupt and returned NS records that were incorrect. And our local name server, not knowing any better, cached that data.

Queries to misconfigured *in-addr.arpa* name servers often result in bad root NS records because the *in-addr.arpa* and *arpa* zones are the closest ancestors of most *in-addr.arpa* subdomains, and name servers very seldom cache either *in-addr.arpa*'s or *arpa*'s NS records. (The roots rarely give them out since they delegate directly to lower-level subdomains.) Once your name server has cached bad root NS records, your name resolution will almost certainly suffer: your name server won't be contacting the "official" root name servers, and who knows what information they will hand out?

Those root NS records may have your name server querying a root name server that is no longer at that IP address or a root name server that no longer exists at all. If you're having an especially bad day, the bad root NS records may point to a real, non-root name server that is close to your network. Even though it won't return authoritative root data, your name server will favor it because of its proximity to your network.

Using host

If our little lecture has convinced you of the importance of maintaining correct delegation, you'll be eager to learn how to use *host* to ensure that you don't join the ranks of the miscreants.

The first step is to use *host* to look up your zone's NS records on a name server for your parent zone and make sure they're correct. Here's how we'd check the *fx.movie. edu* NS records on one of the *movie.edu* name servers:

```
C:\> host -t ns fx.movie.edu. terminator.movie.edu.
```

If everything's okay with the NS records, we'll simply see the NS records in the output:

```
fx.movie.edu   NS   bladerunner.fx.movie.edu
fx.movie.edu   NS   outland.fx.movie.edu
```

This tells us that all the NS records delegating *fx.movie.edu* from *terminator.movie. edu* are correct.

Next, we'll use *host*'s "SOA check" mode to query each of the name servers in the NS records for the *fx.movie.edu* zone's SOA record. This will also check whether the response was authoritative:

```
C:\> host -C fx.movie.edu.
```

Normally, this will produce the NS records above, along with the contents of the *fx. movie.edu* zone's SOA record:

```
fx.movie.edu         NS         bladerunner.fx.movie.edu
bladerunner.fx.movie.edu  hostmaster.fx.movie.edu   (1 10800 3600 608400 3600)
fx.movie.edu         NS         outland.fx.movie.edu
bladerunner.fx.movie.edu  hostmaster.fx.movie.edu   (1 10800 3600 608400 3600)
```

If one of the *fx.movie.edu* name servers—say *outland*—were misconfigured, we might see this:

```
fx.movie.edu   NS   bladerunner.fx.movie.edu
fx.movie.edu   NS   outland.fx.movie.edu
fx.movie.edu SOA record currently not present at outland.fx.movie.edu
fx.movie.edu has lame delegation to outland.fx.movie.edu
```

This indicates that the name server on *outland* is running, but it's not authoritative for *fx.movie.edu*.

If one of the *fx.movie.edu* name servers weren't running at all, we'd see:

```
fx.movie.edu   NS         bladerunner.fx.movie.edu
bladerunner.fx.movie.edu  hostmaster.fx.movie.edu   (1 10800 3600 608400 3600)
fx.movie.edu   NS         outland.fx.movie.edu
fx.movie.edu SOA         record not found at outland.fx.movie.edu, try again
```

In this case, the try again message indicates that *host* sent *outland* a query and didn't get a response back in an acceptable amount of time.

While we could have checked the *fx.movie.edu* delegation using *nslookup*, *host*'s powerful command-line options make the task especially easy.

Managing Delegation

If the special-effects lab gets bigger, we may find that we need additional name servers. We dealt with setting up new name servers in Chapter 8 and even went over what information to send to the parent zone's administrator. But we never explained what the parent needed to do.

It turns out that the parent's job is relatively easy, especially if the administrators of the subdomain send complete information. Imagine that the special-effects lab expands to a new network, 192.254.20/24. They have a passel of new, high-powered graphics workstations. One of them, *alien.fx.movie.edu*, will act as the new network's name server.

The administrators of *fx.movie.edu* (we delegated it to the folks in the lab) send their parent zone's administrators (that's us) a short note:

```
Hi!

We've just set up alien.fx.movie.edu (192.254.20.3) as a name server for fx.movie.
edu.  Would you please update your delegation information?  I've attached the NS
records you'll need to add.

Thanks,

Arty Segue
ajs@fx.movie.edu

----- cut here -----

fx.movie.edu.  86400  IN  NS  bladerunner.fx.movie.edu.
fx.movie.edu.  86400  IN  NS  outland.fx.movie.edu.
fx.movie.edu.  86400  IN  NS  alien.fx.movie.edu.

bladerunner.fx.movie.edu.  86400  IN  A  192.253.254.2
outland.fx.movie.edu.      86400  IN  A  192.253.254.3
alien.fx.movie.edu.        86400  IN  A  192.254.20.3
```

Our job as the *movie.edu* administrator is straightforward: add the NS and A records to *movie.edu*. Once again, it's the New Delegation Wizard to the rescue: select the gray *fx.movie.edu* folder in the DNS console's left pane and then double-click on any of the NS records in the right pane. You'll see a window like the one shown back in Figure 9-6. Select **Add...** to add the new NS record for *alien.fx.movie.edu*.

The final step for the *fx.movie.edu* administrator is to send a similar message to *hostmaster@arin.net* (administrator of the *in-addr.arpa* zone), requesting that the

20.254.192.in-addr.arpa subdomain be delegated to *alien.fx.movie.edu*, *bladerunner. fx.movie.edu*, and *outland.fx.movie.edu*.

Managing the Transition to Subdomains

We won't lie to you—the *fx.movie.edu* example we showed you was unrealistic for several reasons. The main one is the magical appearance of the special-effects lab's hosts. In the real world, the lab would have started out with a few hosts, probably in the *movie.edu* zone. After a generous endowment, an NSF grant, or a corporate gift, they might expand the lab a little and buy a few more computers. Sooner or later, the lab would have enough hosts to warrant the creation of a new subdomain. By that point, however, many of the original hosts would be well known by their names under *movie.edu*.

We briefly touched on using CNAME records in the parent zone (in our *plan9. movie.edu* example) to help people adjust to a host's change of domain. But what happens when you move a whole network or subnet into a new subdomain?

The strategy we recommend uses CNAME records in much the same way, but on a larger scale. Using the DNS console, you can create CNAMEs for hosts. This allows users to continue using the old domain names for any of the hosts that have moved. When they *telnet* or *ftp* (or whatever) to those hosts, however, the command will report that they're connected to a host in *fx.movie.edu*:

```
C:\> telnet plan9

Trying...
Connected to plan9.fx.movie.edu.
Escape character is '^]'.

HP-UX plan9.fx.movie.edu A.09.05 C 9000/735 (ttyu1)

login:
```

Some users, of course, don't notice subtle changes like this, so you should also do some public relations work and notify folks of the change.

How do you create all these aliases? Well, you could do it manually using the DNS console, CNAME record by CNAME record. Or you could use a Perl script to create CNAME records for every host in *fx.movie.edu.dns*:

```
#
# Simple Perl script to create aliases
# Run with <script> <domain name of child zone>
#
die "Usage: $0 <child zone>\n" if $#ARGV!=0;

open(ZDF, "$ARGV[0].dns") || die "Couldn't open $ARGV[0]: $!\n";

($label, $parent) = split(/\./, $ARGV[0], 2);
$parent .= ".dns";
```

```
open(PZDF, ">>$parent") || die "Couldn't open $parent: $!\n";

while (<ZDF>) {
        if (/\s+IN\s+A\s+/) {
            ($host, $rest) = split(/[\s\.]/, $_, 2);
            printf PZDF "%s  IN  CNAME  %s.%s.\n", $host, $host, $ARGV[0];
        }
};
```

Removing Parent Aliases

Although parent-level aliases are useful for minimizing the impact of moving your hosts, they're also a crutch of sorts. Like a crutch, they'll restrict your freedom. They'll clutter up your parent namespace when one of your motivations for implementing a subdomain may have been making the parent zone smaller. And they'll prevent you from using the names of hosts in the subdomain as names for hosts in the parent zone.

After a grace period—which should be well advertised to users—you should remove all the aliases, with the possible exception of aliases for extremely well-known Internet hosts. During the grace period, users can adjust to the new domain names and modify scripts and the like. But don't get suckered into leaving all those aliases in the parent zone; they defeat part of the purpose of DNS because they prevent you and your subdomain administrator from naming hosts autonomously.

You might want to leave CNAME records for well-known Internet hosts or central network resources intact because of the potential impact of a loss of connectivity. On the other hand, rather than moving the well-known host or central resource into a subdomain at all, it might be better to leave it at the parent zone level.

The Life of a Parent

That's a lot of parental advice to digest in one sitting, so let's recap the highlights of what we've talked about. The life cycle of a typical parent goes something like this:

1. You have a single zone with all of your hosts in that zone.

2. You break your zone into a number of subdomains, some of them in the same zone as the parent, if necessary. You provide CNAME records in the parent zone for well-known hosts that have moved into subdomains.

3. After a grace period, you delete any remaining CNAME records.

4. You handle subdomain delegation updates, either manually or by using stubs, and periodically check delegation.

Okay, now that you know all there is to parenting, let's go on to talk about more advanced name server features. You may need some of these tools to keep those kids in line.

Advanced Features and Security

"What's the use of their having names," the Gnat said, "if they won't answer to them?"

In this chapter, we'll cover some of the Microsoft DNS Server's more advanced features and suggest how they might come in handy in your DNS infrastructure. (We do save some of the hardcore firewall material for Chapter 14, and we cover advanced features specific to Windows 2000 in Chapter 11.)

DNS NOTIFY (Zone Change Notification)

Traditionally, slaves have used a polling scheme to determine when they need a zone transfer. The polling interval is called the *refresh time*. Other parameters in the zone's SOA record govern other aspects of the polling mechanism.

Wouldn't it be nice if the primary master name server could tell its slave servers when the information in a zone changed? After all, the primary master name server knows the data has changed: every time a zone is changed with the DNS console, the DNS console notifies the server, which immediately changes the zone in its memory. The primary's notification can come soon after the actual modification instead of waiting for the refresh interval to expire.

RFC 1996 proposed a mechanism that allowed primary master servers to notify their slaves of changes to a zone's data. The Microsoft DNS Server implements this scheme, called DNS NOTIFY for short.

DNS NOTIFY works like this: when a primary master name server notices a change to data in a zone, it sends a special notification message to all slave servers for that zone. It uses the list of NS records in the zone to build the list of slave servers for the zone. The primary master removes the NS record corresponding to the name server listed in the first field in the zone's SOA record (which by convention lists the name of the primary master name server for the zone), as well as the local host. Removing those name servers prevents the primary master from sending a notification message to itself.

The special NOTIFY request is identified by its opcode in the query header. The opcode for most queries is QUERY. NOTIFY messages have a special opcode, NOTIFY. Other than that, the request looks much like a query for the SOA record for the zone: it specifies the zone's domain name, class, and a type of SOA.

When a slave receives a NOTIFY request for a zone from one of its configured master name servers, it sends a NOTIFY response. The response tells the master that the slave received the NOTIFY request and to stop sending NOTIFY messages for the zone. Then the slave proceeds just as if the refresh timer had expired: it queries the master server for the SOA record for the zone the master claimed had changed. If the serial number is higher, the slave performs the zone transfer.

Why doesn't the slave simply take the master's word that the zone has changed? It's possible that a miscreant could forge NOTIFY requests to our slaves, causing lots of unnecessary zone transfers that might amount to a denial-of-service attack against our master server.

If the slave actually transfers the zone, RFC 1996 says that it should issue its own NOTIFY requests to the other authoritative name servers for the zone. The idea is that the primary master may not be able to notify all the slave servers for the zone itself, since it's possible that some slaves can't communicate directly with the primary master and so use another slave as their master. However, the Microsoft DNS Server doesn't implement this, and Microsoft DNS Server slaves don't send NOTIFY messages unless explicitly configured to do so.

Here's how this process works in practice: on our network, *terminator.movie.edu* is the primary master for *movie.edu*, and *wormhole.movie.edu* and *zardoz.movie.edu* are slaves (as shown in Figure 10-1).

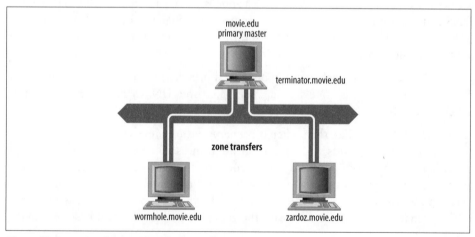

Figure 10-1. movie.edu zone transfer example

When we update *movie.edu* on *terminator*, *terminator* sends NOTIFY messages to *wormhole* and *zardoz*. Both slaves check to see whether *movie.edu*'s serial number has been incremented and, if they find it has, perform a zone transfer.

Let's also look at a more complicated zone transfer scheme. In Figure 10-2, *a* is the primary master name server for the zone and *b*'s master server, but *b* is *c*'s master server. Moreover, *b* has two network interfaces.

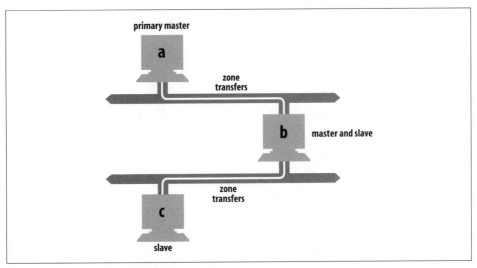

Figure 10-2. Complex zone transfer example

In this scenario, *a* notifies both *b* and *c* after the zone is updated. *b* checks to see whether the zone's serial number has been incremented and initiates a zone transfer. However, *c* ignores *a*'s NOTIFY message because *a* is not *c*'s configured master name server (*b* is). If *b* is explicitly configured to notify *c*, after *b*'s zone transfer completes it sends *c* a NOTIFY message, which prompts *c* to check the serial number *b* holds for the zone.

Older BIND slave name servers, and other name servers that don't support NOTIFY, respond with a "Not Implemented" (NOTIMP) error, wait until their refresh timers expire, and then transfer the zone. The Microsoft DNS Server just ignores the NOTIMP error.

NOTIFY is controlled on a zone-by-zone basis and is enabled by default for every zone. The controls for NOTIFY are somewhat hidden: highlight a zone in DNS console's left pane, select **Action → Properties**, and choose the **Zone Transfers** tab of the zone properties window, which produces a window like the one shown in Figure 10-3.

Select the **Notify...** button to open the window shown in Figure 10-4, which illustrates the NOTIFY configuration for the *movie.edu* zone on the zone's primary, *terminator*. You have two choices for configuring which servers get NOTIFY messages for a zone. The first is to check **Servers listed on the Name Servers tab**, which lets

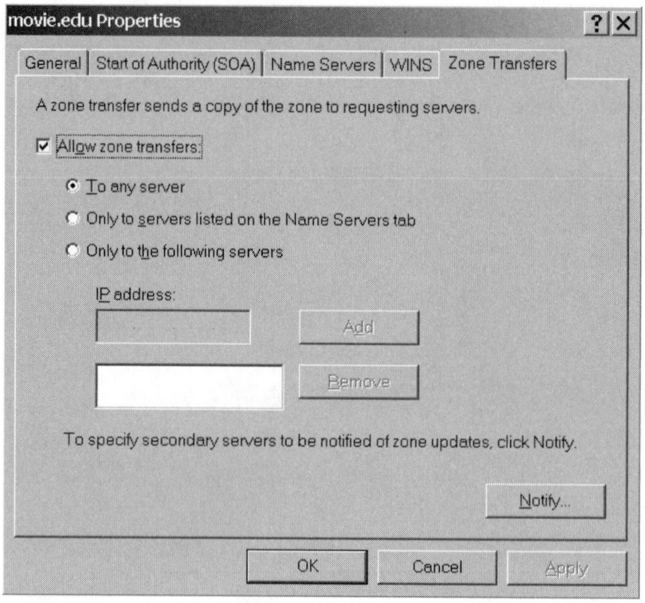

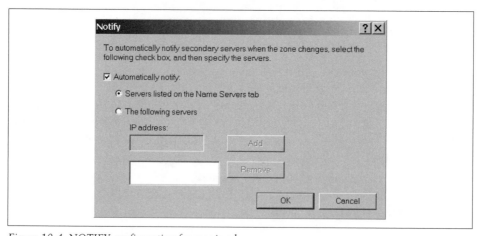

Figure 10-3. Zone transfer configuration for movie.edu

Figure 10-4. NOTIFY configuration for movie.edu

the server decide based on the name servers listed in the zone's NS records. (The **Name Servers** tab of the zone properties window simply shows the name servers listed in the zone's NS records.) The second choice is to specify exactly which slave servers should receive NOTIFY messages. This option is required if you have slave servers not listed in the zone's NS records: such slaves are effectively hidden, and the only way the primary master knows to send NOTIFY messages to them is if you tell it to.

WINS Linkage

Our next topic requires a short detour into the world of Microsoft networking. Networks based on NetBT (NetBIOS over TCP) need to perform name resolution, too: hosts need a way to map NetBIOS names* to IP addresses. The way this name resolution works has evolved over time. In the early days, hosts broadcasted a query on the LAN to resolve a NetBIOS name. This forced all hosts to listen to every broadcast. Since broadcasts don't leave the local LAN, this method didn't allow name resolution beyond the local subnet. The next evolutionary step was the *LMHOSTS* file, which is just a list of NetBIOS names and IP addresses. Every host needed an *LMHOSTS* file to resolve names beyond the local subnet. This model didn't scale very well, either: it was tough to keep the *LMHOSTS* files up-to-date and distribute them. And the introduction of the Dynamic Host Configuration Protocol (DHCP) essentially made basing a network's NetBIOS name resolution on *LMHOSTS* files impossible.

A detailed description of DHCP is beyond the scope of this book,† but suffice it to say that DHCP eliminates the requirement of configuring a static IP address on every one of your hosts. If those hosts support DHCP, they can contact a DHCP server when they boot to obtain an IP address and other configuration parameters, such as the IP addresses of the default router, name servers, and WINS servers.

WINS, which stands for Windows Internet Naming Service, is a Microsoft invention introduced in Windows NT 3.5. The server component of WINS is an implementation of a NetBIOS Name Server as described in RFCs 1001 and 1002. The idea is nothing new; the RFCs date from early 1987. The function of a NetBIOS Name Server is simple: it maps NetBIOS names to IP addresses.

The name and IP address information in a WINS server comes from the various hosts on the network. Once a host sets its IP address using the value sent by a DHCP server, the host registers its name with the WINS server the DHCP server told it about. Actually, any modern NetBT host registers its name with a WINS server, regardless of how it obtained its IP address (e.g., dynamically from a DHCP server or statically from a user-input configuration). Modern NetBT hosts also know to contact a WINS server for NetBIOS name resolution, rather than relying solely on broadcasting or an *LMHOSTS* file.

So where does DNS fit in to all this? Before Windows 2000, it wasn't possible to make the new name-to-IP address mappings generated by the DHCP server visible to

---

* A host's NetBIOS name is simply the name by which it's known for NetBT networking purposes. NetBIOS names are limited to one label of up to 15 octets (that is, no multiple-label names like DNS domain names). On Windows 2000 systems the NetBIOS name is set in the **System Properties** window's **Network Identification** tab (choose **Control Panel → System**). A host's NetBIOS name need not be the same as the hostname portion of its fully qualified domain name in DNS.

† But see another book from O'Reilly & Associates, *TCP/IP Network Administration* by Craig Hunt.

DNS. Microsoft realized there would be some value to enabling a DNS server to query a WINS server, which knows about names for dynamically assigned IP addresses. After all, a NetBIOS name in the WINS server is usually the same as a machine's hostname (the first label of its fully qualified domain name in DNS), which is what it would be in the DNS server if there were an easy way to get it there. (Remember, we're talking about the days before Windows 2000 with its improved integration with DNS.) So a Microsoft DNS Server can be configured to ask a WINS server when it receives a query for a domain name that's not in its zone data.

You may be thinking that a name server contacting a WINS server is kind of silly; isn't there a way for name servers to know what the DHCP servers are doing directly? There is. In a Windows 2000 network, DHCP servers can update name servers after every assignment using the DNS Dynamic Update protocol. We cover this new functionality in Chapter 11. The importance of WINS in Windows 2000 is greatly reduced, too. Windows 2000 hosts can resolve NetBIOS names with DNS rather than WINS, although WINS is still required to support older, legacy clients. You can find more information about how Windows 2000 hosts use DNS for hostname lookups in Chapter 6.

Configuring WINS Lookup

WINS lookup, as it's called, is enabled on a zone-by-zone basis using the **WINS** tab of the zone properties window. When the DNS server receives an address (A) record query for which it doesn't know the answer, if the zone where the record will exist has WINS lookup enabled, the DNS server queries a WINS server. The NetBIOS name sent to the WINS server is the first label of the domain name in the A record query. For example, if the domain name in the A record query is *terminator.movie. edu*, the NetBIOS name queried is *terminator*. If the WINS server responds with an IP address for *terminator*, the DNS server synthesizes an A record for *terminator. movie.edu* and returns it to the original querier.

The WINS lookup configuration for the *movie.edu* zone on the zone's primary master, *terminator*, is shown in Figure 10-5.

WINS lookup is enabled by checking the **Use WINS forward lookup** box. You can specify the IP addresses of up to five WINS servers, and the DNS server will try them in the order listed.

By default, the WINS lookup configuration you establish on the primary master takes effect on the slaves as well. The primary master inserts a special WINS record that gets transferred with the rest of the zone to the slaves. If the slaves are Microsoft DNS Servers, they understand the WINS record and perform WINS lookups accordingly. If the slaves are BIND name servers, they complain about the unknown WINS record. You can suppress sending this WINS record to the slaves by checking **Do not replicate this record**.

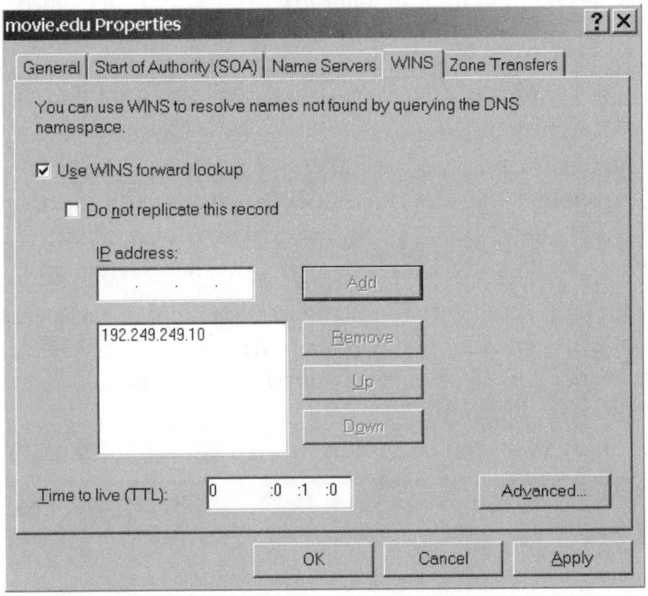

Figure 10-5. WINS lookup settings for movie.edu

The **Time to live (TTL)** field in the lower left corner specifies the TTL for the special WINS record itself. We're not sure why anyone would ever care about this value: a record's TTL applies only to servers that cache it, and the WINS record is meaningful only on a zone's authoritative servers.

Pressing the **Advanced...** button yields a window like that in Figure 10-6. **Cache time-out** controls how long the DNS server will cache the synthesized A records. The default value is 15 minutes. That value may seem small, but it's a good choice: information in the WINS server is transient by nature, so you don't want the DNS server to hold on to it for a long time. If it needs a name again, the DNS server can just ask the WINS server for it. **Lookup time-out** controls how long the DNS server will wait after querying a WINS server. The default is 2 seconds.

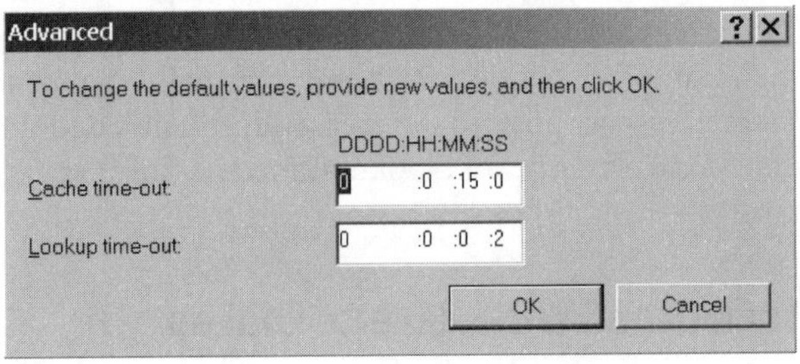

Figure 10-6. Advanced WINS lookup settings

You can enable WINS lookup on *in-addr.arpa* zones, too. It's called WINS reverse lookup, and it's implemented differently than plain WINS lookup. When the name server receives a PTR query it can't answer and WINS reverse lookup is enabled for the zone, it sends a NetBIOS Adapter Status request directly to the IP address referenced by the PTR record. In other words, the name server asks the host directly what its name is. The name server can't ask a WINS server because lookups based on IP address aren't supported: you can't give a WINS server an IP address and get the corresponding NetBIOS name back. WINS servers have obviously never heard of *Jeopardy!* ("The host with IP address 192.249.249.3." "What is *terminator*?")

WINS reverse lookup is configured similarly to WINS lookup: select the **WINS-R** tab of the zone properties window of any *in-addr.arpa* zone. The WINS reverse lookup configuration for the *249.249.192.in-addr.arpa* zone on the zone's primary master, *terminator*, is shown in Figure 10-7.

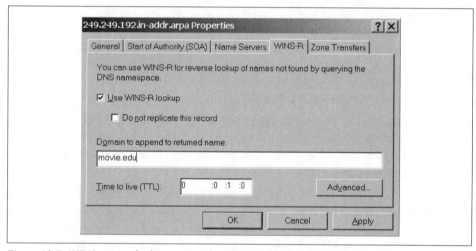

Figure 10-7. WINS reverse lookup settings for 249.249.192.in-addr.arpa

Use WINS-R lookup enables the NetBIOS Adapter Status requests for unknown PTR records in this zone. **Do not replicate this record** has the same effect as its WINS forward-lookup counterpart. If you look in an *in-addr.arpa* zone data file, though, you'll see a WINS-R record instead of a WINS record. The **Domain to append to returned name** field takes a DNS domain name that will be appended to the NetBIOS name returned by the host to form a fully qualified domain name. The **Advanced...** button controls cache and lookup timeouts, just like its WINS forward-lookup counterpart.

Using WINS Lookup and WINS Reverse Lookup

What's WINS lookup good for? In most networks, not a lot. For one thing, Windows 2000 now integrates tightly with DNS so that in a properly configured network, all

Windows 2000 hosts have forward- and reverse-mapping information in DNS. (More information about this new integration with DNS is found in Chapter 11.) But let's say you still have a lot of older Windows hosts on your network. Do you need WINS lookup? Well, we still can't get excited about it. Think about it this way: the names that get resolved the most are the servers, and they usually have fixed IP addresses and thus static DNS entries. They're resolved directly in DNS, not via the WINS lookup detour. Most networks don't have much peer-to-peer networking; your average desktop host usually doesn't offer network services, such as a web server, name server, and so on. It's the need to reach those kinds of network services that require DNS name resolution to work for every host. (Sure, there's a lot of NetBIOS-based file and print sharing among desktop hosts, but that process uses WINS natively.)

If you do need to support WINS lookup in your network, a big problem with it is that the standard BIND name server doesn't support it.* Many people find that they need WINS lookup after they have a DNS infrastructure in place using BIND name servers. One option is to replace all those name servers with the Microsoft DNS Server and enable WINS lookup. That's not realistic for most people. A better, but not perfect, option is to create a new subdomain for DHCP clients resolvable via WINS lookup and delegate the subdomain to a set of Microsoft DNS Servers.

For example, let's say the folks running the domain *acme.com* suddenly find themselves with dozens of PCs doing peer-to-peer networking with DHCP-assigned IP addresses. Since they've already got a BIND infrastructure in place, they decide to create the domain *pcs.acme.com* for these PCs. (The domain name could be anything: *dhcp.acme.com*, *wins.acme.com*, whatever.) They configure a couple of Microsoft DNS Servers for this zone and enable WINS lookup. Finally, they delegate to the *pcs.acme.com* zone from the *acme.com* zone.

In practice, we find WINS reverse lookup is much more useful. It's really nice to have complete reverse-mapping information for your network in DNS. Network-management applications can report names rather than IP addresses. Web servers can log usage statistics by name and make named-based authorization decisions, such as giving access only to hosts in the *movie.edu* domain. Troubleshooting is easier as well. Without WINS reverse lookup, the name server can't reverse map dynamically assigned IP addresses in networks with older Windows hosts. Of course, for you to be able to use WINS reverse lookup in your network, all the name servers for your *in-addr.arpa* zones need to support it.

System Tuning

While the default configuration values will work fine for most sites, yours may be one of the rare sites that needs some further tuning. The following tuning requires

---

* Check Point has ported BIND to Windows 2000 and added WINS lookup and WINS reverse lookup. See *http://www.checkpoint.com/products/metaip/index.html*.

changes to the Registry. All DNS parameters referenced in this section are values of this Registry key:

```
HKEY_LOCAL_MACHINE\SYSTEM\CurrentControlSet\Services\DNS\Parameters
```

More Efficient Zone Transfers

A zone transfer, we said earlier, comprises many DNS messages sent end-to-end over a TCP connection. Traditional zone transfers put only a single resource record in each DNS message. That's a waste of space: you need a full header on each DNS message, even though you're carrying only a single record. It's like being the only person in a Chevy Suburban. A DNS message can carry many more records.

The Microsoft DNS Server understands a relatively new zone-transfer format that puts as many records as possible into a single DNS message. The resulting "many answers" zone transfer takes less bandwidth because there's less overhead and less CPU time because less time is spent unmarshaling DNS messages.

The DNS server uses the "many answers" format by default, which is fine if all your slaves can understand it. Older BIND name servers (prior to Version 4.9.4) can't cope with this format and require the traditional one. Fortunately, you can tell the Microsoft DNS Server to use the traditional method by changing the *BindSecondaries* Registry value. When set to one, the server sends traditional zone transfers to satisfy older BIND servers. The default value is one, but that doesn't affect zone transfers between two Microsoft DNS Servers. They recognize each other, and the master uses the "many answers" format to the slave.

You should change this value only if you have no BIND slaves or if all your BIND slaves are running Version 4.9.4 or later.

Name Server Address Sorting

When you are contacting a host that has multiple network interfaces, using a particular interface may give you better performance. If the multihomed host is local and shares a network (or subnet) with your host, one of the multihomed host's addresses is "closer."

Suppose you have an FTP server on two networks, cleverly called network A and network B, and hosts on both networks access the server often. Hosts on network A will experience better performance if they use the host's interface to network A. Likewise, hosts on network B would benefit from using the host's interface to network B as the address for their FTP client.

In Chapter 4, we mentioned that the Microsoft DNS Server returns all the addresses for a multihomed host. There was no guarantee of the order in which the DNS server would return the addresses, so we assigned aliases (*wh249* and *wh253* for *wormhole*) to the individual interfaces. If one interface is preferable, you (or more realistically, a DNS client) can use an appropriate alias to get the correct address. You can use aliases to choose the "closer" interface but, because of address sorting, they are not always necessary.

The Microsoft DNS Server sorts addresses by default. The server compares the IP address of the querier with the IP addresses of A records in a pending response. It moves those records with the same network as the querier to the top of the list in the response. This comparison is based on the class of network from which each IP address originates. For Class A networks, only the first octet is compared. For Class B networks, the first two octets are compared, and for Class C networks, the first three octets are significant in the comparison. (Nowadays the whole notion of IP network classes is mostly meaningless, having been made obsolete by Classless Inter-Domain Routing, or CIDR. For more information on IP addressing, see Appendix B of O'Reilly's *Internet Core Protocols: The Definitive Guide* by Eric Hall.)

In Figure 10-8, assume that a Microsoft DNS Server is running on *notorious*. When *spellbound* sends a query to *notorious* looking up the addresses of *notorious*, it gets back an answer with *notorious*'s network A address first. When *charade* looks up the addresses of *notorious*, it gets back an answer with *notorious*'s network B address first. In both cases, the name server sorts the addresses in the response based on its comparison of the querier's address with the addresses in the response.

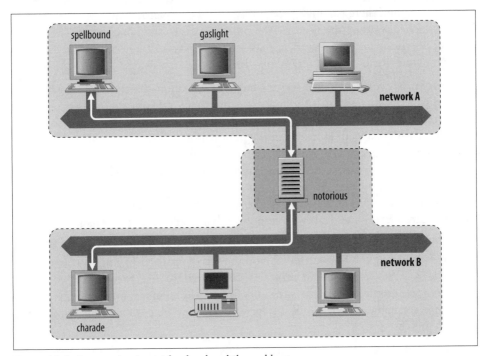

Figure 10-8. Communicating with a local multihomed host

There's a small catch with the DNS server's address sorting: it disables round robin (see "Load Sharing Between Mirrored Servers," later in this chapter). In the Microsoft DNS Server, address sorting is enabled by default and round robin is disabled. If you want round robin and can live without address sorting (unfortunately, they're mutually exclusive), you can disable address sorting with the *LocalNetPriority* registry setting. Set it to zero to disable address sorting and enable round robin. Note, though, that this value doesn't exist in the Registry by default. You need to add it before you can change its value to zero.

Building Up a Large Sitewide Cache with Forwarders

Certain network connections discourage sending large volumes of traffic off-site, either because the network connection is pay-per-packet or because it is a slow link with a high delay, as with a remote office's satellite connection to the company's network. In these situations, you want to limit the off-site DNS traffic to the bare minimum. The Microsoft DNS Server has a feature called *forwarding* to handle this.

If you designate one or more servers at your site as forwarders, all off-site queries are sent to the forwarders first. The idea is that the forwarders handle all off-site queries generated at the site, building up a rich cache of information. For any given query in a remote domain, there is a high probability that the forwarder can answer the query from its cache, avoiding the need for the other servers to send packets off-site. Nothing special is done to these servers to make them forwarders; you modify all the other servers at your site to direct their queries through the forwarders.

A primary master or slave name server's mode of operation changes slightly when it is directed to use a forwarder. If the requested information is already in its database of authoritative data and cache data, it answers with this information; this part of the operation hasn't changed. However, if the information is not in its database, the name server sends the query to a forwarder and waits a short period for an answer before resuming normal operation and contacting the remote servers itself. What the name server is doing that's different is sending a *recursive* query to the forwarder, expecting it to find the answer. At all other times, the name server sends out *nonrecursive* queries to other name servers and deals with responses that refer only to other name servers.

Forwarding is *by server, not by zone*: a server is either forwarding or it isn't. It's configured by selecting the **Forwarders** tab on the server properties window. Figure 10-9 shows how a *movie.edu* name server is configured to use forwarders, assuming *wormhole* and *terminator* are the site's forwarders. (Remember, forwarding is configured on every name server *except* the forwarders themselves—*wormhole* and *terminator* in this case.)

Enable forwarders enables forwarding on this name server. You can specify up to five forwarders. This name server forwards to them in the order in which they're

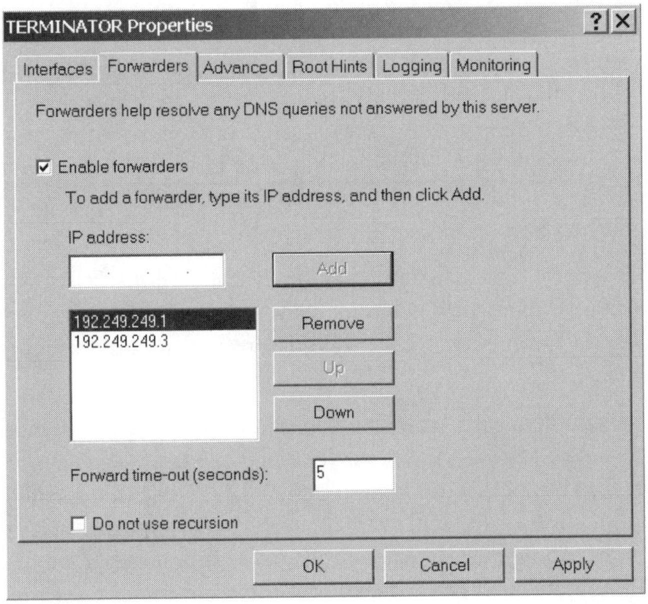

Figure 10-9. Forwarders configuration tab

listed, using a default timeout of five seconds per forwarder; that is, if the first for-warder doesn't respond within five seconds, try the next, wait five more seconds, try the next, and so on. The forwarding timeout can be changed with the **Forward time-out** field. This value is stored in a Registry value, *ForwardingTimeout*, which you can also change. (The list of forwarders is stored in the *Forwarders* value.) We'll talk about the **Do not use recursion** option in the next section.

When you use forwarders, try to keep your site configuration simple. You can end up with configurations that are really twisted. Follow these tips:

- Avoid having "mid-level" servers forward packets (that is, avoid configuring for-warding on your mid-level name servers). Mid-level servers mostly refer name servers to subdomain name servers. If they have been configured to forward packets, do they refer to subdomain name servers, or do they contact the subdo-main name server to find out the answer? Whichever way it works, you're proba-bly making your site configuration too hard for mere mortals (and subdomain administrators) to understand.

- Avoid chaining your forwarders. Don't configure server *a* to forward to server *b*, and configure server *b* to forward to server *c* (or worse yet, back to server *a*).

A More Restricted Name Server

You may want to restrict your name servers even further—stopping them from even *trying* to contact an off-site server if their forwarder is down or doesn't respond. You can do this by telling the server not to fall back to using the recursive resolution process if no forwarders respond: check the **Do not use recursion** box on the **Forwarders** configuration tab (see Figure 10-9). The terminology is confusing: this checkbox has nothing to do with the kind of query being sent to the forwarders. As we said earlier, a name server that's forwarding always sends a recursive query to its forwarders. What this checkbox determines is what happens after that recursive query is sent, which we discuss next. The BIND name server configuration syntax calls this kind of forwarding name server a *forward-only* server, which we think is a good name.

A forward-only server is a variation on a server that forwards. It still answers queries from its authoritative data and cache data. However, it relies completely on its forwarders; it doesn't try to contact other servers for information if the forwarders don't give it an answer.

The slave server contacts each forwarder only once, and it waits a short time for the forwarder to respond. Listing the forwarders multiple times directs the forward-only server to retransmit queries to the forwarders and increases the overall length of time the forward-only name server will wait for an answer from forwarders. You might want to consider listing the forwarders' IP addresses more than once for redundancy: if the first query to a forwarder is lost, the second might still get through and be answered.

However, you must ask yourself if it ever makes sense to use a forward-only server. Such a server is completely dependent on the forwarders. You can achieve much the same configuration (and dependence) by not running a forward-only server at all; instead, configure your hosts' resolvers to point to the forwarders you were using. Thus, you are still relying on the forwarders, but now your applications are querying the forwarders directly instead of having a forward-only name server query them for the applications. You lose the local caching the forward-only server would do as well as the address sorting, but you reduce the overall complexity of your site configuration by running fewer "restricted" name servers.

A Nonrecursive Name Server

By default, resolvers send recursive queries, and name servers do the work required to answer the queries. (If you don't remember how recursion works, refer to Chapter 2.) In the process of finding the answer to recursive queries, the name servers build up a cache of nonauthoritative information about other zones.

In some circumstances, it is undesirable for name servers to do the extra work required to answer a recursive query or to build up a cache of data. The root name servers are an example of these circumstances. The root name servers are too busy to spend extra effort to recursively find the answer to a request. Instead, they send a response based only on the authoritative data they have. The response may contain the answer, but it is more likely that the response contains a referral to other name servers. And since the root servers do not support recursive queries, they do not build up nonauthoritative data caches, which is good because their caches would be huge.*

You can induce the Microsoft DNS Server to run as a nonrecursive name server by setting the *NoRecursion* Registry value to true. By default, the name server supports recursion, and this value is false.

If you choose to make one of your servers nonrecursive, do not configure any of your hosts' resolvers to use it. While you can make your name server nonrecursive, there is no corresponding option to make your resolver work with a nonrecursive name server.†

You can list a nonrecursive name server as one of the servers authoritative for your zone data (that is, you can tell a parent name server to refer queries about your zone to this server). This works because name servers send nonrecursive queries between themselves.

Do not list a nonrecursive name server as a forwarder. When a name server is using another server as a forwarder, it sends the query to the forwarder as a recursive query instead of a nonrecursive query.

Securing Your Name Server

Compared to a modern BIND name server, the Microsoft DNS Server is short on security features, but you do have some options. In this section, we discuss how to prevent unauthorized zone transfers from your servers and how to "lock down" a name server directly connected to the Internet.

Preventing Unauthorized Zone Transfers

It's important to ensure that only your real slave name servers can transfer zones from your primary master name server. Users on remote hosts that can query your name server's zone data can look up data (for example, addresses) only for hosts whose domain names they already know, one at a time. Users who can start zone transfers from your server can list all the hosts in your zones. It's the difference between letting random folks call your company's switchboard and ask for John Q. Cubicle's phone number and sending them a copy of your corporate phone directory.

You control which name servers can perform a zone transfer with settings on the **Zone Transfers** tab of the zone properties window (see Figure 10-3 earlier in this

---

* Note that a root name server doesn't normally receive recursive queries unless a name server's administrator configured it to use a root server as a forwarder, a host's administrator configured its resolver to use the root server as a name server, or a user pointed *nslookup* at the root server.

† In general. Clearly, programs designed to send nonrecursive queries (or ones that can be configured to send nonrecursive queries, like *nslookup*) would still work.

chapter). You can allow any host to perform zone transfers, or only those name servers listed in the zone's NS records, or only a specific set of name servers you list by IP address.

For a primary master name server accessible from the Internet, you definitely want to limit zone transfers to just your slave name servers. You probably don't need to restrict zone transfers on name servers inside your firewall, unless you're worried about your own employees listing your zone data.

Delegated Name Server Configuration

Some of your name servers answer nonrecursive queries from other name servers on the Internet because your name servers appear in NS records delegating your zones to them. We'll call these name servers *delegated* name servers.

You can take special measures to secure your delegated name servers. But first, you should make sure these servers don't receive any recursive queries (i.e., that you don't have any resolvers configured to use these servers and that no name servers use them as forwarders). Some of the precautions we'll take—such as disabling recursive queries—preclude your resolvers from using these servers.

Once you know your name server answers queries only from other name servers, you can turn off recursion. This eliminates a major vector of attack: the most common spoofing attacks involve inducing the target name server to query name servers under the hacker's control by sending the target a recursive query for a domain name in a zone served by the hacker's servers. Disabling recursion is described in the section "A Nonrecursive Name Server" earlier in this chapter. You should also restrict zone transfers of your zones to known slave servers, as described in the previous section.

Load Sharing Between Mirrored Servers

The Microsoft DNS Server has a feature called *round robin* (named after the equivalent feature in the BIND name server): the server rotates address records for the same domain name between responses. For example, if the domain name *foo.bar.baz* has three address records for IP addresses 192.1.1.1, 192.1.1.2, and 192.1.1.3, the round-robin feature causes the name server to give them out first in the order:

```
192.1.1.1 192.1.1.2 192.1.1.3
```

then in the order:

```
192.1.1.2 192.1.1.3 192.1.1.1
```

and then in the order:

```
192.1.1.3 192.1.1.1 192.1.1.2
```

before starting over again with the first order and repeating the rotation ad infinitum.

This functionality is enormously useful if you have a number of equivalent network resources, such as mirrored FTP servers, web servers, or terminal servers, and you'd like to spread the load among them. You establish one domain name that refers to the group of resources and configure clients to access that domain name, and the name server inverse-multiplexes the accesses between the IP addresses you list.

It's a good idea to reduce the records' TTLs, too. This ensures that, if the addresses are cached on an intermediate name server that doesn't support round robin, they'll time out of the cache quickly. If the intermediate name server looks up the name again, your authoritative name server can round-robin the addresses again.

Note that this is really load sharing, not load balancing: the name server gives out the addresses in a completely deterministic way, without regard to the actual load or capacity of the servers servicing the requests. In our example, the server at address 192.1.1.3 could be a 486DX33 running Linux and the other two servers could be HP9000 K420s, and the Linux box would still get a third of the queries.

Note that round robin is disabled by default in favor of name server address sorting. See the end of the earlier section "Name Server Address Sorting" for instructions on how to disable name server address sorting and enable round robin.

## CHAPTER 11

New DNS Features in Windows 2000

In this chapter:
• Active Directory
• Dynamic Update
• Aging and Scavenging
• Incremental Zone Transfer
• Unicode Character Support

The Hatter opened his eyes very wide on hearing this; but all he said was, "Why is a raven like a writing desk?"
"Come, we shall have some fun now!"' thought Alice. "I'm glad they've begun asking riddles—I believe I can guess that," she added aloud.
"Do you mean that you think you can find out the answer to it?" said the March Hare.

Windows 2000 includes many new DNS bells and whistles. The DNS server itself is much improved, with more features than ever that make it more functional and easier to manage. From a client perspective, Windows 2000 as an operating system is more dependent on DNS than any previous operating system from Microsoft. And then there's Active Directory....

Active Directory

Active Directory is *the* major new feature of Windows 2000. It's a hierarchical database of information about all objects in the network: computers, printers, users, and so on. Both users and computers access the information in Active Directory. The Active Directory database is partitioned into *domains* for administrative purposes, and one or more *domain controllers* store information about particular domains. (Compare this to DNS's namespace, which is partitioned into zones, with one or more name servers authoritative for each zone.) The most important fact about Active Directory for our purposes is that it is integrated tightly with DNS. For more—much more—information about Active Directory, see *Windows 2000 Active Directory* by Alistair G. Lowe-Norris (O'Reilly).

Active Directory Domain Names

The most obvious connection between Active Directory and DNS is the naming of domains—Active Directory domains, that is. In the past, under Windows NT, domain names followed the NetBIOS host-naming rules: names consisted of a single label (i.e., no dots) and could contain letters, digits, and limited punctuation. Most Windows dialog boxes forced domain-name input to uppercase, so while they were case-insensitive, you usually saw domain names written in all uppercase. For example, Movie University's Windows NT domain name was *MOVIEU*.

With Windows 2000, all Active Directory domain names are DNS domain names, but—and this is important—not every DNS domain name is an Active Directory domain name.* So while an organization's Active Directory namespace resembles its DNS namespace, the two don't have to be and probably won't be identical. While it's beyond the scope of this book to give an exhaustive explanation of Active Directory namespace design, we can give you some examples to clarify the connection between the naming of Active Directory domains and DNS domains.

Consider Movie University. After reading this far, you're familiar with Movie U.'s DNS namespace: the apex (or top) of the namespace is *movie.edu*, and there are subdomains named *fx.movie.edu*, *classics.movie.edu*, and *comedies.movie.edu*. This namespace is represented in Figure 11-1.

Now let's talk about Movie U.'s Active Directory namespace. An organization's Active Directory domain names correspond to some of its DNS domain names, and the Active Directory domain at the top of an organization's domain tree usually corresponds to a subdomain of the apex of its DNS namespace. In Movie U.'s case, however, the root of the Active Directory domain tree is the same as the apex of the DNS namespace, *movie.edu*. Figure 11-1 shows Movie U.'s Active Directory domain tree beside its DNS namespace. Note how the two diverge, though. For various administrative reasons, the folks over in *fx.movie.edu* need to run their own Active Directory domain. But everyone else at Movie U. is a part of the *movie.edu* Active Directory domain, even though individual hosts fall into different DNS domains.

DNS as Location Broker

You may be wondering why Active Directory domain names are DNS domain names. The answer is that Windows 2000 systems (running in native mode) use DNS as a *location broker*; that is, to find services. Previous versions of Windows used NetBIOS to find domain controllers, but Windows 2000 hosts use DNS. Take the case of a Windows 2000 Professional host at Movie U. that's been joined to the *movie.edu* Active Directory domain. When this system boots up, it sends a series of DNS queries to its configured name server to find a domain controller for the *movie. edu* domain.

---

* And every square is a rectangle, but not all rectangles are squares. All registered mail is certified, but not all certified mail is registered. You get the idea.

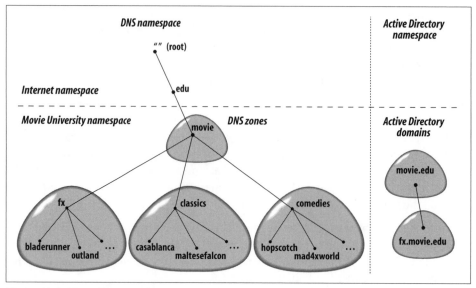

Figure 11-1. Movie University's namespace

The SRV resource record

The particular query sent by the Windows 2000 client is for a resource record type you may not have heard of: the SRV (service location) record. The SRV record, introduced in RFC 2782, is a general mechanism for locating services. Before we can talk in detail about exactly how a Windows 2000 client finds its domain controller using SRV records, we need to describe the SRV record itself.

Locating a service or a particular type of server within a zone is a difficult problem if you don't know which host it runs on. Some zone administrators have attempted to solve this problem by using service-specific aliases in their zones. For example, at Movie U. we created the alias *ftp.movie.edu* and pointed it to the domain name of the host that runs our FTP archive:

```
ftp.movie.edu.    IN    CNAME    plan9.fx.movie.edu.
```

This makes it easy for people to guess a domain name that will get them to our FTP archive and separates the domain name people use to access the archive from the domain name of the host on which it runs. If we were to move the archive to a different host, we could simply change the CNAME record.

Another option, for clients that understand it, is the SRV record. In addition to simply allowing a client to locate the host on which a particular service runs, SRV provides powerful features that allow zone administrators to distribute load and provide backup services, similar to what the MX record provides.

A unique aspect of the SRV record is the format of the domain name to which it's attached. Like the service-specific aliases described earlier, the domain name an SRV record is attached to gives the name of the service sought, but it also includes the protocol it runs over, concatenated with a domain name. The labels representing the service name and the protocol begin with an underscore to distinguish them from labels in the domain name of a host. So, for example:

```
_ftp._tcp.movie.edu
```

represents the SRV records someone *ftp*ing to *movie.edu* should retrieve in order to find the *movie.edu* FTP servers, while:

```
_http._tcp.www.movie.edu
```

represents the SRV records someone accessing the URL *http://www.movie.edu* should look up in order to find the *www.movie.edu* web servers.

The names of the service and protocol must come from the latest Assigned Numbers RFC (the most recent as of this writing is RFC 1700) or be unique names used only locally. Don't use the port or protocol numbers, just the names. When entering SRV records with the DNS console, the service name is limited to eight common services.

The SRV record has four resource record–specific fields: *priority*, *weight*, *port*, and *target*. Priority, weight, and port are unsigned 16-bit numbers (between 0 and 65535). Target is a domain name.

Priority works similarly to the preference in an MX record: the lower the number in the priority field, the more desirable the associated target. When searching for the hosts offering a given service, clients should try targets with the same priority value before trying those with a higher value in the priority field (lower priority values indicate higher priority—confusing, eh?).

Weight allows zone administrators to distribute load to multiple targets. Clients should query targets at the same priority in proportion to their weight. For example, if one target has a priority of zero and a weight of one and another target has a priority of zero but a weight of two, the second target should receive twice as much load (in queries, connections, etc.) as the first. It's up to the service's clients to direct that load: they typically use a system call to choose a random number. If the number is, say, in the top one-third of the range, they try the first target, and if the number is in the bottom two-thirds of the range, they try the second target.

Port specifies the port on which the service being sought is running. This allows zone administrators to run servers on nonstandard ports. For example, an administrator can use SRV records to point web browsers at a web server running on port 8000 instead of the standard HTTP port (80).

Finally, target specifies the domain name of a host on which the service is running (on the port specified in the port field). Target must be the canonical name of the host (not an alias), with address records attached to it.

So, for the *movie.edu* FTP server, we might add two SRV records to the *movie.edu* zone. Adding the first with the DNS console is shown in Figure 11-2.

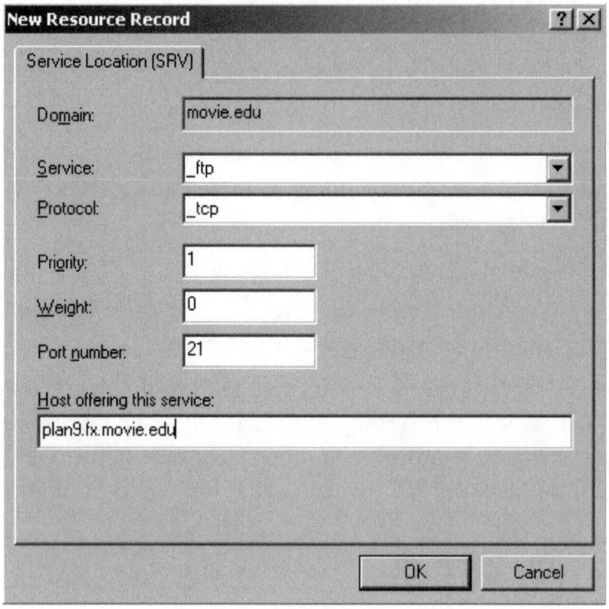

Figure 11-2. Adding an SRV record with the DNS console

After adding the second record, the *movie.edu* zone data file (*movie.edu.dns*) contains these records:

```
_ftp._tcp.movie.edu.  IN  SRV  1  0  21  plan9.fx.movie.edu.
                      IN  SRV  2  0  21  thing.fx.movie.edu.
```

This instructs SRV-capable FTP clients to try the FTP server on *plan9.fx.movie.edu*'s port 21 first when accessing *movie.edu*'s FTP service and then to try the FTP server on *thing.fx.movie.edu*'s port 21 if *plan9.fx.movie.edu*'s FTP server isn't available.

The records:

```
_http._tcp.www.movie.edu.  IN  SRV  0  2  80    www.movie.edu.
                           IN  SRV  0  1  80    www2.movie.edu.
                           IN  SRV  1  1  8000 postmanrings2x.movie.edu.
```

direct web queries for *www.movie.edu* (the web site) to port 80 on *www.movie.edu* (the host) and *www2.movie.edu*, with *www.movie.edu* getting twice the queries *www2.movie.edu* does. If neither is available, queries go to *postmanrings2x.movie.edu* on port 8000.

But don't get excited and add SRV records for your FTP and web servers: few clients actually use SRV records to locate their servers. In fact, we're not aware of any FTP clients or web browsers that look up SRV records. On the other hand, when Microsoft was looking for a way to have Windows 2000 clients find their domain controllers, SRV records fit the bill perfectly.

DNS resource records needed by a domain controller

A Windows 2000 client needs to reach several services on its domain controller. Clients communicate with Active Directory itself using the Lightweight Directory Access Protocol (LDAP).[*] Authentication and authorization are handled by Kerberos.[†] A domain controller needs DNS to "advertise" the availability of these services. The resource records needed by the *movie.edu* Active Directory domain look like this:

```
movie.edu. 600 IN A 192.249.249.3
_ldap._tcp.movie.edu. 600 IN SRV 0 100 389 terminator.movie.edu.
_ldap._tcp.pdc._msdcs.movie.edu. 600 IN SRV 0 100 389 terminator.movie.edu.
_ldap._tcp.6e10690c-40a2-4383-98a7-c716ef9266d1.domains._msdcs.movie.edu.
    600 IN SRV 0 100 389 terminator.movie.edu.
260aad2b-3ce7-41c2-923e-8e7bec165788._msdcs.movie.edu. 600 IN CNAME
    terminator.movie.edu.
_kerberos._tcp.dc._msdcs.movie.edu. 600 IN SRV 0 100 88 terminator.movie.edu.
_ldap._tcp.dc._msdcs.movie.edu. 600 IN SRV 0 100 389 terminator.movie.edu.
_kerberos._tcp.movie.edu. 600 IN SRV 0 100 88 terminator.movie.edu.
_kerberos._udp.movie.edu. 600 IN SRV 0 100 88 terminator.movie.edu.
_kpasswd._tcp.movie.edu. 600 IN SRV 0 100 464 terminator.movie.edu.
_kpasswd._udp.movie.edu. 600 IN SRV 0 100 464 terminator.movie.edu.
_ldap._tcp.Default-First-Site-Name._sites.movie.edu. 600 IN SRV 0 100 389
    terminator.movie.edu.
_kerberos._tcp.Default-First-Site-Name._sites.dc._msdcs.movie.edu.
    600 IN SRV 0 100 88 terminator.movie.edu.
_ldap._tcp.Default-First-Site-Name._sites.dc._msdcs.movie.edu.
    600 IN SRV 0 100 389 terminator.movie.edu.
_kerberos._tcp.Default-First-Site-Name._sites.movie.edu.
    600 IN SRV 0 100 88 terminator.movie.edu.
_ldap._tcp.gc._msdcs.movie.edu. 600 IN SRV 0 100 3268 terminator.movie.edu.
gc._msdcs.movie.edu. 600 IN A 192.249.249.3
_gc._tcp.movie.edu. 600 IN SRV 0 100 3268 terminator.movie.edu.
_ldap._tcp.Default-First-Site-Name._sites.gc._msdcs.movie.edu.
    600 IN SRV 0 100 3268 terminator.movie.edu.
_gc._tcp.Default-First-Site-Name._sites.movie.edu. 600 IN SRV 0 100 3268
    terminator.movie.edu.
```

The *movie.edu* domain has one domain controller, *terminator.movie.edu*. You can see that the target of every SRV record (that is, the host providing the service) is *terminator*. Notice the various services provided by *terminator*: LDAP over TCP, Kerberos over TCP and UDP, etc. For an explanation of the function of each of the records needed by a domain controller, see Microsoft Knowledge Base article Q178169.

Also notice two A records hiding among all those SRV records:

```
movie.edu. 600 IN A 192.249.249.3
gc._msdcs.movie.edu. 600 IN A 192.249.249.3
```

---

[*] LDAP is an Internet standard defined in RFC 2251.

[†] Kerberos is also an Internet standard—see RFC 1510.

The first A record is for LDAP clients that don't understand SRV records. Since Windows 2000 clients do use SRV records to locate the LDAP service on the domain controller, you don't need that domain A record (the one for *movie.edu*) unless you're using other LDAP clients. (And even then, you can just point those clients at the domain controller using its fully qualified name: *terminator.movie.edu*, in this case.) It's good that the A record isn't required, because a lot of folks already have an A record at the apex of their DNS namespace. This record usually points to a web server, not to an Active Directory server. For example, Movie U.'s main web server is accessible via both *www.movie.edu* and *movie.edu*. However, note that the second A record, which points to the Global Catalog service on the domain controller, is required.

This discussion begs the question: how do those SRV records get there? Are you dreading that you'll have to type them in yourself? Never fear—the domain controller adds these records to DNS itself, using a recent DNS protocol enhancement called dynamic update. We'll discuss dynamic update soon, along with more details about how domain controllers update DNS with the records they require.

One final note: if we had multiple domain controllers for *movie.edu*, there would be an additional set of records for each one.

Storing Zones in Active Directory

Zone storage is another Active Directory–DNS integration point. With the previous version of the Microsoft DNS Server in NT Server 4.0 (or a standard BIND name server, for that matter), a name server loads zones from two places. If the name server is a primary master for a zone, it loads that zone from a file on disk. If the name server is a secondary master (or a slave, to use the newer term used by recent DNS-related RFCs), it loads the zone from another authoritative server (usually the primary master) over the network, using a zone transfer. The purpose of this traditional primary/secondary relationship is to facilitate replication. A zone needs multiple authoritative servers for redundancy and to spread the query load. The zone transfer is DNS's built-in replication mechanism: as you know, just change the zone on the primary, and the change eventually percolates to the secondaries.

The Microsoft DNS Server gives you a third option, called *Active Directory integration*. Rather than being stored in a file on the primary master's disk, the zone data is stored in the Active Directory database. This option is available only when the DNS server is running on a domain controller. The reasoning is that since Active Directory already has its own replication topology—a "multimaster" scheme in which each domain controller can accept changes and propagate them to the other domain controllers—why not just take advantage of Active Directory's replication for DNS zones, rather than designing a separate primary/secondary topology?

There are at least a couple of reasons why you'd want to opt for Active Directory integration for your zones. While it does save you from designing and implementing primary/secondary relationships for all your name servers and zones, the main reason is secure dynamic update. Microsoft has extended the standard DNS dynamic update protocol, allowing it to work with the Active Directory security model, but this feature is available only with Active Directory–integrated zones. Secure dynamic update alone is enough reason to store zone information in Active Directory.

One other note about Active Directory–integrated zones: strictly speaking, you don't have to make every name server for a zone Active Directory integrated. Since all authoritative servers allow zone transfers, a server that loads a zone from Active Directory will happily respond to zone transfers. So you can conceivably make only a zone's primary master name server Active Directory integrated and have the secondaries continue to load from the primary. However, it defeats one of the purposes of Active Directory integration—letting Active Directory handle zone replication—to use traditional zone transfers. The other huge advantage of Active Directory integration is secure dynamic update, which isn't possible if only the primary master is Active Directory integrated. So to take full advantage of Active Directory integration, all name servers for a zone should store the zone in Active Directory.

Dynamic Update

Dynamic update is a major new feature implemented in the Microsoft DNS Server. Like many other protocols used by Windows 2000, it's an Internet standard, defined in RFC 2136. Dynamic update is simply a protocol that allows a name server to be updated by sending it a message over the network. This is a big improvement over the traditional method, which requires a human to fire up the DNS console to make the change in person. Dynamic update allows nonhumans—i.e., programs—to easily update DNS information.

No security is built into the dynamic update protocol. It's up to an individual name server to decide whether or not to accept an update message. About the only means of authentication a name server has is to look at the source IP address of the dynamic update message, and that's not a very strong means of authentication at all: it's easy to "spoof" or forge a packet's source IP address. And since a complete dynamic update message travels in a single UDP packet, all an attacker needs to know is an IP address that the name server accepting dynamic updates trusts. The Bad Guy just creates a dynamic update with a spoofed source IP address and sends it to the unsuspecting name server.

This deficiency begs for some stronger security based on cryptography, which fortunately has been developed. The DNS standards community developed a protocol extension to use *transaction signatures* to sign any kind of DNS message—including dynamic updates—sent between two parties: client to server, server to server, dynamic updater to server, etc.

The transaction signatures, or TSIGs for short, in DNS use a technique called HMAC (Keyed-Hashing for Message Authentication),[*] which employs a shared secret and a one-way cryptographic hash function to sign data. A shared secret is like a password known only to the two parties. A one-way cryptographic hash function computes a fixed-size checksum based on any amount of input. What differentiates a cryptographic hash function, such as MD5 or SHA1, from a run-of-the-mill checksum, such as a CRC (Cyclic Redundancy Check), is that it's computationally infeasible to find two different input streams that produce the same hash output. With a CRC checksum, on the other hand, the algorithm is easily reversible: given any checksum, it's trivial to calculate an input stream to generate that checksum. Another property of a good cryptographic hash function is that varying the input by even a small amount—such as changing just one bit—produces a major change in the hash output. In other words, the hash output is like a fingerprint of the original input.

A transaction signature is so-named because it's ephemeral: the signature applies only to a single transaction and is not reusable. Let's say a client wants to send a dynamic update signed with a TSIG to the appropriate name server. After generating the dynamic update message, it appends the secret it shares with the server to the message and runs everything through MD5. The output is the TSIG itself, which is placed into a TSIG resource record that goes in the dynamic update message. Since TSIGs are generated on the fly like this, you see a TSIG record only on a packet sniffer, never in the DNS console or a zone data file. Note that TSIG doesn't encrypt the data being sent: it only authenticates it. HMAC is illustrated in Figure 11-3.

One difficulty with TSIG is distributing the shared secrets. Imagine having hundreds of clients that need to send TSIG-signed dynamic updates to a name server: that requires generating hundreds of keys and distributing them securely to each client. Microsoft found itself in just such a predicament. As we'll see shortly, individual Windows 2000 clients do send dynamic updates to name servers. TSIG is a requirement for these transactions to happen securely, but it's not feasible to statically configure shared secrets on each Windows 2000 client. The solution: Kerberos to the rescue!

As we mentioned earlier, Windows 2000 uses Kerberos for authentication and authorization. Kerberos allows two parties who want to communicate securely to negotiate the necessary information to do so. Every Windows 2000 domain controller is a Kerberos Key Distribution Center, or KDC. Every Windows 2000 client and server is a Kerberos "principal." Every Kerberos principal shares a secret with the KDC. (This shared secret is generated when the host is joined to the domain.) The KDC acts as a trusted third party that allows two principals to communicate securely. For example, suppose a client named Alice wants to send an encrypted

[*] See RFC 2104.

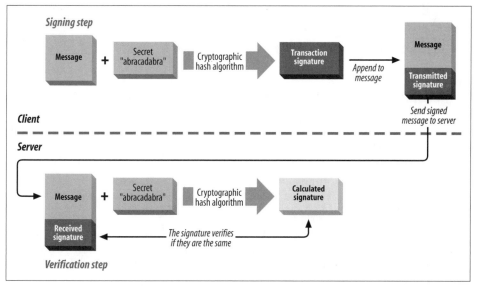

Figure 11-3. HMAC illustrated

message to a client named Bob. Alice asks the KDC to help negotiate a session key[*] with Bob. Alice and Bob don't (yet) trust each other, but they do trust the KDC, which facilitates distributing the session key to both of them. This explanation is quite an oversimplification of how Kerberos actually works, but it does show the underlying concepts.

Microsoft extended TSIG in Windows 2000 to use Kerberos. A Windows 2000 client that wants to send a TSIG-signed dynamic update message to a name server doesn't have to be statically configured to share a secret with that server. The client uses Kerberos to obtain a session key, which serves as a one-time shared secret. This variant of TSIG is called GSS-TSIG and is documented in an Internet-Draft.[†]

Domain Controller Behavior

Earlier we showed the records required by domain controllers for clients to locate them. To ensure that these important records are always present, the Netlogon service running on the domain controller attempts to add them to DNS using dynamic update once per hour. A copy of these records can be found in the file *%SystemRoot%\system32\config\netlogon.dns*.

It's worth describing exactly how the Netlogon service attempts to add these records. As an example, we'll show the steps followed by the *movie.edu* domain controller to

---

[*] As the name implies, a session key is a short-lived key usually used for a single conversation.

[†] GSS stands for Generic Security Service. At the time of this writing, GSS-TSIG was not yet an Internet standard but was on track to become one. Internet-Drafts may be found at *ftp://ftp.ietf.org/internet-drafts/*.

register this SRV record (which happens to be the first one in the list of records we showed previously):

```
_ldap._tcp.movie.edu. 600 IN SRV 0 100 389 terminator.movie.edu.
```

The steps are:

1. Look up the SOA record for _ldap._tcp.movie.edu on the local name server. Though there isn't an SOA record for that domain name, the authority section of the NXDOMAIN (negative) response includes the SOA record of the zone that should contain the _ldap._tcp.movie.edu SRV record, which in this case is *movie.edu*.

2. Look up the address of the name server in the MNAME field of the SOA record, *terminator.movie.edu* (if necessary). Recall that the MNAME field of the SOA record lists the zone's primary master name server, which is where the dynamic update should be sent. Along with the SOA record, the Microsoft DNS Server returns the A record corresponding to the MNAME field in the additional section of the negative response. In that case, no extra A record lookup is needed.

3. Send a dynamic update to *terminator.movie.edu* to add the SRV record for the domain name _ldap._tcp.movie.edu.

These steps are repeated for every record: first the SOA query as a "probe" to discover which zone the record should reside in, then the A-record query, and then the dynamic update itself. Note the significance of the SOA query: this means that you don't have to have a zone corresponding to each Active Directory domain. For example, imagine Movie U. has another Active Directory domain named *fx.movie.edu* but no *fx.movie.edu* zone in the DNS namespace. Now consider the behavior when the *fx.movie.edu* domain controller attempts to register its first SRV record for _ldap._tcp.fx.movie.edu. It sends an SOA query for this domain name but, since there's no *fx.movie.edu* zone, the negative response includes the SOA record for the *movie.edu* zone. As a result, the domain controller attempts to add the _ldap._tcp.fx.movie.edu SRV record to the *movie.edu* zone. In fact, if there were no *movie.edu* zone, the domain controller would even try to update the *edu* zone! It doesn't attempt to send dynamic updates to the root zone, though, which is a good thing.

Two Registry settings are used to control the Netlogon service's dynamic update behavior.[*]

First, to stop Netlogon from attempting to register the necessary records with dynamic update once an hour, create the following Registry key:

```
UseDynamicDns
HKEY_LOCAL_MACHINE\SYSTEM\CurrentControlSet\Services\Netlogon\Parameters
```

---

[*] See Microsoft Knowledge Base article Q246804 for more information about all aspects of Windows 2000 dynamic update behavior.

```
Data type: REG_DWORD
Range: 0 - 1
Default value: 1
```

Set the value to zero. The Netlogon service periodically checks this Registry key, so you don't need to restart the service or reboot the machine.

You'll want to suppress repeated dynamic updates if you don't want to enable dynamic updates on your name server or if it doesn't allow dynamic updates. However, with Microsoft's secure dynamic update, there's really no reason not to enable dynamic updates. If you're running a BIND name server (which doesn't support Microsoft's particular version of secure dynamic update), however, you might want to disable dynamic update and instead add the necessary resource records to your zone by hand. In that case, it's pointless to have the domain controllers continuously attempting to send dynamic updates.[*]

Another useful Registry setting prevents Netlogon from registering A records with dynamic update:

```
RegisterDnsARecords
HKEY_LOCAL_MACHINE\SYSTEM\CurrentControlSet\Services\Netlogon\Parameters

Data type: REG_DWORD
Range: 0 - 1
Default value: 1
```

Set this key to zero to stop Netlogon from registering the two A records from *movie.edu*'s zone:

```
movie.edu. 600 IN A 192.249.249.3
gc._msdcs.movie.edu. 600 IN A 192.249.249.3
```

Recall that the first one is not required, so setting this key to zero stops Netlogon from repeatedly registering an A record for your domain that might conflict with other records, such as those for your web server. On the other hand, the second record is required, so if you disable automatic A-record registration, you have to add the second record by hand. Remember that you can always check *%SystemRoot%\ system32\config\netlogon.dns* for the exact list of records your domain controller expects to be present in DNS.

Windows 2000 Client Behavior

Every Windows 2000 host uses dynamic update to maintain the proper DNS information about itself. The DHCP client service sends the updates, regardless of whether the host actually uses DHCP to obtain any IP addresses. If a Windows 2000 host does not use DHCP, it attempts to register name and address information for

---

[*] The fourth (and latest) edition of our sister book, *DNS and BIND*, discusses Windows 2000 and BIND name server coexistence in Chapter 16.

itself in DNS. Specifically, it sends dynamic updates to the appropriate authoritative name servers to add the appropriate A and PTR records. If the host does get an address from a DHCP server, it still registers the A record itself but allows the DHCP server to register the corresponding PTR record.*

This self-registration with dynamic update is feasible only with Microsoft's secure dynamic update. With Kerberos, the Windows 2000 host attempting the registration can authenticate itself to the DNS server. The DNS server can, in turn, implement a fine-grained authorization policy that allows a host to change only the A and PTR records corresponding to its own domain name and IP address.

This feature extends a client's behavior dealing with its NetBIOS name to the DNS world. If a Windows (including Windows 2000) host is configured to use a WINS server, it registers its NetBIOS name and address with that server.

Dynamic update behavior is controlled from the **DNS** tab of the **Advanced TCP/IP Settings** window for each network interface. Getting to this window takes a fair amount of clicking:

1. Choose **Settings → Network and Dial-up Connections**

2. Double-click on a LAN interface to display its status window.

3. Click **Properties** to display the properties window for the interface. Make sure the **General** tab is selected.

4. Click on **Internet Protocol (TCP/IP)**, then click **Properties** to display the **Internet Protocol (TCP/IP) Properties** window.

5. Click **Advanced**, which displays the **Advanced TCP/IP Settings** window.

6. Select the **DNS** tab, and you'll see a window like the one shown in Figure 11-4.

Most of the settings on the **Advanced TCP/IP Settings** window deal with resolver configuration, which we discussed in Chapter 6. The dynamic update settings are at the bottom of the window. **Register this connection's addresses in DNS** is checked by default, and this setting controls whether or not the client attempts registration with dynamic update (whether it registers both A and PTR records or just an A record is determined by the DHCP settings, as we mentioned previously).

By default, the host registers its fully qualified domain name. Windows 2000 calls the fully qualified domain name the *full computer name*. It's the concatenation of the host's single-label computer name and the primary DNS suffix which, by default, is set to the DNS name of the Active Directory domain to which the computer is joined. The full computer name is displayed on the **Network Identification** tab of the **System** Control Panel document, which is shown in Figure 11-5. To change the computer name, click **Properties**.

---

* Actually, a host will register one A record for each IP address it has.

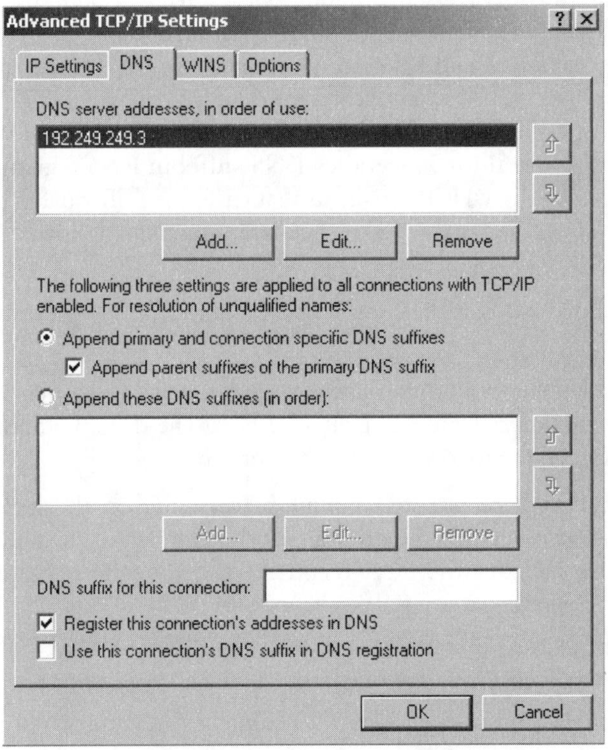

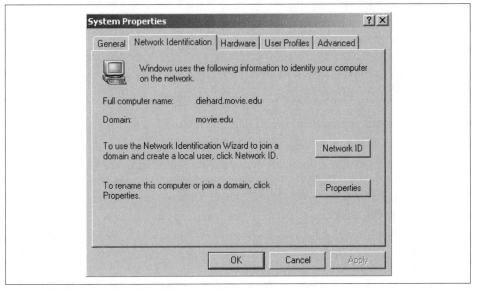

Figure 11-4. Advanced TCP/IP Settings

Figure 11-5. Network Identification tab

If you'd like the host to register an additional FQDN in addition to the primary FQDN (or full computer name), enter another domain name in the **DNS suffix for this connection** field and check **Use this connection's DNS suffix in DNS registration**. The additional FQDN is a concatenation of a single-label computer name and the connection-specific DNS suffix. If you don't specify the **DNS suffix for this connection** but check **Use this connection's DNS suffix in DNS registration**, the DNS suffix is specified by the DHCP server. In that case, the fully qualified domain name registered consists of the host's single-label computer name followed by the contents of the suffix field.

So what gets added when a client registers? Let's reboot a Windows 2000 client in the special-effects lab and see.

Our client is called *mummy.fx.movie.edu*. It has the fixed IP address 192.253.254.13 (it doesn't get its address from our DHCP server). The dynamic update routines on the client go through the following steps at boot time:

1. Look up the SOA record for *mummy.fx.movie.edu* on the local name server. Though there isn't an SOA record for that domain name, the authority section of the response includes the SOA record of the zone that contains *mummy.fx. movie.edu, fx.movie.edu*.

2. Look up the address of the name server in the MNAME field of the SOA record, *bladerunner.fx.movie.edu*.

3. Send a dynamic update to *bladerunner.fx.movie.edu* with two prerequisites: that *mummy.fx.movie.edu* not be an alias (i.e., that it not own a CNAME record) and that it not already have an address record pointing to 192.253.254.13. The dynamic update contains no update section; it's just a probe to see what's out there.

4. If *mummy.fx.movie.edu* already points to its address, stop. Otherwise, send another dynamic update to *bladerunner.fx.movie.edu* with the prerequisites that *mummy.fx.movie.edu* not be an alias and that it not have an A record already. If the prerequisites are satisfied, the update adds an A record pointing *mummy.fx. movie.edu* to 192.253.254.13. If *mummy.fx.movie.edu* already has an A record, the client sends an update to delete that A record and add its own.

5. Look up the SOA record for *254.253.192.in-addr.arpa*.

6. Look up the address of the name server in the MNAME field of the SOA record (though since the MNAME field contains *bladerunner.fx.movie.edu*, which we looked up recently, and Windows 2000 has a caching resolver, this shouldn't require another query).

7. Send a dynamic update to *bladerunner.fx.movie.edu* with the prerequisite that *13.254.253.192.in-addr.arpa* not be an alias. If the prerequisite is satisfied, the update adds a PTR record mapping 192.253.254.13 back to *mummy.fx.movie. edu*. If *13.254.253.192.in-addr.arpa* is an alias, stop.

Registry settings

Several Registry settings affect a Windows 2000 host's dynamic DNS behavior:

Address conflict behavior

> This is one Registry entry you should consider changing if you are aren't using a Windows 2000 Microsoft DNS Server and your name server is therefore forced to accept unsigned dynamic updates. By default, a Windows 2000 host unceremoniously deletes what it considers old A records for itself. For example, if the host we rebooted earlier discovered other A records for *mummy.fx.movie.edu*, it would delete them and then add a new one with its current IP address. The problem is, what if those were legitimate records? The host could be configured with the wrong name; maybe those A records are for the real *mummy.fx.movie.edu*. Setting this key to a value of one disables the overwriting behavior.

```
DisableReplaceAddressesInConflicts
HKEY_LOCAL_MACHINE\SYSTEM\CurrentControlSet\Services\Tcpip\Parameters

Data type: REG_DWORD
Range: 0 - 1
Default value: 0
Scope: Affects all adapters
```

Reregistration interval

> By default, the DHCP client service sends a dynamic update every 24 hours to register a host's A (and PTR, if applicable) records. This behavior is an insurance policy against the records being lost from the zone. There's little reason to change this value.

```
DefaultRegistrationRefreshInterval
HKEY_LOCAL_MACHINE\SYSTEM\CurrentControlSet\Services\Tcpip\Parameters

Data type: REG_DWORD
Range: 0x0 - 0xFFFFFFFF seconds
Default value: 0x15180 (86,400 seconds = 24 hours)
Scope: Affects all adapters
```

Default TTL

> By default, dynamically added resource records have a time to live of 20 minutes. It makes sense to lower this value if you have a large number of hosts changing addresses frequently (such as laptops moving around) and you find DNS information is getting outdated. Recall, however, that this value doesn't affect the authoritative name servers for the zone containing the dynamically added records. Changes to authoritative servers take effect immediately and are propagated quickly, thanks to the NOTIFY protocol. The issue is records remaining in the cache of other name servers after the hosts move.

```
DefaultRegistrationTTL
HKEY_LOCAL_MACHINE\SYSTEM\CurrentControlSet\Services\Tcpip\Parameters

Data type: REG_DWORD
```

```
Range: 0x0 - 0xFFFFFFFF seconds
Default value: 0x4B0 (1,200 seconds = 20 minutes)
Scope: Affects all adapters
```

Maximum number of addresses to register

If a network adapter has multiple virtual addresses, by default only the first is registered using dynamic update. This value sets the maximum number of virtual addresses to register on a per-interface basis. Setting the value to zero disables dynamic updates for this interface.

```
MaxNumberOfAddressesToRegister
HKEY_LOCAL_MACHINE\SYSTEM\CurrentControlSet\Services\Tcpip\Parameters\Adapters\
interface-name

Data type: REG_DWORD
Range: 0x0 - 0xFFFFFFFF
Default value: 0x1
Scope: Affects this adapter only
```

Update security level

By default, a Windows 2000 host first sends unsigned dynamic updates (i.e., it doesn't use Microsoft's security-enhanced method). If those updates fail, it attempts to negotiate a session key and sign the updates. The default value is 0x0. A value of 0x10 means send only nonsecure updates, and a value of 0x100 means send only secure updates. If you have only Windows 2000 name servers (or only non–Windows 2000 name servers), you can set this value accordingly to avoid sending unnecessary updates.

```
UpdateSecurityLevel
HKEY_LOCAL_MACHINE\SYSTEM\CurrentControlSet\Services\Tcpip\Parameters

Data type: REG_DWORD
Range: 0x0 | 0x10 | 0x100
Default value: 0x0
Scope: Affects all adapters
```

A reboot is required to make any of these Registry changes effective.

DHCP Server Behavior

Still another Windows 2000 component that uses dynamic update is the Windows 2000 DHCP server. The dynamic update behavior is set on a per-scope basis. Every scope has a properties window, and dynamic update is configured using the settings on its **DNS** tab. Right-click on a scope in the DHCP console and select **Properties** to produce a window like the one shown in Figure 11-6.

Note that the DHCP server itself has a properties window (right-click on a particular server in the DHCP console and select **Properties**) with an identical **DNS** tab, but the server settings provide defaults only for newly created scopes. The settings of a given scope control the server's dynamic update behavior for addresses given out from that scope. Figure 11-6 shows the default dynamic update settings for an

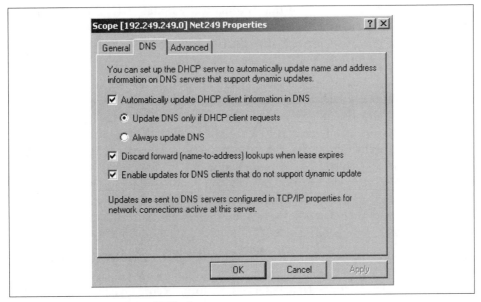

Figure 11-6. Scope properties, DNS tab

unconfigured server. If you don't change them, every scope created has these dynamic update settings.

The wording of the settings is a little confusing. The first one, **Automatically update DHCP client information in DNS**, applies only to DHCP clients that support the DHCP Fully Qualified Domain Name (FQDN) option, which has code number 81. This option has been defined only recently: at the time of this writing, the document describing it is an Internet-Draft and not yet an RFC. The FQDN option lets a DHCP client inform the DHCP server of its fully qualified domain name and also tell the server its intention about registering A and PTR records. This option can also be sent from server to client to let the server respond to the client's request and specify its intentions. In the Microsoft operating system family, only Windows 2000 DHCP clients support the FQDN option, and we've already mentioned how Windows 2000 DHCP clients use it: they specify their FQDN (computer name plus its primary DNS suffix) and inform the server of their intention to register their own A records.

If **Automatically update DHCP client information in DNS** is selected, you must tell the server how to deal with a DHCP client's FQDN option request regarding dynamic update. The default setting is **Update DNS only if DHCP client requests**, which causes the server to honor the client's dynamic update requests. On the other hand, checking **Always update DNS** causes the server to always send dynamic updates for both A and PTR records, regardless of the client's request.

The next setting, **Discard forward (name-to-address) lookups when lease expires**, applies to A records. When a Windows 2000 DHCP server is configured to send dynamic updates—that is, when the **Automatically update DHCP client information in DNS** box is checked—the server always sends a dynamic update to remove a client's PTR record when its lease expires. Checking this box causes the server to remove the client's A record with dynamic update, too.

The final setting, **Enable updates for DNS clients that do not support dynamic update**, applies to any DHCP client that doesn't send the FQDN option—in other words, all versions of Windows before Windows 2000. If this box is checked, the DHCP server always updates A and PTR records for every lease issued to clients that don't pass the FQDN option. Since the client doesn't inform the server of its FQDN, the server has to calculate it by concatenating the values from two other DHCP options: Host Name (code 12) and DNS Domain Name (code 15). The DHCP server uses the value of the Host Name option sent by the client plus the value of the DNS Domain Name option defined in the scope from which the address is being leased. The server ignores any client-set value for the DNS Domain Name option.

Another dynamic update–related feature of the Windows 2000 DHCP server is the *DnsUpdateProxy* built-in security group. This group solves a couple of problems. The first is when multiple DHCP servers perform secure dynamic update. The Microsoft DNS Server's access controls allow only the owner of a dynamically created record to change or delete it. Imagine a DHCP registering a PTR record on a client's behalf, then failing and being replaced by a backup DHCP server. If the original server became the owner of the record when creating it, the backup server would be unable to delete the record when the lease expired. The DnsUpdateProxy group solves this problem: when members of this group register records with dynamic update, they aren't marked as the owner. The first nonmember of DnsUpdateProxy to modify the records becomes the owner. To solve the DHCP server problem mentioned earlier, both computers should be members of the DnsUpdateProxy group. Another problem solved is when a DHCP server registers a PTR record on behalf of a "legacy" (i.e., non–Windows 2000) client that can't perform its own dynamic updates. If the client were later upgraded to Windows 2000, without this feature it wouldn't be able to update its own record.

The "you touch it, you own it" properties of this group can cause problems, though. Since group ownership applies to the entire computer and not just the DHCP server, any records registered by the computer have this no-owner property. Recall that domain controllers register all kinds of important records. So if you run a DHCP server on a domain controller and you make that machine a member of DnsUpdateProxy, anyone can come along and take ownership of the (very important) records registered by the domain controller's Netlogon service. In addition, a DHCP server running on a domain controller uses local system privileges to modify the DNS records and therefore may update records registered by other computers in a secure zone. (This particular problem and its solution are described in Microsoft Knowledge Base article Q255134.) For these reasons, Microsoft recommends that you don't run a DHCP server on a domain controller.

Aging and Scavenging

Zones with dynamic update enabled are prone to stale records; that is, A or PTR records that are dynamically added but not properly removed when no longer necessary. Most DHCP clients—including Windows clients—don't release their addresses on shutdown, which means they don't send the corresponding dynamic update message to remove their A records (nor does the DHCP server send a dynamic update message to remove the PTR record). Imagine a transient host, such as a laptop, that receives but never releases an address, leaving A and PTR records in DNS. Microsoft refers to these records as *stale*, and the DNS server in Windows 2000 can track their age and remove, or *scavenge*, them when they are no longer necessary.

The DNS server knows a record is not stale when it receives a dynamic update request for it. A Windows 2000 host sends a dynamic update message for its A record (and PTR record, if configured with a static address) every 24 hours by default. Windows 2000 hosts also send dynamic updates on lease renewal. An update of an existing record is called a *refresh*. (Before sending the update to make any changes, clients actually probe for a record's existence by sending a dynamic update message with only a prerequisite section. The DNS server counts such a message as a refresh, too.) A refresh is the signal to the server that a particular client is still alive and using its records.

The idea behind aging and scavenging is to remove records that haven't been refreshed within a certain interval. The primary master server stores a timestamp for each resource record in zones with aging and scavenging enabled. Every time a record is created, modified, or refreshed, the server updates the timestamp with the current time. If the primary master is Active Directory integrated, it replicates these timestamps to the other servers (since all primary masters may need to perform aging and scavenging). A large number of dynamic updates means a large number of refresh events and corresponding timestamp updates, which means a lot of replication traffic if the zone is Active Directory integrated.

To reduce the replication burden of this algorithm, Microsoft introduced the concept of a "no-refresh" interval. After a record is refreshed and its timestamp is updated, the server will not process additional refresh events (nor update the record's timestamp) for the length of the no-refresh interval. Note that each record has its own refresh or no-refresh timer ticking away. The record can still be changed, though, which does cause its timestamp to be updated. Remember, a refresh is just a dynamic update that doesn't cause any changes[*] because the records specified in the update are already present in the zone. The no-refresh interval is like a cooling-off period that cuts down on replication: since refresh events aren't recorded during this interval, a record's timestamp isn't updated and therefore doesn't have to be replicated.

---

[*] Or the prerequisite check we described.

The DNS server's default refresh and no-refresh interval are both seven days. Aging and scavenging is enabled on a zone-by-zone basis. At a configurable interval, the server makes a scavenging pass to remove any stale records in zones enabled for aging and scavenging. Stale records have a timestamp older than the current time minus the no-refresh interval minus the refresh interval. Figure 11-7 shows the phases of a record from creation through refreshing to scavenging. Since this record was never refreshed, it's eligible for scavenging. Figure 11-8 corresponds to another record from a live client that is sending periodic dynamic updates to keep its A record refreshed. This record won't be scavenged.

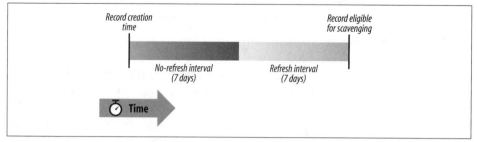

Figure 11-7. Nonrefreshed record

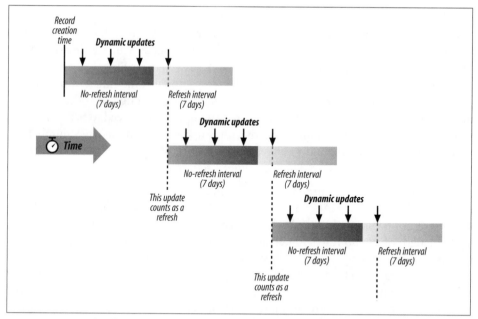

Figure 11-8. Periodically refreshed record

Configuring Aging and Scavenging

Aging and scavenging is disabled by default, since its improper use is dangerous. If you set the refresh and no-refresh intervals too low, records that aren't stale can be inadvertently removed. A global setting controls aging and scavenging for the entire DNS server. It's located on the **Advanced** tab of the server properties window, which is shown in Figure 11-9. The **Scavenging period** setting controls how often the server makes a scavenging pass through all authoritative zones.

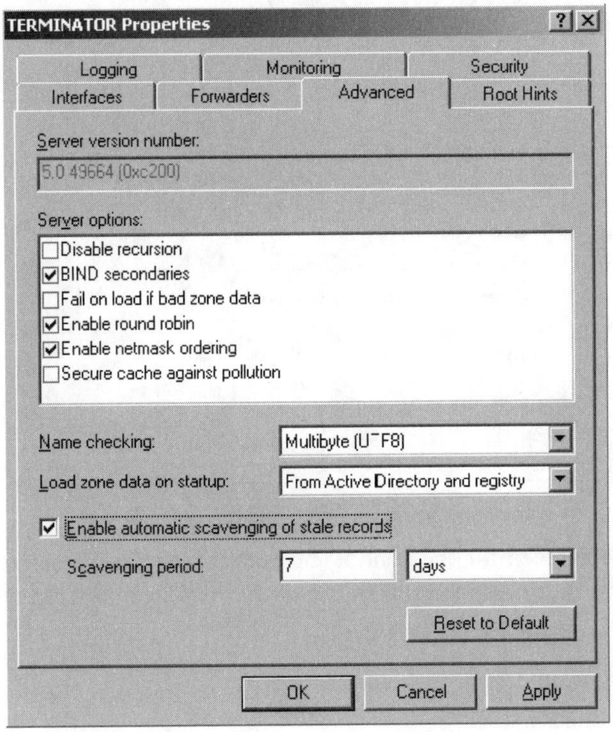

Figure 11-9. Enabling aging and scavenging for an entire server

Once aging and scavenging has been enabled on a given server, you must still enable it for a particular zone. From the **General** tab of a zone's properties window, click the **Aging** button to produce a window like the one shown in Figure 11-10. Click **Scavenge stale resource records** to enable aging and scavenging for this zone. The refresh and no-refresh intervals are set on a per-zone basis.

In addition, a DNS server may be configured to apply the zone parameters values to all the existing and future zones.

When Scavenging Occurs

The server stores a parameter called *StartScavenging* for each primary zone, which is the time after which the zone is eligible for scavenging. A DNS server performs a zone-scavenging pass only if the current time is greater than StartScavenging. (In addition, scavenging must be enabled for the server and the zone, and dynamic

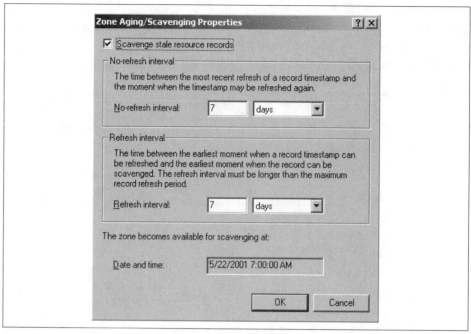

Figure 11-10. Enabling aging and scavenging for a particular zone

update must be enabled for the zone.) The StartScavenging parameter is set to the current time plus the refresh interval of the zone when the following events happen:

- When scavenging is enabled for the zone
- When dynamic update is enabled for the zone
- When the zone is loaded
- When the zone is resumed

Other Notes on Aging and Scavenging

Static records (i.e., those added with the DNS console) are considered "permanent." They have a creation/refresh timestamp of zero and are ignored during a scavenging pass.

The DNS server needs to retain each record's creation/refresh timestamp across server restarts, which means writing this information to disk. For Active Directory–integrated zones, this information goes in—surprise!—Active Directory. For standard zones, the server has to store the information in the zone data file. Thus, for standard zones with aging and scavenging enabled, the zone data file format includes an extra field that is incompatible with non–Windows 2000 name servers. An outbound zone transfer of a zone with aging and scavenging enabled is not affected, so you can still have non–Windows 2000 name servers as secondaries. But if aging and scavenging is enabled for a zone, you can't take the actual zone file from a Windows 2000 name server and load it on, say, a BIND name server.

Incremental Zone Transfer

The Microsoft DNS Server in Windows 2000 supports a new kind of zone transfer. *Incremental zone transfer*, or IXFR for short, is specified in RFC 1995, and it does exactly what you'd expect based on its name. A traditional zone transfer always transfers the entire contents of a zone, even if only one record has changed. Incremental zone transfers allow a name server to send a list of just the records that have changed since the last zone transfer (whether it was a full or incremental one).

This new feature is critical for zones that change frequently. Imagine the scenario with dynamic update: every dynamic update is a change to the zone that requires a zone transfer. Doing a full zone transfer with every small change wastes bandwidth and CPU time. The situation is compounded when the zone being updated and transferred is large.

For IXFR to function, the master servers need to keep track of the differences between successive versions of the zone. A secondary requests an incremental zone transfer and presents its current serial number. The master server calculates and sends the changes needed on the secondary to make its version of the zone current. If the master server can't calculate the changes for whatever reason—perhaps the secondary has an old version of the zone and the primary hasn't kept a record of changes that far back—the primary is allowed to say "Sorry, but you've got to accept a full zone transfer."

A Microsoft DNS Server acting as a secondary requests an incremental zone transfer by default. If the master server doesn't support incremental zone transfer, the Microsoft DNS Server asks for a standard full zone transfer. A Microsoft DNS Server acting as a primary master stores a record of changes going back several versions. The number of versions the server keeps in memory depends on the zone's size: it keeps 25% of the total number of resource records of the zone, up to a total of 64,000. For example, given a zone of 100 resource records, the server would store changes corresponding to the last 25 versions of the zone. It responds with a full zone transfer instead of an incremental when it doesn't have the necessary information to produce the list of changes to the zone or when the list of changes would be larger than a full zone transfer.

Active Directory–integrated zones introduce an extra wrinkle. Any of these zones' authoritative servers can accept a dynamic update for the zone. The change is stored locally and replicated to the other servers using Active Directory. This situation means that different servers can potentially apply changes to the zone in a different order. To maintain a consistent view of changes to a zone, a secondary must always use the same master server. If a particular master server becomes unavailable and a secondary is forced to use another, it automatically requests a full zone transfer for the first transfer from that server to avoid inconsistencies.

Unicode Character Support

The Microsoft DNS Server allows any character from the Unicode character set to be used in a domain name. These characters are represented in UTF-8, a particular method of encoding Unicode characters.* The vast majority of DNS domain names are represented with a subset of the ASCII character set: alphanumeric characters (i.e., the uppercase and lowercase letters A–Z and the digits 0–9) and the hyphen. In fact, the DNS specification has always permitted any binary value to be used in domain names, though RFC 1035—one of the core RFCs that define DNS—recommends that domain names be limited to the characters just listed to avoid problems using the domain names with other protocols. For example, the Internet standards dealing with valid hostname syntax (RFCs 952 and 1123) restrict hostnames to the same ASCII alphanumeric subset. Since this hostname syntax is referenced in Internet standards for electronic mail, domain names used in email addresses must use this same limited syntax.

Until Windows 2000, however, networking in Microsoft operating systems was based on NetBIOS, which has more liberal hostname-syntax rules than strict alphanumerics and the hyphen. As we mentioned earlier in this chapter, limited punctuation is allowed in NetBIOS names, as well. Since DNS is the protocol used to name hosts in Windows 2000, sites that upgrade can run into trouble with hosts named according to NetBIOS syntax rules that are no longer valid according to the accepted DNS syntax rules. As a result, Microsoft extended the DNS server and the DNS console user interfaces to support a wider character set—everything in Unicode.

The Microsoft DNS Server can check the syntax of domain names in zones for which it is authoritative. This behavior, called *name checking*, is controlled on the **Advanced** tab of the server properties window (see Figure 11-9). The default value is to check according to UTF-8 syntax rules, but domain names can also be restricted to alphanumerics and the hyphen or name checking can be disabled completely.

A word of caution is in order here: just because the Microsoft DNS Server allows you to use all kinds of crazy characters in domain names, it doesn't mean you should. Many other protocols have certain expectations for syntax of domain names, and violating these expectations can cause applications to exhibit strange and unpredictable behavior. We recommend sticking to the accepted alphanumerics and the hyphen until standards for using additional characters are developed by the IETF (they're working on such standards at the time of this writing). If you absolutely must use other characters, do so only for hostnames used inside your organization, not those visible to the entire Internet.

---

* More information about the Unicode Standard is available at *http://www.unicode.org*.

nslookup

"Don't stand chattering to yourself like that," Humpty Dumpty said, looking at her for the first time, "but tell me your name and your business."

"My name is Alice, but—"

"It's a stupid name enough!" Humpty Dumpty interrupted impatiently. "What does it mean?"

"Must a name mean something?" Alice asked doubtfully.

"Of course it must," Humpty Dumpty said with a short laugh....

To be proficient at troubleshooting name server problems, you'll need a special tool to make DNS queries, one that gives you complete control. We'll cover *nslookup* in this chapter because it's distributed with Windows 2000 and with many other operating systems.

Note that this chapter isn't comprehensive; there are aspects of *nslookup*—mostly obscure and seldom used—that we won't cover. You can always consult the manual pages for information on those aspects.

Is nslookup a Good Tool?

Much of the time you'll use *nslookup* to make queries in the same way the resolver makes them. Sometimes, though, you'll use *nslookup* to query other name servers as a name server would. Which one you emulate will depend on the problem you're trying to debug. You might wonder, "How accurately does *nslookup* emulate a resolver or a name server? Does *nslookup* actually use the Windows resolver library routines?" No, *nslookup* uses its own routines for querying name servers, but those routines are based on the resolver routines. Consequently, *nslookup*'s behavior is very similar to the resolver's behavior, but it does differ slightly. We'll point out some of those differences. As for emulating name server behavior, *nslookup* allows us to query another server with the same query message that a name server would use, but the retransmission scheme is quite different. Like a name server, though, *nslookup* can pull a copy of the zone data. So *nslookup* does not exactly emulate either the resolver or the name server, but it does emulate them well enough to make a good troubleshooting tool. Let's delve into those differences to which we've alluded.

Multiple Servers

nslookup talks to only one name server at a time. This is the major difference between *nslookup*'s behavior and the resolver's behavior. The resolver makes use of all the name servers listed in the Windows resolver configuration window. If two name servers are listed, the resolver tries the first name server, then the second, then the first, then the second, until it receives a response or gives up. The resolver does this for every query. On the other hand, *nslookup* tries the first name server listed and keeps retrying until it finally gives up on the first name server and tries the second. Once it gets a response, it locks onto that server and doesn't try the other. But you *want* your troubleshooting tool to talk with only one name server, so you can reduce the number of variables when analyzing a problem. If *nslookup* used more than one name server, you wouldn't have as much control over your troubleshooting session. So talking to only one server is the right thing for a troubleshooting tool to do.

Timeouts

The *nslookup* timeouts are similar to the resolver timeouts when the resolver is querying only one name server. A name server's timeouts, however, are based on how quickly the remote server answered the last query, a dynamic measure. *nslookup* will never match name server timeouts, but that's not a problem either. When you're querying remote name servers with *nslookup*, you probably care only what the response was, not how long it took.

The Search List

nslookup implements the search list just as the resolver code does. Name servers don't implement search lists, so, to act like a name server, the *nslookup* search function must be turned off—more on that later.

Zone Transfers

nslookup will do zone transfers just like a name server. Unlike the name server, though, *nslookup* does not check SOA serial numbers before pulling the zone data; you'll have to do that manually, if you want to.

Using NetBIOS Names

This last point doesn't compare *nslookup* to the resolver or name server but rather to ways of looking up names in general. *nslookup*, as distributed by Microsoft, only uses DNS; you can't use it to look up NetBIOS names via broadcast, *LMHOSTS*, or WINS. Before using *nslookup* to try to find your lookup problem, you need to determine if your problem is really with DNS. For example, if an application is using a different IP address than you expect, perhaps it's treating a value as a NetBIOS name and not a DNS domain name. To diagnose this kind of problem, you need to understand how the Windows resolver, which we discussed in Chapter 6, works. Just remember that *nslookup* talks only to name servers.

Interactive Versus Noninteractive

Let's start our tutorial on *nslookup* by looking at how to start it and how to exit from it. You can run *nslookup* either interactively or noninteractively. If you want to look up only one piece of data, you should use the noninteractive form. If you plan on doing something more extensive, such as changing servers or options, use an interactive session.

To start an interactive session, just type *nslookup*:

```
C:\> nslookup
Default Server:  terminator.movie.edu
Address:  192.249.249.3

> ^Z
```

If you need help, type *?* or *help*.

When you want to exit, type ^Z (Ctrl-Z) and press Enter. You can also exit from *nslookup* with ^C or ^*Break* (Ctrl-Break). This behavior is different from *nslookup*'s operation on a Unix host, where if you send *nslookup* an interrupt, it catches it, stops whatever it is doing (like a zone transfer), and gives you the > prompt. There's no way to just interrupt Microsoft's *nslookup*: you just have to stop *nslookup* completely and restart it.

For a noninteractive lookup, include the name you are looking up on the command line:

```
C:\> nslookup carrie
Server:  terminator.movie.edu
Address:  192.249.249.3

Name:    carrie.movie.edu
Address:  192.253.253.4
```

Option Settings

nslookup has its own set of dials and knobs called *option settings*. All the option settings can be changed. We'll discuss here what each of the options means. We'll use the rest of the chapter to show you how to use them.

```
C:\> nslookup
Default Server:  terminator.movie.edu
Address:  192.249.249.3

> set all
Default Server:  terminator.movie.edu
Address:  192.249.249.3

Set options:
  nodebug
  defname
  search
  recurse
  nod2
  novc
  noignoretc
  port=53
  type=A
  class=IN
  timeout=2
  retry=1
  root=A.ROOT-SERVERS.NET.
  domain=movie.edu
  MSxfr
  IXFRversion=1
  srchlist=movie.edu

> ^Z
```

Before we get into the options, we need to cover the introductory lines. The default name server is *terminator.movie.edu*. This means that every query sent by *nslookup* will be sent to *terminator*.

The options come in two flavors: *Boolean* and *value*. The options that do not have an equals sign after them are Boolean options. They have the interesting property of being either "on" or "off." The value options can take on different, well, values. How can we tell which Boolean options are on and which are off? The option is *off* when a "no" precedes the option's name. *nodebug* means that debugging is off. As you might guess, the option *search* is on.

How you change Boolean or value options depends on whether or not you are using *nslookup* interactively. In an interactive session, you change an option with the *set* command, as in *set debug* or *set domain=classics.movie.edu*. From the command line, you omit the word *set* and precede the option with a hyphen, as in *nslookup –debug* or *nslookup –domain=classics.movie.edu*. The options can be abbreviated to their shortest unique string—for example, *nodeb* for *nodebug*. In addition to its abbreviation, the *querytype* option can also be entered simply as *type*.

Let's go through each of the options:

[no]debug

Debugging is turned off by default. If it is turned on, *nslookup* displays the complete contents of the response messages from the name server. See *[no]d2* for a discussion of debug level 2.

[no]defname

This option reflects *nslookup*'s BIND heritage. By default, *nslookup* adds the default domain name to names without a dot in them. Before search lists existed, the BIND resolver code would only add the default domain to names without any dots in them; this option reflects that behavior. *nslookup* can implement the presearch list behavior (with *search* off and *defname* on), or it can implement the search list behavior (with *search* on).

[no]search

The *search* option "overshadows" the default domain name (*defname*) option. That is, *defname* applies only if *search* is turned off. By default, *nslookup* appends the domain names in the search list (*srchlist*) to names that don't end in a dot. *nslookup*'s search list is constructed from the **Domain Suffix Search Order** field of the Windows resolver configuration window.

[no]recurse

nslookup requests recursive service by default. This turns on the recursion-desired bit in query messages. The Windows resolver sends recursive queries in the same way. Name servers, however, send nonrecursive queries to other name servers.

[no]d2

Debugging at level 2 is turned off by default. If it is turned on, you see the query messages sent to the name server in addition to the regular debugging output. Turning on *d2* also turns on *debug*. Turning off *d2* turns off *d2* only; *debug* is left on. Turning off *debug* turns off both *debug* and *d2*.

[no]vc

By default, *nslookup* makes queries using UDP instead of over a TCP connection (virtual circuit). Most Windows resolver queries are made with UDP, so the default *nslookup* behavior matches the resolver.

[no]ignoretc

By default, *nslookup* doesn't ignore truncated messages. If a message is received that has the "truncated" bit set—indicating that the name server couldn't fit all the important information in the UDP response message—*nslookup* doesn't ignore it; it retries the query using a TCP connection instead of UDP.

port=53

The DNS service is on port 53. You can start a name server on another port—for debugging purposes, for example—and *nslookup* can be directed to use that port.

type=A

By default, *nslookup* looks up A (address) resource record types. In addition, if you type in an IP address (and the *nslookup* query type is address or pointer), *nslookup* will invert the address, append *in-addr.arpa*, and look up PTR (pointer) data instead.

class=IN

The only class that matters is Internet. Well, there's the Hesiod (HS) class, too, if you are an MITer or run Ultrix.

timeout=2

If the name server doesn't respond within two seconds, *nslookup* resends the query and doubles the timeout (to four and then eight seconds). The Windows resolver uses different timeouts when querying a single name server—see Chapter 6.

retry=1

The query is sent just once before giving up. After each retry, the timeout value is doubled. Again, the Windows resolver behaves slightly differently as discussed in Chapter 6.

root=A.ROOT-SERVERS.NET.

A convenience command called *root* switches your default server to the server named here. Executing the root command from *nslookup*'s prompt is equivalent to executing *server A.ROOT-SERVERS.NET.* You can change the default "root" server with *set root=server*.

domain=movie.edu

This is the default domain name appended if the *defname* option is on. If the *defname* option is not on, no default domain name is appended.

[no]MSxfr

The Microsoft DNS Server implements a feature that Microsoft calls "fast" zone transfers. Those of you familiar with the BIND name server know this as the "many answers" zone-transfer format, in which multiple records are packed into the answer section of a single DNS message during a zone transfer. (The method implemented by older BIND name servers uses one DNS message per record, which is somewhat wasteful of bandwidth.) This option indicates whether or not to request one of these "fast" zone transfers.

IXFRversion=1

The Microsoft DNS Server also supports a protocol called incremental zone transfer (IXFR). IXFR requests include a version number. The default value of 1 corresponds to the IXFR version supported by the Microsoft DNS Server. At this point, there's no reason to change this value.

srchlist=movie.edu

If *search* is on, these are the domain names appended to names that do not end in a dot. The domain names are listed in the order in which they will be tried and are separated by slashes.

Avoiding the Search List

nslookup implements the search list, as the resolver does. When you are debugging, the search list can get in your way. You need to either turn the search list off completely (*set nosearch*) or add a trailing dot to the fully qualified domain name you are looking up. We prefer the latter, as you'll see in our examples.

Common Tasks

You'll come to use *nslookup* for little chores almost every day: for example, finding out the IP address or MX records for a given domain name or querying a particular name server for data. We'll cover these common tasks before moving on to the more occasional stuff.

Looking Up Different Data Types

By default, *nslookup* looks up the address for a name or the name for an address. You can look up any data type by changing the *querytype*, as we show in this example:

```
C:\> nslookup
Default Server:  terminator.movie.edu
Address:  192.249.249.3

> misery      --Look up address
Server:  terminator.movie.edu
Address:  192.249.249.3

Name:    misery.movie.edu
Address:  192.253.253.2

> 192.253.253.2      --Look up name
Server:  terminator.movie.edu
Address:  192.249.249.3

Name:    misery.movie.edu
Address:  192.253.253.2

> set q=mx      --Look up MX data
> wormhole
```

```
Server:  terminator.movie.edu
Address:  192.249.249.3
wormhole.movie.edu      MX preference = 10, mail exchanger = wormhole.movie.edu
wormhole.movie.edu      internet address = 192.249.249.1
wormhole.movie.edu      internet address = 192.253.253.1

> set q=any     --Look up data of any type
> diehard
Server:  terminator.movie.edu
Address:  192.249.249.3

diehard.movie.edu       internet address = 192.249.249.4
diehard.movie.edu       MX preference = 10, mail exchanger = diehard.movie.edu
diehard.movie.edu       internet address = 192.249.249.4
```

These are only a few of the valid DNS data types, of course. For the complete list, see Appendix A.

Authoritative Versus Nonauthoritative Answers

If you've used *nslookup* before, you might have noticed that it sometimes precedes its answers with the phrase "Non-authoritative answer":

```
C:\> nslookup
Default Server:  relay.hp.com
Address:  15.255.152.2

> slate.mines.colorado.edu.
Server:  relay.hp.com
Address:  15.255.152.2

Non-authoritative answer:
Name:    slate.mines.colorado.edu
Address:  138.67.1.3
```

This phrase indicates that the name server is not authoritative for the data in the answer. (Recall that a name server is authoritative for data when it's a primary master or slave for the zone containing the data.) There are two reasons why you'll see a nonauthoritative response. The first is that the name server you queried didn't have the data you were looking for and had to query a remote name server to get it. The remote name server is authoritative for the data (that's the reason it was queried!) and returns it with the "authoritative answer" bit set in the DNS message header. The Microsoft DNS Server you queried puts this data in its cache and returns it to you marked nonauthoritative. If you ask for the same data again, this time the name server can answer from its cache and will mark the data nonauthoritative: that's the second reason you'll see a nonauthoritative answer.

Authoritative answers are not announced by *nslookup*: the absence of the nonauthoritative message means the answer is authoritative.

This brings up a significant difference between the Microsoft DNS Server and the BIND name server. When you send a query to a BIND name server and it has to contact an authoritative name server to find the answer, the BIND name server returns the answer to you marked authoritative (unlike the Microsoft DNS Server). The BIND name server, in effect, passes the authoritative response directly back to you. Then, like the Microsoft DNS Server, it caches the response, and subsequent queries for the data result in a nonauthoritative answer.

Notice that we ended the domain name with a trailing dot each time we looked it up. The response would have been the same had we left it off. Sometimes it is critical that you use the trailing dot while debugging, but not always. Rather than stopping to decide if *this* name needs a trailing dot, we always add one if we know the name is fully qualified (except, of course, for the example where we turn off the search list).

Switching Servers

Sometimes you want to query another name server directly—for example, if you think it is misbehaving. You can switch servers with *nslookup* by using the *server* or *lserver* commands. The difference between *server* and *lserver* is that *lserver* queries your "local" server—the one you started out with—to get the address of the server you want to switch to; *server* uses the default server instead of the local server. This difference is important to know because the server to which you just switched may not be responding, as we'll show in this example:

```
C:\> nslookup
Default Server:  relay.hp.com
Address:  15.255.152.2
```

When we start up, our first server, *relay.hp.com*, becomes our *lserver* (this will matter later on in this session):

```
> server galt.cs.purdue.edu.
Default Server:  galt.cs.purdue.edu
Address:  128.10.2.39

> cs.purdue.edu.
Server:  galt.cs.purdue.edu
Address:  128.10.2.39

DNS request timed out.
    timeout was 2 seconds.
*** Request to galt.cs.purdue.edu timed-out
>
```

At this point we try to switch back to our original name server. But there is no name server running on *galt* to look up *relay*'s address:

```
> server relay.hp.com.
DNS request timed out.
    timeout was 2 seconds.
*** Can't find address for server relay.hp.com.: Timed out
```

Instead of being stuck, though, we use the *lserver* command to have our local server look up *relay*'s address:

```
> lserver relay.hp.com.
Default Server:  relay.hp.com
Address:  15.255.152.2

>
```

Since the server on *galt* did not respond—it's not even running a name server—it wasn't possible to look up the address of *relay* to switch back to using *relay*'s name server. Here's where *lserver* comes to the rescue: the local name server, *relay*, was still responding, so we used it. Instead of using *lserver*, we could have recovered by using *relay*'s IP address directly—server 15.255.152.2.

You can even change servers on a per-query basis. To specify that you'd like *nslookup* to query a particular server for information about a given domain name, you can specify the server as the second argument on the line, after the domain name to look up—like so:

```
C:\> nslookup
Default Server:  relay.hp.com
Address:  15.255.152.2

> saturn.sun.com. ns.sun.com.
Server:  ns.sun.com
Address:  192.9.9.3

Name:    saturn.sun.com
Address:  192.9.25.2

> ^Z
```

And, of course, you can change servers from the command line. You can specify the server to query as the argument after the domain name to look up, like this:

```
C:\> nslookup -type=mx fisherking.movie.edu. terminator.movie.edu.
```

This instructs *nslookup* to query *terminator.movie.edu* for MX records for *fisherking. movie.edu*.

To specify an alternate default server and enter interactive mode, you can use a hyphen in place of the domain name to look up:

```
C:\> nslookup - terminator.movie.edu.
```

One final note about switching servers: those of you who are familiar with using *nslookup* to talk to BIND name servers have probably entered an address of 0.0.0.0 or 127.0.0.1 to mean "this host." The Microsoft DNS Server never responds to queries sent to the loopback address—you need to use the IP address of one of the host's network interfaces.

Less-Common Tasks

The following sections describe tricks you'll probably have to use less often but are still handy to have in your repertoire. Most of these will be helpful when you're trying to troubleshoot a DNS problem; they'll enable you to grub around in the messages the resolver sees and mimic a name server querying another name server or transferring zone data.

Seeing the Query and Response Messages

If you need to, you can direct *nslookup* to show you the queries it sends out and the responses it receives. Turning on *debug* shows you the responses. Turning on *d2* shows you the queries as well. When you want to turn off debugging completely, you have to use *set nodebug*, since *set nod2* turns off only level 2 debugging. After the following trace, we'll explain some parts of the message output. If you want, you can pull out your copy of RFC 1035, turn to page 25, and read along with our explanation.

```
C:\> nslookup
Default Server:  terminator.movie.edu
Address:  192.249.249.3

> set q=mx
> acmebw.com.
Server:  terminator.movie.edu
Address:  192.249.249.3

------------
Got answer:
    HEADER:
        opcode = QUERY, id = 9, rcode = NOERROR
        header flags:  response, want recursion, recursion avail.
        questions = 1,  answers = 2,  authority records = 0,  additional = 2

    QUESTIONS:
        acmebw.com, type = MX, class = IN
    ANSWERS:
    -> acmebw.com
        type = MX, class = IN, dlen = 29
        MX preference = 10, mail exchanger = store-forward.MSPRING.NET
        ttl = 86400 (1 day)
    -> acmebw.com
        type = MX, class = IN, dlen = 17
        MX preference = 0, mail exchanger = domain-relay.MSPRING.NET
        ttl = 86400 (1 day)
    ADDITIONAL RECORDS:
    -> store-forward.MSPRING.NET
        type = A, class = IN, dlen = 4
        internet address = 207.69.231.6
        ttl = 3600 (1 hour)
```

```
    ->  domain-relay.MSPRING.NET
          type = A, class = IN, dlen = 4
          internet address = 207.69.231.10
          ttl = 3600 (1 hour)


    ------------
    Non-authoritative answer:
    acmebw.com
          type = MX, class = IN, dlen = 29
          MX preference = 10, mail exchanger = store-forward.MSPRING.NET
          ttl = 86400 (1 day)
    acmebw.com
          type = MX, class = IN, dlen = 17
          MX preference = 0, mail exchanger = domain-relay.MSPRING.NET
          ttl = 86400 (1 day)

    store-forward.MSPRING.NET
          type = A, class = IN, dlen = 4
          internet address = 207.69.231.6
          ttl = 3600 (1 hour)
    domain-relay.MSPRING.NET
          type = A, class = IN, dlen = 4
          internet address = 207.69.231.10
          ttl = 3600 (1 hour)


    >
    > set d2
    > acmebw.com.
    Server:  terminator.movie.edu
    Address:  192.249.249.3
```

This time the query is also shown:

```
    ------------
    SendRequest( ), len 28
        HEADER:
            opcode = QUERY, id = 9, rcode = NOERROR
            header flags:  query, want recursion
            questions = 1,  answers = 0,  authority records = 0,  additional = 0

        QUESTIONS:
            acmebw.com, type = MX, class = IN


    ------------
    ------------
    Got answer (130 bytes):
```

The answer is the same as in the previous example.

The text between the dashes are the query and response messages. As promised, we will go through the message contents. DNS messages are composed of five sections:

Header section

    The Header section is present in every query and response. The operation code is always QUERY. The only other opcodes are inverse query (IQUERY) and status

---

(STATUS), but those aren't used. The ID is used to associate a response with a query and to detect duplicate queries or responses. You have to look in the header flags to see which messages are queries and which are responses. The string "want recursion" indicates that the querier wants the name server to do all the work. The flag is parroted in the response. The string "auth. answer," when present, means that the response is authoritative—in other words, that the response comes from the name server's authoritative data, not from its cache data. (This response isn't authoritative, so that string is absent.) The response code, rcode, can be one of no error, server failure, name error (also known as "NXDOMAIN" or "nonexistent domain"), not implemented, or refused. The server failure, name error, not implemented, and refused response codes cause the nslookup "Server failed," "Nonexistent domain," "Not implemented," and "Query refused" errors, respectively. The last four entries in the Header section are counters—they indicate how many resource records there are in each of the next four sections.

Question section

There is always one question in a DNS message; it includes the name and the requested data type and class. There is never more than one question. Handling more than one question in a DNS message would require a redesign of its format. For one thing, the single authority bit would have to be changed, because the Answer section could contain a mix of authoritative answers and nonauthoritative answers. In the present design, setting the authoritative answer bit means that the name server is an authority for the domain name in the Question section.

Answer section

This section contains the resource records that answer the question. There can be more than one resource record in the response. For example, if the host is multihomed, there will be more than one address resource record.

Authority section

The Authority section is where name server records are returned. When a response refers the querier to some other name servers, those name servers are listed here.

Additional section

The Additional records section adds information that may complete information included in other sections. For instance, if a name server is listed in the Authority section, the name server's address is added to the Additional records section. After all, to contact the name server, you need to have its address.

For you sticklers for detail, there *is* a time when the number of questions in a query message isn't one: in an inverse query, when it's zero. In an inverse query, there is one answer in the query message, and the Question section is empty. The name server fills in the question. But, as we said, inverse queries are almost nonexistent. The Microsoft DNS Server doesn't even support them.

Querying Like a Name Server

You can make *nslookup* send out the same query message a name server would. Name server query messages are not much different from resolver messages. The primary difference in the query messages is that resolvers request recursion and name servers seldom do. Recursion is the default with *nslookup*, so you have to explicitly turn it off. The difference in *operation* between a resolver and a name server is that the resolver implements the search list and the name server doesn't. By default, *nslookup* implements the search list, so that, too, has to be turned off. Of course, judicious use of the trailing dot will have the same effect.

In raw *nslookup* terms, this means that to query like a resolver, you use *nslookup*'s default settings. To query like a name server, use *set norecurse* and *set nosearch*. On the command line, that's *nslookup –norecurse –nosearch*.

When a name server gets a query, it looks for the answer in its cache. If it doesn't have the answer and it is authoritative for the zone, the name server responds that the name doesn't exist or that there is no data for that type. If the name server doesn't have the answer and it is *not* authoritative for the zone, it starts walking up the namespace looking for NS records. There will always be NS records somewhere higher in the domain tree. As a last resort, it will use the NS records at the root domain, the highest level.

If the name server received a nonrecursive query, it would respond to the querier by giving the NS records that it had found. On the other hand, if the original query was a recursive query, the name server would then query the remote name servers in the NS records that it found. When the name server receives a response from one of the remote name servers, it caches the response and repeats this process, if necessary. The remote server's response will contain either the answer to the question or a list of name servers lower in the namespace and closer to the answer.

Let's assume for our example that we are trying to satisfy a recursive query and that we didn't find any NS records until we checked the *gov* domain. That is in fact the case when we ask the name server on *relay.hp.com* about *www.whitehouse.gov*—it doesn't find any NS records until the *gov* domain. From there we switch servers to a *gov* name server and ask the same question. It directs us to the *whitehouse.gov* servers. We then switch to a *whitehouse.gov* name server and ask the same question:

```
C:\> nslookup
Default Server:  relay.hp.com
Address:  15.255.152.2

> set norec              --Query like a name server: turn off recursion
> set nosearch           --Turn off the search list
> www.whitehouse.gov     --We don't need to dot-terminate since we've turned search off
Server:  relay.hp.com
Address:  15.255.152.2

Name: www.whitehouse.gov
```

```
Served by:
- H.ROOT-SERVERS.NET
  128.63.2.53
  gov
- B.ROOT-SERVERS.NET
  128.9.0.107
  gov
- C.ROOT-SERVERS.NET
  192.33.4.12
  gov
- D.ROOT-SERVERS.NET
  128.8.10.90
  gov
- E.ROOT-SERVERS.NET
  192.203.230.10
  gov
- I.ROOT-SERVERS.NET
  192.36.148.17
  gov
- F.ROOT-SERVERS.NET
  192.5.5.241
  gov
- G.ROOT-SERVERS.NET
  192.112.36.4
  gov
- A.ROOT-SERVERS.NET
  198.41.0.4
  gov
```

Switch to a *gov* name server. You may have to turn recursion back on temporarily, if the name server doesn't have the address already cached:

```
> server e.root-servers.net
Default Server:  e.root-servers.net
Address: 192.203.230.10
```

Ask the same question of the *gov* name server. It will refer us to name servers closer to our desired answer:

```
> www.whitehouse.gov.
Server:  e.root-servers.net
Address:  192.203.230.10

Name:    www.whitehouse.gov
Served by:
- SEC1.DNS.PSI.NET
        38.8.92.2
        WHITEHOUSE.GOV
- SEC2.DNS.PSI.NET
        38.8.93.2
        WHITEHOUSE.GOV
```

Switch to a *whitehouse.gov* name server—either of them will do:

```
> server sec1.dns.psi.net.
Default Server:  sec1.dns.psi.net
```

```
Address:  38.8.92.2

> www.whitehouse.gov.
Server:  sec1.dns.psi.net
Address:  38.8.92.2

Name:    www.whitehouse.gov
Addresses:  198.137.240.91, 198.137.240.92
```

We hope this example gives you a feeling for how name servers look up names. If you need to refresh your understanding of what this looks like graphically, flip back to Figures 2-12 and 2-13.

Before we move on, notice that we asked each of the servers the very same question: "What's the address for *www.whitehouse.gov?*" What do you think would happen if the *gov* name server itself had already cached *www.whitehouse.gov*'s address? The *gov* name server would have answered the question out of its cache instead of referring us to the *whitehouse.gov* name servers. Why is this significant? Suppose you messed up a particular host's address in your zone. Someone points it out to you, and you clean up the problem. Even though your name server now has the correct data, some remote sites find the old, messed-up data when they look up the name. One of the name servers higher up in the domain tree has cached the incorrect data; when it receives a query for that host's address, it returns the incorrect data instead of referring the querier to your name servers. What makes this problem hard to track down is that only one of the "higher up" name servers has cached the incorrect data, so only some of the remote lookups get the wrong answer—the ones that use this server. Fun, huh? Eventually, though, the "higher up" name server will time out the old record. If you're pressed for time, you can contact the administrators of the remote name server and ask them to kill and restart their name servers to flush the cache. Of course, if the remote name server is an important, much-used name server, they may tell you where to go with that suggestion.

Zone Transfers

You can use *nslookup* to transfer a whole zone with the *ls* command. This feature is useful for troubleshooting, for figuring out how to spell a remote host's name, or just for counting how many hosts are in some remote zone. Since the output can be substantial, *nslookup* allows you to redirect the output to a file.

Beware: a lot of hosts won't let you pull a copy of their zones, either for security reasons or to limit the load on their name server hosts. The Internet is a friendly place, but administrators have to defend their turf.

nslookup filters zone transfer data: it shows you only some of the zone unless you tell it otherwise. By default, you see only address and name server data. You will see all of the zone data if you tell *nslookup* to display data of *any* type. The *nslookup* help (available in the main Windows 2000 help) or command summary (shown by typing *help* at the *nslookup* prompt) tells you all the parameters to the *ls* command. We are going to show only the *–t* parameter, since the others can be emulated with *–t*. The *–t* option takes one argument: the data type to filter on. So, to pull a copy of a zone and see all the MX data, use *ls –t mx*. Let's do some zone transfers:

```
C:\> nslookup
Default Server:  terminator.movie.edu
Address:  192.249.249.3

> ls movie.edu.      --List NS and A records for movie.edu
[terminator.movie.edu]
 movie.edu.                  NS      server = terminator.movie.edu
 movie.edu.                  NS      server = wormhole.movie.edu
 carrie                      A       192.253.253.4
 diehard                     A       192.249.249.4
 misery                      A       192.253.253.2
 robocop                     A       192.249.249.2
 shining                     A       192.253.253.3
 terminator                  A       192.249.249.3
 wh249                       A       192.249.249.1
 wh253                       A       192.253.253.1
 wormhole                    A       192.253.253.1
 wormhole                    A       192.249.249.1
> ls -t any movie.edu  > /temp/movie.edu.txt     --List all data into \temp\
```

--movie.edu.txt
```
[terminator.movie.edu]
Received 25 records.
```

Those forward slashes in the *ls* command aren't a misprint—*nslookup* was originally written for Unix as part of the BIND distribution. Microsoft must have missed the slashes when porting *nslookup* to Windows 2000.

Troubleshooting nslookup Problems

The last thing you want is to have problems with your troubleshooting tool. Unfortunately, some types of failures render the troubleshooting tool mostly useless. Other types of *nslookup* failures are, at best, confusing because they don't give you any direct information to work with. While there may be a few problems with *nslookup* itself, most of the problems you encounter will be with name server configuration and operation. We'll cover a few odd problems here.

Looking Up the Right Data

This isn't really a problem, per se, but it can be awfully confusing. If you use *nslookup* to look up a type of data for a domain name and the domain name exists but no data of the type you're looking for exists, you'll get an error like this:

```
C:\> nslookup
Default Server:  terminator.movie.edu
```

```
Address:  192.249.249.3

> movie.edu.

*** No address (A) records available for movie.edu.
```

So what types of records *do* exist? You can use *set type=any* to find out:

```
> set type=any
> movie.edu.
Server:  terminator.movie.edu
Address:  192.249.249.3

movie.edu        nameserver = terminator.movie.edu
movie.edu        nameserver = wormhole.movie.edu
movie.edu
        primary name server = terminator.movie.edu
        responsible mail addr = administrator.movie.edu
        serial  = 6
        refresh = 3600 (1 hour)
        retry   = 600 (10 mins)
        expire  = 86400 (1 day)
        default TTL = 3600 (1 hour)
movie.edu        MX preference = 10, mail exchanger = wormhole.movie.edu
terminator.movie.edu    internet address = 192.249.249.3
wormhole.movie.edu      internet address = 192.253.253.1
wormhole.movie.edu      internet address = 192.249.249.1
wormhole.movie.edu      internet address = 192.249.249.1
wormhole.movie.edu      internet address = 192.253.253.1
```

Why are the IP addresses for *terminator* and *wormhole* returned? If you receive the NS records for *movie.edu* listing these two hosts as that zone's name servers, chances are the next thing you'll want are those hosts' IP addresses. The name server anticipates that and sends along address records in the Additional section. The same thing goes for the *movie.edu* MX record pointing to *wormhole*: if you get that record, you'll want *wormhole*'s IP address next. That explains why *wormhole*'s IP addresses show up twice, but this is arguably a bug in the Microsoft DNS Server.

No PTR Data for Name Server's Address

Here's a cryptic message:

```
C:\> nslookup
*** Can't find server name for address 192.249.249.3: Non-existent domain
*** Can't find server name for address 192.249.249.3: Non-existent domain
*** Default servers are not available
Default Server:  UnKnown
Address:  192.249.249.3

>
```

The "Non-existent domain" message means that there's no PTR record for *3.249.249. 192.in-addr.arpa*. In other words, *nslookup* couldn't find the name for 192.249.249.3, which is the first name server the resolver is configured to query. The only reason *nslookup* looks up this address is to print the "Default Server" startup message. Obviously, this name server's data is messed up, at least for the *249.249.192.in-addr.arpa* zone, so *nslookup* prints "UnKnown".

At least we've got the *nslookup* prompt: even if the server doesn't know its own name, it might still be able to answer other queries. This behavior is a vast improvement over the standard version of *nslookup* in the BIND distribution (the one shipped with most versions of Unix). That version of *nslookup* refuses even to run unless it can successfully reverse map the default server's IP address.

Still, the "Default servers are not available" message in the example is misleading. After all, a name server is there to say the address doesn't exist. More often, you'll see the error "timed out" if the name server isn't running on the host or the host can't be reached. Only then does the "Default servers are not available" message make sense.

Timeouts

What if your resolver is pointing to a name server that isn't running or a host that can't be reached? We kinda gave the answer away in the previous section, but here's what happens:

```
C:\> nslookup
DNS request timed out.
    timeout was 2 seconds.
*** Can't find server name for address 192.249.249.4: Timed out
DNS request timed out.
    timeout was 2 seconds.
*** Can't find server name for address 192.249.249.4: Timed out
*** Default servers are not available
Default Server:  UnKnown
Address:  192.249.249.4

>
```

The resolver is configured to use the name server 192.249.249.4 (and only that name server). *nslookup* tries valiantly to contact it—it goes through its timeout sequence twice in attempt to get the name server to reverse map its own IP address. Finally *nslookup* gives up, prints "UnKnown" for the default server, and gives you a prompt. You can't really do anything productive without changing servers at this point—after all, no server is running at that IP address—but at least you've got a prompt. Again, this is a better than the standard *nslookup*, which would have dumped us back to the command line.

Note that if your resolver is configured to send queries to more than one name server, *nslookup* tries the servers in order until it finds one that responds:

```
C:\> nslookup
DNS request timed out.
```

```
        timeout was 2 seconds.
*** Can't find server name for address 192.249.249.1: Timed out
Default Server:  terminator.movie.edu
Address:  192.249.249.3

>
```

Occasionally you'll see timeouts during the course of an *nslookup* session. If you are looking up some remote information, the name server could fail to respond because it is still trying to look up the item and *nslookup* gave up waiting. How can you tell the difference between a name server that isn't running and a name server that is running but didn't respond? Use the *ls* command to point out the difference. In this case, no name server is running, or the host couldn't be reached:

```
C:\> nslookup
Default Server:  terminator.movie.edu
Address:  192.249.249.3

> ls foo.
ls: connect: No error
*** Can't list domain foo.: Unspecified error
```

If a name server is running, you'll see the following error message:

```
C:\> nslookup
Default Server:  terminator.movie.edu
Address:  192.249.249.3

> ls foo.
[terminator.movie.edu]
*** Can't list domain foo.: Non-existent domain
```

That is, unless there's a top-level *foo* domain in your world.

Query Refused

You generally see a "query refused" error message under two conditions. The first is when you attempt a zone transfer and the server refuses for security reasons (for example, because you checked **Only Allow Access From Secondaries Included on Notify List** in the zone properties **Notify** window). This is what you'll see:

```
C:\> nslookup
Default Server:  terminator.movie.edu
Address:  192.249.249.3

> ls movie.edu      --This attempts a zone transfer
[terminator.movie.edu]
*** Can't list domain movie.edu: Query refused
>
```

You might also see a "query refused" error from a name server running a recent version of BIND, which has the ability to restrict queries to different zones based on the querier's source IP address.

Unspecified Error

You may run into a rather unsettling problem called "unspecified error." We have an example of this error here:

```
C:/> nslookup
Default Server: terminator.movie.edu
Address: 192.249.249.3

> set type=ns
> .
Server: terminator.movie.edu
Address: 192.249.249.3

Non-authoritative answer:
(root)  nameserver = NS.NIC.DDN.MIL
(root)  nameserver = B.ROOT-SERVERS.NET
(root)  nameserver = E.ROOT-SERVERS.NET
(root)  nameserver = D.ROOT-SERVERS.NET
(root)  nameserver = F.ROOT-SERVERS.NET
(root)  nameserver = C.ROOT-SERVERS.NET
(root)  nameserver = G.ROOT-SERVERS.NET
(root)  nameserver = hpfcsx.fc.hp.com
(root)  nameserver = hp-pcd.cv.hp.com
(root)  nameserver = hp-ses.sde.hp.com
(root)  nameserver = hpsatc1.gva.hp.com
(root)  nameserver = named_master.ch.apollo.hp.com
(root)  nameserver = A.ISI.EDU
(root)  nameserver = SRI-NIC.ARPA
(root)  nameserver = GUNTER-ADAM.ARPA

Authoritative answers can be found from:
(root)  nameserver = NS.NIC.DDN.MIL
(root)  nameserver = B.ROOT-SERVERS.NET
(root)  nameserver = E.ROOT-SERVERS.NET
(root)  nameserver = D.ROOT-SERVERS.NET
(root)  nameserver = F.ROOT-SERVERS.NET
(root)  nameserver = C.ROOT-SERVERS.NET
(root)  nameserver =

*** Error: record size incorrect (1050690 != 65519)

*** terminator.movie.edu can't find .: Unspecified error
```

What happened here is that there was too much data to fit into a UDP datagram.* The name server stopped filling in the response when it ran out of room. The name server *didn't* set the truncation bit in the response message, or *nslookup* would have retried the query over a TCP connection. The name server must have decided that

---

* What are all those *hp.com* name servers doing in there? This example illustrates a problem besides just filling a UDP datagram: under some conditions, older BIND name servers can easily be contaminated with "bogus" root name servers. This output shows a query to such a name server.

---

enough of the "important" information fit. You won't see this kind of error very often. You'll see it if you create too many NS records for a zone, so don't create too many. (Advice like this makes you wonder why you bought this book, right?) How many is too many depends upon how well the names can be "compressed" in the message, which in turn depends upon how many name servers share the same domain in their domain name. The root name servers were renamed to all be in the *root-servers.net* domain for this very reason—more names fit in DNS messages if they share a common domain, which allows more root name servers to support the Internet. As a rule of thumb, don't go over 10 NS records.

Best of the Net

System administrators have a thankless job. They are asked certain questions, usually quite simple ones, over and over again. And sometimes, in a creative mood, they come up with a clever way to help their users. When the rest of us find out about their ingenuity, we can only sit back, smile admiringly, and wish we had thought of it ourselves. Here is one such case, where a system administrator found a way to communicate the solution to the sometimes perplexing puzzle of how to end an *nslookup* session:

```
C:\> nslookup
Default Server:  envy.ugcs.caltech.edu
Address:  131.215.134.135

> quit
Server:  envy.ugcs.caltech.edu
Addresses:  131.215.134.135, 131.215.128.135

Name:    ugcs.caltech.edu
Addresses:  131.215.128.135, 131.215.134.135
Aliases:  quit.ugcs.caltech.edu
          use.exit.to.leave.nslookup.-.-.-.ugcs.caltech.edu

> exit
```

CHAPTER 13

Troubleshooting DNS

> *"Of course not," said the Mock Turtle. "Why, if a fish*
> *came to me, and told me he was going on a journey,*
> *I should say, 'With what porpoise?'"*
> *"Don't you mean 'purpose'?" said Alice.*
> *"I mean what I say," the Mock Turtle replied,*
> *in an offended tone.*
> *And the Gryphon added, "Come, let's hear*
> *some of your adventures."*

In the last chapter, we demonstrated how to use *nslookup* to make queries. In this chapter, we'll show you how to use *nslookup*—plus traditional TCP/IP networking tools like trusty ol' *ping*—to troubleshoot real-life problems with DNS.

Troubleshooting, by its nature, is a tough subject to teach. You start with any of a world of symptoms and try to work your way back to the cause. We can't cover the whole gamut of problems you may encounter on the Internet, but we will certainly do our best to show you how to diagnose the most common of them. And along the way, we hope to teach you troubleshooting techniques that will be valuable in tracking down more obscure problems that we don't document.

Is DNS Really Your Problem?

Before we launch into a discussion of how to troubleshoot a DNS problem, we should make sure you know how to tell whether a problem is caused by DNS, not by another naming service. On Windows hosts, figuring out whether the culprit is actually DNS can be difficult. Windows supports a whole panoply of naming services: DNS, WINS, *HOSTS*, *LMHOSTS*, and more. The stock Windows 2000 *nslookup*, however, doesn't pay any attention to these other naming services. You can run *nslookup* on a Windows 2000 box and query the name server 'till the cows come home while the service with the problem is using a different naming service.

How do you know where to put the blame? First, you need to consider what kind of program is having the problem. If it's a TCP/IP client, such as *telnet* or *ftp*, the possible culprits are DNS and the *HOSTS* file. If it's a utility that supports NetBIOS naming, such as *net* (as in *net use*), the likely suspects also include WINS and the *LMHOSTS* file. Other clients, such as *ping*, that also take either a DNS name or a NetBIOS name as an argument can use any of these naming services.

Next, consider the order in which Windows uses the naming services. You should look through the various services in that order when troubleshooting the problem.

These hints should help you identify the guilty party or at least exonerate one suspect. If you narrow down the suspects and DNS is still implicated, you'll just have to read this chapter.

Checking the Cache

As we've said earlier, you can check the contents of your name server's cache with the DNS console. This can come in handy if you suspect that your name server has cached bad or out-of-date data from another server. To inspect a server's cache, click the plus sign to the left of the name of the server in the DNS console's left pane. You'll see a folder named **Cached Lookups**. Either click on the plus sign to the left of it or double-click the folder icon or the label to expand the next level. This shows you the top-level domains for which your name server has cached data. Expand your way to the domain name to which the cached data you're looking for is attached. In Figure 13-1, we've clicked our way down to *acmebw.com* to look for cached data.

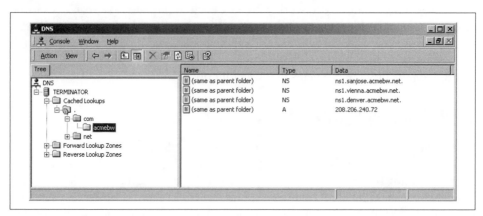

Figure 13-1. NS and A records for acmebw.com in the cache

As you can see in the right pane, our name server has cached three NS records and one A record for *acmebw.com*. If we double-clicked **net** and then **acmebw**, we could find the cached addresses of these name servers, too.

If you'd like to see the TTL on the cached data, double-click on a record in the right pane. Provided the DNS console is in advanced view mode (select **View** → **Advanced**), the resulting window shows the record's TTL. For example, in Figure 13-2, we've double-clicked the **acmebw.com** A record.

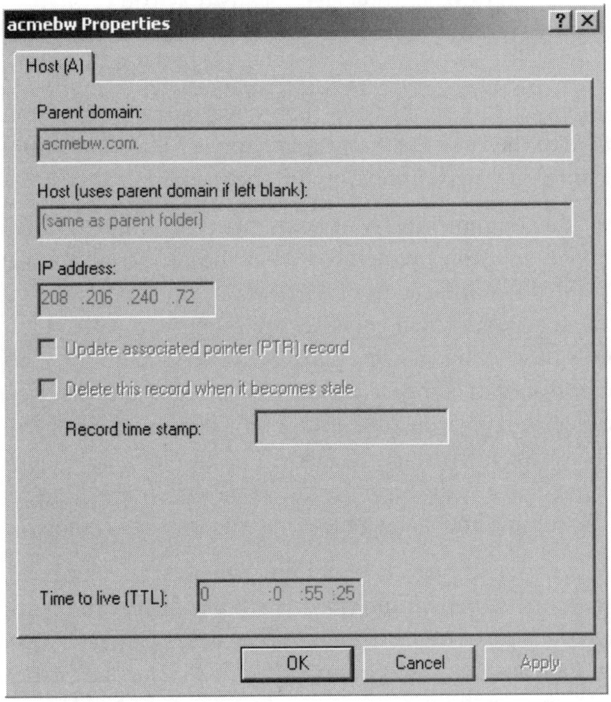

Figure 13-2. The TTL on a cached record

Be sure to refresh the DNS console with **Action** → **Refresh** or **F5** before checking the TTL, or the TTL you see may be bigger than the current TTL.

If you right-clicked the record, you may have noticed a **Delete Record** selection. Now there's something you can't do in BIND. Using the DNS console, you can actually delete cached data record by record! If you know that some records in your name server's cache are out of date, you can delete them and let your name server pick up updated records from an authoritative name server.

Potential Problem List

Let's go through some common real-world DNS problems. Many of these problems are easy to recognize and correct. We cover these problems as a matter of course—they're some of the most common problems because they're caused by some of the most common mistakes. Here are the contestants, in no particular order.

1. Forget to Increment Serial Number

This particular problem will occur only if you make changes to your zone data file by hand, without using the DNS console. The DNS console remembers to increment the serial number in the SOA record each time it changes zone data, so you don't have to worry about it. However, this also means that you probably won't be in the habit of updating the serial number, so you may forget when making that one-off manual modification.

The main symptom of this problem is that slave name servers don't pick up any changes you make to the zone on the primary server. The slaves think the zone data hasn't changed since the serial number is still the same.

How do you check if you remembered to increment the serial number? Unfortunately, that's not so easy. If you don't remember what the old serial number was and your serial number gives you no indication of when it was updated, there's no direct way to tell whether it has changed.* When you start the primary, it will load the updated zone data file regardless of whether you've changed the serial number. About the best you can do is to use *nslookup* to compare the data returned by the primary and by a slave. If they return different data, you probably forgot to increment the serial number. If you can remember a recent change you made, you can look for that data. If you can't remember a recent change, you can try transferring the zone from a primary and from a slave, sorting the results, and using a file-comparison tool to compare them.

The good news is that, although determining whether the zone was transferred is tricky, making sure the zone is transferred is simple. Just increment the serial number on the primary's copy of the zone by double-clicking the SOA record in the DNS console and manually editing the serial number field. The slaves should pick up the new data within their refresh interval, or sooner if they use NOTIFY.

2. Forget to Restart Primary Master Server

Like the last problem, you'll see this problem only if you make changes to your zone data files by hand. The DNS console adds and deletes data on the fly, so there's no need to restart your primary master name server.

If you're not using the DNS console, though, you may forget to restart your primary master name server after editing a zone data file. The name server won't know to load the new data—it doesn't automatically check the file to see if it has changed. Consequently, any changes you've made won't be reflected in the name server's data: new zones won't be loaded, and new records won't percolate out to the slaves.

---

* On the other hand, if you encode the date into the serial number, as many people do (for example, 1998010500 is the first rev of data on January 5, 1998), you may be able to tell at a glance whether you updated the serial number when you made the change. However, the DNS console makes this almost impossible since it just increments by one for each change.

To check when you last restarted the name server, scan the Event Viewer output for the last entry that looks like this:

```
The DNS Server has started.
```

The date and time on these events will tell you the last time you restarted the name server.

If the time of the restart doesn't correlate with the time you made the last change, use the DNS console to stop and restart the name server and reload its data. Check that you incremented the serial numbers on the zone data files you changed, too.

3. DNS Server Loses Manual Changes

One final but important note about making manual changes: remember that the Microsoft DNS Server periodically updates its zone data files. Each time you make changes to a zone's data using the DNS console, a write is pending: before the DNS server exits, it must rewrite the zone's data file or it will lose the changes you made. Think of this as a dirty page in memory: the operating system must write it to disk before exiting.

If you make a manual change to a zone data file while a write is pending, you'll mysteriously lose the change when the name server exits. Say you add delegation to a new subdomain of *movie.edu* while the server is running and a write is pending. After you've made the change, you have to stop the server and start it again to get it to read the zone data again. But as the server exits, it rewrites the *movie.edu* zone data file, and your delegation disappears. If you're watching the Event Viewer carefully (like you should be), you'll see this message before the server stops:

```
The DNS server wrote version 37 of zone movie.edu to file movie.edu.dns.
```

Once you force the server to rewrite its zone data files with **Action → Update Server Data Files**, the server is in sync with the zone data files and doesn't have to rewrite them on exit. So, if you're going to make manual changes to the zone data files, you should either stop the server first (although that means your server won't answer queries while you make the change), or use the DNS console to sync the server with the zone data files and then make the change.

4. Slave Server Can't Load Zone Data

If a slave name server can't get the current serial number for a zone from its master server, you won't be warned about it initially. However, if the problem persists and the slave can't determine within the expire interval whether or not its data is up to date, it will expire the zone. On a Microsoft DNS Server, you'll see a message like this in the Event Viewer:

```
Zone movie.edu expired before it could obtain a successful zone transfer or update
from a master server acting as its source for the zone. The zone has been shut down.
```

Once the zone has expired, you'll start getting SERVFAIL errors when you query the name server for data in the zone:

```
C:\> nslookup robocop wormhole.movie.edu.
Server:  wormhole.movie.edu
Addresses:  192.249.249.1, 192.253.253.1

*** wormhole.movie.edu can't find robocop.movie.edu: Server failed
```

There are three leading causes of this problem: a loss in connectivity to the master server due to network failure, an incorrect IP address configured for the master server, and a syntax error in the zone data file on the master server.

First, use the DNS console to check the address of the master server(s) from which the slave is attempting to load data. Right-click the domain name of the zone in the left pane, choose **Properties**, and look at the **General** tab, shown in Figure 13-3.

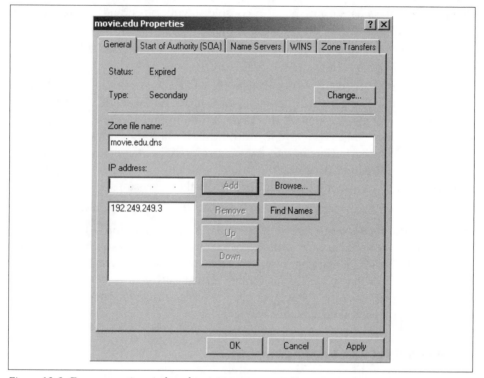

Figure 13-3. Zone properties window showing master server(s)

Make sure that's really the IP address of the master name server. If it is, check connectivity to that IP address:

```
C:\> ping 192.249.249.3
Pinging 192.249.249.3 with 32 bytes of data:
```

```
Request timed out.
Request timed out.
Request timed out.
Request timed out.
```

If the master server isn't reachable, make sure that the server's host is really running (for example, is powered on) or look for a network problem.

You may also want to check that the master server is returning authoritative responses to queries for data in the zone. If the master server is responding as not authoritative for the zone, the slave won't transfer the zone from it. Here's how you could use *nslookup* to check for an authoritative response for the zone's SOA record from the master server:

```
C:\> nslookup -norec -type=SOA movie.edu. 192.249.249.3
```

This command sends a nonrecursive query for the SOA record for *movie.edu* to the name server at 192.249.249.3. We need to send a nonrecursive query so that the name server at 192.249.249.3 doesn't try to forward the query to another server.

If this master server is correctly configured, the answer to this query should be authoritative. (Remember that unless *nslookup* reports "Non-authoritative answer," the answer is authoritative.) A nonauthoritative reply may indicate that the master server had a problem loading the zone, usually because of a syntax error in the zone data file. Contact the administrator of the master server and have him check his Event Viewer or syslog output for indications of a syntax error. We've never seen a Windows 2000 name server go nonauthoritative for a zone based on a syntax error in a zone data file, but older BIND name servers exhibit this behavior. So if your name server is a slave to a zone whose primary master is a BIND name server that's not claiming authority for the zone, a syntax error could be your problem.

If the answer to the query is authoritative but the slave server still can't transfer the zone successfully, you can use the *nslookup*'s *ls* command to try to transfer the zone manually (*ls*, as we said in Chapter 12, performs a zone transfer). If you see an error like this, it's a good bet that the master server restricts zone transfers:

```
C:\> nslookup - 192.249.249.3
Default Server: terminator.movie.edu
Address: 192.249.249.3
> ls movie.edu
[terminator.movie.edu]
*** Can't list domain movie.edu: Query refused
>
```

Contact the administrator of the master server and ask whether she is restricting zone transfers. Ask her to check the options on the **Zone Transfers** tab of the **Properties** window for the zone you're trying to transfer (if she's running the Microsoft DNS Server). If the remote server is running BIND, ask if she's using the *xfrnets* or *allow-transfer* features to restrict zone transfers.

Once the problem has been cleared up and your server successfully transfers the zone, you'll see messages like these in the Event Viewer:

```
A more recent version, version 212 of zone movie.edu was found at DNS server at 192.
249.249.3. Zone transfer is in progress.

The DNS server wrote version 212 of zone movie.edu to file movie.edu.dns.
```

5. Add Address to Zone, but Forget to Add Corresponding PTR Record

Because the mappings from hostnames to IP addresses are disjointed from the mappings from IP addresses to hostnames in DNS, it's easy to forget to add a PTR record for a new host. Adding the A record is intuitive, but many people who are used to host tables assume that adding an address record takes care of the reverse mapping, too. That's not true—you need to add a PTR record for the host to the appropriate *in-addr.arpa* zone. Thankfully, the DNS console makes that easy by providing a checkbox to **Create associated pointer (PTR) record** when you choose **New Host…**.

Neglecting to add the PTR record for a host usually causes that host to fail authentication checks. For example, users on the host won't be able to *rsh* or *rcp* to other hosts. The servers these programs talk to need to be able to map the connection's IP address to a domain name to check authorization files.

In addition, many large FTP archives, including *ftp.uu.net*, refuse anonymous *ftp* access to hosts whose IP addresses don't map back to domain names. *ftp.uu.net*'s FTP server emits a message that reads, in part:

```
530- Sorry, we're unable to map your IP address 140.186.66.1 to a hostname
530- in the DNS. This is probably because your nameserver does not have a
530- PTR record for your address in its tables, or because your reverse
530- nameservers are not registered. We refuse service to hosts whose
530- names we cannot resolve.
```

That makes the reason you can't use anonymous *ftp* pretty evident. Other FTP sites, however, don't bother printing informative messages; they simply deny service.

nslookup is handy for checking whether or not you've forgotten the PTR record:

```
C:\> nslookup
Default Server:  terminator.movie.edu
Address:  192.249.249.3

> beetlejuice      --Check for a hostname-to-address mapping
Server:  terminator.movie.edu
Address:  192.249.249.3

Name:    beetlejuice.movie.edu
Address: 192.249.249.23
```

```
> 192.249.249.23      --Now check for a corresponding address-to-hostname mapping
Server:  terminator.movie.edu
Address:  192.249.249.3

*** terminator.movie.edu can't find 192.249.249.23: Non-existent domain
```

On the primary master for *249.249.192.in-addr.arpa*, a quick check of the DNS console or the *249.249.192.in-addr.arpa.dns* file will tell you if the PTR record has been added to the zone yet.

6. Wrong Domain Name in RDATA of Record

When you add CNAME, MX, and NS records with the DNS console, remember to specify the fully qualified domain name of the host for the resource record–specific data. The DNS console assumes that the name you type as the RDATA field is fully qualfied. So if you try to create a CNAME record as shown in Figure 13-4, the CNAME record looks like this in the zone data file:

```
bigt     IN  NS  terminator.
```

This is probably not what you intended, since there's no top-level *terminator* domain. You probably assumed the DNS console would append the name of the zone to the name if you left off the dot. Nope.

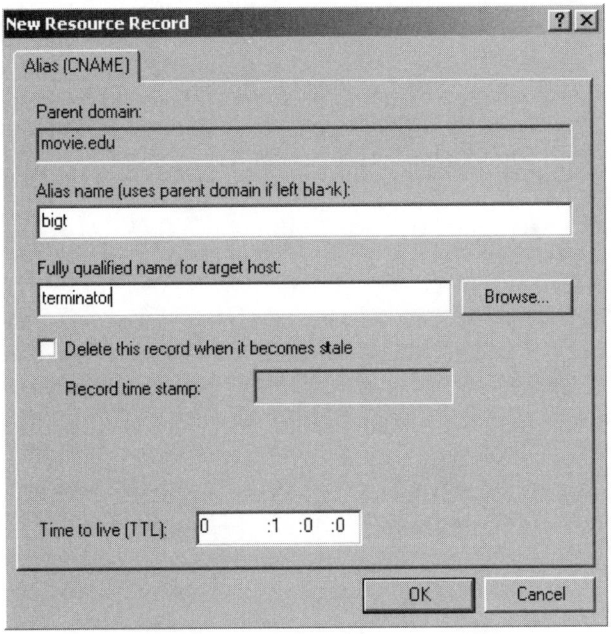

Figure 13-4. Creating a CNAME record (the wrong way)

These mistakes are easy to discover if you simply examine the zone data file (after **Action → Update Server Data Files**) or use *nslookup*:

```
C:\> nslookup -type=ns movie.edu.
Server:  terminator.movie.edu
Address:  192.249.249.3

movie.edu        nameserver = wormhole.movie.edu
movie.edu        nameserver = terminator
wormhole.movie.edu        internet address = 192.253.253.1
wormhole.movie.edu        internet address = 192.249.249.1
```

7. Loss of Network Connectivity

Though the Internet is more reliable today than it was back in the wild and woolly days of the ARPANET, network outages are still relatively common. These failures usually look like poor performance:

```
C:\> nslookup nisc.sri.com.
Server:  terminator.movie.edu
Address:  192.249.249.3

DNS request timed out.
    timeout was 2 seconds.
DNS request timed out.
    timeout was 4 seconds.
DNS request timed out.
    timeout was 8 seconds.
*** Request to terminator.movie.edu timed-out
```

Using *nslookup*, you can look up the names and addresses of the name servers your name server needs to talk to in order to resolve the name:

```
C:\> nslookup
Default Server:  terminator.movie.edu
Address:  192.249.249.3

> set type=ns
> sri.com.
Server:  terminator.movie.edu
Address:  192.249.249.3

Non-authoritative answer:
sri.com nameserver = NS.sri.com
sri.com nameserver = NS.CSL.sri.com
sri.com nameserver = TURTLE.MCC.COM
sri.com nameserver = NS1.sri.com

NS.sri.com        internet address = 128.18.30.66
NS.CSL.sri.com    internet address = 130.107.4.94
NS.CSL.sri.com    internet address = 192.12.33.94
TURTLE.MCC.COM    internet address = 128.62.1.215
NS1.sri.com       internet address = 128.18.30.65
```

```
> com.
Server: terminator.movie.edu
Address:  192.249.249.3

Non-authoritative answer:
com      nameserver = C.ROOT-SERVERS.NET
com      nameserver = D.ROOT-SERVERS.NET
com      nameserver = E.ROOT-SERVERS.NET
com      nameserver = I.ROOT-SERVERS.NET
com      nameserver = F.ROOT-SERVERS.NET
com      nameserver = G.ROOT-SERVERS.NET
com      nameserver = J.GTLD-SERVERS.INTERNIC.NET
com      nameserver = A.ROOT-SERVERS.NET
com      nameserver = H.ROOT-SERVERS.NET
com      nameserver = B.ROOT-SERVERS.NET

C.ROOT-SERVERS.NET        internet address = 192.33.4.12
D.ROOT-SERVERS.NET        internet address = 128.8.10.90
E.ROOT-SERVERS.NET        internet address = 192.203.230.10
I.ROOT-SERVERS.NET        internet address = 192.36.148.17
F.ROOT-SERVERS.NET        internet address = 192.5.5.241
G.ROOT-SERVERS.NET        internet address = 192.112.36.4
J.GTLD-SERVERS.INTERNIC.NET     internet address = 198.41.0.21
A.ROOT-SERVERS.NET        internet address = 198.41.0.4
H.ROOT-SERVERS.NET        internet address = 128.63.2.53
B.ROOT-SERVERS.NET        internet address = 128.9.0.107
```

Then you can check your host's connectivity to those servers. Odds are, *ping* won't have much better luck than your name server did. If it does, you should check that the remote name servers are really running.

```
C:\> ping 128.18.30.66      --ping first sri.com name server
Pinging 128.18.30.66 with 32 bytes of data:

Request timed out.
Request timed out.
Request timed out.
Request timed out.
C:\> ping 130.107.4.94      --ping second sri.com name server
Pinging 130.107.4.94 with 32 bytes of data:

Request timed out.
Request timed out.
Request timed out.
Request timed out.
```

Now all that's left to do is to locate the break in the network. Utilities like *tracert* can help you determine whether the problem is on your network, on the destination network, or somewhere in the middle.

You should also use common sense when tracking down the break. If, for example, your *ping* testing showed that you couldn't reach any of the Internet's root name servers, it's not likely that each root's local network went down or that the Internet's commercial backbone networks collapsed entirely. Occam's razor says that the simplest condition that could cause this behavior—namely, the loss of *your* network's link to the Internet—is the most likely cause.

8. Missing Subdomain Delegation

Even though your ICANN-accredited registrar does its best to process your requests as quickly as possible, it may take a week or two for your subdomain's delegation to appear in the root name servers. Depending on your parent (whether an ICANN-accredited registrar or some other zone administrator), your mileage may vary. Some parents are quick and responsible; others are slow and inconsistent. Just like in real life, though, you're stuck with them.

Until your delegation data appear in your parent zone's name servers, your name servers will be able to look up data in the Internet domain namespace, but no one else on the Internet (outside of your domain) will know how to look up data in *your* namespace.

That means that even though you can send mail outside of your domain, the recipients won't be able to reply to it. Furthermore, no one will be able to *telnet* to, *ftp* to, or even *ping* your hosts by name.

Remember that this applies equally to any *in-addr.arpa* subdomains you may run. Until the parent delegates those subdomains to your servers, name servers on the Internet won't be able to reverse-map addresses on your networks.

To determine whether or not your zone's delegation has made it into your parent zone's name servers, query a parent name server for the NS records for your zone. If the parent name server has the data, any name server on the Internet can find it:

```
C:\> nslookup
Default Server:  terminator.movie.edu
Address:  192.249.249.3

> server a.root-servers.net.      --Query a root name server
Default Server:  a.root-servers.net
Address:  198.41.0.4

> set norecurse              --Instruct the server to answer out of
> set type=ns               --its own data and to look for NS records
> 249.249.192.in-addr.arpa.       --for 249.249.192.in-addr.arpa
Server:  a.root-servers.net
Address:  198.41.0.4

*** a.root-servers.net can't find 249.249.192.in-addr.arpa.: Non-existent domain
```

Here, the delegation clearly hasn't been added yet. You can either wait patiently or, if an unreasonable amount of time has passed since you requested delegation from your parent zone, you can contact your parent zone's administrator and ask what's up.

9. Incorrect Subdomain Delegation

Incorrect subdomain delegation is another familiar problem on the Internet. Keeping delegation up-to-date requires human intervention—informing your parent zone's administrator of changes to your set of authoritative name servers. Consequently, delegation information often becomes inaccurate as administrators make changes without letting their parents know. Far too many administrators believe that setting up delegation is a one-shot deal: they let their parents know which name servers are authoritative once, when they set up their zones, and then they never talk to them again. They don't even call on Mother's Day.

An administrator may add a new name server, decommission another, and change the IP address of a third, all without telling the parent zone's administrator. Gradually, the number of name servers correctly delegated to by the parent zone dwindles. In the best case this leads to long resolution times, as querying name servers struggle to find an authoritative name server for the zone. If the delegation information becomes badly out-of-date and the last authoritative name server host is brought down for maintenance, the information within the zone will be inaccessible.

If you suspect bad delegation, whether from your parent to your zone, from your zone to one of your children, or from a remote zone to one of its children, you can check with *nslookup*:

```
C:\> nslookup
Default Server:  terminator.movie.edu
Address:  192.249.249.3

> server a.gtld-servers.net.      --Set server to the parent name
                                  --server you suspect has bad delegation
Default Server:  a.gtld-servers.net
Address:  198.41.0.4

> set type=ns      --Look for NS records
> hp.com.          --for the zone in question
Server:  a.gtld-servers.net
Address:  198.41.0.4

Non-authoritative answer:
hp.com          nameserver = RELAY.HP.COM
hp.com          nameserver = HPLABS.HPL.HP.COM
hp.com          nameserver = NNSC.NSF.NET
hp.com          nameserver = HPSDLO.SDD.HP.COM

Authoritative answers can be found from:
hp.com          nameserver = RELAY.HP.COM
hp.com          nameserver = HPLABS.HPL.HP.COM
hp.com          nameserver = NNSC.NSF.NET
hp.com          nameserver = HPSDLO.SDD.HP.COM
RELAY.HP.COM      internet address = 15.255.152.2
HPLABS.HPL.HP.COM      internet address = 15.255.176.47
NNSC.NSF.NET      internet address = 128.89.1.178
```

```
HPSDLO.SDD.HP.COM          internet address = 15.255.160.64
HPSDLO.SDD.HP.COM          internet address = 15.26.112.11
```

Let's say you suspect that the delegation to *hpsdlo.sdd.hp.com* is incorrect. Query *hpsdlo* for data in the *hp.com* zone, and check the answer:

```
> server hpsdlo.sdd.hp.com.
Default Server:  hpsdlo.sdd.hp.com
Addresses:  15.255.160.64, 15.26.112.11

> set norecurse
> set type=soa
> hp.com.
Server:  hpsdlo.sdd.hp.com
Addresses:  15.255.160.64, 15.26.112.11

Non-authoritative answer:
hp.com
        origin = relay.hp.com
        mail addr = hostmaster.hp.com
        serial = 1001462
        refresh = 21600 (6 hours)
        retry  = 3600 (1 hour)
        expire  = 604800 (7 days)
        minimum ttl = 86400 (1 day)

Authoritative answers can be found from:
hp.com          nameserver = RELAY.HP.COM
hp.com          nameserver = HPLABS.HPL.HP.COM
hp.com          nameserver = NNSC.NSF.NET
RELAY.HP.COM      internet address = 15.255.152.2
HPLABS.HPL.HP.COM      internet address = 15.255.176.47
NNSC.NSF.NET      internet address = 128.89.1.178
```

If *hpsdlo* really were authoritative, it would have responded with an authoritative answer. The administrator of the *hp.com* zone can tell you whether *hpsdlo* should be an authoritative name server for *hp.com*, so that's who you should contact.

Interoperability Problems

The Microsoft DNS Server has at least one known interoperability issue with BIND name servers: zone transfers sometimes fail because of the proprietary WINS record.

When a Microsoft DNS Server is configured to consult a WINS server for names it can't find in a given zone, it inserts a special record into the zone data file. The record looks like this:

```
@   IN   WINS   <IP address of WINS server>
```

Unfortunately, WINS is not a standard record type in the IN class. Consequently, any BIND slaves that transfer this zone will choke on the WINS record and refuse to load the zone. Here's the message the administrator of the BIND server would see in his syslog output:

```
May 23 15:58:43 terminator named-xfer[386]: "fx.movie.edu IN 65281" - unknown type
(65281)
```

The workaround for this problem is to configure the Microsoft DNS Server to filter out the proprietary record before transferring the zone. You do this by selecting the zone in the left pane of the DNS console, right-clicking it, and selecting **Properties**. Click on the **WINS** tab in the resulting properties window, which is shown in Figure 13-5.

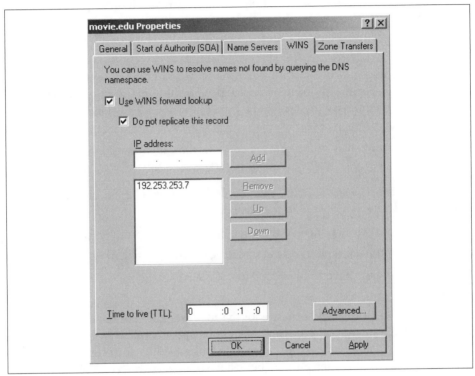

Figure 13-5. "Do not replicate this record" checkbox

Checking **Do not replicate this record** will filter out the WINS record for that zone. However, any Microsoft DNS Server slaves won't see the record, even though they could use it.

Problem Symptoms

Some problems, unfortunately, aren't as easy to identify as the ones we've listed. You'll probably experience some misbehavior that you won't be able to attribute directly to its cause, often because any of a number of problems may cause the symptoms you see. For cases like this, we'll suggest some of the common causes of these symptoms and ways to isolate them.

Can't Look Up Local Name

The first thing to do when a program like *telnet* or *ftp* can't look up a local name is to use *nslookup* to try to look up the same name. When we say "the same name," we mean *literally* the same name—don't add a domain name and a trailing dot if the user didn't type either one. Don't query a different name server than the user did.

As often as not, the user will have mistyped the name or misunderstood how the search list works and just needs direction. Occasionally, you'll turn up real host configuration errors, such as a mistake in the resolver configuration (e.g., the wrong IP address for a name server). You can check for errors like this using *nslookup*'s *set all* command.

If *nslookup* points to a problem with the name server, rather than with the host configuration, check for the problems associated with the type of name server. If the name server is the primary master for the zone but it doesn't respond with data you think it should:

- Check that the zone or zone data file contains the data in question.
- Ensure that the domain names in the records are correct (problem 6).

If the name server is a slave server, you should first check whether or not its master has the correct data. If it does, and the slave doesn't:

- Make sure you've incremented the serial number on the primary (problem 1).
- Look for a problem on the slave in updating the zone (problem 4).

If the primary *doesn't* have the correct data, of course, diagnose the problem on the primary.

If the problem server isn't authoritative for the zone that contains the data, check that your parent zone's delegation to your zone exists and is correct (problems 8 and 9). Remember that to that name server, your zone looks just like any other remote zone. Even though the host it runs on may be inside your zone, the name server must be able to locate an authoritative server for your zone from your parent zone's servers.

Can't Look Up Remote Names

If your local lookups succeed but you can't look up names outside your local zones, there is a different set of problems to check:

- Can you *ping* the remote zone's name servers? Maybe you can't reach the remote zone's servers because of connectivity loss (problem 7).
- Is the remote zone new? Maybe its delegation hasn't yet appeared (problem 8). Alternatively, the delegation information for the remote zone may be wrong or out of date, due to neglect (problem 9).
- Does the domain name actually exist on the remote zone's servers? Does it exist on all of them (problems 1, 2, and 4)?

Wrong or Inconsistent Answer

If you get the wrong answer when looking up a local name or you get an inconsistent answer, depending on which name server you ask or when you ask, first check the synchronization between your name servers:

- Are they all holding the same serial number for the zone? Did you forget to increment the serial number on the primary after you made a manual change (problem 1)? If you did, the name servers may all have the same serial number, but they will answer differently out of their authoritative data.

- Did you forget to restart the primary after making a manual change (problem 2)? Then the primary will return (via *nslookup*, for example) a different serial number than the serial number in the zone data file.

- Are the slaves having trouble updating from the primary (problem 4)?

- Is the name server's round-robin feature rotating the addresses of the domain name you're looking up?

If you get these results when looking up a name in a remote zone, you should check whether the remote zone's name servers have lost synchronization. You can use tools like *nslookup* to determine whether the remote zone's administrator has forgotten to increment the serial number, for example. If the name servers answer differently from their authoritative data but show the same serial number, the serial number probably wasn't incremented. If the primary's serial number is much lower than the slaves', the primary's serial number was probably accidentally reset. We usually assume a zone's primary name server is running on the host listed as the origin in the SOA record.

You probably can't determine conclusively that the primary hasn't been restarted, though. It's also difficult to pin down updating problems between remote name servers. In cases like this, if you've determined that the remote name servers are giving out incorrect data, contact the zone administrator and (gently) relay what you've found. This will help the administrator track down the problem on the remote end.

Lookups Take a Long Time

Long name resolution periods are usually due to one of two problems:

- Connectivity loss (problem 7), which you can diagnose with tools like *ping* and *tracert*

- Incorrect delegation information (problem 9), which points to the wrong name servers or the wrong IP addresses

Usually, sending a few *ping*s will point to one or the other of these causes. Either you can't reach the name servers at all, or you can reach the hosts but the name servers aren't responding.

Sometimes, though, the results are inconclusive. For example, the parent name servers may delegate to a set of name servers that don't respond to *ping*s or queries, but connectivity to the remote network seems all right (a *tracert*, for example, will get you to the remote network's "doorstep"—the last router between you and the host). Is the delegation information so badly out-of-date that the name servers have long since moved to other addresses? Are the hosts simply down? Or is there really a remote network problem? Usually, finding out will require a call or a message to the administrator of the remote zone. (And remember, *whois* gives you phone numbers!)

That's about all we can think of to cover. It's certainly a less than comprehensive list, but we hope it'll help you solve the more common problems you encounter with DNS and give you ideas about how to approach the rest. Boy, if we'd only had a troubleshooting guide when *we* started!

Miscellaneous

> *"The time has come," the Walrus said,*
> *"To talk of many things: Of shoes—and ships—*
> *and sealing-wax—Of cabbages—and kings—*
> *And why the sea is boiling hot—*
> *And whether pigs have wings."*

It's time we tied up loose ends. We've already covered the mainstream of DNS, but we haven't explored a handful of interesting niches. Some of these, like instructions on how to set up DNS on a network without Internet connectivity, may actually be useful; others may just be interesting. We can't in good conscience send you out into the world without completing your education!

Using CNAME Records

We talked about CNAME resource records in Chapter 4. We didn't tell you all about CNAME records, though; we saved that for this chapter. When you set up your first name servers, you didn't care about the subtle nuances of the magical CNAME record. Maybe you didn't realize there was more to it than we explained; maybe you didn't care. Some of this trivia is interesting, some is arcane. We'll let you decide which is which.

CNAMEs Attached to Interior Nodes

If you've ever renamed your zone because of a company reorganization, you may have considered creating a single CNAME record that pointed from the zone's old domain name to the new domain name. For instance, if the *fx.movie.edu* zone were renamed to *magic.movie.edu*, we'd be tempted to create a single CNAME record to map all the old names to the new names:

```
fx.movie.edu.   IN CNAME magic.movie.edu.
```

With this record in place, you'd expect a lookup of *empire.fx.movie.edu* to result in a lookup of *empire.magic.movie.edu*. Unfortunately, this doesn't work—you *can't* have a CNAME record attached to an interior node like *fx.movie.edu* if it owns other records. Remember that *fx.movie.edu* has an SOA record and NS records, so attaching a CNAME record to it violates the rule that a domain name be either an alias or a canonical name, not both. So, instead of using a single CNAME record to rename a complete zone, you'll have to do it the old-fashioned way—a CNAME record for each individual host within the zone:

```
empire.fx.movie.edu.       IN  CNAME  empire.magic.movie.edu.
bladerunner.fx.movie.edu.  IN  CNAME  bladerunner.magic.movie.edu.
```

If the subdomain isn't delegated and consequently doesn't have an SOA record and NS records attached to it, you can create an alias for *fx.movie.edu*, but it will apply only to the domain name *fx.movie.edu* and not to domain names in *fx.movie.edu*.

Hopefully, the tool you use to manage your DNS data files will handle creating CNAME records for you.

CNAMEs Pointing to CNAMEs

You may have wondered whether it was possible to have an alias (CNAME record) pointing to another alias. This might be useful in situations where an alias points from a domain name outside of your zone to a domain name inside your zone. You may not have any control over the alias outside of your zone. What if you want to change the domain name to which it points? Can you simply add another CNAME record?

The answer is yes: you can chain together CNAME records. The Microsoft DNS Server supports it, and the RFCs don't expressly forbid it. But, while you *can* chain CNAME records, is it a wise thing to do? The RFCs recommend against it because of the possibility of creating a CNAME loop and because it slows resolution. You may be able to do it in a pinch, but you probably won't find much sympathy on the Net if something breaks.

CNAMEs in the Resource Record Data

For any other record besides a CNAME record, you must have the canonical domain name in the resource record data. Applications and name servers won't operate correctly otherwise. As we mentioned back in Chapter 5, for example, many mailers recognize only the canonical name of the local host on the right side of an MX record. If a mailer doesn't recognize the local host, it won't strip out the right MX records when paring down the MX list and may deliver mail to itself or to less-preferred hosts, causing mail to loop.

Looking Up CNAMEs

At times you may want to look up a CNAME record itself, not data for the canonical name. With *nslookup*, this is easy to do. You can set the query type either to *cname* or to *any* and then look up the name:

```
C:\> nslookup
Default Server:  wormhole.movie.edu
Address:  192.249.249.1

> set query=cname
> bigt
Server:  wormhole.movie.edu
Address:  192.249.249.1

bigt.movie.edu  canonical name = terminator.movie.edu
> set query=any
> bigt
Server:  wormhole.movie.edu
Address:  192.249.249.1

bigt.movie.edu  canonical name = terminator.movie.edu
```

Finding Out a Host's Aliases

One thing you can't easily do with DNS is find out a host's aliases. With the host table, it's easy to find both the canonical name of a host and any aliases. No matter which you look up, they're all there together on the same line, as shown in the following excerpt from *HOSTS*:

```
192.249.249.3  terminator.movie.edu terminator bigt
```

With DNS, however, if you look up the canonical name, all you get is the canonical name. There's no easy way for the name server or the application to know whether aliases exist for that canonical name:

```
C:\> nslookup
Default Server:  wormhole.movie.edu
Address:  192.249.249.1

> terminator
Server:  wormhole.movie.edu
Address:  192.249.249.1

Name:     terminator.movie.edu
Address:  192.249.249.3
```

If you use *nslookup* to look up an alias, you'll see that alias and the canonical name. *nslookup* reports both the alias and the canonical name in the packet. But you won't see any other aliases that might point to that canonical name.

```
C:\> nslookup
Default Server:  wormhole.movie.edu
Address:  192.249.249.1

> bigt
Server:  wormhole.movie.edu
Address:  192.249.249.1

Name:     terminator.movie.edu
```

```
Address:  192.249.249.3
Aliases:  bigt.movie.edu
```

About the only way to find out all the CNAMEs for a host is to transfer the whole zone and pick out the CNAME records where that host is the canonical name. You can have *nslookup* filter on CNAME records:

```
C:\> nslookup
Default Server:  wormhole.movie.edu
Address:  192.249.249.1

> ls -t cname movie.edu
[wormhole.movie.edu]
 bigt                          terminator.movie.edu
 wh                            wormhole.movie.edu
 dh                            diehard.movie.edu
```

Even this method will show you only the aliases within that zone—there could be aliases in a different zone, pointing to canonical names in this zone.

Wildcards

Something else we haven't covered yet is DNS *wildcards*. At times you want a single resource record to cover any possible name, rather than creating zillions of resource records that are all the same except for the domain name to which they apply. DNS reserves a special character, the asterisk (*), to be used in a DNS data file as a wildcard name. It will match any number of labels in a name, as long as it isn't an exact match with a name already in the DNS database.

Most often, you'd use wildcards to forward mail to non-Internet-connected networks. Suppose your site is not connected to the Internet, but you have a host that will relay mail between the Internet and your network. You could add a wildcard MX record to the *movie.edu* zone for Internet consumption that points all your mail to the relay. Here is an example:

```
    *.movie.edu.  IN  MX  10 movie-relay.nea.gov.
```

Since the wildcard matches one or more labels, this resource record would apply to names like *terminator.movie.edu*, *empire.fx.movie.edu*, or *casablanca.bogart.classics. movie.edu*. The danger with wildcards is that they clash with search lists. This wildcard also matches *cujo.movie.edu.movie.edu*, making wildcards dangerous to use in your internal zone data. Remember that some mailers apply the search list when looking up MX records:

```
C:\> nslookup
Default Server:  wormhole.movie.edu
Address:  192.249.249.1

> set type=mx        --Look up MX records
> cujo.movie.edu     --for cujo
Server:  wormhole.movie.edu
```

```
Address:  192.249.249.1

cujo.movie.edu.movie.edu     --This isn't a real host's name!
        preference = 10, mail exchanger = movie-relay.nea.gov
```

What are the limitations of wildcards? Wildcards do not match names for which there is already data. Suppose you *did* use wildcards within your zone data:

```
*.movie.edu.    IN  MX  10 mail-hub.movie.edu.
et.movie.edu.   IN  MX  10 et.movie.edu.
jaws.movie.edu IN  A   192.253.253.113
```

Mail to *terminator.movie.edu* will be sent to *mail-hub*, but mail to *et.movie.edu* will be sent directly to *et*. An MX lookup of *jaws.movie.edu* would result in a response that says there is no MX data for that name. The wildcard doesn't apply because an A record exists. Can you use wildcards safely within your zone data? Yes. We'll cover that case a little later in this chapter.

A Limitation of MX Records

While we are on the topic of MX records, let's talk about how they can result in mail taking a longer path than necessary. The MX records are a list of data returned when a name is looked up. The list is not ordered according to which exchanger is closest to the sender. Here is an example of this problem. Your non-Internet-connected network has two hosts capable of relaying Internet mail to your network. One host is in the U.S., and one host is in France. Your network is in Greece. Most of your mail comes from the U.S., so you have someone maintain your zone and install two wildcard MX records—with the highest preference to the U.S. relay and a lower preference to the France relay. Since the U.S. relay is at a higher preference, *all* mail will go through that relay (as long as it is reachable). If someone in France sends you a letter, it will travel across the Atlantic to the U.S. and back because there is nothing in the MX list to indicate that the French relay is closer to that sender.

DNS and Internet Firewalls

The Domain Name System wasn't designed to work with Internet firewalls. It's a testimony to the flexibility of DNS that you can configure DNS to work with, or even through, an Internet firewall.

That said, configuring the Microsoft DNS Server to work in a firewalled environment, although not difficult, takes a good, complete understanding of DNS. Describing it also requires a large portion of this chapter, so here's a roadmap.

We start by describing the two major families of Internet firewall software: packet filters and application gateways. The capabilities of each family have a bearing on how you'll need to configure your DNS servers to work through the firewall. The next section details the two most common DNS architectures used with firewalls, forwarders and internal roots, and describes the advantages and disadvantages of each. Finally, we discuss split namespaces and the configuration of the bastion host, the host at the core of your firewall system.

Types of Firewall Software

Before you start configuring your DNS servers to work with your firewall, it's important that you understand what your firewall is capable of. Your firewall's capabilities will influence your choice of DNS architecture and will determine how you implement it. If you don't know the answers to the questions in this section, track down someone in your organization who does know and ask. Better yet, work with your firewall's administrator when designing your DNS architecture to ensure it will coexist with the firewall.

Note that this is far from a complete explanation of Internet firewalls. These few paragraphs describe only the two most common types of Internet firewalls and only in enough detail to show how the differences in their capabilities impact name servers. For a comprehensive treatment of Internet firewalls, see Elizabeth Zwicky, Simon Cooper, D. Brent Chapman, and Deborah Russell's *Building Internet Firewalls* (O'Reilly).

Packet filters

The first type of firewall we'll cover is the packet-filtering firewall. Packet-filtering firewalls operate largely at the transport and network levels of the TCP/IP stack (layers three and four of the OSI reference model, if you dig that). They decide whether to route a packet based upon packet-level criteria such as the transport protocol (e.g., whether it's TCP or UDP), the source and destination IP addresses, and the source and destination ports (see Figure 14-1).

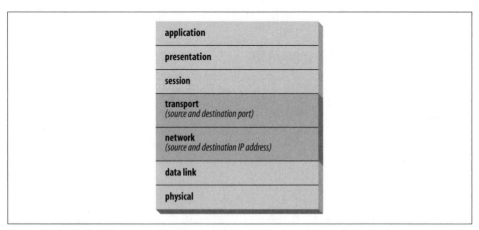

Figure 14-1. Packet filters operate at the network and transport layers of the stack

What's most important to us about packet-filtering firewalls is that you can typically configure them to selectively allow DNS traffic between hosts on the Internet and your internal hosts. That is, you can let an arbitrary set of internal hosts communicate with Internet name servers. Some packet-filtering firewalls can even permit your name servers to query name servers on the Internet, but not vice versa. All router-based Internet firewalls are packet-filtering firewalls. Check Point's FireWall-1, Cisco's PIX, and Sun's SunScreen are popular commercial packet-filtering firewalls.

Application gateways

Application gateways operate at the application protocol level, several layers higher in the OSI reference model than most packet filters (Figure 14-2). In a sense, they "understand" the application protocol in the same way a server for that particular application would. An FTP application gateway, for example, can make the decision to allow or deny a particular FTP operation, like a *RETR* (a *get*) or a *STOR* (a *put*).

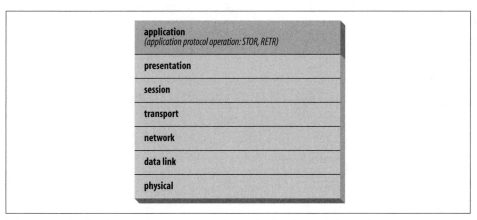

Figure 14-2. Application gateways operate at the application layer of the stack

The bad news, and what's important for our purposes, is that most application gateway–based firewalls handle only TCP-based application protocols. DNS, of course, is largely UDP-based, and we know of no application gateways for DNS. This implies that if you run an application gateway–based firewall, your internal hosts will likely not be able to communicate directly with name servers on the Internet.

The popular Firewall Toolkit from Trusted Information Systems (TIS, now part of Network Associates) is a suite of application gateways for common Internet protocols such as Telnet, FTP, and HTTP. Network Associates' Gauntlet product is also based on application gateways, as is Axent's Eagle Firewall.

Note that these two categories of firewalls are really just generalizations. The state of the art in firewalls changes very quickly, and by the time you read this, you may have a firewall that includes an application gateway for DNS. Which family your firewall falls into is important only because it *suggests* what that firewall is capable of; what's more important is whether your particular firewall will let you permit DNS traffic between arbitrary internal hosts and the Internet.

A Bad Example

The simplest configuration is to allow DNS traffic to pass freely through your firewall (assuming you can configure your firewall to do that). That way, any internal name server can query any name server on the Internet, and any Internet name server can query any of your internal name servers. You don't need any special configuration.

Unfortunately, this is a bad idea, for two reasons:

Version control
> The developers of the Microsoft DNS Server are constantly finding and fixing security-related bugs in the code. Consequently, it's important to run a recent version of the server, especially for name servers that are directly exposed to the Internet. If one or just a few of your name servers communicate directly with name servers on the Internet, upgrading them to a new version is easy. If all of the name servers on your network do, upgrading all of them is vastly more difficult.

Possible vector for attack
> Even if you're not running a name server on a particular host, a hacker might be able to take advantage of the fact that you allow DNS traffic through your firewall to attack that host. For example, a co-conspirator working on the inside could set up a Telnet daemon listening on the host's DNS port, allowing the hacker to *telnet* right in.

For the rest of this chapter, we'll try to set a good example.

Internet Forwarders

Given the dangers of allowing bidirectional DNS traffic through the firewall unrestricted, most organizations elect to limit the internal hosts that can "talk DNS" to the Internet. With an application gateway firewall, or any firewall without the ability to pass DNS traffic, the only host that can communicate with Internet name servers is the bastion host (see Figure 14-3).

With a packet-filtering firewall, the firewall's administrator can configure the firewall to let any set of internal name servers communicate with Internet name servers. Often, this is a small set of hosts that run name servers under the direct control of the network administrator (see Figure 14-4).

Internal name servers that can query name servers on the Internet directly don't require any special configuration. Their root hints files contain the Internet's root name servers, which enables them to resolve Internet domain names. Internal name servers that *can't* query name servers on the Internet, however, need to know to forward queries they can't resolve to one of the name servers that can. This is done

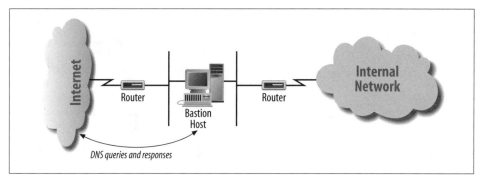

Figure 14-3. A small network, showing the bastion host

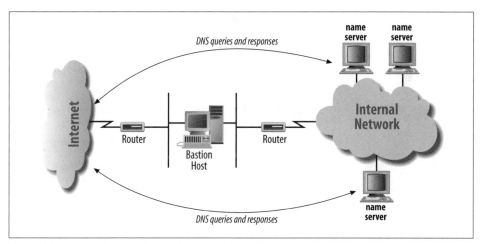

Figure 14-4. A small network, showing select internal name servers

with the **Forwarders** tab on the server's **Properties** window, described in Chapter 10.

Figure 14-5 illustrates a common forwarding setup, with internal name servers forwarding queries to a name server running on a bastion host.

At Movie U., we put in a firewall to protect ourselves from the Big Bad Internet several years ago. Ours is a packet-filtering firewall, and we negotiated with our firewall administrator to allow DNS traffic between Internet name servers and two of our name servers, *terminator.movie.edu* and *wormhole.movie.edu*. Figure 14-6 shows how we configured the other internal name servers at the university.

When configuring different internal name servers, we vary the order in which the forwarders appear to help spread the load among them.

When an internal name server receives a query for a name it can't resolve locally, such as an Internet domain name, it forwards that query to one of our forwarders, which can resolve the name using name servers on the Internet. Simple!

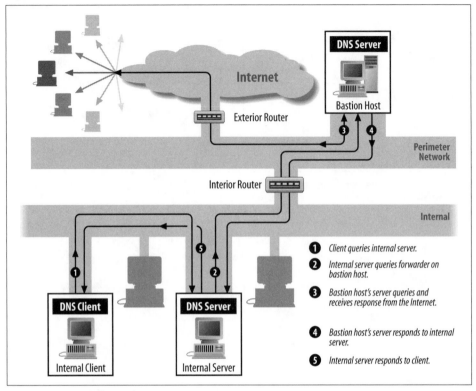

Figure 14-5. *Using forwarders*

The trouble with forwarding

Unfortunately, it's a little too simple. Forwarding starts to get in the way once you delegate subdomains or build an extensive network. To explain what we mean, take a look at *zardoz.movie.edu*. *zardoz.movie.edu* is a slave for *movie.edu* and uses our two forwarders. What happens when *zardoz.movie.edu* receives a query for a name in *fx.movie.edu*? *zardoz.movie.edu*, as an authoritative *movie.edu* name server, has the NS records that delegate *fx.movie.edu* to its authoritative name servers. But it's also been configured to forward queries it can't resolve locally to *terminator.movie.edu* and *wormhole.movie.edu*. Which will it do?

It turns out that *zardoz.movie.edu* will ignore the delegation information and forward the query to *terminator.movie.edu*. That'll work since *terminator.movie.edu* will receive the recursive query and ask an *fx.movie.edu* name server on *zardoz.movie.edu*'s behalf. But it's not particularly efficient, since *zardoz.movie.edu* could easily have sent the query directly.

Now imagine the scale of the network is much larger: a corporate network that spans continents, with tens of thousands of hosts and hundreds or thousands of

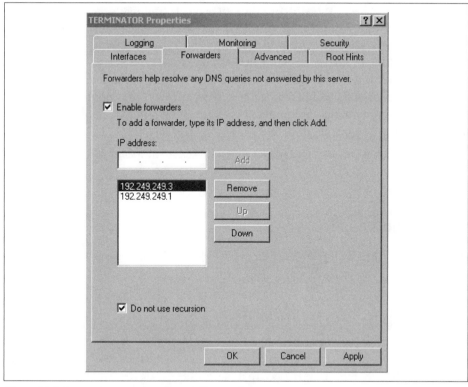

Figure 14-6. Internal name server forwarding configuration

name servers. All of the internal name servers that don't have direct Internet connectivity—the vast majority of them—use a small set of forwarders. There are several things wrong with this picture:

Single point of failure

If the forwarders fail, your name servers lose the ability to resolve both Internet domain names and internal domain names that they don't have cached or in authoritative data.

Concentration of load

The forwarders will have an enormous query load placed on them. This is both because of the large number of internal name servers that use them and because the queries are recursive and require a good deal of work to answer.

Inefficient resolution

Imagine two internal name servers, authoritative for *west.acmebw.com* and *east. acmebw.com*, respectively, both on the same network segment in Boulder, Colorado. Both are configured to use the company's forwarder in Bethesda, Maryland. To resolve a name in *east.acmebw.com*, the *west.acmebw.com* name server sends a query to the forwarder in Bethesda. The forwarder in Bethesda then sends a query back to Boulder to the *east.acmebw.com* name server, the original querier's neighbor. The *east.acmebw.com* name server replies by sending a response back to Bethesda, which the forwarder sends back to Boulder.

In a traditional configuration with root name servers, the *west.acmebw.com* name server would quickly have learned that an *east.acmebw.com* name server was next door and would favor it (because of its low roundtrip time). Using forwarders "short-circuits" the normally efficient resolution process.

The upshot is that forwarding is fine for small networks and simple namespaces but probably inadequate for large networks and complex namespaces. We found this out the hard way at Movie U. as our network grew and we were forced to implement internal roots.

Internal Roots

If you want to avoid the scalability problems of forwarding, you can set up your own root name servers. These internal roots will serve only the name servers in your organization. They'll know about only the portions of the namespace relevant to your organization.

What good are they? By using an architecture based on root name servers, you gain the scalability of the Internet namespace (which should be good enough for most companies), plus redundancy, distributed load, and efficient resolution. You can have as many internal roots as the Internet has roots—13 or so—whereas having that many forwarders may be an undue security exposure and a configuration burden. Most of all, the internal roots don't get used frivolously. Name servers need to consult an internal root only when they time out the NS records for your top-level zones. Using forwarders, name servers may have to query a forwarder once *per resolution*.

The moral of our story is that if you have, or intend to have, a large namespace and lots of internal name servers, internal root name servers will scale better than any other solution.

Where to put internal root name servers

Since name servers "lock on" to the closest root name server by favoring the one with the lowest roundtrip time, it pays to pepper your network with internal root name servers. If your organization's network spans the U.S., Europe, and the Pacific Rim, consider locating at least one internal root name server on each continent. If you have three major sites in Europe, give each of them an internal root.

Forward-mapping delegation

Here's how an internal root name server is configured. An internal root delegates directly to any zones you administer. For example, on the *movie.edu* network, the root zone's data file would contain:

```
movie.edu.   86400  IN  NS  terminator.movie.edu.
             86400  IN  NS  wormhole.movie.edu.
             86400  IN  NS  zardoz.movie.edu.
terminator.movie.edu.  86400  IN  A  192.249.249.3
wormhole.movie.edu.    86400  IN  A  192.249.249.1
                       86400  IN  A  192.253.253.1
zardoz.movie.edu.      86400  IN  A  192.249.249.9
                       86400  IN  A  192.253.253.9
```

On the Internet, this information would appear in the *edu* name servers' zone data files. On the *movie.edu* network, of course, there aren't any *edu* name servers, so you delegate directly to *movie.edu* from the root.

Notice that this example doesn't contain delegation to *fx.movie.edu* or any other subdomain of *movie.edu*. The *movie.edu* name servers know which name servers are authoritative for all *movie.edu* subdomains, and all queries for information in those subdomains pass through the *movie.edu* name servers, so there's no need to delegate them here.

in-addr.arpa delegation

We also need to delegate from the internal roots to the *in-addr.arpa* zones that correspond to the networks at the university:

```
249.249.192.in-addr.arpa.  86400  IN  NS  terminator.movie.edu.
                           86400  IN  NS  wormhole.movie.edu.
                           86400  IN  NS  zardoz.movie.edu.
253.253.192.in-addr.arpa.  86400  IN  NS  terminator.movie.edu.
                           86400  IN  NS  wormhole.movie.edu.
                           86400  IN  NS  zardoz.movie.edu.
254.253.192.in-addr.arpa.  86400  IN  NS  bladerunner.fx.movie.edu.
                           86400  IN  NS  outland.fx.movie.edu.
                           86400  IN  NS  alien.fx.movie.edu.
20.254.192.in-addr.arpa.   86400  IN  NS  bladerunner.fx.movie.edu.
                           86400  IN  NS  outland.fx.movie.edu.
                           86400  IN  NS  alien.fx.movie.edu.
```

Notice that we *did* include delegation for the *254.253.192.in-addr.arpa* and *20.254. 192.in-addr.arpa* zones, even though they both correspond to the *fx.movie.edu* zone. We didn't need to delegate to *fx.movie.edu* because we'd already delegated to its parent, *movie.edu*. The *movie.edu* name servers delegate to *fx.movie.edu*, so by transitivity the roots delegate to *fx.movie.edu*. Since neither of the other *in-addr.arpa* zones is a parent of *254.253.192.in-addr.arpa* or *20.254.192.in-addr.arpa*, we needed to delegate both zones from the root.

As we've explained earlier, we don't need to add address records for the three Special Effects name servers, *bladerunner.fx.movie.edu*, *outland.fx.movie.edu*, and *alien. fx.movie.edu*, because a remote name server can already find their addresses by following delegation from *movie.edu*.

The root.dns file

All that's left is to add an SOA record for the root zone and NS records for this internal root name server and any others:

```
.   IN  SOA  rainman.movie.edu.  hostmaster.movie.edu.  (
                1        ; serial
                10800    ; refresh
                3600     ; retry
                604800   ; expire
                86400 )  ; default TTL

    IN  NS  rainman.movie.edu.
    IN  NS  awakenings.movie.edu.

rainman.movie.edu.    IN  A  192.249.249.254
awakenings.movie.edu. IN  A  192.253.253.254
```

rainman.movie.edu and *awakenings.movie.edu* are the hosts running internal root name servers. We shouldn't run an internal root on a bastion host because if a name server on the Internet accidentally queries it for data it's not authoritative for, the internal root will respond with its list of roots—all internal!

So the whole *root.dns* file (by convention, we call the root zone's data file *root.dns*) looks like this:

```
.   IN  SOA  rainman.movie.edu.  hostmaster.movie.edu.  (
                1        ; serial
                10800    ; refresh
                3600     ; retry
                604800   ; expire
                86400 )  ; default TTL

    IN  NS  rainman.movie.edu.
    IN  NS  awakenings.movie.edu.

rainman.movie.edu.    IN  A  192.249.249.254
awakenings.movie.edu. IN  A  192.253.253.254

movie.edu.  IN  NS  terminator.movie.edu.
            IN  NS  wormhole.movie.edu.
            IN  NS  zardoz.movie.edu.

terminator.movie.edu.  IN  A  192.249.249.3
wormhole.movie.edu.    IN  A  192.249.249.1
                       IN  A  192.253.253.1
zardoz.movie.edu.      IN  A  192.249.249.9
                       IN  A  192.253.253.9

249.249.192.in-addr.arpa.  IN  NS  terminator.movie.edu.
                           IN  NS  wormhole.movie.edu.
                           IN  NS  zardoz.movie.edu.
253.253.192.in-addr.arpa.  IN  NS  terminator.movie.edu.
                           IN  NS  wormhole.movie.edu.
```

```
                             IN  NS  zardoz.movie.edu.
    254.253.192.in-addr.arpa.  IN  NS  bladerunner.fx.movie.edu.
                             IN  NS  outland.fx.movie.edu.
                             IN  NS  alien.fx.movie.edu.
     20.254.192.in-addr.arpa.  IN  NS  bladerunner.fx.movie.edu.
                             IN  NS  outland.fx.movie.edu.
                             IN  NS  alien.fx.movie.edu.
```

Creating the root zone with the DNS console on both of the internal root name servers, *rainman* and *awakenings*, is just like creating any primary zone: right-click on the server's name in the left pane, then choose **New Zone....** For the zone's domain name, choose . (a single dot). The DNS console helpfully uses *root.dns* as the default filename for this zone.

If you don't have a lot of idle hosts sitting around that you can turn into internal roots, don't despair! Any internal name server (i.e., one that's not running on a bastion host or outside your firewall) can serve double duty as an internal root *and* as an authoritative name server for whatever other zones you need it to load. Remember, a single name server can be authoritative for many, many zones, including the root zone.

Configuring other internal name servers

Once you've set up internal root name servers, configure all the name servers on hosts anywhere on your internal network to use them. Any name server running on a host without direct Internet connectivity (i.e., behind the firewall) should list the internal roots in its root hints file:

```
; Internal cache.dns file, for Movie U. hosts without direct
; Internet connectivity
;
; Don't use this file on a host with Internet connectivity!
;

.  99999999  IN  NS  rainman.movie.edu.
   99999999  IN  NS  awakenings.movie.edu.

rainman.movie.edu.      99999999  IN  A  192.249.249.254
awakenings.movie.edu.   99999999  IN  A  192.253.253.254
```

Name servers running on hosts using this root hints file will be able to resolve domain names in *movie.edu* and in Movie U.'s *in-addr.arpa* domains but not outside of those domains.

How internal name servers use internal roots

To tie together how this whole scheme works, let's go through an example of name resolution on an internal caching-only name server using these internal root name servers. First, the internal name server receives a query for a domain name in *movie.edu*, say the address of *gump.fx.movie.edu*. If the internal name server doesn't have any "better" information cached, it starts by querying an internal root name server. If it has communicated with the internal roots before, it has a roundtrip time associated with each, which tells it which of the internal roots is responding to it most quickly. It sends a nonrecursive query to that internal root for *gump.fx.movie.edu*'s address. The internal root answers with a referral to the *movie.edu* name servers on *terminator.movie.edu*, *wormhole.movie.edu*, and *zardoz.movie.edu*. The caching-only name server follows up by sending another nonrecursive query to one of the *movie.edu* name servers for *gump. fx.movie.edu*'s address. The *movie.edu* name server responds with a referral to the *fx. movie.edu* name servers. The caching-only name server sends the same nonrecursive query for *gump.fx.movie.edu*'s address to one of the *fx.movie.edu* name servers and finally receives a response.

Contrast this with the way a forwarding setup would have worked. Let's imagine that instead of using internal root name servers, our caching-only name server were configured to forward queries first to *terminator.movie.edu* and then to *wormhole. movie.edu*. In that case, the caching-only name server would have checked its cache for the address of *gump.fx.movie.edu* and, not finding it, would have forwarded the query to *terminator.movie.edu*. *terminator.movie.edu* would have queried an *fx. movie.edu* name server on the caching-only name server's behalf and returned the answer. Should the caching-only name server need to look up another name in *fx. movie.edu*, it would still ask the forwarder, even though the forwarder's response to the query for *gump.fx.movie.edu*'s address probably contained the names and addresses of the *fx.movie.edu* name servers.

The trouble with internal roots

Unfortunately, just as forwarding has its problems, internal root architectures have their limitations. Chief among these is the fact that your internal hosts can't see the Internet namespace. On some networks this isn't an issue, because most internal hosts don't have direct Internet connectivity. The few that do can have their resolvers configured to use a name server on the bastion host. Some of these hosts will probably need to run proxy servers to allow other internal hosts access to services on the Internet.

On other networks, however, the Internet firewall or other software may require that all internal hosts have the ability to resolve names in the Internet namespace. For these networks, an internal root architecture won't work.

A Split Namespace

Many organizations would like to advertise different zone data to the Internet than they do internally. In most cases, much of the internal zone data is irrelevant to the Internet because of the organization's Internet firewall. The firewall may not allow direct access to most internal hosts and may also translate internal, unregistered IP addresses into a range of IP addresses registered to the organization. Therefore, the organization may need to trim out irrelevant information from the external view of the zone or change internal addresses to their external equivalents.

Unfortunately, the Microsoft DNS Server doesn't support automatic filtering and translation of zone data. Consequently, many organizations manually create what have become known as "split namespaces." In a split namespace, the real namespace is available only internally while a pared-down, translated version of it, called the *shadow namespace*, is visible to the Internet.

The shadow namespace contains the name-to-address and address-to-name mappings of only those hosts that are accessible from the Internet through the firewall. The addresses advertised may be the translated equivalents of internal addresses. The shadow namespace may also contain one or more MX records to direct mail from the Internet through the firewall to a mail server.

Since Movie U. has an Internet firewall that greatly limits access from the Internet to the internal network, we elected to create a shadow namespace. For the *movie.edu* zone, the only information we need to give out is about the domain name *movie.edu* (an SOA record and a few NS records), the bastion host (*postmanrings2x.movie.edu*), and our new external name server, *ns.movie.edu*, which also functions as an external web server, *www.movie.edu*. The address of the external interface on the bastion host is 200.1.4.2, while the address of the name/web server is 200.1.4.3. The shadow *movie.edu* zone data file looks like this:

```
@    IN    SOA    ns.movie.edu.    hostmaster.movie.edu. (
                         1         ; Serial
                         10800     ; Refresh
                         3600      ; Retry
                         604800    ; Expire
                         86400 )   ; Default TTL

     IN    NS     ns.movie.edu.
     IN    NS     ns1.isp.net.          ; our ISP's name server is a movie.edu slave

     IN    A      200.1.4.3
     IN    MX     10 postmanrings2x.movie.edu.
     IN    MX     100 mail.isp.net.

www            IN    CNAME movie.edu.

postmanrings2x IN    A      200.1.4.2
               IN    MX     10 postmanrings2x.movie.edu.
               IN    MX     100 mail.isp.net.

;postmanrings2x.movie.edu handles mail addressed to ns.movie.edu
ns             IN    A      200.1.4.3
               IN    MX     10 postmanrings2x.movie.edu.
               IN    MX     100 mail.isp.net.

*              IN    MX     10 postmanrings2x.movie.edu.
               IN    MX     100 mail.isp.net.
```

Note that there's no mention of any of the subdomains of *movie.edu*, including any delegation to the name servers for those subdomains. That information isn't necessary, since there's nothing in any of the subdomains you can get to from the Internet and inbound mail addressed to hosts in the subdomains is caught by the wildcard.

The *4.1.200.in-addr.arpa.dns* file, which we need to reverse map the two Movie U. IP addresses that hosts on the Internet might see, looks like this:

```
$TTL 1d
@    IN    SOA    ns.movie.edu.    hostmaster.movie.edu. (
                            1       ; Serial
                            10800   ; Refresh
                            3600    ; Retry
                            604800  ; Expire
                            86400 ) ; Default TTL

     IN    NS     ns.movie.edu.
     IN    NS     ns.isp.net.

2    IN    PTR    postmanrings2x.movie.edu.
3    IN    PTR    ns1.movie.edu.
```

One precaution we need to take is to make sure that the resolver on our bastion host isn't configured to use the server on *ns.movie.edu*. Since that server can't see the real, internal *movie.edu*, using it would render *postmanrings2x.movie.edu* unable to map internal names to addresses or internal addresses to names.

Configuring the bastion host

The bastion host is a special case in a split-namespace configuration. The bastion host has a foot in each environment: one network interface connects it to the Internet and another connects it to the internal network. Now that we have split our namespace in two, how can our bastion host see both the Internet namespace and our internal namespace? If we configure it with the Internet's root name servers in its root hints file, it will follow delegation from the Internet's *edu* name servers to an external *movie.edu* name server with shadow zone data. It would be blind to our internal namespace, which it needs to see to log connections, deliver inbound mail, and more. On the other hand, if we configure it with our internal roots it won't see the Internet namespace, which it clearly needs to do in order to function as a bastion host. What to do?

If we have internal name servers that can resolve both internal and Internet domain names—using the forwarding configuration earlier in this chapter, for example—we can simply configure the bastion host's resolver to query those name servers. But if we use forwarding internally, depending on the type of firewall we're running we may also need to run a forwarder on the bastion host itself. If the firewall won't pass DNS traffic, we'll need to run at least a caching-only name server, configured with the Internet roots, on the bastion host so that our internal name servers will have somewhere to forward their unresolved queries.

If our internal name servers aren't configured to forward zones, the name server on our bastion host must be configured as a slave for *movie.edu* and any *in-addr.arpa* zones in which it needs to resolve addresses. This way, if it receives a query for a domain name in *movie.edu*, it'll use its local authoritative data to resolve the name. (If our internal name servers support forward zones and are configured correctly, the name server on our bastion host will never receive queries for names in *movie.edu*.) If the domain name is in a subdomain of *movie.edu*, it'll follow NS records in the zone data to query an internal name server for the name. Therefore, it doesn't need to be configured as a slave for any *movie.edu* subdomains, such as *fx.movie.edu*, just the "topmost" zone (see Figure 14-7).

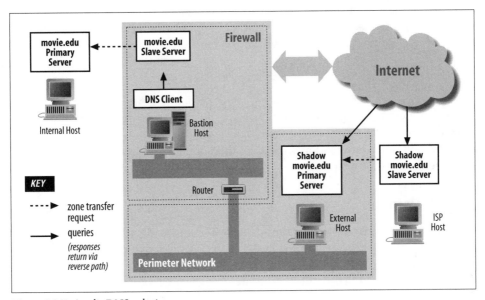

Figure 14-7. A split DNS solution

Dial-up Connections

Another relatively recent development in networking that presents a challenge to DNS is the dial-up Internet connection. When the Internet was young and DNS was born, there was no such thing as a dial-up connection. With the enormous explosion in the Internet's popularity and the propagation of Internet service providers who offer dial-up Internet connectivity to the masses, a whole new breed of problems with name service has been introduced.

We'll separate dial-up connections into two categories: simple dial-up, by which we mean a single computer that connects to the Internet occasionally, when a user manually initiates a connection; and dial-on-demand, which means one or more computers that connect to the Internet automatically whenever they generate traffic bound for the Internet. Often, the device that makes this dial-on-demand connectivity possible is a small dial-up router with an analog modem or ISDN interface, such as an Ascend Pipeline 25.

Simple Dial-up

The easiest way to deal with simple dial-up is to configure your dial-up computer's resolver to use a name server provided by your ISP. Most ISPs run name servers for their subscribers' use. If you're not sure whether your ISP provides name servers for your use or if you don't know what their IP addresses are, check their web site, send them email, or give them a call.

Some operating systems, including all modern versions of Windows, will let you define a set of name servers for a particular dial-up provider. So, for example, you can configure one set of name servers to use when you dial up Netcom and another to use when you dial up your office. Unfortunately, if you're still using Windows 95, defining name servers for your LAN connection overrides all your precious dial-up settings.*

This configuration is usually adequate for most casual dial-up users. Name resolution fails unless the dial-up connection is up, but that's not likely to be a problem since there's no use for Internet name service without Internet connectivity. If you have special needs that aren't addressed by this configuration, take a look at the recommendations in the next section.

Dial-on-Demand

A more sophisticated dial-up solution is dial-on-demand. Dial-on-demand Internet connections often use dedicated hardware, such as a small dial-up router, to provide connectivity whenever it's needed. If you initiate a connection to the Internet from the "remote" end of a dial-on-demand router, it dials up another router on the Internet and routes your packets across. If the connection is idle for more than a specified amount of time, the router drops the connection.

The challenge with DNS is to keep a local name server from continuously bringing the dial-on-demand connection up and down like a yo-yo. This could be costly, because you sometimes pay a premium for connection setup with technologies like ISDN.

The most important strategy for minimizing this off-net traffic is to configure your resolvers to use a minimal search list (or DNS suffix list, as it's called in Windows). The default Windows search list (which you get when you don't specify an explicit list of DNS suffixes to search) searches the ancestors of your local domain, which can cause unnecessary remote traffic. For instance, say your local domain is *tinyoffice.majorcorp.com*, and you have a dial-on-demand connection to Majorcorp's

---

* A handy shareware utility called *Netswitcher* allows Windows 95 users to change resolver settings easily. For more information, see *http://www.netswitcher.com*.

enterprise network. On hosts without an explicit DNS suffix list, your default search list is:

```
tinyoffice.majorcorp.com
majorcorp.com
```

A user typing *telnet foo.tinyoffice.majorcorp.com* to log into the workstation next to him might inadvertently cause lookups of both of these addresses:

```
foo.tinyoffice.majorcorp.com.tinyoffice.majorcorp.com
foo.tinyoffice.majorcorp.com.majorcorp.com
```

before the correct domain name, *foo.tinyoffice.majorcorp.com*, is looked up.[*] Since your local name server is probably authoritative for *tinyoffice.majorcorp.com*, it can tell that the first domain name, *foo.tinyoffice.majorcorp.com.tinyoffice.majorcorp.com*, is bogus. (It ends in *com.tinyoffice.majorcorp.com*, so it would require the existence of a *com* subdomain of your local domain, and there isn't one.) But it can't tell about the second domain name without talking to a *majorcorp.com* name server first. If there isn't one locally, it'll have to bring up that dial-on-demand connection.

The easiest way to prevent these unnecessary queries is to trim the parent domain out of your search list explicitly by setting a DNS suffix list in the resolver configuration. In this example, a DNS suffix list *tinyoffice.majorcorp.com* (just one entry) would probably cause fewer failed off-site lookups.

If many of the names your users look up are in your parent zone, you might also consider configuring your local name server as a slave for your parent zone. At least that way you'll bring up the link at most only once per refresh interval to resolve names in your parent zone. The same logic could be applied to nearly any zone your local name server queries often.

Network Names and Numbers

The original DNS definitions didn't provide the ability to look up network names based on a network number—a feature that was provided by the original *HOSTS.TXT* file. More recently, a procedure for storing network names has been defined; this procedure also works for subnets and subnet masks, so it goes significantly beyond *HOSTS.TXT*. Moreover, it doesn't require any modification to the DNS server software at all; it's based entirely on the clever use of pointer and address records.

If you remember, to map an IP address to a name in DNS, you reverse the IP address, append *in-addr.arpa*, and look up the PTR data. This same technique is used to map a network number to a network name; for example, to map network 15.0.0.0 to "HP

---

[*] The exact behavior depends on which version of Windows the user is running. Older versions of Windows exhibit this behavior, but newer versions of Windows try to resolve any domain names containing at least one dot by themselves before appending the search list. You'll find more details about resolver behavior in Chapter 6.

Internet." To look up the network number, include the trailing zeros to make it four bytes and look up PTR data just as you would with a host's IP address. For example, to find the network name for the old ARPANET, network 10.0.0.0, look up PTR data for *0.0.0.10.in-addr.arpa*. You'd get back an answer like *ARPANET.ARPA*.

If the ARPANET were subnetted, you'd also find an address record at *0.0.0.10.in-addr.arpa*. The address would be the subnet mask (255.255.0.0, for instance). If you were interested in the subnet name instead of the network name, you'd apply the mask to the IP address and look up the subnet number.

This technique allows you to map the network number to a name. To provide a complete solution, there must be a way to map a network name to its network number. This, again, is accomplished with PTR records. The network name has PTR data that points to the network number (reversed, with *in-addr.arpa* appended).

Let's see what the data might look like in HP's zone data files (the HP Internet has network number 15.0.0.0) and step through mapping a network number to a network name.

Here are the partial contents of the *hp.com.dns* file:

```
;
; Map HP's network name to 15.0.0.0.
;
hp-net.hp.com.              IN  PTR 0.0.0.15.in-addr.arpa.
```

Following are the partial contents of the *corp.hp.com.dns* file:

```
;
; Map corp's subnet name to 15.1.0.0.
;
corp-subnet.corp.hp.com.  IN  PTR 0.0.1.15.in-addr.arpa.
```

Here are the partial contents of the *15.in-addr.arpa.dns* file:

```
;
; Map 15.0.0.0 to hp-net.hp.com.
; HP's subnet mask is 255.255.248.0.
;
0.0.0.15.in-addr.arpa.    IN  PTR hp-net.hp.com.
                          IN  A   255.255.248.0
```

And here are the partial contents of the *1.15.in-addr.arpa.dns* file:

```
;
; Map the 15.1.0.0 back to its subnet name.
;
0.0.1.15.in-addr.arpa.    IN  PTR corp-subnet.corp.hp.com.
```

Here's the procedure to look up the subnet name for the IP address 15.1.0.1:

1. Apply the default network mask for the address's class. Address 15.1.0.1 is a Class A address, so the mask is 255.0.0.0. Applying the mask to the IP address makes the network number 15.

2. Send a query (*type=a* or *type=any*) for *0.0.0.15.in-addr.arpa*.

   The query response contains address data. Since address data is at *0.0.0.15.in-addr.arpa* (the subnet mask—255.255.248.0), apply the subnet mask to the IP address. This yields 15.1.0.0.

3. Send a query (*type=a* or *type=any*) for *0.0.1.15.in-addr.arpa*.

   The query response does not contain address data, so 15.1.0.0 is not further subnetted.

4. Send a PTR query for *0.0.1.15.in-addr.arpa*.

   The query response contains the network name for 15.1.0.1: *corp-subnet.corp. hp.com*.

In addition to mapping between network names and numbers, you can also list all the networks for your domain with PTR records:

```
movie.edu.  IN  PTR  0.249.249.192.in-addr.arpa.
            IN  PTR  0.253.253.192.in-addr.arpa.
```

Now for the bad news: despite the fact that RFC 1101 contains everything you need to know to set this up, we know of only one software package that actually *uses* this type of network name encoding, and very few administrators go to the trouble of adding this information. Until software actually makes use of DNS-encoded network names, about the only reason for setting this up is to show off. But that's a good enough reason for many of us.

Additional Resource Records

There are a number of resource records that we haven't covered yet in this book. The first of these, HINFO, has been around since the beginning but hasn't been widely used. The others were defined in RFC 1183 and several successive RFCs. Most are experimental, but some are on the standards track and are coming into more prevalent use. We'll describe them here to give you a little head start in getting used to them.

Host Information

HINFO stands for *host information*. The record-specific data is a pair of strings identifying the host's hardware type and operating system. The strings are supposed to come from the MACHINE NAMES and OPERATING SYSTEM NAMES listed in the Assigned Numbers RFC (currently RFC 1700), but this requirement is not enforced; you can use your own abbreviations. The RFC isn't at all comprehensive, so it's quite possible you won't find your system in the list anyway. Originally, host information records were intended to let services like FTP determine how to interact with a remote system. This would have made it possible to negotiate data type transformations automatically, for example. Unfortunately, this didn't happen—few sites supply accurate HINFO values for all their systems. Some network administrators use HINFO records to help them keep track of the machine types, instead of recording the machine types in a database or a notebook. Here are two examples of HINFO records (note that the values in the **CPU type** and **Operating system** fields must be surrounded with quotes if they include any whitespace):

```
;
; These machine names and system names did not come from RFC 1700
;
wormhole  IN  HINFO  ACME-HW  ACME-GW
cujo      IN  HINFO  "Watch Dog Hardware"  "Rabid OS"
```

You'd see the window shown in Figure 14-8 if you added an HINFO record with the DNS console.

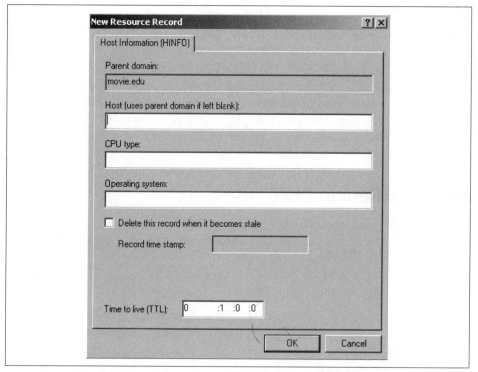

Figure 14-8. Adding an HINFO record with the DNS console

If you include whitespace in the values you type in the **CPU type** and **Operating system** fields, the DNS console will automatically put double quotes around them, so don't use double quotes in either field—you'll get double double quotes.

Before you go adding them to your zone—particularly a zone visible from the Internet—you should know that HINFO records can present a security risk. By providing easily accessible information about a system, you may be making it easier for a hacker to break into it.

AFSDB

AFSDB has a syntax like that of the MX record and semantics a bit like that of the NS record. An AFSDB record gives either the location of an AFS cell database server or of a DCE cell's authenticated name server. The type of server the record points to, and the name of the host running the server, are contained in the record-specific data portion of the record.

So what's an AFS cell database server? Or AFS, for that matter? AFS originally stood for the Andrew File System, designed by the good folks at Carnegie-Mellon University as part of the Andrew Project. (It's now an IBM product.) AFS is a network filesystem, like NFS, but one that handles the latency of wide-area networks much better than NFS does and provides local caching of files to enhance performance. An AFS cell database server runs the process responsible for tracking the location of filesets (groups of files) on various AFS file servers within a cell (a logical group of hosts). So being able to find the AFS cell database server is the key to finding any file in the cell.

And what's an authenticated name server? It holds location information about all sorts of services available within a DCE cell. A DCE cell? That's a logical group of hosts that share services offered by The Open Group's Distributed Computing Environment (DCE).

And now, back to our story. To access another cell's AFS or DCE services across a network, you must first find out where that cell's cell database servers or authenticated name servers are. Hence the new record type. The domain name to which the record is attached gives the name of the cell the server knows about. Cells are often share names with DNS domains, so this usually doesn't look at all odd.

As we said, the AFSDB record's syntax is like the MX record's syntax. In place of the preference value, you specify the number 1 for an AFS cell database server or 2 for a DCE authenticated name server.

In place of the mail exchanger host, you specify the name of the host running the server. Simple!

Say an *fx.movie.edu* system administrator sets up a DCE cell (which includes AFS services) because she wants to experiment with distributed processing to speed up graphics rendering. She runs both an AFS cell database server and a DCE name server on *bladerunner.fx.movie.edu*, another cell database server on *empire.fx.movie.edu*, and another DCE name server on *aliens.fx.movie.edu*. She should set up the AFSDB records as follows:

```
; Our DCE cell is called fx.movie.edu, same as the domain name of the zone
fx.movie.edu.  IN  AFSDB  1 bladerunner.fx.movie.edu.
               IN  AFSDB  2 bladerunner.fx.movie.edu.
               IN  AFSDB  1 empire.fx.movie.edu.
               IN  AFSDB  2 aliens.fx.movie.edu.
```

X25, ISDN, and RT

These three record types were created specifically in support of research on next-generation internets. Two of the records, X25 and ISDN, are simply address records specific to X.25 and ISDN networks, respectively. Both take record-specific data appropriate to the type of network. The X25 record type uses an X.121 address (X. 121 is the ITU-T recommendation that specifies the format of addresses used in X.25 networks.) The ISDN record type uses an ISDN address.

ISDN stands for Integrated Services Digital Network. Telephone companies around the world use ISDN protocols to allow their telephone networks to carry both voice and data, creating an integrated network. Although ISDN's availability is spotty throughout the U.S., it has been widely adopted in some international markets. Since ISDN uses the telephone companies' networks, an ISDN address is just a phone number and, in fact, consists of a country code, followed by an area code or city code, then by a local phone number. Sometimes there are a few extra digits you wouldn't see in a phone number at the end, called a subaddress. The subaddress is specified in a separate field in the record-specific data.

Examples of the X25 and ISDN record types are:

```
relay.pink.com.   IN  X25   31105060845

delay.hp.com.     IN  ISDN  141555514539488
hep.hp.com.       IN  ISDN  141555514539488 004
```

These records are intended for use in conjunction with the Route Through (RT) record type. RT is syntactically and semantically similar to the MX record type: it specifies an intermediate host that will route *packets* (instead of mail) to a destination host. So now, instead of being able to route mail only to a host that isn't directly connected to the Internet, you can route any kind of IP packet to that host by using another host as a forwarder. The packet could be part of a Telnet or FTP session or perhaps even a DNS query!

Like MX, RT includes a preference value, which indicates how desirable delivery to a particular host is. For example, the records:

```
housesitter.movie.edu.  IN  RT  10 relay.pink.com.
                        IN  RT  20 delay.hp.com.
```

instruct hosts to route packets bound for *housesitter.movie.edu* through *relay.pink. com* (the first choice) or through *delay.hp.com* (the second choice).

The way RT works with X25 and ISDN (and even A) records is like this:

1. Internet host A wants to send a packet to host B, which is not connected to the Internet.

2. Host A looks up host B's RT records. This search also returns all address records (A, X25, and ISDN) for each intermediate host.

3. Host A sorts the list of intermediate hosts and looks for its own domain name. If it finds it, it removes it and all intermediate hosts at higher preference values. This is analogous to *sendmail*'s "paring down" a list of mail exchangers.

4. Host A examines the address record(s) for the most-preferred intermediate host that remains. If host A is attached to a network that corresponds to the type of address record indicated, it uses that network to send the packet to the intermediate host. For example, if host A were trying to send a packet through *relay.pink.com*, it would need connectivity to an X.25 network.

5. If host A lacks appropriate connectivity, it tries the next intermediate host specified by the RT records. For example, if host A lacked X.25 connectivity, it might fall back to connecting via ISDN to *delay.hp.com*.

This process continues until the packet is routed to the most-preferred intermediate host. The most-preferred intermediate host may then deliver the packet directly to the destination host's address (which may be A, X25, or ISDN).

DNS Message Format and Resource Records

This appendix outlines the format of DNS messages and enumerates all the resource record types. The resource records are shown in their textual format, as you would specify them in a zone data file, and in their binary format, as they appear in DNS messages. You'll find a few resource records here that weren't covered in the book because they are experimental or obsolete.

We've included the portions of RFC 1035, written by Paul Mockapetris, that deal with the textual format of master files (what we called *zone data files* in the book) or with the DNS message format (for those of you who need to parse DNS packets).

Master File Format

(From RFC 1035, pages 33–35)

The format of these files is a sequence of entries. Entries are predominantly line-oriented, though parentheses can be used to continue a list of items across a line boundary, and text literals can contain CRLF within the text. Any combination of tabs and spaces acts as a delimiter between the separate items that make up an entry. The end of any line in the master file can end with a comment. The comment starts with a semicolon (;).

The following entries are defined:

    blank[comment]

    $ORIGIN domain-name [comment]

    $INCLUDE file-name [domain-name] [comment]

    domain-namerr [comment]

    blankrr [comment]

Blank lines, with or without comments, are allowed anywhere in the file.

Two control entries are defined: $ORIGIN and $INCLUDE. $ORIGIN is followed by a domain name and resets the current origin for relative domain names to the stated name. $INCLUDE inserts the named file into the current file and may optionally specify a domain name that sets the relative domain name origin for the included file. $INCLUDE may also have a comment. Note that an $INCLUDE entry never changes the relative origin of the parent file, regardless of changes to the relative origin made within the included file.

The last two forms represent RRs. If an entry for an RR begins with a blank, then the RR is assumed to be owned by the last stated owner. If an RR entry begins with a *domain-name*, then the owner name is reset.

rr contents take one of the following forms:

```
[TTL] [class] type RDATA
[class] [TTL] type RDATA
```

The RR begins with optional TTL and class fields, followed by a type and RDATA field appropriate to the type and class. Class and type use the standard mnemonics; TTL is a decimal integer. Omitted class and TTL values default to the last explicitly stated values. Since type and class mnemonics are disjoint, the parse is unique.

*domain-name*s make up a large share of the data in the master file. The labels in the domain name are expressed as character strings and separated by dots. Quoting conventions allow arbitrary characters to be stored in domain names. Domain names that end in a dot are called absolute, and are taken as complete. Domain names that do not end in a dot are called relative; the actual domain name is the concatenation of the relative part with an origin specified in an $ORIGIN, $INCLUDE, or argument to the master file-loading routine. A relative name is an error when no origin is available.

character-string is expressed in one of two ways: as a contiguous set of characters without interior spaces, or as a string beginning with " and ending with ". Inside a "-delimited string any character can occur, except for " itself, which must be quoted using a backslash (\).

Because these files are text files, several special encodings are necessary to allow arbitrary data to be loaded. In particular:

.

> Of the root.

@

> A free-standing @ is used to denote the current origin.

\X

> Where X is any character other than a digit (0–9), \ is used to quote that character so that its special meaning does not apply. For example, \. can be used to place a dot character in a label.[*]

---

[*] Not implemented by BIND 4.8.3.

\DDD

> Where each *D* is a digit in the octet corresponding to the decimal number described by *DDD*. The resulting octet is assumed to be text and is not checked for special meaning.[*]

( )

> Parentheses are used to group data that crosses a line boundary. In effect, line terminations are not recognized within parentheses.[†]

;

> A semicolon is used to start a comment; the remainder of the line is ignored.

Character Case

(From RFC 1035, page 9)

For all parts of the DNS that are part of the official protocol, all comparisons between character strings (e.g., labels, domain names, etc.) are done in a case-insensitive manner. At present, this rule is in force throughout the domain system without exception. However, future additions beyond current usage may need to use the full binary octet capabilities in names, so attempts to store domain names in 7-bit ASCII or use of special bytes to terminate labels, etc., should be avoided.

Types

Following is a complete list of resource record types. The textual representation is used in master files. The binary representation is used in DNS queries and responses. These resource records are described on pages 13–21 of RFC 1035.

A (address)

(From RFC 1035, page 20)

Textual representation:

    owner ttl class A address

Example:

    localhost.movie.edu.   IN A 127.0.0.1

Binary representation:

    Address type code: 1

---

[*] Not implemented by BIND 4.8.3.

[†] BIND 4.8.3 allows parentheses only on SOA and WKS resource records.

where:

ADDRESS
>A 32 bit Internet address.

CNAME (canonical name)

(From RFC 1035, page 14)

Textual representation:

>*owner ttl class* CNAME *canonical-dname*

Example:

>wh.movie.edu. IN CNAME wormhole.movie.edu.

Binary representation:

```
CNAME type code: 5
    +--+--+--+--+--+--+--+--+--+--+--+--+--+--+--+--+
    /                     CNAME                     /
    /                                               /
    +--+--+--+--+--+--+--+--+--+--+--+--+--+--+--+--+
```

where:

CNAME
>A *domain-name* which specifies the canonical or primary name for the owner. The owner name is an alias.

HINFO (host information)

(From RFC 1035, page 14)

Textual representation:

>*owner ttl class* HINFO *cpu os*

Example:

>grizzly.movie.edu. IN HINFO VAX-11/780 UNIX

Binary representation:

```
HINFO type code: 13
    +--+--+--+--+--+--+--+--+--+--+--+--+--+--+--+--+
    /                      CPU                      /
    +--+--+--+--+--+--+--+--+--+--+--+--+--+--+--+--+
    /                      OS                       /
    +--+--+--+--+--+--+--+--+--+--+--+--+--+--+--+--+
```

where:

CPU
>A *character-string* which specifies the CPU type.

OS
>A *character-string* which specifies the operating system type.

MB (mailbox domain name—experimental)

(From RFC 1035, page 14)

Textual representation:

```
owner ttl class MB mbox-dname
```

Example:

```
al.movie.edu.  IN  MB  robocop.movie.edu.
```

Binary representation:

```
MB type code: 7
    +--+--+--+--+--+--+--+--+--+--+--+--+--+--+--+--+
    /                     MADNAME                    /
    /                                                /
    +--+--+--+--+--+--+--+--+--+--+--+--+--+--+--+--+
```

where:

MADNAME

A *domain-name* which specifies a host which has the specified mailbox.

MD (mail destination—obsolete)

MD has been replaced with MX.

MF (mail forwarder—obsolete)

MF has been replaced with MX.

MG (mail group member—experimental)

(From RFC 1035, page 16)

Textual representation:

```
owner ttl class MG mgroup-dname
```

Example:

```
admin.movie.edu.  IN  MG  al.movie.edu.
                  IN  MG  ed.movie.edu.
                  IN  MG  jc.movie.edu.
```

Binary representation:

```
MG type code: 8
    +--+--+--+--+--+--+--+--+--+--+--+--+--+--+--+--+
    /                     MGMNAME                    /
    /                                                /
    +--+--+--+--+--+--+--+--+--+--+--+--+--+--+--+--+
```

where:

MGMNAME

> A *domain-name* which specifies a mailbox which is a member of the mail group speci-
> fied by the domain name.

MINFO (mailbox or mail list information—experimental)   (From RFC 1035, page 16)

Textual representation:

```
owner ttl class MINFO resp-mbox error-mbox
```

Example:

```
admin.movie.edu.  IN  MINFO  al.movie.edu. al.movie.edu.
```

Binary representation:

```
MINFO type code: 14
    +--+--+--+--+--+--+--+--+--+--+--+--+--+--+--+--+
    /                   RMAILBX                     /
    +--+--+--+--+--+--+--+--+--+--+--+--+--+--+--+--+
    /                   EMAILBX                     /
    +--+--+--+--+--+--+--+--+--+--+--+--+--+--+--+--+
```

where:

RMAILBX

> A *domain-name* which specifies a mailbox which is responsible for the mailing list or
> mailbox. If this domain name names the root, the owner of the MINFO RR is respon-
> sible for itself. Note that many existing mailing lists use a mailbox X-request for the
> RMAILBX field of mailing list X, e.g., Msgroup-request for Msgroup. This field
> provides a more general mechanism.

EMAILBX

> A *domain-name* which specifies a mailbox which is to receive error messages related to
> the mailing list or mailbox specified by the owner of the MINFO RR (similar to the
> ERRORS-TO: field which has been proposed). If this domain name names the root,
> errors should be returned to the sender of the message.

MR (mail rename—experimental)   (From RFC 1035, page 17)

Textual representation:

```
owner ttl class MR new-mbox
```

Example:

```
eddie.movie.edu.  IN  MR  eddie.bornagain.edu.
```

Binary representation:

```
MR type code: 9
```

```
+--+--+--+--+--+--+--+--+--+--+--+--+--+--+--+--+
/                    NEWNAME                    /
/                                               /
+--+--+--+--+--+--+--+--+--+--+--+--+--+--+--+--+
```

where:

NEWNAME
> A *domain-name* which specifies a mailbox which is the proper rename of the specified mailbox.

MX (mail exchanger)

(From RFC 1035, page 17)

Textual representation:

```
owner ttl class MX preference exchange-dname
```

Example:

```
ora.com.  IN  MX  0  ora.ora.com.
          IN  MX  10 ruby.ora.com.
          IN  MX  10 opal.ora.com.
```

Binary representation:

```
MX type code: 15
   +--+--+--+--+--+--+--+--+--+--+--+--+--+--+--+--+
   |                   PREFERENCE                  |
   +--+--+--+--+--+--+--+--+--+--+--+--+--+--+--+--+
   /                    EXCHANGE                   /
   /                                               /
   +--+--+--+--+--+--+--+--+--+--+--+--+--+--+--+--+
```

where:

PREFERENCE
> A 16 bit integer which specifies the preference given to this RR among others at the same owner. Lower values are preferred.

EXCHANGE
> A *domain-name* which specifies a host willing to act as a mail exchange for the owner name.

NS (name server)

(From RFC 1035, page 18)

Textual representation:

```
owner ttl class NS name-server-dname
```

Example:

```
movie.edu.  IN   NS  terminator.movie.edu
```

Binary representation:

```
NS type code: 2
```

```
+--+--+--+--+--+--+--+--+--+--+--+--+--+--+--+--+
/                     NSDNAME                    /
/                                                /
+--+--+--+--+--+--+--+--+--+--+--+--+--+--+--+--+
```

where:

NSDNAME
A *domain-name* which specifies a host which should be authoritative for the specified class and domain.

NULL (null—experimental)   (From RFC 1035, page 17)

Binary representation:

```
NULL type code: 10
    +--+--+--+--+--+--+--+--+--+--+--+--+--+--+--+--+
    /                     anything                  /
    /                                               /
    +--+--+--+--+--+--+--+--+--+--+--+--+--+--+--+--+
```

Anything at all may be in the RDATA field so long as it is 65535 octets or less.

NULL is not implemented by BIND.

PTR (pointer)   (From RFC 1035, page 18)

Textual representation:

owner ttl class PTR *dname*

Example:

```
1.249.249.192.in-addr.arpa.  IN PTR wormhole.movie.edu.
```

Binary representation:

```
PTR type code: 12
    +--+--+--+--+--+--+--+--+--+--+--+--+--+--+--+--+
    /                     PTRDNAME                   /
    +--+--+--+--+--+--+--+--+--+--+--+--+--+--+--+--+
```

where:

PTRDNAME
A *domain-name* which points to some location in the domain name space.

SOA (start of authority)   (From RFC 1035, pages 19–20)

Textual representation:

owner ttl class SOA *source-dname mbox (serial refresh retry expire minimum)*

Example:

```
movie.edu. IN SOA terminator.movie.edu. al.robocop.movie.edu. (
                        1        ; Serial
                        10800    ; Refresh after 3 hours
                        3600     ; Retry after 1 hour
                        604800   ; Expire after 1 week
                        86400 )  ; Minimum TTL of 1 day
```

Binary representation:

SOA type code: 6

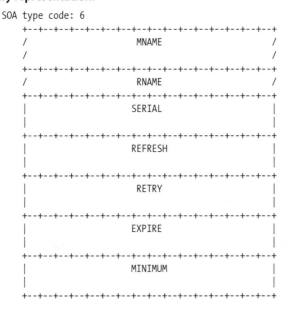

where:

MNAME

> The *domain-name* of the name server that was the original or primary source of data for this zone.

RNAME

> A *domain-name* which specifies the mailbox of the person responsible for this zone.

SERIAL

> The unsigned 32 bit version number of the original copy of the zone. Zone transfers preserve this value. This value wraps and should be compared using sequence space arithmetic.

REFRESH

> A 32 bit time interval before the zone should be refreshed.

RETRY

> A 32 bit time interval that should elapse before a failed refresh should be retried.

EXPIRE

> A 32 bit time value that specifies the upper limit on the time interval that can elapse before the zone is no longer authoritative.

MINIMUM

The unsigned 32 bit minimum TTL field that should be exported with any RR from this zone.

TXT (text)

(From RFC 1035, page 20)

Textual representation:

```
owner ttl class TXT txt-strings
```

Example:

```
cujo.movie.edu.  IN  TXT  "Location: machine room dog house"
```

Binary representation:

```
TXT type code: 16
    +--+--+--+--+--+--+--+--+--+--+--+--+--+--+--+--+
    /                    TXT-DATA                   /
    +--+--+--+--+--+--+--+--+--+--+--+--+--+--+--+--+
```

where:

TXT-DATA

One or more *character-string*s.

WKS (well-known services)

(From RFC 1035, page 21)

Textual representation:

```
owner ttl class WKS address protocol service-list
```

Example:

```
terminator.movie.edu.  IN  WKS 192.249.249.3  TCP ( telnet smtp ftp shell domain )
```

Binary representation:

```
WKS type code: 11
    +--+--+--+--+--+--+--+--+--+--+--+--+--+--+--+--+
    |                    ADDRESS                    |
    +--+--+--+--+--+--+--+--+--+--+--+--+--+--+--+--+
    |    PROTOCOL        |                          |
    +--+--+--+--+--+--+--+--+                          |
    |                    |                          |
    /                  BIT MAP                      /
    /                                               /
    +--+--+--+--+--+--+--+--+--+--+--+--+--+--+--+--+
```

where:

ADDRESS

A 32 bit Internet address.

PROTOCOL

An 8 bit IP protocol number.

BIT MAP

A variable length bit map. The bit map must be a multiple of 8 bits long.

New Types from RFC 1183

AFSDB (Andrew File System Data Base—experimental)

Textual representation:

```
owner ttl class AFSDB subtype hostname
```

Example:

```
fx.movie.edu.  IN  AFSDB  1 bladerunner.fx.movie.edu.
               IN  AFSDB  2 bladerunner.fx.movie.edu.
               IN  AFSDB  1 empire.fx.movie.edu.
               IN  AFSDB  2 aliens.fx.movie.edu.
```

Binary representation:

```
AFSDB type code: 18
    +--+--+--+--+--+--+--+--+--+--+--+--+--+--+--+--+
    |                   SUBTYPE                     |
    +--+--+--+--+--+--+--+--+--+--+--+--+--+--+--+--+
    /                   HOSTNAME                    /
    /                                               /
    +--+--+--+--+--+--+--+--+--+--+--+--+--+--+--+--+
```

where:

SUBTYPE

Subtype 1 is an AFS cell database server. Subtype 2 is a DCE authenticated name server.

HOSTNAME

A *domain-name* that specifies a host that has a server for the cell named by the owner of the RR.

ISDN (Integrated Services Digital Network address—experimental)

Textual representation:

```
owner ttl class ISDN ISDN-address sa
```

Example:

```
delay.hp.com.  IN  ISDN  141555514539488
hep.hp.com.    IN  ISDN  141555514539488 004
```

Binary representation:

```
ISDN type code: 20
    +--+--+--+--+--+--+--+--+--+--+--+--+--+--+--+--+
    /                   ISDN ADDRESS                /
    +--+--+--+--+--+--+--+--+--+--+--+--+--+--+--+--+
    /                    SUBADDRESS                 /
    +--+--+--+--+--+--+--+--+--+--+--+--+--+--+--+--+
```

where:

ISDN ADDRESS
> A *character-string* that identifies the ISDN number of *owner* and DDI (Direct Dial In), if any.

SUBADDRESS
> An optional *character-string* specifying the subaddress.

RP (Responsible Person—experimental)

Textual representation:

```
owner ttl class RP mbox-dname txt-dname
```

Example:

```
; The current origin is fx.movie.edu
@            IN  RP   ajs.fx.movie.edu.     ajs.fx.movie.edu.
bladerunner  IN  RP   root.fx.movie.edu.    hotline.fx.movie.edu.
             IN  RP   richard.fx.movie.edu. rb.fx.movie.edu.
ajs          IN  TXT  "Arty Segue, (415) 555-3610"
hotline      IN  TXT  "Movie U. Network Hotline, (415) 555-4111"
rb           IN  TXT  "Richard Boisclair, (415) 555-9612"
```

Binary representation:

```
RP type code: 17
    +--+--+--+--+--+--+--+--+--+--+--+--+--+--+--+--+
    /                     MAILBOX                   /
    /                                               /
    +--+--+--+--+--+--+--+--+--+--+--+--+--+--+--+--+
    /                    TXTDNAME                   /
    /                                               /
    +--+--+--+--+--+--+--+--+--+--+--+--+--+--+--+--+
```

where:

MAILBOX
> A *domain-name* that specifies the mailbox for the responsible person.

TXTDNAME
> A *domain-name* for which TXT RRs exist. A subsequent query can be performed to retrieve the associated TXT resource records at *txt-dname*.

RT (Route Through—experimental)

Textual representation:

    owner ttl class RT preference intermediate-host

Example:

    sh.prime.com.   IN RT 2   Relay.Prime.COM.
                    IN RT 10 NET.Prime.COM.

Binary representation:

    RT type code: 21
        +--+--+--+--+--+--+--+--+--+--+--+--+--+--+--+--+
        | PREFERENCE |
        +--+--+--+--+--+--+--+--+--+--+--+--+--+--+--+--+
        /   INTERMEDIATE   /
        /   /
        +--+--+--+--+--+--+--+--+--+--+--+--+--+--+--+--+

where:

PREFERENCE
    A 16 bit integer that specifies the preference given to this RR among others at the same
    owner. Lower values are preferred.

EXCHANGE
    A *domain-name* that specifies a host that will serve as an intermediate in reaching the
    host specified by *owner*.

X25 (X.25 address—experimental)

Textual representation:

    owner ttl class X25 PSDN-address

Example:

    relay.pink.com. IN X25   31105060845

Binary representation:

    X25 type code: 19
        +--+--+--+--+--+--+--+--+--+--+--+--+--+--+--+--+
        /   PSDN ADDRESS   /
        +--+--+--+--+--+--+--+--+--+--+--+--+--+--+--+--+

where:

PSDN ADDRESS
    A *character-string* that identifies the PSDN (Public Switched Data Network) address
    in the X.121 numbering plan associated with *owner*.

New Types from RFC 1664

PX (pointer to X.400/RFC 822 mapping information)

Textual representation:

```
owner ttl class PX preference RFC822 address X.400 address
```

Example:

```
ab.net2.it.  IN  PX  10   ab.net2.it.  O-ab.PRMD-net2.ADMDb.C-it.
```

Binary representation:

```
PX type code: 26
  +--+--+--+--+--+--+--+--+--+--+--+--+--+--+--+--+
  |                   PREFERENCE                  |
  +--+--+--+--+--+--+--+--+--+--+--+--+--+--+--+--+
  /                     MAP822                    /
  /                                               /
  +--+--+--+--+--+--+--+--+--+--+--+--+--+--+--+--+
  /                    MAPX400                    /
  /                                               /
  +--+--+--+--+--+--+--+--+--+--+--+--+--+--+--+--+
```

where:

PREFERENCE
    A 16 bit integer which specifies the preference given to this RR among others at the same owner. Lower values are preferred.

MAP822
    A *domain-name* element containing *rfc822-domain*, the RFC 822 part of the RFC 1327 mapping information.

MAPX400
    A *domain-name* element containing the value of *x400-in-domain-syntax* derived from the X.400 part of the RFC 1327 mapping information.

New Types from RFC 2052

SRV (service location)

Textual representation:

```
owner ttl class SRV priority weight port target
```

Example:

```
_http._tcp.movie.edu.  IN  SRV 1 2 80 www.fx.movie.edu.
                       IN  SRV 1 1 8080 www1.fx.movie.edu.
```

Binary representation:

SRV type code: 33

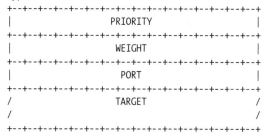

where:

PRIORITY

As for MX, the priority of this target host. A client MUST attempt to contact the target host with the lowest-numbered priority it can reach; target hosts with the same priority SHOULD be tried in pseudorandom order. The range is 0–65535.

WEIGHT

Load balancing mechanism. When selecting a target host among those that have the same priority, the chance of trying this one first SHOULD be proportional to its weight. The range of this number is 1–65535. Domain administrators are urged to use Weight 0 when there isn't any load balancing to do, to make the RR easier to read for humans (less noisy).

PORT

The port on this target host of this service. The range is 0–65535. This is often as specified in Assigned Numbers but need not be.

TARGET

As for MX, the domain name of the target host. There MUST be one or more A records for this name. Implementors are urged, but not required, to return the A record(s) in the Additional Data section. Name compression is to be used for this field. A Target of "." means that the service is decidedly not available at this domain.

Classes

(From RFC 1035, page 13)

CLASS fields appear in resource records. The following CLASS mnemonics and values are defined:

IN

1: the Internet

CS

2: the CSNET class (obsolete—used only for examples in some obsolete RFCs)

CH

3: the CHAOS class

HS

4: the Hesiod class

DNS Messages

To write programs that parse DNS messages, you need to understand the message format. DNS queries and responses are most often contained within UDP datagrams. Each message is fully contained within a UDP datagram. If the query and response are sent over TCP, they are prefixed with a 2-byte value indicating the length of the query or response, excluding the 2-byte length. The format and content of the DNS message are as follows.

Message Format

(From RFC 1035, page 25)

All communications inside of the domain protocol are carried in a single format called a message. The top level format of the message is divided into 5 sections (some of which are empty in certain cases), shown below:

```
+---------------------+
|        Header       |
+---------------------+
|       Question      | the question for the name server
+---------------------+
|        Answer       | RRs answering the question
+---------------------+
|      Authority      | RRs pointing toward an authority
+---------------------+
|      Additional     | RRs holding additional information
+---------------------+
```

The Header section is always present. The header includes fields that specify which of the remaining sections are present, and also specify whether the message is a query or a response, a standard query or some other opcode, etc.

The names of the sections after the header are derived from their use in standard queries. The Question section contains fields that describe a question to a name server. These fields are a query type (QTYPE), a query class (QCLASS), and a query domain name (QNAME). The last three sections have the same format: a possibly empty list of concatenated resource records (RRs). The Answer section contains RRs that answer the question; the Authority section contains RRs that point toward an authoritative name server; and the Additional records section contains RRs which relate to the query, but are not strictly answers for the question.

Header Section Format

(From RFC 1035, pages 26–28)

The header contains the following fields:

```
                          1  1  1  1  1  1
      0  1  2  3  4  5  6  7  8  9  0  1  2  3  4  5
    +--+--+--+--+--+--+--+--+--+--+--+--+--+--+--+--+
    |                      ID                       |
    +--+--+--+--+--+--+--+--+--+--+--+--+--+--+--+--+
    |QR|   Opcode  |AA|TC|RD|RA|    Z   |   RCODE   |
    +--+--+--+--+--+--+--+--+--+--+--+--+--+--+--+--+
    |                    QDCOUNT                    |
    +--+--+--+--+--+--+--+--+--+--+--+--+--+--+--+--+
    |                    ANCOUNT                    |
    +--+--+--+--+--+--+--+--+--+--+--+--+--+--+--+--+
    |                    NSCOUNT                    |
    +--+--+--+--+--+--+--+--+--+--+--+--+--+--+--+--+
    |                    ARCOUNT                    |
    +--+--+--+--+--+--+--+--+--+--+--+--+--+--+--+--+
```

where:

ID

A 16 bit identifier assigned by the program which generates any kind of query. This identifier is copied into the corresponding reply and can be used by the requester to match up replies to outstanding queries.

QR

A one bit field which specifies whether this message is a query (0), or a response (1).

OPCODE

A four bit field which specifies the kind of query in this message. This value is set by the originator of a query and copied into the response. The values are:

0

A standard query (QUERY)

1

An inverse query (IQUERY)

2

A server status request (STATUS)

3–15

Reserved for future use

AA (Authoritative Answer)

This bit is valid in responses, and specifies that the responding name server is an authority for the domain name in the Question section. Note that the contents of the Answer section may have multiple owner names because of aliases. The AA bit corresponds to the name which matches the query name, or the first owner name in the Answer section.

TC (TrunCation)

This bit specifies that this message was truncated due to length greater than that permitted on the transmission channel.

RD (Recursion Desired)

This bit may be set in a query and is copied into the response. If RD is set, it directs the name server to pursue the query recursively. Recursive query support is optional.

RA (Recursion Available)

This bit is set or cleared in a response, and denotes whether recursive query support is available in the name server.

Z

Reserved for future use. Must be zero in all queries and responses.

RCODE (Response Code)

This 4 bit field is set as part of responses. The values have the following interpretation:

0

No error condition

1

Format Error—The name server was unable to interpret the query.

2

Server Failure—The name server was unable to process this query due to a problem with the name server.

3

Name Error—Meaningful only for responses from an authoritative name server, this code signifies that the domain name referenced in the query does not exist.

4

Not Implemented—The name server does not support the requested kind of query.

5

Refused—The name server refuses to perform the specified operation for policy reasons. For example, a name server may not wish to provide the information to the particular requester, or a name server may not wish to perform a particular operation (e.g., zone transfer) for particular data.

6–15

Reserved for future use.

QDCOUNT

An unsigned 16 bit integer specifying the number of entries in the Question section.

ANCOUNT

An unsigned 16 bit integer specifying the number of resource records in the Answer section.

NSCOUNT

An unsigned 16 bit integer specifying the number of name server resource records in the Authority records section.

ARCOUNT

An unsigned 16 bit integer specifying the number of resource records in the Additional records section.

Question Section Format

(From RFC 1035, pages 28–29)

The Question section is used to carry the "question" in most queries, i.e., the parameters that define what is being asked. The section contains QDCOUNT (usually 1) entries, each of the following format:

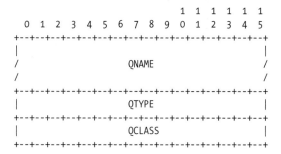

where:

QNAME

A domain name represented as a sequence of labels, where each label consists of a length octet followed by that number of octets. The domain name terminates with the zero length octet for the null label of the root. Note that this field may be an odd number of octets; no padding is used.

QTYPE

A two octet code which specifies the type of the query. The values for this field include all codes valid for a TYPE field, together with some more general codes which can match more than one type of RR.

QCLASS

A two octet code that specifies the class of the query. For example, the QCLASS field is IN for the Internet.

QCLASS values   (From RFC 1035, page 13)

QCLASS fields appear in the Question section of a query. QCLASS values are a superset of CLASS values; every CLASS is a valid QCLASS. In addition to CLASS values, the following QCLASS is defined:

*   255 Any class

QTYPE values (From RFC 1035, pages 12–13)

QTYPE fields appear in the Question part of a query. QTYPES are a superset of TYPEs, hence all TYPEs are valid QTYPEs. Also, the following QTYPEs are defined:

AXFR
> 252 A request for a transfer of an entire zone

MAILB
> 253 A request for mailbox-related records (MB, MG, or MR)

MAILA
> 254 A request for mail agent RRs (obsolete—see MX)

*
> 255 A request for all records

Answer, Authority, and Additional Section Format

(From RFC 1035, pages 29–30)

The Answer, Authority, and Additional sections all share the same format: a variable number of resource records, where the number of records is specified in the corresponding count field in the header. Each resource record has the following format:

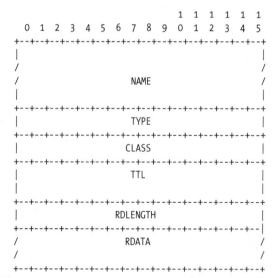

where:

NAME
> A domain name to which this resource record pertains.

TYPE
> Two octets containing one of the RR type codes. This field specifies the meaning of the data in the RDATA field.

CLASS

Two octets which specify the class of the data in the RDATA field.

TTL

A 32 bit unsigned integer that specifies the time interval (in seconds) that the resource record may be cached before it should be discarded. Zero values are interpreted to mean that the RR can only be used for the transaction in progress, and should not be cached.

RDLENGTH

An unsigned 16 bit integer that specifies the length in octets of the RDATA field.

RDATA

A variable length string of octets that describes the resource. The format of this information varies according to the TYPE and CLASS of the resource record. For example, if the TYPE is A and the CLASS is IN, the RDATA field is a 4 octet ARPA Internet address.

Data Transmission Order

(From RFC 1035, pages 8–9)

The order of transmission of the header and data described in this document is resolved to the octet level. Whenever a diagram shows a group of octets, the order of transmission of those octets is the normal order in which they are read in English. For example, in the following diagram, the octets are transmitted in the order they are numbered.

```
 0                   1
 0 1 2 3 4 5 6 7 8 9 0 1 2 3 4 5
+-+-+-+-+-+-+-+-+-+-+-+-+-+-+-+-+
|       1       |       2       |
+-+-+-+-+-+-+-+-+-+-+-+-+-+-+-+-+
|       3       |       4       |
+-+-+-+-+-+-+-+-+-+-+-+-+-+-+-+-+
|       5       |       6       |
+-+-+-+-+-+-+-+-+-+-+-+-+-+-+-+-+
```

Whenever an octet represents a numeric quantity, the left most bit in the diagram is the high order or most significant bit. That is, the bit labeled zero is the most significant bit. For example, the following diagram represents the value 170 (decimal).

```
 0 1 2 3 4 5 6 7
+-+-+-+-+-+-+-+-+
|1 0 1 0 1 0 1 0|
+-+-+-+-+-+-+-+-+
```

Similarly, whenever a multi-octet field represents a numeric quantity, the left most bit of the whole field is the most significant bit. When a multi-octet quantity is transmitted the most significant octet is transmitted first.

Resource Record Data

Data Format

In addition to two- and four-octet integer values, resource record data can contain *domain-name*s or *character-string*s.

Domain name (From RFC 1035, page 10)

Domain names in messages are expressed in terms of a sequence of labels. Each label is represented as a one octet length field followed by that number of octets. Since every domain name ends with the null label of the root, a domain name is terminated by a length byte of zero. The high order two bits of every length octet must be zero, and the remaining six bits of the length field limit the label to 63 octets or less.

Message compression (From RFC 1035, page 30)

In order to reduce the size of messages, the domain system utilizes a compression scheme which eliminates the repetition of domain names in a message. In this scheme, an entire domain name or a list of labels at the end of a domain name is replaced with a pointer to a prior occurrence of the same name.

The pointer takes the form of a two octet sequence:

```
+--+--+--+--+--+--+--+--+--+--+--+--+--+--+--+--+
| 1  1|                 OFFSET                   |
+--+--+--+--+--+--+--+--+--+--+--+--+--+--+--+--+
```

The first two bits are ones. This allows a pointer to be distinguished from a label, since the label must begin with two zero bits because labels are restricted to 63 octets or less. (The 10 and 01 combinations are reserved for future use.) The OFFSET field specifies an offset from the start of the message (i.e., the first octet of the ID field in the domain header). A zero offset specifies the first byte of the ID field, etc.

Character string (From RFC 1035, page 13)

character-string is a single length octet followed by that number of characters. *character-string* is treated as binary information, and can be up to 256 characters in length (including the length octet).

Installing the DNS Server from CD-ROM

This brief appendix guides you through installing the Microsoft DNS Server from CD-ROM.

1. Insert the Windows 2000 Server CD-ROM into your CD-ROM drive.

2. After a moment you'll see the CD's installation window. Click the **Install Add-On Components** option.

3. When the **Windows Components Wizard** window appears, scroll down and double-click on **Networking Services**.

4. In the resulting **Networking Services** window, check the box to the left of **Domain Name System (DNS)** and click **OK** to close the window.

5. Click **Next** in the **Windows Components Wizard** window. After the installation is finished, you'll be prompted to click **Finished** to end the wizard.

6. After the installation, you'll need to reboot. Following the reboot, the DNS server will be running, and you'll see **DNS** in the **Administrative Tools** menu.

Converting from BIND to the Microsoft DNS Server

This appendix covers the steps necessary to convert a BIND Version 4 name server to a Microsoft DNS Server. This process is straightforward, since the Microsoft DNS Server can read a BIND Version 4–style configuration file to obtain its configuration. If you're running BIND Version 8 or 9, you're no doubt aware that the configuration file format is drastically different. Unfortunately, the Microsoft DNS Server can't read this version of the BIND configuration file. You should still read through this appendix to see what's involved in the conversion, but you'll need to manually "downgrade" your BIND configuration file to a format readable by the Microsoft DNS Server.

Step 1: Change the DNS Server Startup Method to File

The first step is directing the DNS server to obtain its configuration from a file rather than the Registry or an Active Directory server (or a combination of both). Start the DNS console, right-click on the server name in the left pane, and choose **Properties**. In the server properties window, click on the **Advanced** tab, which produces a window like the one shown in Figure C-1.

Change the **Load zone data on startup** parameter to **From file** and click **OK**.

Step 2: Stop the Microsoft DNS Server

The next step is stopping the DNS server: right-click on the server name in the DNS console's left pane and choose **All Tasks → Stop**.

Step 3: Change the Zone Data File Naming Convention

This step is optional. Chances are, your BIND zone data files don't follow the same naming convention used by the Microsoft DNS Server. Recall from Chapter 4 that

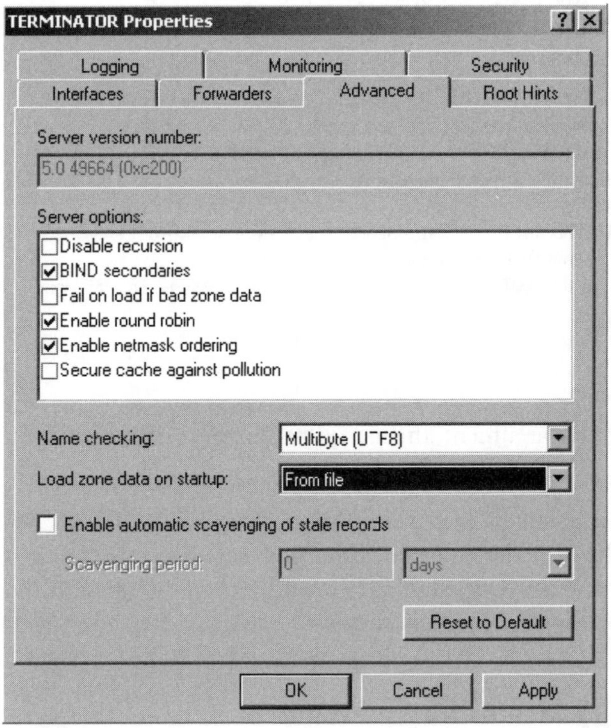

Figure C-1. Changing the DNS server startup method

the Microsoft convention is the name of the zone followed by the *.dns* extension—for example, *movie.edu.dns*. You can continue to use your current naming convention, but if you add new zones with the DNS console, they'll have the *.dns* extensions unless you go out of your way to make the names conform to your scheme. If you're not particularly attached to your naming scheme and don't want to fight the DNS console every time you create a new zone, this Perl script will rename your zone data files in the *.dns* style and modify your *named.boot* file accordingly:

```
# name-convert.pl -- Convert zone data file naming convention in a BIND
#                    named.boot file to Microsoft *.dns format
#

die "usage: name-convert.pl path-to-named.boot\n" unless $ARGV[0];

open (BOOTIN, $ARGV[0]) || die "Can't open boot file for reading: $!\n";
open (BOOTOUT, ">boot") || die "Can't open boot file for writing: $!\n";

while (<BOOTIN>) {
    $dir="$1/" if /^directory\s+(.+).*$/;
    &changeit (1, $1, $2) if /^primary\s+(.+)\s+(.+)$/;
    &changeit (2, $1, $5, $2) if /^secondary\s+([\w\.]+)\s+((((\d{1,3}\.){3}\
    d{1,3}\s+)+)(.+)$/;
```

```
        &changeit (3, "cache", $1) if /^cache\s+\.\s+(.+)$/;
}

sub changeit {
    local ($zonetype, $zonename, $oldfilename, $mastersips) = @_;
    $newfilename="$zonename.dns";
    rename ($dir.$oldfilename, $dir.$newfilename) || print "Error renaming
    $oldfilename to $newfilename!\n";
    if ($zonetype == 1) {
        print BOOTOUT "primary $zonename $newfilename\n";
    } elsif ($zonetype == 2) {
        print BOOTOUT "secondary $zonename $mastersips $newfilename\n";
    } else {
        print BOOTOUT "cache . $newfilename\n";
    }
}
```

The script takes one argument, the name of the name server boot file. For example:

```
name-convert.pl /etc/named.boot
```

It outputs a file called *boot* in the current directory, which is a Microsoft DNS Server boot file with the zone data filenames changed. It's probably easiest to run the script on the BIND name server (which is probably running Unix and therefore has Perl installed), then copy over *boot* and the newly renamed **.dns* zone data files.

Step 4: Copy the Files

The next step is copying the necessary files from the BIND name server to the Windows 2000 server. You'll need to copy the name server configuration file, called the *boot* file (which is usually */etc/named.boot*) and all the zone data files for which the BIND server is a primary master. The zone data files will be in the directory specified by the *directory* directive in the boot file. The files should be copied to the *%SystemRoot%\system32\dns* directory on the Windows 2000 server. The *named. boot* file goes in that directory, too, but you need to rename it to just *boot*. One final note: only the *primary*, *secondary*, and *cache* directives are supported. Any other directives are ignored.

Step 5: Get a New Root Name Server Cache File

Now is a good time to make sure you've got the latest and greatest root name server cache file. Follow the instructions in Chapter 4 to retrieve the file from *ftp.rs.inter-nic.net*. Be sure the name matches the one in the boot file's *cache* directive. If you went through the name conversion process (step two), the file should be called *cache.dns*.

Step 6: Restart the DNS Server

Restart the DNS server. The server will now read the BIND boot file for its configuration information and—here's the nice part—update its configuration information in the Registry to match what it read from the boot file.

If you want to the server to use the boot file permanently, you're finished now. You can even add or delete zones using the DNS console; the server will update the boot file. That's a nice improvement over Windows NT, which silently converted back to loading startup data from the Registry if you made any changes with its DNS Manager administration tool.

Step 7: Change the DNS Server Startup Method to Registry

Finally, you can configure the DNS server to load its configuration information from the Registry or Active Directory (or both). Using the instructions from step one above, change the boot method back to **From registry** or **From Active Directory and registry**.

APPENDIX D
Top-Level Domains

This table lists all the two-letter country codes and all the top-level domains that aren't countries. Not all of the countries are registered in the Internet namespace at the time of this writing, but there aren't many missing.

Domain	Country or organization	Domain	Country or organization
AC	Ascension Island	BF	Burkina Faso
AD	Andorra	BG	Bulgaria
AE	United Arab Emirates	BH	Bahrain
AF	Afghanistan	BI	Burundi
AG	Antigua and Barbuda	BJ	Benin
AI	Anguilla	BM	Bermuda
AL	Albania	BN	Brunei Darussalam
AM	Armenia	BO	Bolivia
AN	Netherlands Antilles	BR	Brazil
AO	Angola	BS	Bahamas
AQ	Antarctica	BT	Bhutan
AR	Argentina	BV	Bouvet Island
ARPA	ARPA Internet	BW	Botswana
AS	American Samoa	BY	Belarus
AT	Austria	BZ	Belize
AU	Australia	CA	Canada
AW	Aruba	CC	Cocos (Keeling) Islands
AZ	Azerbaijan	CD	Congo, Democratic Republic of the
BA	Bosnia and Herzegovina	CF	Central African Republic
BB	Barbados	CG	Congo
BD	Bangladesh	CH	Switzerland
BE	Belgium	CI	Cote d'Ivoire

Domain	Country or organization	Domain	Country or organization
CK	Cook Islands	GE	Georgia
CL	Chile	GF	French Guiana
CM	Cameroon	GG	Guernsey, Alderney, and Sark (British Channel Islands)
CN	China	GH	Ghana
CO	Colombia	GI	Gibraltar
COM	Generic (formerly Commercial)	GL	Greenland
CR	Costa Rica	GM	Gambia
CU	Cuba	GN	Guinea
CV	Cape Verde	GOV	U.S. Federal Government
CX	Christmas Island	GP	Guadeloupe
CY	Cyprus	GQ	Equatorial Guinea
CZ	Czech Republic	GR	Greece
DE	Germany	GS	South Georgia and the South Sandwich Islands
DJ	Djibouti	GT	Guatemala
DK	Denmark	GU	Guam
DM	Dominica	GW	Guinea-Bissau
DO	Dominican Republic	GY	Guyana
DZ	Algeria	HK	Hong Kong
EC	Ecuador	HM	Heard and McDonald Islands
EDU	Education	HN	Honduras
EE	Estonia	HR	Croatia
EG	Egypt	HT	Haiti
EH	Western Sahara	HU	Hungary
ER	Eritrea	ID	Indonesia
ES	Spain	IE	Ireland
ET	Ethiopia	IL	Israel
FI	Finland	IM	Isle of Man
FJ	Fiji	IN	India
FK	Falkland Islands (Malvinas)	INT	International entities
FM	Micronesia, Federated States of	IO	British Indian Ocean Territory
FO	Faroe Islands	IQ	Iraq
FR	France	IR	Iran
FX	France, metropolitan	IS	Iceland
GA	Gabon	IT	Italy
GB	United Kingdom[a]	JE	Jersey (British Channel Island)
GD	Grenada	JM	Jamaica

[a] In practice, the United Kingdom uses "UK" for its top-level domain.

Domain	Country or organization	Domain	Country or organization
JO	Jordan	MR	Mauritania
JP	Japan	MS	Montserrat
KE	Kenya	MT	Malta
KG	Kyrgyzstan	MU	Mauritius
KH	Cambodia	MV	Maldives
KI	Kiribati	MW	Malawi
KM	Comoros	MX	Mexico
KN	Saint Kitts and Nevis	MY	Malaysia
KP	Korea, Democratic People's Republic of	MZ	Mozambique
KR	Korea, Republic of	NA	Namibia
KW	Kuwait	NATO	North Atlantic Treaty Organization
KY	Cayman Islands	NC	New Caledonia
KZ	Kazakhstan	NE	Niger
LA	Lao People's Democratic Republic	NET	Generic (formerly Networking Organizations)
LB	Lebanon	NF	Norfolk Island
LC	Saint Lucia	NG	Nigeria
LI	Liechtenstein	NI	Nicaragua
LK	Sri Lanka	NL	Netherlands
LR	Liberia	NO	Norway
LS	Lesotho	NP	Nepal
LT	Lithuania	NR	Nauru
LU	Luxembourg	NU	Niue
LV	Latvia	NZ	New Zealand
LY	Libyan Arab Jamahiriya	OM	Oman
MA	Morocco	ORG	Generic (formerly Organizations)
MC	Monaco	PA	Panama
MD	Moldova, Republic of	PE	Peru
MG	Madagascar	PF	French Polynesia
MH	Marshall Islands	PG	Papua New Guinea
MIL	U.S. Military	PH	Philippines
MK	Macedonia, the Former Yugoslav Republic of	PK	Pakistan
ML	Mali	PL	Poland
MM	Myanmar	PM	St. Pierre and Miquelon
MN	Mongolia	PN	Pitcairn
MO	Macau	PR	Puerto Rico
MP	Northern Mariana Islands	PS	Palestinian Authority
MQ	Martinique	PT	Portugal

Domain	Country or organization	Domain	Country or organization
PW	Palau	TK	Tokelau
PY	Paraguay	TM	Turkmenistan
QA	Qatar	TN	Tunisia
RE	Reunion	TO	Tonga
RO	Romania	TP	East Timor
RU	Russian Federation	TR	Turkey
RW	Rwanda	TT	Trinidad and Tobago
SA	Saudi Arabia	TV	Tuvalu
SB	Solomon Islands	TW	Taiwan, Province of China
SC	Seychelles	TZ	Tanzania, United Republic of
SD	Sudan	UA	Ukraine
SE	Sweden	UG	Uganda
SG	Singapore	UK	United Kingdom
SH	St. Helena	UM	United States Minor Outlying Islands
SI	Slovenia	US	United States
SJ	Svalbard and Jan Mayen Islands	UY	Uruguay
SK	Slovakia	UZ	Uzbekistan
SL	Sierra Leone	VA	Holy See (Vatican City State)
SM	San Marino	VC	Saint Vincent and The Grenadines
SN	Senegal	VE	Venezuela
SO	Somalia	VG	Virgin Islands (British)
SR	Suriname	VI	Virgin Islands (U.S.)
ST	Sao Tome and Principe	VN	Vietnam
SU	Union of Soviet Socialist Republics	VU	Vanuatu
SV	El Salvador	WF	Wallis and Futuna Islands
SY	Syrian Arab Republic	WS	Samoa
SZ	Swaziland	YE	Yemen
TC	Turks and Caicos Islands	YT	Mayotte
TD	Chad	YU	Yugoslavia
TF	French Southern Territories	ZA	South Africa
TG	Togo	ZM	Zambia
TH	Thailand	ZR	Republic of Zaire
TJ	Tajikistan	ZW	Zimbabwe

Index

We'd like to hear your suggestions for improving our indexes. Send email to *index@oreilly.com*.

DNS Service Search Order, 118
DNS suffix, 102–105
DnsUpdateProxy group, 216
documentation
    BIND, 36
    firewalls, 268
    network numbers, 49
domain controllers, 207–209
    Active Directory, 198
    resource records needed by, 203–204
domain name labels, resource record data
            and, 312
Domain Name System (see DNS)
domain names, 5, 12
    Active Directory, 198
    choosing, 38–52
    collisions, 3
    consistency of, 3, 22
    FQDNs, 12, 105
    geographic, 18
    mail exchangers, 93, 95–97
    mapping, 30, 64
    MX records (see MX records)
    reading, 19
    resolving (see resolution)
    resource record data and, 312
    resource records and, 73
    servers for (see name servers)
    subdomains, 16
    trailing dot (.) in, 12, 292
    wrong one in RDATA of record, 253
domain namespace, 11–17
    CIDR and, 50
    Internet, 17–19
    shadow namespace, 279
    visibility of, 280
Domain Suffix Search Order (Windows
            95), 114
domains, 4, 13–16
    adding, 89, 160–161
    default, 228
    delegating, 20, 23, 162–165, 256, 275
    in-addr.arpa, 51, 275
        delegating, 169
        subdomains of, 170
    information about, obtaining, 41, 46
    international (see geographic domain
            names)
    levels of, 16
    naming, 159
    non-U.S., 18

parenting, 157–180
    managing transition to
            subdomains, 179
    registering, 49–52
    root, 4, 11, 129
    searching for, 224
    state- and city-level, 19
    testing setup, 81–83
    top-level (see TLDs)
    zones vs., 21
dot (.)
    root domain, 4, 75–78
    trailing, 74
        in domain names, 12
        indicating absolute domain name, 292
dotted-octet representation, 30
Dynamic Host Configuration Protocol (see
            DHCP)

E

edu domain, 17
email, 92–100
    administrator address, 63
    mail exchangers, 93, 95–97
    MX records, 93–95
        adding, 95–97
    routing loops, 98–100
error messages, 80
errors
    disasters, 152–156
    nonexistent domain (nslookup), 240–242
    rcodes for, 234
    SERVFAIL, 250
    subdomain delegation, 257–258
    unspecified (nslookup), 243
Event Log, 80, 132–134
Event Viewer (DNS console), 80
example programs, obtaining, xiv
expire value, 88, 151
expiring cached data, 33
    changing TTL, 148–152
extranet, 2

F

filenaming conventions, BIND and Microsoft
            DNS Server, 314
files
    cache.dns, 75–78, 123
    db.cache, updating, 129
    named.root, 78

queries, 111
  caching and, 32–34
  inverse, 235
  iterative (nonrecursive), 27, 192
  mimicking server with
      nslookup, 236–238
  name servers, 109–112
  nonauthoritative nslookup answers, 230
  recursive, 26–28, 196
  refused, 242
  trace of, 233–235
  volume of (see traffic)
querytype option (nslookup), 228, 229
Question section (DNS messages), 235, 309

R

RCODE field, 308
rcodes (response codes), 234
recurse option (nslookup), 227
recursion, 26, 196
  queries, 192
    name server configuration and, 196
  resolution, 26–28
    caching and, 32–34
refresh interval, 87, 151, 181
  no-refresh interval, 217
  slave servers, 143
refused queries, 242
registration, 39
  of additional FQDNs, 212
  of name servers, 146–148
  of network numbers, 49–52
registries, 39, 49
  choosing, 48
Registry settings
  Netlogon service, 208
  Windows 2000 dynamic
      updates, 213–214
remote host names, 82, 260
resolution, 25–32
  caching and, 32–34
  iterative (nonrecursive), 27
  recursive, 26–28
  root name servers, 25
  roundtrip time, 29
  (see also resolvers)
resolvers, 4, 25, 101, 118
  caching, 112
  configuring, 102–112, 164
    DNS suffix, 102–105
    local name servers, 118

    name servers to query, 109–112
    remote name servers, 118
    sample configurations, 118–119
    search list, 105–108
  nslookup vs., 224, 225
  response acceptance, 114
  round robin, 113
  stub, 25
  subnet prioritization, 113
  Windows 95, 114–115
  Windows 98, 116
  Windows NT, 116
  (see also resolution)
resource records, 16
  adding, 66–69
    manually, 124–126
  case sensitivity, 72
  CNAMEs in, 264
  data format for, 312
  deleting
    manually, 124–126
    stale, 217–221
  domain names in, 73
  needed by domain controllers, 203–204
  properties of, 89
  scavenging, 217–221
  storing, 69
  types of, 285–289, 293–304
  zone creation and, 62–65
resources (see documentation)
responses
  inconsistent, 261
  time for (see performance)
  tracing, 233–235
Responsible Person (RP) records, 128, 302
restricted servers, 192–194
retry interval, 88, 151, 228
reverse-mapping, 65, 75
RIPE Network Coordination Centre, 49
root command (nslookup), 228
root domain, 4, 11, 129
Root Hints window (DNS console), 78
root name server hints file, 75–78
root name servers, 25, 194, 274–278
  setting with nslookup, 228
  temporary, 155
root.dns file, 276–277
round robin, 113, 196
roundtrip time, 29
routing loops, 98–100
RP records, 128, 302
RT records, 288, 303

S

scalability, forwarding and, 274
Scope Properties window (Microsoft DNS Server), 215
search list, 105–108
    setting manually, 108
search option (nslookup), 227
searching
    for domains, 224
    for IP addresses, 37
    turning off, 229
secondary name servers (see slave/secondary name servers)
second-level domains, 16
    (see also domains; subdomains)
security, 138, 195–197
    dynamic update protocol and, 205
    encryption, 206
    firewalls, 267–281
    forwarders, 270–274
    root name servers, 274–278
    transaction signatures, 205
semicolon (;)
    in comments, 293
    in zone data files, 72
sendmail program, 95
serial numbers, 126
    incrementing, 248
    integer, 127
    nslookup and, 224
server command (nslookup), 231
Server Properties window (Microsoft DNS Server), 91, 123
servers (see name servers)
SERVFAIL errors, 250
set all command (nslookup), 260
set command (nslookup), 226
shadow namespace, 279
sibling nodes, 12
signals to primary name server, forgetting, 248
Simple Mail Transfer Protocol (SMTP), 93
slave/secondary name servers, 24
    adding, 143, 169
    expired zones, 249–252
    loading data, 126
    loading from other slaves, 143
    partial-slave servers, 145
    running, 83–88
    serial numbers, 126
    setting up, 165

zone transfers and, 181–184
    (see also name servers)
SMTP (Simple Mail Transfer Protocol), 93
SOA records, 41, 47, 86–88, 298
    Netlogon service and, 208
    serial numbers (see serial numbers)
    values in, changing, 151
    zone creation and, 62
software
    firewall, 268
    name server, 138
sorting addresses, 190–192
split namespace, 278–281
srchlist option (nslookup), 229
SRI-NIC host, 3
SRV records, 200–202
    adding with DNS console, 201
    fields in, 201
start of authority records (see SOA records)
starting/stopping DNS server, 79, 122
    from DOS command line, 80
state-level domains, 19
statistics, 134
stub resolvers, 25
subdomains, 4, 16
    choosing, 39–48
    delegating, 20, 22, 23
    non-U.S., 18
    reading, 19
    size, 158
    SOA records, 41
    (see also domains; parenting)
subnet prioritization, 113
subnetting networks
    Class A and B, 171
    Class C, 172–175
    on/off nonoctet boundaries, 171–175
    on/off octet boundaries, 170
system administration (see administration)
System Log, 132–134

T

TCP (Transmission Control Protocol)
    application gateway firewalls and, 269
    virtual circuits, 227
TCP/IP, 1
    DNS and, 10
    nslookup and, 227
temporary root servers, 155
testing domain setup, 81–83
time to live (see TTL)

Z

zone data files, 24, 61, 69–72, 122
    changing origin in, 131
    controls, 130–135
    event log for, 133
    format of, 72–74, 291–305
       domains, appending, 73
    manual changes to, making, 249
    syntax errors in, 134, 250
Zone Properties window (Microsoft DNS
       Server), 90, 250
zone transfers, 24, 83, 181–184, 190
    incremental, 221
    nslookup and, 224, 238
    unauthorized, 195
zones, 5, 21–25
    creating, 59–65, 84–85
    domains vs., 21
    expired, 249–252
    properties of, 89
    registering, 51
    reverse-mapping, 65
    SOA records, 41, 47
    stale resource records and, 217
    storing in Active Directory, 204
    updating, 124–130
    (see also zone data files; zone transfers)

About the Authors

Matt Larson works for VeriSign's Global Registry Services division, the folks who maintain the database of all *com*, *net*, and *org* domain names and run the name servers for those three zones. In 1997 he started Acme Byte & Wire, a company specializing in DNS consulting and training, with Cricket Liu. Before being acquired by VeriSign in 2000, Acme Byte & Wire counted many large companies as its customers, including ten of the Fortune 100. Matt's first job out of college was with Hewlett-Packard, first as Cricket's successor as *hp.com* hostmaster, then as a consultant in HP's Professional Services Organization.

Matt graduated from Northwestern University in 1992 with a Bachelor of Arts in computer science and a Bachelor of Music in church music/organ performance. He lives in Bethesda, Maryland with his wife, Sonja Kahler, and their two pugs. In his spare time, he enjoys playing the 10-rank pipe organ in his house.

Cricket Liu matriculated at the University of California's Berkeley campus, that great bastion of free speech, unencumbered Unix, and cheap pizza. He joined Hewlett-Packard after graduation and worked for HP for nine years.

Cricket began managing the *hp.com* zone after the Loma Prieta earthquake forcibly transferred the zone's management from HP Labs to HP's Corporate Offices (by cracking a sprinkler main and flooding Labs' computer room). Cricket was *hostmaster@hp.com* for over three years, and then joined HP's Professional Services Organization to found HP's Internet consulting program.

Cricket left HP in 1997 to found Acme Byte & Wire with his friend (and coauthor) Matt Larson. When Acme Byte & Wire was acquired by VeriSign, Cricket became the company's Director of DNS Product Management. He is now an independent consultant.

Cricket, his wife, Paige, and their son, Walt, live in Colorado with two Siberian Huskies, Annie and Dakota. On warm weekend afternoons, you'll probably find them on the flying trapeze or wakeboarding behind Betty Blue.

Colophon

Our look is the result of reader comments, our own experimentation, and feedback from distribution channels. Distinctive covers complement our distinctive approach to technical topics, breathing personality and life into potentially dry subjects.

The animal on the cover of *DNS on Windows 2000* is an African white-necked raven (*Corvus albicollis*), a subspecies of raven, the largest of the crow-like birds at about 24 inches long. The sexes look alike; the female is slightly smaller. Perceived as spirited or even impudent, the raven has a distinctive, hoarse, carrying call. They are excellent flyers, hovering and gliding, and are safe in flight from predators. Ravens are scavengers and eat carrion and small live animals, as well as some plants. They sometimes hide and store excess food, and will occasionally carry food in their feet.

African raven nests, built in niches in rocks, are crafted of an underlying stick structure, covered by grass, dirt, and rocks, then smaller twigs with soft materials such as moss or rags, and finally a layer of grass or similar plant material. Ravens lay 3–6 mottled grayish-green eggs, and the young hatch after 18–20 days of incubation. Both parents (a pair mated for life) will change the nest lining materials to adjust for changes in temperature and climate.

The raven is a popular figure, both profane and sacred, in many legends. Ravens, along with their relatives jays and crows, have long been considered omens of evil in folklore, possibly due to the supposed annual tribute in feathers paid to the Devil; this legend is probably based on the molting of feathers every summer, during which the raven stays relatively well hidden—only this and nothing more. The Old Testament lists ravens among "unclean" birds; ravens also fed Elijah by the brook. Other ancient and medieval cultures considered the raven a symbol of virility or wisdom. An ancient Norse saga describes the use of ravens by ocean navigators as guides to land, and Norse mythology describes ravens as scouts for Odin. Native American folklore tells that the raven created the world and its creatures.

Because they prey on locusts, mice, and rats, the white-necked raven is generally welcomed in Africa (despite the occasional theft of domestic fowl). Like that of many other wild animals, the raven's habitat is dwindling with expansion of the human population.

Rachel Wheeler was the production editor and proofreader for *DNS on Windows 2000*, and Mary Anne Weeks Mayo was the copyeditor. Mary Brady provided quality control, and Sada Preisch, Kimo Carter, and Edie Shapiro provided production assistance. Nancy Crumpton wrote the index.

Edie Freedman designed the cover of this book. The cover image is a 19th-century engraving from the Dover Pictorial Archive. Emma Colby produced the cover layout with QuarkXPress 4.1 using Adobe's ITC Garamond font.

Melanie Wang designed the interior layout, based on a series design by David Futato. Anne-Marie Vaduva converted the files from Microsoft Word to FrameMaker 5.5.6 using tools created by Mike Sierra. The text font is Linotype Birka; the heading font is Adobe Myriad Condensed; and the code font is Lucas-Font's TheSans Mono Condensed. The illustrations that appear in the book were produced by Robert Romano and Jessamyn Read using Macromedia FreeHand 9 and Adobe Photoshop 6. The tip and warning icons were drawn by Christopher Bing. This colophon was written by Nancy Kotary.

Whenever possible, our books use a durable and flexible lay-flat binding. If the page count exceeds this binding's limit, perfect binding is used.